Able to Lead

Able to Lead

Disablement, Radicalism, and
the Political Life of E.T. Kingsley

RAVI MALHOTRA and BENJAMIN ISITT

UBCPress · Vancouver · Toronto

30 29 28 27 26 25 24 23 22 21   5 4 3 2 1

Printed in Canada on FSC-certified ancient-forest-free paper
(100% post-consumer recycled) that is processed chlorine- and acid-free.

Library and Archives Canada Cataloguing in Publication

Title: Able to lead : disablement, radicalism, and the political life of E.T. Kingsley /
Ravi Malhotra and Benjamin Isitt.
Names: Malhotra, Ravi, author. | Isitt, Benjamin, 1978- author.
Description: Includes bibliographical references and index.

Identifiers: Canadiana (print) 20210164875 | Canadiana (ebook) 20210164891 |
ISBN 9780774865760 (hardcover) | ISBN 9780774865777 (paperback) |
ISBN 9780774865784 (PDF) | ISBN 9780774865791 (EPUB)

Subjects: LCSH: Kingsley, E. T. | LCSH: Politicians—Canada—Biography. |
LCSH: Politicians—United States—Biography. | LCSH: Socialists—Canada—
Biography. | LCSH: Socialists—United States—Biography. | LCSH: Amputees—
Canada—Biography. | LCSH: Amputees—United States—Biography. |
CSH: Canada—Politics and government—1896-1911. | LCGFT: Biographies.

Classification: LCC FC551.K56 M35 2021 | DDC 971.05/6092—dc23

Canadä

UBC Press gratefully acknowledges the financial support for our publishing
program of the Government of Canada (through the Canada Book Fund),
the Canada Council for the Arts, and the British Columbia Arts Council.

This book has been published with the help of a grant
from the Canadian Federation for the Humanities and Social Sciences,
through the Awards to Scholarly Publications Program, using funds provided
by the Social Sciences and Humanities Research Council of Canada.

UBC Press
The University of British Columbia
2029 West Mall
Vancouver, BC V6T 1Z2
www.ubcpress.ca

For Ross Johnson and people of all abilities who lead

Contents

List of Illustrations

List of Abbreviations

AFL	American Federation of Labor
AOUW	Ancient Order of United Workmen
BCA	British Columbia Archives
BCFL	British Columbia Federation of Labor
BLE	Brotherhood of Locomotive Engineers
BLF	Brotherhood of Locomotive Firemen
BRT	Brotherhood of Railway Trainmen
CCF	Co-operative Commonwealth Federation
CLP	Canadian Labor Party
CSF	Canadian Socialist Federation
CSL	Canadian Socialist League
FELA	*Federal Employers' Liability Act*
FLP	Federated Labor Party of British Columbia
ILP	Independent Labor Party of British Columbia
IWA	International Workmen's Association
IWW	Industrial Workers of the World
LAC	Library and Archives Canada
MLA	Member of the Legislative Assembly
MLL	Miners' Liberation League
MMLPA	Miners' and Mine Laborers' Protective Association
NILP	Nanaimo (Independent) Labor Party

NPR	Northern Pacific Railroad
OBU	One Big Union
PPP	Provincial Progressive Party
RCMP	Royal Canadian Mounted Police
RG	Record Group
RNWMP	Royal North West Mounted Police
RSL	Revolutionary Socialist League
RSPC	Revolutionary Socialist Party of Canada
SDPC	Social Democratic Party of Canada
SFUSC	Simon Fraser University Special Collections
SLP	Socialist Labor Party of America
SPA	Socialist Party of America
SPBC	Socialist Party of British Columbia
SPC	Socialist Party of Canada
STLA	Socialist Trade and Labor Alliance
TLC	Trades and Labor Congress of Canada
UBCSC	University of British Columbia Special Collections
VDLC	Vancouver and District Labor Council
VTLC	Vancouver Trades and Labor Council
WFM	Western Federation of Miners
WHS	Wisconsin Historical Society

Acknowledgments

This book has had a long gestation. Originally, Ravi Malhotra, a legal scholar who focuses on disability rights law with no specialist training in history, read about E.T. Kingsley in Ian McKay's magisterial account of Canadian early-twentieth-century working-class movements, *Reasoning Otherwise*, one day in 2010. After discussions with many historians, he became convinced that Kingsley as a disabled radical was a topic that demanded sustained scholarly attention. With the publication of Michael Oliver's *The Politics of Disablement* in 1990, disability studies had taken off, and a book about Kingsley was timely. Yet a trained historian knowledgeable about the period was badly needed to set the project on a firm footing. This was particularly true given that Malhotra has always been based in Ottawa, far from the field of Kingsley's extensive political activities. Malhotra soon identified Victoria-based Benjamin Isitt as the ideal writing partner. One thing led to another, and we soon found ourselves holding a nearly $70,000 Standard Research Grant from the Social Sciences and Humanities Research Council of Canada. This assistance is gratefully acknowledged and enabled us to hire a large interdisciplinary research team that scoured the continent for archives containing references to Kingsley. After a long period of research and writing, the book that you hold in your hands emerged.

A mini-conference held at the annual meeting of the Canadian Law and Society Association in Winnipeg in June 2014 also helped to crystallize our ideas and increase awareness of Kingsley. We also curated and launched the E.T. Kingsley Historical Archive (www.abletolead.ca), in partnership with the University of Ottawa and with the assistance of programmer Shawn DeWolfe, an online collection of archival sources with interpretive material to make Kingsley's story accessible in the digital age. We thank our research assistants, Lucas Adams, Margherita Barbagallo, Joe Berry, Victoria Chan, Patrick Craib, Carolyn Cunliffe, Amy Derickx, Dianne Hajdasz, Allison McMahon, Devanne O'Brien, Tom Rorke, Morgan Rowe, Justin Schwartz, Daniel Tucker-Simmons, Ann Twigg née Andrzejewska, Patrick Webber, Katherine "Kit" White, and Paul Whiteley. Their commitment and professionalism were extraordinary. Patrick Craib, Tom Rorke, and Morgan Rowe in particular provided invaluable feedback and gems from the archives. Participants at the Kingsley mini-conference included Patrick Craib, Anne Finger, Dustin Galer, Esyllt Jones, Mark Leier, Geoffrey Reaume, Megan Rusciano, and Eric Tucker. We also wish to thank Mark Aldrich, Ian Angus, Paul Buhle, Peter Campbell, Bruce Feldthusen, David Frank, Douglas Hedin, Nate Holdren, Richard Jochelson, Jeffrey Johnson, Mark Lause, Mark Leier, Ross McCormack, Ian McKay, Dale Martin, Bryan Palmer, Jeremy Patzer, Mark Pittenger, Larry Royston, Carlos Schwantes, Marlys Hesch Sebasky, David Serlin, Alan Wald, Mark Weber, John Williams-Searle, Barry Wright, and Robin Wylie. Mikko Heinonen (whom Malhotra met at Harvard Law School) generously made available a translator, Outi Talola, at his Helsinki law firm to translate an article from *Vapaus,* the Finnish Canadian socialist newspaper. James Tracy kindly provided photographs of the building now located at 115 Turk Street in San Francisco where Kingsley presided over Metropolitan Temple meetings of the Socialist Labor Party in the 1890s as well as of various sites in San Jose where Kingsley lived at the end of the 1890s. John Williams-Searle kindly drew our attention to a striking illustration of a labouring amputee published in an 1891 issue of the *Locomotive Firemen's Magazine*. David A. Franz provided valuable details on how to find the site of Kingsley's 1890 railway accident.

The insightful feedback of the anonymous peer reviewers is appreciated, strengthening the manuscript in important ways, along with the efforts of Randy Schmidt, Meagan Dyer, Carmen Tiampo, and other hard-working staff at UBC Press. Nate Holdren was kind enough to provide valuable feedback on chapters. Helpful archivists include Ewa Delanowski and Eric Swanick of Simon Fraser University, where the Hawthornthwaite

Papers are housed; Cheryl Beredo, director of the Kheel Center at Cornell University; Kyle Pugh of the University of Toronto's Thomas Fisher Rare Book Library; Trevor Livelton of the City of Victoria Archives; Stephen Irwin at the Library and Archives Canada; and Tim Davenport of the Marxists Internet Archive. Each of these remarkable individuals encouraged us along this long road. Ilia Starr deserves special credit for invaluable input in helping us to secure the grant from the Social Sciences and Humanities Research Council. Alex Lubet and his team, Kirk Allison, Peter Shea, and Susannah Smith, were kind enough to invite Malhotra to speak about E.T. Kingsley at the University of Minnesota in 2013 during a sabbatical in which a public affairs television broadcast was also filmed. Bruce Feldthusen, then dean of the Faculty of Law, Common Law Section, University of Ottawa, remained steadfast in his enthusiastic support and willing to extend every possible form of assistance to our project. His passion and commitment were continued after 2013 by his extraordinary successors, Doyenne Nathalie Des Rosiers and Dean Adam Dodek.

Both authors wish to express their deep appreciation to family members and friends for their support throughout the research and writing phases of this book, particularly Mohan, Lalitha (who passed away in 2016), Christine, Linda, Julian, and Aviva. Finally, some of the best pioneering work on E.T. Kingsley was done in the 1970s by Ross Johnson, who tragically did not live to see the publication of this work. Dr. Johnson's legacy lives on in these pages, and we will always remain in his debt.

Able to Lead

E.T. Kingsley was a master on the platform – simple, direct phrases – master of repartee. This one instance that comes to mind – out of many, and one will be enough. Whenever an election took place at that time, in Vancouver, the Vancouver local of the party ... organized a debate or meeting between candidates. Almost always the other parties agreed to this. The boys organized the meeting, ushered it, did everything, took a collection, and thus got some funds to carry on their work.

This particular year I have in mind, there was a Conservative, was named Cowan, I think the Liberal was Joe Martin, and there was an independent running, besides E.T. Kingsley[,] for the Socialist party. This independent was a young lawyer with a good shock of curly hair and as they drew lots as to the order of speech, this fellow drew the first one and Kingsley was number two. Well the meeting opened and this boy took it upon himself to tell the crowd that he would not attempt to deal with questions of history and economics and these deep matters. "I leave that," he said, "to my bald-headed friend."

Well the old man, and he got up, he had artificial legs, they'd been cut off on the railroad on this side of the line, and he would stand holding onto a chair, and he said, "Ladies and gentlemen, I've addressed hundreds of meetings on this side of the line and the other side of the line, and I've never found it necessary to refer to the physical characteristics of any of my opponents." But he says, "This young squirt has taken it upon himself to make reference to my baldness, which is very obvious. I want to tell him that there are two kinds of baldness. Bald on the outside," and he points to his head ... Then he pointed to the fella and said, "and bald on the inside. You can see my kind of baldness every time I take off my hat. His kind of baldness is evident every time he opens his mouth."

That was old Kingsley. And I could tell you all kinds of stories about him.[1]

– W.A. Pritchard

1

Kingsley in Context
Labour History, Legal History, and Critical Disability Theory

This interdisciplinary work examines the forgotten and important story of Eugene Thornton Kingsley (1856–1929), a double amputee, railroader, printer, and immigrant who transcended the considerable barriers that he faced as a person with a disability to stand out as a leading light of the political left in turn-of-the-century western Canada and the United States. Variously described by socialist comrades as the "Old Man" or "Old War Horse," by the bourgeois press as "the legless wonder of social economics," by Canada's chief wartime press censor as "an out-and-out red Bolshevik Socialist of pronounced literary capacity and unquestionably one of the most dangerous men in Canada," and by the Winnipeg labour press as "the best exponent of scientific Socialism on the American continent," Kingsley described himself in the frontispiece to his magnum opus, *The Genesis and Evolution of Slavery* (1916), as "An Uncompromising Enemy of Class Rule and Class Robbery."[1] Bill Pritchard, a comrade of Kingsley's in the Socialist Party of Canada (SPC), described his oratorical approach: "He was very forceful – a very forceful fellow. That was his line – simple propaganda laced with these similes of his. They'd come out quick, right in the middle of things. There'd always be a good crowd when he spoke in those early days."[2]

In the pages that follow, we combine legal history, labour history, and critical disability theory – three usually distinct fields – to illuminate the hitherto (and unfairly) obscure political life of Kingsley. Born in the antebellum United States, he was radicalized after becoming a double amputee in a railway accident and joined Daniel De Leon's Socialist Labor Party

(SLP) in California, where Kingsley fought for free speech and ran twice for the US House of Representatives. In 1902, he moved first to Nanaimo, where he worked as a fishmonger, and then to Vancouver, where he operated a printshop and became a leading member of the Socialist Party of Canada, editing its newspaper, the *Western Clarion*. Kingsley ran for the House of Commons and Legislative Assemblies of Alberta and British Columbia no fewer than six times. In this book, we trace his life story through the prisms of history, critical disability theory, and law, illustrating how tort law, immigration law, and national security law deeply regulated his life while also providing him with opportunities to transform the world. In the process, we provide an original window into the experience of a disabled worker – and the radical movement that he joined and led – connecting one man's life experiences on North America's corporate industrial frontier with the wider currents of disablement, industrialism, and radicalism that shook the continent at the turn of the twentieth century.

On 15 October 1890, Eugene T. Kingsley's life changed dramatically and irrevocably. The political trajectory of the North American working class would change as well, even if Kingsley was not cognizant of his destiny. He was working as a brakeman on the remote Spring Gulch line of the Northern Pacific Railroad (NPR) in rural Montana, which had just been admitted to the United States as a state in November 1889.[3] Sparsely populated, this was frontier country, and the NPR transcontinental line had been completed through Helena only in 1883.[4] Kingsley, nearly thirty-four and a married father of two young boys, was injured when he fell between two moving cars.[5] He was rushed to the NPR hospital in Missoula, and his left leg had to be amputated between the knee and hip and the right leg between the ankle and knee.[6] During his recuperation in the Missoula hospital, Kingsley began to read the work of Karl Marx. Parallels between his own life circumstances and the dangers of capitalism might have propelled Kingsley toward the left, but unfortunately evidence of his political awakening is scarce.

What we do know is that Kingsley soon became an active member of the Socialist Labor Party, led by Curacao-born immigrant Daniel De Leon.[7] Known for their rigid politics and relentless opposition to the capitalist system, the De Leonists had a pronounced influence on Kingsley's political outlook and conceptual universe. The party encompassed a strong commitment to the complete transformation of the capitalist state while showing an aversion to the day-to-day trade union battles that Kingsley and his De Leonist co-thinkers perceived as hopelessly reformist. Kingsley was soon engaged in public speaking on the street corners of San Francisco, where he had migrated to after growing estranged from his family. In due course, he became a party organizer and ran for the US House of Representatives on the SLP ticket in 1896 and 1898 and ran municipally in San Francisco and San Jose. His meandering personal and political paths would take him first to Seattle, where he became active in the Revolutionary Socialist League (RSL), then to Vancouver Island in 1902, and finally to Vancouver, where he became a founder and leader of the Socialist Party of Canada, running three times for the House of Commons and three times for the Legislative Assembly of British Columbia. One of the most prominent socialist intellectuals of his day, Kingsley merits scholarly attention beyond the glimpses that he has been accorded to date. We hope that this book serves to rectify this omission, illuminating Kingsley's contribution as well as the tenacious capacity of people to rise above adversity and demonstrate an ability to lead within an environment systematically designed for able-bodied people.

Challenging History

Historian Peter Campbell identifies Kingsley in the second sentence of his invaluable book *Canadian Marxists and the Search for a Third Way* but chooses other figures for the four biographies that structure the work.[8] This methodological choice is symptomatic of the general marginalization of Kingsley within the scholarship on the North American left. He is a character who appears frequently on the stage only to be consigned a cameo role as the spotlight shines on others. The preponderance of Kingsley appearances in dozens of existing works on the history of labour and the left amply demonstrates his substantial contribution to the political landscape of turn-of-the-century North America – and hence the need for our study focusing on his atypical life story and his eclectic political life.

Historian Ian McKay identifies Kingsley as "the pivotal theorist in the Socialist Party of Canada," and Ross McCormack identifies him as "the real founder" of and a central ideological influence in the party, which enjoyed considerable influence in British Columbia and Canada in the first decade of the twentieth century.[9] McCormack notes how Kingsley, known by his nickname the Old Man, edited the SPC organ, the *Western Clarion*, from 1903 to 1908 and continued supporting the paper, at enormous personal cost, both physically and financially, until 1912. He was also one of the most popular SPC speakers and travelled widely in western Canada and occasionally beyond to stump for socialism and the abolition of capitalism, nurturing what would come to be known in some quarters as "the British Columbia School" of socialism.[10] Political scientist Paul Fox describes Kingsley as "a brilliant speaker and writer" and "a devoted Marxist" under whose "pugnacious direction" the *Western Clarion* "quickly became a resounding Marxist trumpet, blasting out revolutionary marches to more than two-thousand wage-earning subscribers every week."[11]

Much of the historiography of the Canadian left has focused on the tradition of social democracy of the Co-operative Commonwealth Federation (CCF)/New Democratic Party or the official communist history of the Communist Party of Canada. The earlier Canadian left, or what McKay aptly calls the "first formation" left of the early twentieth century, has received relatively little scholarly attention.[12] Yet as McKay elegantly demonstrates, this first formation left had a deep influence on early-twentieth-century Canadian culture. One of its central ideas was that social evolution would see the emergence of socialism from the self-destruction of the capitalist monopolies.[13] In this book, we offer a corrective to the dominance of social democracy and communism in the scholarship on the Canadian left while contributing to legal history and disability history through a historical and legal analysis of the political life of one man.

Kingsley was one of the most influential physically disabled[14] intellectuals of the left in North American history. The story of this American-born radical and double amputee who mobilized socialist forces along the Pacific Coast highlights a distinct and compelling contribution to political life in Canada and the United States during the era of capitalist consolidation. Alongside our treatment of this socio-political context, we consider the history of prosthetics and how this emerging technology provided options to men such as Kingsley – who lived more than half of his life as a double amputee – to participate fully in political life despite an environment that imposed significant barriers, in terms of both physical ability and expectations, to physically disabled people. We also employ a critical reading of tort cases to understand the opportunities and constraints for a worker who lost his limbs in light of Kingsley's lawsuit for $85,000 in the Minnesota state court.

Kingsley left the Socialist Labor Party during a factional fight in 1900 and then played a role in leading dozens of socialists into a De Leonist splinter group, the Revolutionary Socialist League, in Seattle. In 1902, he was invited to relocate to Nanaimo, British Columbia, by Canadian radical coal miners who would go on to establish the now forgotten but once influential Socialist Party of Canada. Kingsley soon moved to Vancouver, and as editor of the SPC political organ, the *Western Clarion*, he rallied workers against the horrors of the capitalist system and encouraged them to have the confidence in their own talents and abilities to establish a new society. We use critical disability theory, which we elaborate below, to explore how the racist and ableist immigration regime of the day shaped Kingsley's ability to operate as a radical. As the First World War broke out, the national security state gathered momentum. We show how Kingsley was affected by state monitoring of his activities while participating in some of the most important political events of the day. Although now forgotten, he commented on or participated in many political crises, including free-speech battles in San Francisco and Vancouver in the 1890s and 1900s; race riots against Chinese, Japanese, and South Asian immigrants on the streets of Vancouver in 1907; a bitter coal miners' strike on Vancouver Island in 1912–14; the controversial rejection of hundreds of Sikh, Muslim, and Hindu immigrants attempting to enter Canada on the *Komagata Maru* in 1914; the First World War and conscription crisis; the eventual censorship and suppression of dissidents such as Kingsley and his comrades in the Socialist Party of Canada; and the famous Winnipeg General Strike and One Big Union of 1919.

One of our primary objectives in writing this book is to demonstrate how critical disability theory can illuminate Kingsley's life and help scholars to appreciate better how amputees have been able to make significant contributions to public discourse. The paucity of scholarship on Canadian disability history suggests that this work breaks fresh ground in our knowledge of the experience and agency of double amputees at the turn of the twentieth century.

Kingsley and the Politics of Disablement

Kingsley has presented a genuine challenge to scholars because his life spanned two countries and involved facets of labour history, left history, disability history, intellectual history, and the law of torts, immigration, and national security. What was life like for amputees in the 1890s? Much depended on the social position of the amputee. As we will explore in this book, social class and gender had significant impacts on how amputees were treated, in terms of both receiving a prosthetic limb at all and the type and quality of the limb. Among adult men in the United States, amputees were often war veterans from the American Civil War or had been injured in the large number of industrial accidents common during this period. According to one study, between 1880 and 1914, a worker died in Pittsburgh-area coal mines on average nearly every day, and many more were undoubtedly injured.[15] As Edward Slavishak notes, the amputee was a powerful visible symbol of the failings of American industrial capitalism in the Gilded Era.[16]

What Slavishak so eloquently describes as the double logic of prosthesis is emblematic of the realities of disabled people in this time period. On the one hand, artificial limbs reminded the viewer of the realities of disablement and, in an era of intense ableism, the associated shame of impairment. On the other hand, artificial limbs offered the possibility of "mechanical transcendence," normality, and mobility without the casual observer's knowledge of the prosthetic user's impairments as we shall see in the case of Kingsley, in a world filled with structural barriers faced by disabled people.[17] Instead of enduring whispers and rude stares, the double amputee with artificial limbs in 1890 had the potential for normality in a world of ableism.[18] Advertisements for artificial limb manufacturers of the day such as A.A. Marks and Feick Brothers promised a restoration of masculinity and a comfortable prosthetic at a cost commensurate with a working-class person's income.[19] Some prosthetics cost as little as $15 (approximately $450 in 2021 dollars).[20] Four themes associated with the prosthetic user were a person whose body appeared to be whole, prosthetics as products of American technological power, a person whose whole body allowed a potentially elevated social status, and a body that worked and could return to wage labour.[21] Kingsley arguably rejected conventional wage labour and sought to transform capitalist exploitation as part of his understanding that a conventional path of wage labour was closed to him.

Theory and Method

We employ a critical disability studies perspective that illustrates how structural barriers, including but not limited to legal structures, both shaped and constrained opportunities for Kingsley throughout his life. It should not be forgotten that he was politically radicalized – and consequently impelled down an entirely different trajectory in life – because of the amputation of his legs. Although this point has yet to be developed in the literature, we suggest that a critical disability studies reading of his life will deepen our understanding of his political beliefs, choices, and interventions.[22] Critical disability theory – and more broadly the social model of disablement – seek to demonstrate how society handicaps people with impairments, drawing a distinction between socially created handicaps and physiological impairments.[23] At its core, critical disability theory posits that physiological impairment does not determine destiny any more than women's physiology precludes their equality with men. It also reveals how what might be called "compulsory ablebodiedness," or the establishment of a set of routines for tasks to be completed within given times, gradually took hold with the rise of industrial capitalism. This discourse of compulsory ablebodiedness constituted a new biopolitics.[24] Although there has been a dramatic growth in disability studies scholarship in recent years, Canadian disability history remains an emerging field. We will therefore apply critical disability theory to each of the themes identified above.

In the context of tort laws, we evaluate how concepts such as free labour might have encouraged railway unions and other unions in the United States to oppose tort reform that would assist their disabled coworkers.[25] We also consider how the language of tort law changed over time and how critical disability theory can help to reinterpret changes in tort law. Our purpose here is to shed light on the world of Kingsley and the contributions of critical disability theory to the literature on tort law.

In the context of immigration, the arbitrary use of medical classifications to admit some disabled immigrants, a matter contested by politicians as early as the turn of the twentieth century, appears to be illustrated in

Kingsley's case. However, perhaps immigration laws were enforced only sporadically, and socialists in Nanaimo might have arranged for Kingsley to work as a fish shop proprietor to avoid the restrictive immigration regime.

With respect to the security state, we probe its changing discourses and priorities during Kingsley's life. How might his impairments have influenced political organizing monitored by the state? Politically active as early as the 1890s, Kingsley was clearly monitored by Canadian authorities.

We adopt what William Fisher has described as a contextual paradigm to history in order to evaluate Kingsley's life and largely unexplored political ideas. A contextual approach situates intellectual theories within a larger framework by exploring which personal, political, and cultural factors led to the ideas. In other words, one attempts to reconstruct the context and then interpret the text in light of it.[26] By excavating the conceptual vocabularies of subjects and their milieus, one can obtain a deeper understanding of how the ideas were developed. Illustrations of this approach include Reva B. Siegel's analysis of how early American feminists used the discursive rhetoric of utopian communitarianism, abolitionism, and separate sphere ideology to make their case for women's property rights.[27] Similarly, Ian McKay demonstrates that a distinct first formation socialism was influenced by Herbert Spencer's and Charles Darwin's evolutionary theories, which helped to explain the complexity of a rapidly industrializing society and made enlightening the population about the issues of the day a key goal of socialist activists in this era.[28] This framework facilitates an understanding of how Kingsley might have transposed concepts that he learned while an active participant in and leader of the De Leonist left in California and later Washington to the BC context after 1902. A contextual approach to history is important because the distinctions between the reformist left and the revolutionary left prior to the 1917 Bolshevik Revolution were fluid. Moreover, his own politics changed over time as Kingsley eventually joined the Federated Labor Party in 1918 and then operated outside of formal partisan structures when he ran for Parliament one last time in 1926 at the age of seventy. His later political life has been poorly understood, and a deeper appreciation of how he interpreted the post-1917 world and the failure of the Winnipeg General Strike will contribute to a richer understanding of the dynamics of the left in that period overall.

We apply the contextualist approach to each of the three broad legal issues that we have identified to date. In the case of torts, we evaluate how the principle of negligence evolved doctrinally in the United States in the context of workplace accidents. We also consider how the concept of "free labour" influenced the ideology of American railway unions, some of which were not sympathetic to injured members.[29] Our purpose is not to make a contribution of comparative tort law doctrine but to probe the evolution of tort law in the part of the United States where Kingsley lived and litigated at the time of his accident. In the case of immigration, we examine how immigration regulations changed over time and how the discretion to exclude "undesirable" immigrants accorded to medical professionals was altered as conflicts between immigration officials and medical professionals emerged.[30] How was the legal category of ineligible immigrants contested over time as the needs of the state varied? How strong was the belief in restricting immigration to those who could be economically productive? In the case of the security state, we explore two dimensions: first, how the security state evolved between Kingsley's arrival in British Columbia in 1902 and his death in 1929; second, how the radical press for which Kingsley wrote, such as the *Western Clarion*, the *British Columbia Federationist*, and the *Labor Star*, portrayed the rising security state.[31] We consider to what extent and at what stage anti-communist discourse supplanted concerns about Asian immigrants as well as how Kingsley responded to the ontological shift in the political world marked by the 1917 Bolshevik Revolution.

In this transnational study, we engage a wealth of archival records related to the history of workplace injury and litigation, railroading, and the history of labour and the left in western Canada and the United States. We scoured all known writings of or about Kingsley in more than a dozen regional and national labour and left-wing newspapers, notably the *Western Clarion, BC Federationist,* Seattle *Socialist,* Winnipeg *Voice,* and *Labor Star.* We also examined the daily press in Minnesota, Montana, California, and British Columbia for coverage of Kingsley's lawsuit against the Northern Pacific Railroad Company as well as coverage of his electoral runs for public office in Canada and the United States. Aided by a large team of research assistants and archivists, we consulted court records at the University of Minnesota Law Library, NPR records at the Minnesota

Historical Society and University of Montana at Missoula, and records of the Brotherhood of Railway Trainmen in the United Transport Union Collection at Ithaca, New York. Turning to Kingsley's involvement with the socialist movement in the United States and Canada, we consulted the Socialist Labor Party of America Records at the Wisconsin Historical Society and records of the Socialist Party of Canada, Vancouver Trades and Labor Council, and kindred organizations and individuals at the University of British Columbia and Simon Fraser University archives. For national security records and government records illuminating other aspects of Kingsley's life, we consulted collections at Library and Archives Canada and British Columbia Archives. Finally, we engaged the field of oral history and listened to surviving interviews with fellow leftists such as William Pritchard who knew Kingsley personally and struggled with (and at times against) him.

This book is structured chronologically and thematically, moving from Kingsley's disablement and radicalization as a railway worker in Montana to his political (and later business) career in California's Bay Area, Seattle, and British Columbia. Following this introductory chapter, in Chapter 2 we provide an account of Kingsley's workplace injury at Spring Gulch, the resulting hospitalization and litigation, and the process of radicalization whereby Kingsley became a revolutionary. We also examine the politics of prosthetics for nineteenth-century amputees and its relationship to conceptions of masculinity. In Chapter 3, we explore Kingsley's activism in California as the state organizer for Daniel De Leon's Socialist Labor Party and his election campaigns for the US House of Representatives in 1896 and 1898 and for the municipal councils of San Francisco and San Jose in 1894 and 1900 respectively. Included in this discussion is a reflection on how limits on free speech shaped Kingsley's activism and an analysis of his eventual split from De Leon, culminating in the creation of a splinter group, the Revolutionary Socialist League, in Seattle. In Chapter 4, we move with Kingsley to British Columbia, exploring the racist and ableist immigration legal framework of the day while postulating how he slipped across the line to serve as a propagandist for Nanaimo coal miners and later to establish the printshop that sustained him for the next decade. We consider his early organizing work in Nanaimo in the context of the coal economy, which contributed to a politically radical and industrially militant

working class on Vancouver Island. In Chapter 5, we explore the transformation of the BC left in the opening years of the twentieth century,
focusing on Kingsley's role in the formation and leadership of the Socialist Party of Canada, which elected members to the Legislative Assembly
of British Columbia from mining districts and pursued an uncompromising
policy of "one-plank Marxism": abolition of the wage system. Aspects of
Kingsley's political thought, polemical style, and business pursuits are also
rigorously interrogated in this chapter. In Chapter 6, we focus on Kingsley's
campaigns for political office and clashes with the law in British Columbia
in the context of widening state surveillance and repression of radical
labour activists before, during, and after the First World War. Finally, in
Chapter 7, we consider Kingsley's last decade of left political militancy tied
to the demise of the Socialist Party of Canada and his final run for elected
office in the 1926 parliamentary elections as an independent Labor candidate. We conclude the book with a discussion of why Kingsley's life has
been marginalized in the historiography and speculate on what critical
disability theory can teach us and how it can influence historical and legal
research in the future.

In the pages that follow, we provide a sweeping and rare journey through
an essential period of North American history – from the turbulent
industrial frontier of Montana in the late nineteenth century, to the
street-corner battles of San Francisco, to political intrigue in urban Vancouver from the prewar years to the "not-so-roaring twenties" – organized
around the atypical but extraordinary life of Kingsley. In the process, *Able
to Lead* breaks new ground in disability history, legal history, intellectual
history, and labour and left political history. It challenges prevailing perceptions of the capabilities of disabled people in western Canada and the
United States while forcing a rethinking of the character of the early North
American left. It is our hope that this work prompts legal scholars, disability studies academics, and historians to reconsider the contributions
of disabled people to public life in Canada and the United States at the
turn of the twentieth century. As Kingsley's unusual life story suggests,
disabled people are able, willing, and determined to lead.

2

Incident at Spring Gulch
Disablement, Litigation,
and the Birth of a Revolutionary

It was an otherwise ordinary autumn night on 15 October 1890 as a Northern Pacific Railroad Company train chugged its way up the Spring Gulch line from Missoula, Montana, toward the Idaho state line, taking the just-completed "river track" that bypassed the mainline to the north, opening up the area's rich ore deposits.[1] Aboard a flatbed car near the front of the train, a thirty-three-year-old brakeman named Eugene Kingsley scrambled frantically across the moving cars. Because of an allegedly defective drawbar, the cars separated after Kingsley set a brake, but he did not see the gap because of the darkness.[2] He fell between the cars and was run over by the train, crushing his legs. He was not expected originally to survive his injuries.[3]

In this chapter, we explore Kingsley's early life and how it might have shaped his political development. We then situate his accident in the context of the time, a period so dangerous that President Benjamin Harrison regarded it as a crisis in his State of the Union address to Congress. We also consider how free-labour ideology, developments in prosthetic technology, and conceptions of masculinity affected Kingsley. Finally, we explore tort litigation at the time and demonstrate how early American tort law was dominated by doctrines that safeguarded the interests of employers. The failure of tort law led to its replacement in the early twentieth century by a statist workmen's compensation system that provided security to employees but also stifled the kind of worker control from below that men like Kingsley had espoused.

Kingsley's Origins

Eugene Thornton Kingsley was born in 1856 in the town of Pomfret, Chautauqua County, New York State, southwest of Buffalo, the first and only son of Hophni and Henrietta Kingsley.[4] Census records indicate that Kingsley moved about a great deal as a child and young man, living at various times in New York State, Ohio, Wisconsin, Minnesota, and Montana before ultimately moving to California.[5] His consistent migration westward is emblematic of the journey to the western frontier undertaken by countless workers searching for a better life during the late nineteenth century.[6]

Eugene had two younger sisters, Cora, born in 1858, and Clara, born in 1860.[7] Although relatively little is known about Cora Kingsley Cornwell, Clara Kingsley Fuller led a remarkable life in her own right as a newspaper publisher in the small town of Little Falls, Minnesota, book author, historian, wife of a Republican state representative and later senator, property owner, postmistress, suffragist, and sometime political radical.[8]

In 1878, Eugene married Almyra "Myra" Doane in Hudson, Wisconsin, not far from Minneapolis–St. Paul, Minnesota.[9] They lived for a time with Myra's family in the village of Caldwell, Ohio, between Columbus and Pittsburgh, with Kingsley working as a farmer, and they had two sons.[10] Their oldest son, Percy, was born in 1880, followed by Robert in 1884.[11] That year the family moved to St. Paul, where Kingsley worked as a fireman with the Chicago, St. Paul, Minneapolis, and Omaha Railway.[12] What might have been a tranquil farm life surrounded by a loving family would ultimately be shattered as a result of his fateful decision to accept employment as a railworker, particularly when he left the Omaha Road to work as a brakeman on the Northern Pacific Railroad in Montana in March 1889.[13] Although we have no record of what motivated this dramatic and life-altering decision, it was likely the harsh economic climate of the day that forced many marginal and presumably dispossessed farmers like Kingsley to take on dangerous industrial work on the railways. The proletarianization of impoverished farmworkers was a common theme in late-nineteenth-century America.[14] Kingsley was now the father of two young children and had to provide for his family. Brakemen were generally regarded as semi-skilled labour, senior to firemen but still relatively low on the occupational hierarchy compared with the better-paid conductors and engineers; the 1894 schedule for trainmen employed by the Northern Pacific Railroad indicates a monthly pay of sixty dollars for brakemen.[15]

Kingsley's migration westward also reflected rapid colonization and economic expansion on America's resource frontier. Montana, which Congress recognized as a state in November 1889, was at the nexus of economic growth in the final decade of the nineteenth century. Like elsewhere, economic development was predicated on the colonization of Indigenous lands, which in Montana required military suppression of Indigenous nations during bloody and protracted "Indian Wars" in the 1870s. At sites such as Little Big Horn, Sioux and Cheyenne warriors under the command of Chiefs Sitting Bull, Crazy Horse, and others forcefully challenged the authority of American corporate and military power, leaving nearly 1,000 Indigenous and US Army combatants dead, including an entire regiment

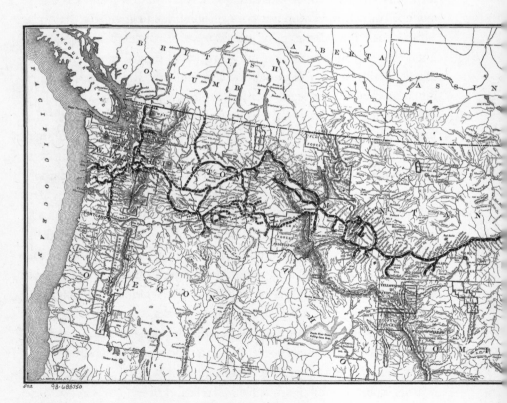

FIGURE 1   Map of Northern Pacific Railroad network, 1900. | Library of Congress, 98688750.

led by Lieutenant Colonel George Custer. The Northern Pacific Railroad was at the vanguard of American colonization of the Montana territory; survey parties initiated by company president Jay Cooke into the Yellowstone Valley beginning in 1871 played a major role in provoking Indigenous armed resistance. The US Army endorsed the expansionary aims of the Northern Pacific Railroad, with General William Sherman, commander of the army, advising his friend and subordinate, Lieutenant Colonel Philip Sheridan, in 1872, "I think our interest is to favor the undertaking of the Road, as it will help to bring the Indian problem to a final solution."[16] American colonization was pursued militarily but also through a deliberate policy of exterminating the Plains buffalo herds, depriving the Sioux and Cheyenne of their primary food supply, with Sherman advocating a policy of sending "soldiers to the plains, with orders to shoot buffaloes until they became too scarce to support the redskins,"

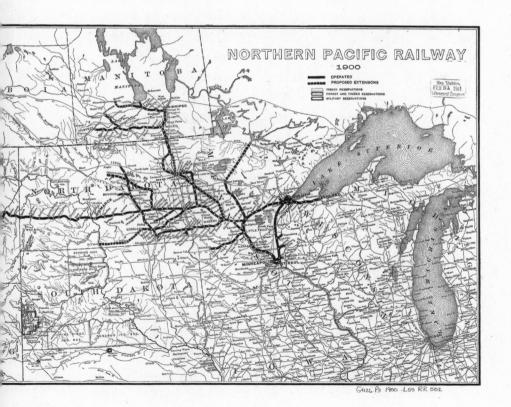

a strategy predicated on defeating a guerrilla foe "by making it impossible for him to exist in the country he operates in."[17]

By 1880, the Northern Pacific line had reached the Montana border from the Dakota Territory in the east, and the track across the territory was completed in 1883, providing a line of communication to open up the newly conquered lands to economic exploitation by American capital.[18] Mineral wealth, particularly gold, silver, and copper, provided the engine for expansion in the years culminating in statehood. Helena, the future state capital, was purported to have more millionaires per capita than any other city in the world in 1888, and production of ores reached $41 million a year later, making Montana the leading mining state in America at the time that it achieved statehood.[19] Although the railway company would be bogged down in litigation about the selection of lands containing minerals, completion of the Northern Pacific line was nonetheless a significant achievement.[20] By 1890, Northern Pacific was feverishly extending its network into northwestern Montana, driven by competition from the Great Northern Railway to open up new branch lines closer to the sources of ore within the state and in nearby Idaho (a branch line connecting Missoula to Coeur d'Alene would be completed in 1891). The discovery of large silver and zinc deposits at Iron Mountain near Superior (six kilometres east of Spring Gulch) intensified Northern Pacific's expansion in the area.[21] Working conditions in the mines in the Mountain West region of the western United States, the mountainous western states between the coastal states and the Great Plains, also led to the foundation of the radical Western Federation of Miners (WFM) in Butte in May 1893.[22]

Kingsley's Disablement

This was the context for the incident at Spring Gulch on 15 October 1890. Eugene Kingsley was ordered to ride on flat cars in front of the engine, but after he set a brake two cars separated because of a defective drawbar. It pulled out to a distance of five feet as Kingsley attempted to cross from one car to another. He could not see this because of the darkness. He fell between the cars and onto the tracks and was run over by the train. Both of his legs were crushed.[23] Kingsley originally was not expected to survive the accident.[24] However, he cheated fate, undergoing a series of operations and amputations at the Northern Pacific Railroad hospital in Missoula at

FIGURE 2 Northern Pacific Railroad train at Spring Gulch, Montana – the location of the workplace accident that left Kingsley disabled. | Museum of the Rockies, RVN09569.

THE MISSOULA GAZETTE.

TIME TABLES.

N. P. Time Table.

	Arrives.	Departs.
No. , Pacific Express,	7:25, p. m.	7:30 p. m.
No. 2, Atlantic "	5:55 "	6:00 "
No. 3, Pacific Limited	6:45 a m	6:50 a m
No. 4, Atlantic Limited	11:00 a m	11:05 a m
No. 5, Butte Express	1:05 p m	
No. 6, Helena "		7.00 a. m.

M. & B. R. V. R. R.

S Bound,	Stations,	N Bound
Leave 3:00 p m	Missoula.	11:00 a m Arr.

FIGURE 3 Schedule for Northern Pacific Railroad trains at Missoula, Montana, on 15 October 1890, the day of Kingsley's disablement. It might have been on one of these trains that Kingsley was injured. | *Missoula Weekly Gazette.*

a time when rehabilitation medicine and diagnostic tools were still in their infancy.[25] X-rays, for instance, were not discovered until 1895, several years after his accident and rehabilitation.[26] According to press reports describing his subsequent tort litigation against his former employer, Kingsley's left leg was removed between the knee and the hip and the right leg between the ankle and the knee.[27] His protégé and legendary socialist in his own right, Bill Pritchard, told interviewers that Kingsley ambulated with

FIGURE 4 Northern Pacific Railroad hospital, Missoula, Montana, where Kingsley convalesced following his workplace injury and where he embraced Marxism. | Montana Historical Society, H-3206.

artificial limbs (an adaptation confirmed in other sources), which might explain in part why reports of his extensive political activities in both the United States and Canada frequently omitted references to any impairment.[28] The Missoula hospital where Kingsley underwent rehabilitation, and which subsequently burned down and was later rebuilt in 1893, was one of four Northern Pacific Railroad hospitals established by the Northern Pacific Beneficial Association to treat injured employees and their families as well as retirees.[29]

It was during his lengthy convalescence in the Missoula hospital between October 1890 and April 1891 that Kingsley became politicized while reading classic socialist works by Karl Marx, including his magnum opus, *Capital*. According to an account in the Winnipeg *Voice* a decade and a half later, "after some time it was found that the surgeons had further amputations, resulting in a long period of enforced idleness which was made use of to study Marx's Capital which a friend lent him to beguile the weary hours. The result was a ready enthusiastic disciple of the Socialist philosophy and a profound thinker on economic lines."[30] Kingsley's political awakening following his disablement paralleled a larger process of radicalization under way in the United States in this era, particularly in the mining west, as the conditions that working-class people experienced on the western industrial frontier matched the economic prognosis offered by Marx and Engels.

Labour historian Melvin Dubofsky has explored this connection:

During the Populist and Progressive eras (1890–1917) when radicalism took root among Western workers, reform crusades ... challenged the capitalist order. This order, described fifty years earlier by Marx and Engels, was dying throughout the industrial world, the United States included; and social groups struggled to control or shape the economic order to come. None w[as] sure of the future, but all wanted it to accord with their concept of a just and good society. In America many options *appeared* to exist, for in 1890 and 1900 the triumph of the modern corporation and the corporate state was still in the future. And Western workers were among those Americans who opted for an alternative to the capitalist order ... Nowhere was the economic and social change which produced American radicalism in the late nineteenth century so rapid and so unsettling as in the mining West.[31]

A deeper understanding of the process of Kingsley's radicalization is lost to history. Kingsley left no first-hand account of the incident at Spring Gulch, his hospitalization and disablement, or his journey toward embracing the Marxist critique of capitalism. The local press is also unhelpful. Although the issue of the *Missoula Weekly Gazette* following the incident at Spring Gulch included reports on how the Northern Pacific Railroad would distribute $3 million in surplus to stockholders, elections for directors of that company, and accidents involving a Northern Pacific train at Boulder Mountain, Montana, and other accidents in Pennsylvania and Indiana, there was no mention of Kingsley's accident and hospitalization.[32] Company records are also notoriously sparse for details of personnel below the executive ranks.[33] But the outcome of this political transformation was clear: an unwavering devotion to the socialist cause for the rest of his life.

CAPITAL:

A CRITICAL ANALYSIS OF CAPITALIST
PRODUCTION

By KARL MARX

TRANSLATED FROM THE THIRD GERMAN EDITION, BY
SAMUEL MOORE AND EDWARD AVELING

AND EDITED BY
FREDERICK ENGELS

NEW YORK: APPLETON & CO.
LONDON: SWAN SONNENSCHEIN & CO.
1889.

FIGURE 5 Kingsley read Karl Marx's
Das Kapital while convalescing in
hospital. The exposition of the process
of capitalist exploitation radicalized
Kingsley, sparking his transformation
into a revolutionary socialist. |
Capital, Volume 1 (1889).

Kingsley left the Missoula hospital in the spring of 1891 for his family home in River Falls, Wisconsin, passing through Little Falls, Minnesota, on 3 April, where he visited his sister Clara, a school principal.[34] What followed is unclear, given the paucity of source material, as Kingsley adapted to his new life as a double amputee and political radical. A glimpse of his personal experience of hardship can perhaps be gleaned from comments in the *Western Clarion* nearly two decades later in response to statistics showing that 2 million workers had suffered non-fatal injuries as a result of workplace accidents in 1908: "The grand total of pain and misery represented is something appalling. Nor are the victims the only sufferers; wages stop when the head of the family goes to the hospital."[35] In 1892, Kingsley worked for a time with the law firm McDonald & Barnard in St. Paul (which represented him in tort litigation against his former employer) while living in nearby River Falls.[36]

What we do know with certainty is that, at some point in the early 1890s, Kingsley became permanently estranged from his wife, Myra, and their two sons, who relocated from River Falls to Minneapolis, where she started work as a schoolteacher, while Kingsley moved to the West Coast, specifically to San Francisco, by 1893.[37] The following year Myra filed for divorce in the US district court in Minneapolis, citing cruel and inhuman treatment by her husband; no further details of the circumstances of Eugene's relationship with Myra or the divorce have been found.[38] At the time, cruelty in Minnesota law had to involve both objective and subjective elements in order to justify divorce. For instance, physical abuse of a wife or neglecting to provide her with food, clothing, housing, and medical care could qualify.[39] We simply do not have the evidence to analyze the situation further. Counsel for the divorce was T.A. Garrity, a local criminal lawyer who was only twenty-four at the time.[40] We also have not found any record of Kingsley ever having future romantic relationships.

And we do not know how and why he ended up in California. The Socialist Labor Party (which Kingsley would lead in California) had an active branch in Minneapolis at the time, but there is no record that he joined it.[41] We are left to speculate on the trajectory that led him from the fateful night at Spring Gulch into a leadership position in that party in California four years later. His experience of class relations, disablement, and convalescence seemed to result in the erosion of family bonds and his transformation into a revolutionary and impossibilist socialist. Impossibilism, associated with the political thought of Daniel De Leon, refers to the notion that capitalism cannot be reformed through the introduction of piecemeal social reforms but must be completely transformed.

We are also left to speculate on Kingsley's association with organized labour both before and immediately after his workplace injury, which is unfortunate in light of his strong aversion to labour union activity later in his life. At the time of Kingsley's disabling injury, labour organization among American railworkers was uneven, particularly among semi-skilled brakemen and other trades, since railway brotherhoods focused their activities on the most skilled workers. It was not until a bit later in the 1890s that the efforts of Eugene Debs and others would help to organize all workers in the industry, notably in the American Labor Union, founded in 1893. We have found no evidence that Kingsley was involved with railworkers' unions, but he likely belonged to a local of the Brother-hood of Railway Trainmen based in Missoula, the established home ter-minal for Northern Pacific in the state. Consulting the records of the brotherhood (founded as the Brotherhood of Railroad Brakemen in 1883 before changing its name to the Brotherhood of Railway Trainmen earlier in 1890 when it opened its membership to workers employed in fourteen different running trades) produced no mention of Kingsley.[42] There was also no reference to him in the files that we consulted of the associated Brotherhood of Locomotive Firemen (BLF) (Debs's union), including in the "Honorary Register of the Disabled," a ledger maintained from October 1897 to November 1904 with the names, lodges, dates, and types of injury for members of the union who had been disabled on the job.[43]

The significance of these early American railway unions as benevolent associations to protect the interests of workers and families facing the substantial risk of injury, disability, or death cannot be understated. One of the founding purposes for the railworkers who formed the Brotherhood of Railway Trainmen was to "protect their families by the exercise of a sys-tematic benevolence, so very needful in a calling so hazardous as ours."[44] BLF records, including many signed by Debs as grand secretary and treas-urer of the union, attest to the central importance of providing economic support for disabled workers in the day-to-day work of the union – in a period before the advent of workplace safety legislation, insurance programs, the *Wagner Act,* and formalization of union structures and relationships with employers.[45] Railworkers' journals were full of material highlighting the hazards faced on the job. For example, a notice from the Illinois Central Railroad Company to trainmen in 1889, reproduced by the BRT organ, the *Railroad Trainmen's Journal* (Galesburg, Illinois), described in meticu-lous, legalistic detail the risks confronting railworkers. For example,

> all employees, when coupling engines or cars must notice the speed at which they are moving, and if moving at a dangerous speed, no attempt must be made to couple them ... The attention of employees is also specially called to the necessity for care on account of the icy and sleety conditions of cars in winter; of the unevenness of ground where couplings are to be made; of the inequalities of surface between and at the end of ties.[46]

The notice was designed to shield the company from potential liability, informing workers of the risks that they faced in deciding whether to "enter into or remain in the Company's employ." The railworkers' journal, meanwhile, described the notice as "a cold-blooded document ... [It is] a striking illustration of the undeniable fact that railroad men must have a powerful and defensive organization."[47]

Although historian John Williams-Searle has suggested that railworkers shied away from thinking about and dealing with workplace injuries and amputations, driven by aspirations of a brave and agile masculine physicality, BRT and BLF records suggest otherwise. Our research suggests that a major motivating factor behind the formation and operation of these fraternal organizations of railworkers was to provide a collective response to the risk of disabling workplace injuries.[48] The link between disabling injuries and working-class activism, as exemplified by Kingsley's story, was a common feature in railway unions: long-standing BRT president Alexander Whitney, though no radical, had lost two fingers during a railway accident while working as a brakeman in Iowa in 1893.[49]

Industrial Accidents and the Politics of Masculinity

Eugene Kingsley was hardly unique, of course, in experiencing an injury as a result of a railway accident. From 1882 to 1912, close to 50 percent of all deaths among members of the Brotherhood of Locomotive Firemen and Enginemen were caused by railway accidents, nearly seven times the next most common cause of death, typhoid fever.[50] John Witt observes that workplace injuries were the leading category of injury and death in turn-of-the-century America, causing as much as one-half to two-thirds of all injuries.[51] As Mark Aldrich has noted, American railways were far more dangerous than their British counterparts for railworkers.[52] Railway accidents in the United States were so common in this era that, by the First World War, nearly 14,000 physicians, or one-tenth of all physicians in the United States, worked for railway organizations.[53] Sarah Rose observes that among brakemen missing fingers were so common that employers regarded them as a valued sign of an experienced brakeman.[54] At the same time, some employers were eager to replace older workers with relatively inexperienced workers, as Kingsley would have been at the time of his accident in 1890, in order to implement speed-up plans and increase productivity.[55]

The culture of masculinity and independence among many American railworkers in the years following the American Civil War also fostered a sense that risk was a routine expectation of the job and a source of dignity.[56] Free-labour ideology, a legacy of historical debates about slavery in the American South, powerfully shaped the discourse of American unions in the late nineteenth century. A contested concept, one version stood for the proposition that "consensual relationships among autonomous private actors" would serve as the bedrock for American labour relations.[57] Labour unions, in contrast, tended to emphasize substantive outcomes that empowered working-class citizens to be economically independent within a market framework.[58] Williams-Searle has cogently analyzed how many railworkers conformed to an ideal type known as the hustler, acting with great speed and dexterity to accomplish the job at hand even if such conduct entailed the risk of serious injury.[59] The very concept of hard physical work as a sign of manliness was deeply entrenched in Americans' sense of their identity. Unions laid claim to notions of citizenship by highlighting the strength, confidence, and contributions of their hard-working members.[60]

Although like Kingsley brakemen were paid significantly less than locomotive engineers and, again like Kingsley, frequently injured or even killed in accidents that received little press attention because few or no passengers were killed, there was nevertheless a tense camaraderie among railworkers.[61] This led by the 1880s to a measure of union solidarity across the chief railway trades, including the Brotherhood of Locomotive Engineers (BLE), the Brotherhood of Locomotive Firemen, the Order of Railway Conductors, and the union that we presume Kingsley joined, the Brotherhood of Railway Trainmen (which operated as the Brotherhood of Railway Brakemen until 1890).[62] However, the mutual hostility and competition between the running trades frequently and tragically undermined working-class solidarity and strike actions against the railways.[63]

One dimension of this competition was manliness, articulated at times through attitudes toward disability. The cultural construction of risk, as Aldrich describes the laissez-faire culture of nineteenth-century America, was therefore shaped by attitudes of masculinity and the solidarity that accidents engendered.[64] Beneath it all, as disability theorists have stressed, was a draconian conception of compulsory able-bodiedness in industrial capitalism, in which profit making was king.

The running trades held an apparently contradictory attitude toward disabled railworkers in the late nineteenth century. There was a perception that at least some disability claims were entirely fraudulent.[65] As well, disabled members were often regarded with disdain and contempt since they were perceived as having failed to live up to the creed of competence and manliness of the railway trades by becoming injured in the first place. The perception was that a skilled tradesman would have been more diligent in his work performance and would not have been so careless as to sustain such an injury.[66] This attitude was also reflected in judicial rulings on tort actions against railway companies.[67]

At its root, this attitude reflected the wider cultural context within which a panoply of institutions developed in the United States over the nineteenth century to classify, confine, and discipline disabled people.[68] Rules requiring the completion of work at a given pace socially constructed the norm of the able-bodied trainman and excluded those who could not keep up with these standards from the labour market. Precise motion standards prescribing how the body should move and requiring completion of tasks within stated times were very much a part of the Taylorist revolution of scientific management that became widespread in late-nineteenth-century America as industrialization accelerated at a rapid clip and manufacturing and transportation required rigid factory discipline in order to meet production standards.[69] Those whose bodies could not comply with the new rigid ethos of efficiency were consigned to a life of poverty or incarceration in a wide variety of institutional settings such as asylums, poorhouses, penitentiaries, and state schools for those with particular impairments, such as blindness or deafness.[70] Moreover, as Rose has observed, if a male breadwinner became seriously injured, then he and his dependent family were likely to experience a dramatic fall in their standard of living even if he obtained work because any new job was likely to pay only a fraction of his previous skilled labour job.[71] Kingsley, a newly divorced disabled man, appears to have struggled with finances after his injury for the remainder of his life. Given this context, it is hardly surprising that disablement was regarded as a threat to the brakeman as a successful breadwinner for his family.[72]

Yet paying into insurance schemes for disabled members gradually came to be regarded as acceptable, especially given the alternative of company relief programs seen as arbitrary both in favouring certain employees and in undermining the power of unions even though they were largely funded by compulsory payments by union members themselves.[73] In an era before the adoption of state workers' compensation schemes, this approach provided a modicum of dignified support for injured workers.[74] To receive a company gratuity payment, the only real alternative, a worker typically had to sign a waiver with respect to any tort claim that he might have had against the railway company.[75] As the Industrial Revolution resulted in a massive toll of workplace injury and death on the rails, workers' attitudes toward disablement gradually changed with respect to the importance of providing appropriate funding for injured workers, if only because so many fellow trainmen were now suffering serious impairments that, as medical technology improved, they were surviving in significant numbers. It became evident that not all accidents could be attributed to a lack of skill or adequate manliness.[76]

In 1867, the Brotherhood of Locomotive Engineers established the Mutual Life Insurance Association as an autonomous organization with its own offices and annual meetings. During its first five years, it paid out $475,000 to 182 policies. This worked out to approximately $2,600 per policy, a considerable sum in this period.[77] Remarkably, Williams-Searle documents how trade unionists were able creatively to reformulate insurance payments within the ontological framework of masculinity that dominated American society. Whereas in earlier times to become disabled was to transgress the boundaries of masculinity, railway unions now began to argue that real manliness included a commitment to taking responsibility for one's risky future.[78] This discursive shift allowed unions to move forward with insurance programs without any threat to the masculinity of their members. At the same time, only a minority of union members subscribed to the BLE insurance plan.[79] In contrast, the BRT insurance plan was compulsory with union membership, likely reflecting the significantly greater dangers faced on the railway undertaken by brakemen such as Kingsley.[80] The *Railroad Brakemen's Journal,* the BRT publication, was filled with letters and articles admonishing those brakemen foolish enough to become injured after shamefully failing to keep up with their dues.[81] Again an ideology of compulsory able-bodiedness undermined the possibility of solidarity.

Nevertheless, as Kingsley's life makes evident, thousands of trainmen acquired physical impairments during the Gilded Age. Some railway companies did offer alternative employment to injured trainmen capable of performing other work. Office work, a form of disability accommodation a century or more before it would become enshrined in statutory law, was assigned to some disabled trainmen. When reading rooms became common on some railway lines to keep off-duty trainmen away from the saloons, they were often staffed by elderly trainmen, many of whom likely also had physical impairments.[82] Many railway companies would offer this informal accommodation only to those deemed not to have contributed to their injuries as a result of their own negligence.[83] Clearly, however, this policy would not have worked for trainmen more severely injured given the structural barriers in the physical environment and an unwillingness to include disabled employees in adapted employment. This left the unions for the various running trades with a policy challenge to address while preserving their attitudes toward the masculinity of their able-bodied members. The tension between these conflicting positions manifested itself in the debates about building and funding a home for disabled railway workers. Williams-Searle shows how controversial funding a home was among unionized railworkers because the very existence of the disabled men posed a threat to the masculinity and professionalism of the able-bodied members.[84] A heady mix of masculinity and compulsory able-bodiedness precluded unions from exercising solidarity in a more substantive way despite having the resources to do so.

The framework of masculinity so compellingly articulated by Williams-Searle also allows us to theorize the roots of Kingsley's political trajectory. In effect, by choosing to reject the system and joining the most radical anti-capitalist political tendency of the 1890s, Kingsley was able to redefine manhood and ability on his own terms. Although large numbers of injured railworkers were consigned to the margins as their wage-earning capacity destroyed their self-conceptions as independent men, Kingsley defied the odds by taking a path on which he would become a respected political leader prized for his oratorical and organizational abilities regardless of his physical impairments. He might have compensated for a perceived loss of his masculinity by masking his impairment, and there is hardly any record of Kingsley discussing his accident or impairment in detail despite spending decades in public life. This does suggest a direct relationship among his disablement, masculinity, and politics. Although no diaries and little correspondence by him have survived, it seems that faced with a traumatic physical accident he found conventional social roles closed to him as a physically disabled man.[85] Yet the path that Kingsley selected eventually brought him international fame that he was very unlikely to have achieved as either a Minnesota farmer or a brakeman on the Northern Pacific Railroad. The ideology of rank-and-file socialism also made a lot of sense for someone no longer capable of meeting capitalist standards of production. The universalist ethos of prewar socialism embraced the value of everyone, regardless of employment status, in a struggle against the capitalist system and therefore was likely highly attractive to someone in Kingsley's position, especially in light of the deep economic depression that engulfed the United States after the Panic of 1893.[86]

One dimension of his biography perhaps sheds some light on what is otherwise a mysterious tale. Clara Kingsley, Eugene's illustrious sister, married in 1894 a Minnesota Republican member of the State House of Representatives, Wheaton Fuller, later elected to the State Senate.[87] It is possible that Kingsley's brother-in-law's success as a politician, albeit one of a different stripe, provided some impetus for Kingsley to run for political office at a pivotal moment in his life. No correspondence between the siblings survives, but Clara, widowed at a relatively young age in 1908, later became a militant suffragist, even travelling to Washington to be arrested at the White House in 1917 and owning shares in the radical journal the *Liberator*.[88] This suggests that, despite the physical distance between Clara and Eugene, the two may have remained in touch. To be sure, Clara Kingsley Fuller was a pioneering feminist and likely made her own choices based on her own political development in the United States. Still, her marriage to State Senator Fuller might have influenced Eugene's political ambitions, and his own radicalization might well have affected Clara through now lost correspondence. We now turn to a discussion of the evolution of safety technology.

The Emergence of Safety Appliances

Kingsley's disablement occurred in the midst of a flurry of advocacy by railworkers and unions to address the most glaring threat to worker safety at that time: manually operated brakes and couplers, the source of Kingsley's injury. A staggering 369 American railworkers were killed and 7,842 injured in 1890 alone in accidents while coupling and uncoupling cars.[89] As the Brotherhood of Railway Trainmen's grand secretary-treasurer testified at an Interstate Commerce Commission inquiry into the issue in 1889, "9 out of 10 railroad accidents could be prevented by the use of automatic brakes and couplers on freight cars." He concluded his remarks with a poignant statement on the eve of Kingsley's disablement: "There is an army of cripples in this country, caused by the present style of brakes and couplers, whose empty sleeves, mangled limbs, stumps, and crutches mutely appeal to your honorable body."[90] Legislative action would arrive too late to save Kingsley's legs – with Congress mandating automatic brakes on freight trains in the *Safety Appliance Act* in 1893.

Aldrich makes the important point that one might conceptualize the economics of railways in the nineteenth century as a trade-off between railway safety and output as railways sought to maximize profit by preferring increased output over costly safety measures.[91] This model has to be modified to consider the fact that managers operated with imperfect information, and certain types of technological innovation, such as improved signalling, simultaneously increased both safety and productivity.[92] Nevertheless, to the extent that railways prioritized reducing accidents in the late nineteenth century, they were focused mostly on finding ways to avoid injuries to passengers through the installation of air brakes and automatic couplers on passenger cars.[93] Accidents that resulted in the deaths of brakemen were simply seen as an inevitable cost of doing business.[94]

By 1875, the Miller automatic coupler was commonly used on passenger trains.[95] During most of the nineteenth century, the link and pin coupler, however, predominated on freight trains. This coupler required a brakeman to stand between the railcars and guide the drawbar, a long heavy bar, through the drawhead while dropping the pin at the same time so that the two cars were connected. However, drawbars could become unfastened, or pins could break, resulting in serious injury or death.[96]

Clearly, freight trains required an automatic coupler system to reduce injury and death among trainmen. One major stumbling block was the fact that freight cars were frequently interchanged. This meant that drawbars were of different heights, grab iron locations varied, and many types of bumpers existed on the various cars.[97] Consequently, work began first on standardizing the height of drawbars. Although agreement on this height was reached in 1871, progress stalled during the 1870s since railway companies were reluctant to purchase expensive and complex new safety products.[98] Ironically, entrepreneurial success also played a role in delaying the adoption of automatic couplers: although thousands of couplers were approved by the Patent Office by the early 1880s, railway authorities could not decide on which one to select.[99]

After various failed attempts at railway safety legislative reform since the 1870s, in 1893 Congress finally enacted safety legislation requiring automatic couplers and air brakes through the passage of the *Safety Appliance Act* following a campaign by railworkers, state railway commissioners, and others, such as the Interstate Commerce Commission, which released timely statistics in an 1889 report on the shocking scope of railway injuries across the United States.[100] Created in 1887 to address the regulation of freight rates, the commission organized a conference of state regulators of railways in 1889 to find ways to address the problem. The Interstate Commerce Commission was encouraged by its state counterparts to advocate for legislative reform.[101] Speeches by President Harrison to Congress on the growing accident crisis in American society also created a political climate favourable to legislative reform.[102] In the 1889 State of the Union address, Harrison noted that nearly 10,000 brakemen had signed a petition to the commission calling for the installation of automatic couplers and air brakes on freight trains.[103] In his address to Congress, Harrison also remarked that some 2,000 brakemen had been killed and 20,000 injured in the year ending in June 1888, a staggering death toll that one might regard as akin to a small war.[104] Yet statistics were typically produced as a result of employer self-reporting and almost certainly underestimated the number of injuries.[105]

The safety campaign was led by Lorenzo Coffin, a pragmatic former member of the Iowa Railway Commission, who regarded the campaign for legislative reform as a manifestation of his Christian beliefs and attempted to craft a bill that would be acceptable to the railway companies. Frustratingly, even after the *Safety Appliance Act* was enacted, it did not come into effect for several more years since the railway companies repeatedly demanded extensions for compliance until 1900, citing threats to their economic health and to that of the nation if they were forced to comply with the provisions of the act.[106] In 1899, the Brotherhood of Locomotive Firemen noted in the *Locomotive Firemen's Magazine* that 31 percent of America's 1 million freight cars remained unequipped with couplers and that 56 percent had not yet been equipped with brakes, demonstrating the ongoing hazard to railworkers.[107] Edward Moseley, secretary of the Interstate Commerce Commission, acknowledged that, as late as 1902, no railway company had been prosecuted for violating the *Safety Appliance Act*.[108] This wave of legislative reform culminated in the *Federal Employers' Liability Act* (*FELA*) of 1908, which allowed a railway employee to have a cause of action in which he could demonstrate that the *Safety Appliance Act* had been violated and that the violation had played a role in the injury.[109] Unfortunately, reforms in railway safety that led to the widespread introduction of automatic couplers, technology that likely would have prevented injuries such as Kingsley's, were far too late for Kingsley. Railway safety could accomplish only so much. In many cases, medical intervention was inevitable.

The State of Medical Science

What was the state of medical science at the time of Kingsley's injury? Ducker observes that, in the early 1880s, there were few medical resources available for injured railworkers in the western railway towns. Because most towns had no hospitals, injured workers were cared for on an ad hoc basis, sometimes in hotels.[110] By June 1888, just over two years prior to Kingsley's accident, 200 physicians attended the first meeting of the National Association of Railway Surgeons in Chicago.[111] Aldrich identifies three major benefits of railway medical hospitals. First, they were economically efficient since they saved railway companies the cost of hiring physicians and ordering prescription medications on an ad hoc basis. Second, they significantly reduced legal costs by lowering the risk of litigation in an era before workers' compensation laws were enacted. They did so not only by demonstrating an ethic of care toward injured railway workers but also by carefully monitoring patients to prevent fraudulent claims. Third, they served a public relations function to reassure the average citizen that the railway had the public interest at heart, even though the annual death toll from railway accidents was staggering and railway physicians were often effective in torpedoing legislation regarded as hostile to railway interests.[112] Railway surgeons therefore had to engage in complex ethical situations in which their duty to provide quality care to patients was often in conflict with their duty to save the railway companies money, prevent fraud, and protect their employers from potential tort litigation.[113]

At the same time, railway surgery had become a distinct specialty with its own professional interests apart from those of physicians in general. By early 1891, the National Association of Railway Surgeons had attained close to 1,000 dues-paying members.[114] A rival organization for railway surgeons, with more stringent membership criteria, was founded in 1894.[115] Together they constituted an epistemic community as well as a lobbying group, seeking to encourage railways wherever possible to appoint surgeons as the chief officers of railway medical departments to ensure the maintenance of professional standards.[116] As we noted earlier, the Northern Pacific Beneficial Association, originally established in 1882, sponsored the creation of four hospitals at key junctions along the railway line in Missoula, Montana; Brainerd, Minnesota; Glendive, Montana; and Tacoma, Washington.[117] Other railways, such as the Atlantic & Pacific and Santa Fe, also established hospitals in major towns along the line, such as Albuquerque, Las Vegas, and Ottawa, Kansas. Typically, compulsory paycheque deductions from railworkers, combined with occasional employer contributions, were used to fund the railway hospitals.[118] As with the funding of disability insurance and disabled workers' homes, however, this was highly controversial. Railworkers in Kansas lobbied the state legislature in 1891 to prohibit compulsory railway company hospital associations.[119] Yet it would be an error to assume that this reflected some sort of ideological commitment to laissez-faire politics among working-class trainmen. Ducker has persuasively shown that it was not necessarily the concept but the rudimentary delivery mechanism that alienated so many railway workers. In many cases, admission to a hospital required a trainman to travel hundreds of miles from his family and strained marriages and family bonds.[120] Kingsley's own marriage came to an end in 1894, after the long agony of hospitalization in distant Montana, despite briefly returning to Minneapolis–St. Paul in the early 1890s.

The Class and Gender Politics of Prosthetics

The dedication of the railway surgeon was constrained by the technology available at the time to treat double amputees such as Kingsley. In this section, we illustrate how prosthetics in the nineteenth century were constructed as a tool for restoring manliness. This paradigm rested on a tremendous irony: men such as Kingsley were injured because of defective machinery, yet they were expected to have confidence in machinery to empower them. Immediately striking is how even the stump was related to the amputee's class position. Vanessa Warne observes how surgeons as early as the 1860s were cognizant that stumps designed for working-class people were often cruder, on the assumptions that they would be getting only a basic prosthetic or none at all and that the class mobility of working-class amputees was minimal.[121] Edward Slavishak also stresses that high-quality artificial limbs were simply unaffordable for most industrial workers and that many companies provided minimal funding for their purchase.[122] The fact that Kingsley, an injured railworker who had been a farmer, apparently obtained artificial limbs that enabled him to lead a political party is remarkable. It seems that his earliest artificial limbs were wooden and that only some years after moving to British Columbia did he eventually upgrade, in 1908, to more sophisticated, contemporary, and presumably enabling prosthetic legs as his financial situation improved.[123]

The artificial limb held out the promise of what Slavishak has eloquently called "mechanical transcendence," offering injured workers the chance for a new life post-injury.[124] Legal scholar and jurist Oliver Wendell Holmes Jr. famously referred to a prosthetic designer as a "surgeon-artist," conveying the esteem with which the creators of prosthetics were regarded: innovative and creative like musicians and painters.[125] Legal regulation played an important part in fostering innovation as hundreds of patents were filed between 1846 and 1873 for prosthetic devices.[126] Manufacturers such as A.A. Marks customized both the product and the advertising campaign as needed. There were two distinct waves of amputees. The first

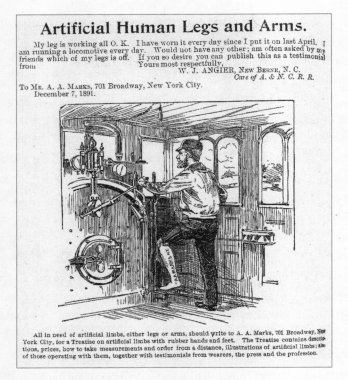

Artificial Human Legs and Arms.

My leg is working all O. K. I have worn it every day since I put it on last April. I am running a locomotive every day. Would not have any other; am often asked by my friends which of my legs is off. If you so desire you can publish this as a testimonial from

W. J. ANGIER, NEW BERNE, N. C.
Care of A. & N. C. R. R.

To MR. A. A. MARKS, 701 Broadway, New York City.
December 7, 1891.

All in need of artificial limbs, either legs or arms, should write to A. A. Marks, 701 Broadway, New York City, for a Treatise on artificial limbs with rubber hands and feet. The Treatise contains descriptions, prices, how to take measurements and order from a distance, illustrations of artificial limbs; also of those operating with them, together with testimonials from wearers, the press and the profession.

FIGURE 6   Advertisement for artificial limbs, showing a railworker with a wooden leg, exemplifying the hazards confronting workers on the railway and other dangerous sectors of industrial capitalism at the turn of the twentieth century. | *Locomotive Firemen's Magazine.*

occurred during the aftermath of the American Civil War, when breech-loading firearms resulted in many lost limbs, and the second took place in the late nineteenth century and continued into the twentieth century as rapid industrialization resulted in high rates of accidents across industries.[127] Lisa Herschbach documents a significant increase in patent applications for artificial limbs in the 1860s as the state sought to work closely with manufacturers of prosthetics to support Civil War veterans who had lost limbs during the conflict.[128]

As Lieffers so elegantly demonstrates, there was tension between traditionalists in the medical profession, as embodied by the professional regulations of the American Medical Association, and entrepreneurs who crafted thoughtful solutions for their disabled patients by inventing and patenting new artificial limbs. Traditionalists in the medical profession regarded the holding of patents by physicians, arguably best placed to pursue advances in rehabilitation sciences, as unethical and promulgated this value system in the American Medical Association Code of Ethics in 1847, which stipulated that the holding of a patent was "derogatory to professional character."[129] Clearly, the profit-making dimension of holding patents troubled many physicians. Entrepreneurs and manufacturers of prostheses, such as Benjamin Franklin Palmer, himself an amputee, pushed back against this ethos, working valiantly for their patients on the fringes of medicine while remaining outside the formal profession.[130] Lieffers illustrates how the role of prosthetic manufacturer was situated delicately between a social model and a medical model of disablement, encompassing elements of both paradigms.[131] Although scholars such as Katherine Ott are right to point out that designers and manufacturers of assistive devices such as artificial limbs and canes, both of which Kingsley used, typically ignored the perspective of the disabled user in product design and created devices without according due attention to day-to-day functionality, aesthetics, and fashion, at least occasionally artificial limb manufacturers themselves were disabled people.[132]

However, this spurt in artificial limb manufacturing soon expanded beyond the market for veterans in the late nineteenth century to include both middle-class professionals who had experienced accidents and injured blue-collar workers. When appealing to a wealthy clientele, manufacturers energetically sought to emphasize artificial limbs as articles of conspicuous consumption, rebranded as fashion accessories and status symbols. Manufacturers nevertheless struggled with the fact that impairment was stigmatized, and it was impossible to erase entirely the fact that amputees required artificial limbs for mobility.[133] There was a tense contradiction, accordingly, between the artificial limb as a luxury good and a medical necessity. For working-class men, the focus was on restoring manly productivity, which required that limb manufacturers invest in the intense shame of disfigurement and the need to avoid pitying stares to buttress the case for artificial limbs as the perfect mechanism of concealment. This is similar to the various beauty products, cosmetic surgery, and weight-loss products marketed to women today that rely on female shame and insecurity about body image.[134] The two ideas worked in tandem to ensure a profitable market for artificial limb manufacturers.[135] This was supplemented by the stigma of widespread municipal ordinances of the day, referred to by disability scholars as the Ugly Laws, which prohibited people with visible disabilities from appearing in public.[136]

Slavishak has determined four identities of manhood that advertisers articulated in marketing and promoting artificial limbs. First was the consumer as a whole and complete man. This appealed to traditional conceptions of masculinity and the role of men in society. Herschbach comments that "limb manufacturers were thus impresarios of a kind of theatre, systematically interpreting and dramatizing commodities and commodity environments in ways that disguised and transformed them into what they were not."[137] Second was the opportunity for elevated social status with the acquisition of an artificial limb. Advertisements for prosthetics typically featured well-dressed men in top hats and business suits, suggesting the opportunities that awaited those who invested in the devices.[138] Third was the artificial limb as a product of American technological innovation of which every patriotic man could be proud. And fourth was the restoration of a man's capacity to earn wages and consequently assume the male breadwinner role.[139] As Daniel Rodgers notes, a ubiquitous belief among nineteenth-century American policy makers was that "work was the core of moral life."[140]

In the last trope, one sees an early anticipation of the emphasis on productivity as the basis of citizenship that would become hegemonic within rehabilitation fields over the twentieth century and entail the use of disability ratings to assess and assign workers' pensions and threaten those who scored too poorly with confinement in segregated institutional settings.[141] This trope was also deeply imbricated with the free-labour ideology that carried enormous epistemic power in nineteenth-century labour movements. To be a man was to be economically productive and autonomous. At all costs, one was to avoid the trope of the "burdensome cripple." Indeed, rehabilitation experts such as Major John Todd of the Canadian pension board expressed concern that the reservation of particular occupations for disabled men risked the creation of what he termed a "special class of cripples," inherently stigmatized and devalued.[142]

Rose cogently identifies three key factors that shaped disablement policy in the late-nineteenth-century and early-twentieth-century United

States and collectively tended to increase poverty and marginalization among disabled people. First, the rise of industrial wage labour made it more difficult for families to care for disabled people. It also became more difficult for disabled people to find employment if they could not meet standardized production requirements imposed by factory owners and railway employers. Second, the rise of standardized production requirements precluded employers from informally accommodating employees such as Kingsley who had physical impairments. And third, the eventual passage of workers' compensation legislation in the United States after 1910 stigmatized disability and made it difficult for disabled people to re-enter the labour market.[143] By allowing at least some disabled men to maintain employment, artificial limbs served to block the most negative impacts of life-altering injuries.

The gendered dimensions of amputation also merit closer attention. It is hardly surprising that the vast majority of nineteenth-century amputees were men since the Civil War and industrial accidents were the major sources of injury. Hundreds of thousands of men sustained non-fatal injuries in the Union army alone.[144] However, it is important to recognize the extent to which Victorian attitudes perceived an amputation as feminizing, and women amputees faced even greater stigma and were frequently regarded as unworthy of marriage or incompetent mothers.[145] The phantom pains and twitching associated with amputations were perceived by many as similar to the malingering and akin to the hysteria commonly associated with women at the time.[146] Erin O'Connor comments that stump pathology compromised men by deceiving them into thinking that they were whole while betraying them by making them act in ways that Victorian culture perceived as feminine.[147] In short, in the nineteenth century, it was not evident that an amputation did not have effects on a person's mental capacities. This might partly explain Kingsley's consistent reticence about his accident in the vast majority of his speeches, newspaper articles, and even extant personal correspondence. Kingsley chose to become a socialist activist, and his silence about his impairment might well have been part of a conscious desire to downplay any perception of a diminishment of his keen intellect in an ableist society that devalued the contributions and potential of physically disabled men.

Tort Litigation

Whereas safety legislation and medical rehabilitation represented two aspects of American society's mechanism to cope with widespread injuries, the third key prong was tort litigation. In 1891, newspapers reported that Eugene Kingsley was suing his former employer, headquartered in St. Paul, for $85,000 in Minnesota state court.[148] Considering the effect of cumulative inflation, this is a truly staggering sum, perhaps more than $2 million in 2021 dollars.[149] Although we have been unable to locate the original court records, which appear to have been destroyed, one can obtain an understanding of the case through newspaper reports, a general understanding of tort law principles, and other decided tort cases of the era. Kingsley claimed damages against the Northern Pacific Railroad Company of $75,000 for the loss of both legs and $10,000 for pains of body and mind.[150] He was represented by the firm McDonald & Barnard, based in St. Paul. The law firm is identified as his employer in the city directory for 1892, and perhaps he worked for the firm as a law clerk.[151] This suggests that perhaps McDonald & Barnard waived part or all of their fees to Kingsley because he was staff. According to Peter Karsten, contingency fee contracts, which would allow someone without significant financial means to sue a large corporation in exchange for a share of the ultimate settlement, were declared barratrous and void in Minnesota in 1899. This refers to the practice of encouraging frivolous litigation. Such lawyers were stigmatized as ambulance chasers in this era.[152] Although not definitely disproving that Kingsley had such an arrangement, it seems to be rather unlikely.

At least one stage of his litigation was heard by Judge William D. Cornish.[153] Originally from Massachusetts, Cornish was a member of the Minnesota House of Representatives from 1883 to 1887. He was appointed to the bench in 1890 but left it relatively quickly. In 1893, he was appointed special master of chancery of Northern Pacific–Union Pacific executive receivership cases. Cornish later became a vice-president of the Union Pacific–Southern Pacific Railway System, Oregon Short Line, and Oregon Railroad and Navigation Companies as well as a director of numerous railway companies.[154] One source written only four years after he left the bench lavishly praises him, observing that his work was a hallmark for "fairness, close investigation, and deep judicial knowledge."[155] Although there is insufficient information to comment on his objectivity, Judge Cornish's post-retirement connections to the railway industry are striking and indicate how closely economic and legal elites were linked.

The outcome of Kingsley's litigation is not entirely clear because of the patchy archival record. However, a news report from July 1892 on "the case of John [*sic*] Kingsley against The Northern Pacific Railway [*sic*] Company, tried in the United States circuit court," noted that "the jury returned a verdict of $5,000 in favour of the plaintiff."[156] Given the preponderance of railway accidents at the time, the relatively common surname, and the absence of evidence that Kingsley received a financial windfall (which would be equivalent to $140,000 US in 2021), we cannot conclude that this was the outcome in his case. But given the timing and appearance of the article in the *St. Paul Daily Globe,* it is possible that this verdict applied to Kingsley, notwithstanding the variation in given name. Moreover, there is the distinct possibility that the company would have appealed against any award, a common occurrence at the time, as labour lawyer George Alger noted in a 1908 article on negligence suits by workers against their employers.[157] Case law supports the conclusion that any award that Kingsley received would have been small. Indeed, a report the following year entitled "The Price of a Leg" discussed "an unusually large verdict" rendered against Northern Pacific when a jury awarded $18,900 to a man who had his leg amputated following an injury while employed by the company.[158] Karsten observes that the median award for damages for plaintiffs between 1823 and 1896 for negligent acts by corporations was $5,000. Moreover, he stresses that juries awarded far greater damages when the tortfeasor was a corporation and approximately seven to eight times the damages awarded by English juries.[159]

To appreciate fully Kingsley's claims, we need to understand nineteenth-century tort law principles as America underwent an unprecedented economic transformation and as new technologies rapidly spread across manufacturing plants and mills, transportation such as carriages and ships, and mining to reorganize the workplace. All of these new technologies posed a dramatically new legal problem: the potential for injuries to complete strangers.[160] Yet the profound impact of legal realism on tort law, in turning away from scientific conceptualism and abstract principles to focus on real people's lived situations and empirical methods, would not come until later in the twentieth century.[161] We can only provide an overview of some of the salient points in the space available.

One of the most influential thinkers in the evolution of American tort law was undoubtedly the famed legal scholar of the nineteenth century, Oliver Wendell Holmes Jr. He maintained that losses for accidents must lie where they fall.[162] Holmes developed a systematic organizing principle, negligence, to structure a conceptual framework for tort law.[163] He found support for such a sentiment in cases such as the 1842 decision of the influential jurist Massachusetts Supreme Court Chief Justice Lemuel Shaw in *Farwell v Boston and Worcester Rail Road*.[164] That case created the notorious fellow servant rule; it stood for the proposition that employees assume the ordinary risks of their employment, including a fellow servant's negligence, because the worker is in a better position than the employer to monitor his coworker's competence.[165] The fellow servant rule thus obscured the managerial power of the employer in the workplace and displaced the onus for ensuring safety from the employer to the employee, even though in reality workers often had no control over the conduct of their coworkers and even might not have met them. It also focused attention on the instructions of immediate lower-level supervisors rather than on employers' overall control of the workplace, which had a significant effect on workplace safety or lack thereof.[166]

However, in the 1884 case of *Chicago & Milwaukee R R v Ross*,[167] the Supreme Court considered whether there was a "superior servant" exception to the fellow servant rule. This likely would have been the operating decision at the time of Kingsley's accident. In this case, a bitterly divided court ruled 5–4 that the exception did apply, concluding that a conductor was the superior of an engineer. A freight train collided with a gravel train in November 1880, resulting in the death of one person and severe and permanent injuries to the plaintiff, an engineer, who sued the railway company. After a detailed review of cases such as *Farwell* and others, the majority of the court concluded that a conductor could not be said to be the social equal or fellow servant of engineers, firemen, brakemen, or porters. A conductor was the personal representative of the corporation and had significant authority and direction over how these other workers performed their tasks.[168]

Another critical decision in 1842 was the English ruling in *Winter-bottom v Wright*.[169] The defendant was contracted by the English postmaster general to provide and maintain a coach to deliver the mail. When the coach collapsed, the plaintiff was injured, and he sued the defendant, alleging that the defendant had not maintained the coach in proper condition.[170] The Court of Exchequer unanimously held that the plaintiff had failed to state a claim because the defendant owed a duty only to the postmaster general.[171] The privity rule stood for the proposition that there was no liability for injuries where the plaintiff was not the immediate purchaser of the service in question.[172] This formalist line of reasoning prevented injured plaintiffs from recovering damages and was not reversed until the twentieth century.[173] Yet scholars of tort law such as Karsten have suggested that nineteenth-century juries were actually quite generous, rivalling twentieth-century damage awards. Indeed, some judges criticized juries when they awarded excessively *low* damages.[174]

Two other key tort doctrines were the contributory negligence rule and the assumption of risk doctrine. Each once again operated to shield employers from liability. The contributory negligence rule stated that even the slightest negligence by the injured plaintiff precluded recovery for damages against an employer. In numerous cases in the nineteenth century, this rule operated to preclude employer liability regardless of the seriousness of the plaintiff's injuries.[175] Courts almost always found that a worker who had violated a company rule was not entitled to recovery for damages because of contributory negligence.[176] The renowned legal scholar Morton Horwitz famously argued that the development of tort law facilitated the ability of bourgeois interests to protect their property rights in the face of a potentially massive wave of claims in a rapidly industrializing society.[177] In the Canadian context, scholars of tort law such as the legendary Cecil Wright, dean of the University of Toronto Law School for decades and one of the most influential theorists of tort law in Canada, have been highly skeptical of government intervention to assist those who have been victims of torts. Writing in the context of automobile accidents, Wright regarded such legislation as potentially undermining traditional tort principles.[178] We surmise that this laissez-faire philosophy would apply to the far more vulnerable group of injured railworkers.

The assumption of risk doctrine, also known by the Latin maxim *volenti non fit injuria,* barred employer liability when employers gave employees notice of defects in their equipment or employees learned of the defects. Courts also sometimes precluded liability when they concluded that employees had constructive knowledge of the defects.[179] Needless to say, such interpretations made it very challenging for injured workers to recover damages against an employer in tort, especially since the economic reality of late-nineteenth-century America meant that few workers would be in a position to withdraw their labour after learning of such risks.

Rules of evidence, such as the *res gestae* rule, also made it difficult for injured plaintiffs to succeed in litigation. This evidentiary rule posited that statements were admissible only if an agent made them at the time of, or in relation to, some act then being performed in the scope of the agent's duty. Interpreted strictly, this meant that statements indicating an employer's liability shortly after an accident were not admissible in court. Absurdly, this was true with respect to statements indicating liability made prior to an accident or even just minutes after an accident.[180] The rigidity of the rule served to deflect justice for injured workers and to protect employers from liability.

Another doctrinal issue was employers who maintained that they had secured contractual waivers of liability and therefore could not be held liable in tort for accidents that injured their employees. In fact, railway companies often attempted to take the same position vis-à-vis passengers by issuing waivers of liability on tickets. Contracts made dramatic changes such as reducing statutory limitation periods to a paltry thirty days, waived state safety regulations, and required medical examinations by company physicians. Waivers were sometimes struck down by courts for a variety of reasons, including paternalistic impulses to set boundaries within the framework of tort law on an individual's exercise of contractual freedom.[181] Collectively, these doctrinal issues might partly explain why the majority of accidents never resulted in tort litigation. Kingsley was an anomaly in having the courage to file a suit against his employer.

Corrupt practices in personal injury litigation unfortunately also made it difficult for injured plaintiffs to succeed. Although there were certainly disreputable members of the plaintiff bar who knowingly pursued fraudulent claims, the enormous asymmetrical power imbalance between injured workers and employers made unethical behaviour by the defence bar particularly problematic. This included employers who paid coworkers to be unavailable to testify on behalf of an injured worker with a meritorious claim and even Faustian bargains between a plaintiff and defence counsel to abandon a valid tort claim in exchange for a promise of steady future work for the lawyer.[182]

These factors combined to stack the legal deck against workers such as Kingsley, who attempted to prove in tort that they had suffered harm as a result of their employers' negligence and were entitled to compensation. As the *Railroad Trainmen's Journal* noted, a majority of injuries and deaths of railworkers were legally attributed to their own negligence, based on the doctrines noted above, when in fact the work process mandated the dangerous conditions: "The fact is that in almost every instance the hurried demands of the service required the performance that resulted in injury or death ... If he had not taken the risk the work could not have been done."[183] This seems to conform to the circumstances of Kingsley's injury at Spring Gulch as well as observations noted in Walter Licht's 1977 doctoral dissertation on the work process on American railways in an earlier period.[184]

The elaborate system of rules, notices, and waivers that employers imposed on railworkers to shield themselves from liability and to shift the burden onto workers was impractical in operation. For example, a notice of the Illinois Central Railroad Company from 1889 (which we can assume was mirrored in the Northern Pacific Railroad's internal procedures) specified the duty of employees to inspect "the pins, links, drawheads, and other appliances connected therewith," to ensure that "the ties, rails, track and road bed ... are in good, safe condition, and the cars are so loaded that such work may be safely done," and "not [to] work" until any defect was remedied.[185] Although this might have provided a theoretical path for a worker to escape injury or death, conformity to such rules was wholly impractical in light of power relations in the railway industry and the demands of daily operations, as the BRT journal noted: "If the railroad employees, every one of them, would strictly obey each rule ... the railroad business of this country would be tied up solid inside of a week and no one knows this better than the railroads themselves."[186] The journal offered the sober assessment that in the current legal environment "it is cheaper to kill workmen than to protect them."[187] Labour lawyer George Alger noted in the *Railroad Trainmen's Journal* that only in "a very small percentage" of cases did injured workers obtain a substantial award through the courts, even though "a great many accidents happen[ed]."[188]

Litigation against an employer was not something to be undertaken lightly. One trade union observed that, "when a workman goes to law with his employer, he, as it were, declares war against the person on whom his future probably depends."[189] This was compounded by the fact that many employees frequently had relatives who were coworkers. Any litigation threatened the employment of all concerned.[190] Consequently, it was typically workers who had more severe impairments and were unlikely to return to the workforce, such as Kingsley, who were plaintiffs in litigation against employers because they literally had nothing to lose.

Although we will never know the outcome of Kingsley's litigation, it is possible to analyze the extant case law to provide a reasonable understanding of how a court in 1890 might have interpreted his case. The two key issues were likely whether Northern Pacific was negligent both in failing to keep the drawbar in proper repair and in providing unsafe work premises because it was too dark to see that the cars had separated. Although it was not an insurmountable barrier, Kingsley would have had to demonstrate affirmatively that Northern Pacific had failed in its duty to inspect and repair its equipment. On the second issue, much likely would have depended on whether he regularly worked at night and therefore could have been regarded as accustomed to the work environment. However, if this were not the case and Kingsley could have demonstrated that Northern Pacific had not met its duty to inspect its equipment, he might well have recovered damages. Unfortunately, as we have seen, employers could rely on a number of doctrinal exceptions to avoid liability.

Still, despite doctrinal challenges and intimidating employers, accident litigation against employers increased dramatically in the late nineteenth century. In New York City's state courts, such litigation increased elevenfold as a proportion of the court's docket between 1870 and 1910.[191] There was also a concomitant increase in the number of attorneys in the late nineteenth century, particularly among children of immigrants.[192] Because the more elite areas of law were often barred to such lawyers in an era when racial discrimination and anti-Semitism were rampant, personal injury law became a stable and lucrative opportunity for many new Jewish lawyers. Having been raised in more working-class families than the typical attorney, in many cases they also had the ties to working-class communities that facilitated the work.[193] Yet relatively few workers succeeded in tort actions, and those who did failed to recover much. This is a bitter truth. In most cases, the accidents resulted in their permanent departure from the labour market. Even Kingsley, who rebuilt his life to become a renowned political leader and activist in California and British Columbia, struggled with financial issues for the rest of his life. Ultimately, the limitations of the tort system in the industrial workplace would lead to demands for its replacement by a system of workers' compensation.

In this chapter, we examined the circumstances of Kingsley's disablement and its implications in Gilded Age America. Since Kingsley was a brakeman, the politics of masculinity and class delineated a certain role that shaped his identity in this dangerous occupation. As a man using artificial limbs, products developed as a result of both scientific innovations related to prosthetics science and legal innovations related to patent law, Kingsley encountered a specific set of barriers that he overcame in a manner shaped by his experiences as a working-class man. A culture of masculinity governed how disabled men who used prosthetics were perceived, enabling his mastery of his prosthetics. This facilitated the public to see Kingsley as a serious working-class radical intellectual, as we demonstrate in Chapter 3.

3

California Radical
Fighting for Free Speech and Running for Congress in the Socialist Labor Party

Eugene Kingsley played a dramatic role as a socialist and free-speech activist in California in the 1890s through his activism in Daniel De Leon's Socialist Labor Party (SLP), including his election campaigns for the House of Representatives in California in 1896 and 1898 and his municipal runs in San Francisco and San Jose. His acquisition of a disability in the late nineteenth century affected his life chances and prospects. Limits on free speech also shaped his activism, including charges laid against him for street corner speaking. In leading campaigns for free speech in San Francisco in the 1890s, Kingsley and his SLP comrades anticipated by many years the far better known Free Speech fights led by the Industrial Workers of the World (IWW) in the early twentieth century.

Kingsley's political advocacy and career were truly remarkable. In an era with relatively crude medical technology and an environment in which physically disabled people were often cast aside or institutionalized, his fortitude in launching a political career was highly exceptional.[1] The paucity of known personal letters and writings by Kingsley, especially prior to his move to British Columbia, makes it particularly challenging to evaluate his precise motivations with certainty. However, the marriage of his sister Clara to a successful Minnesota politician, Wheaton Fuller, in 1894 perhaps encouraged Kingsley to rethink fundamentally his life goals and priorities in the aftermath of his disablement in 1890.

The Panic of 1893, an economic crisis resulting in a sharp increase in poverty, unemployment, and homelessness, as well as greater interest in socialist ideas and membership in organizations such as the Socialist Labor

Party, likely also had an impact in radicalizing working people such as Kingsley, as it did others, such as Big Bill Haywood.[2] There is also a geographic factor: Kingsley's protracted convalescence in the Missoula railway hospital following the accident at Spring Gulch, and his subsequent adaptation to life as a double amputee, occurred in the radical political cauldron of the mining west. On the eve of the Panic of 1893, representatives of independent miners' unions from across the western states convened in Butte, Montana, to forge a new, militant, unified organization – the Western Federation of Miners (WFM) – that had a major radicalizing influence in working-class communities where its members lived, worked, and struggled. "Almost every local of the sizeable Western Federation of Miners had its corresponding socialist club or party," political scientist Paul Fox noted.[3] The federation built on a foundation of class unity that had been nurtured by the Knights of Labor in communities across North America in the preceding decade. The Western Federation of Miners was also politically aligned with the populist movement, providing a powerful alternative leadership to the moderate approach of the American Federation of Labor (AFL) led by Samuel Gompers. In advocating militancy in the workplace and radicalism in the political sphere, the Western Federation of Miners harnessed and helped to foster a renewed combativeness within the American working class.[4] According to labour historian Melvyn Dubofsky, "the Western Federation transformed the naïve idealism of the Knights and native radicalism of the populists into a brand of radicalism shared by socialist workers throughout the industrial world."[5]

Personal factors also influenced Kingsley's emergence as a political activist. The fact that artificial limbs made his physical impairment partly invisible to a casual observer might have also enhanced his confidence in public speaking and activism. In any case, what is known is that Kingsley was divorced by his wife and became permanently estranged from his children, who moved from Wisconsin to Minnesota, whereas he moved to the San Francisco Bay Area by 1894, when a newspaper report documents his first run for office at the city council level. We can find no evidence that Kingsley ever had relationships with women again. Although he was unsuccessful in the election, as would be the case throughout his political life in both California and British Columbia, it marked the beginning of more than thirty years of political commitment to propagandizing, organizing, and electoral campaigning for working-class emancipation. Over time, Kingsley would develop his notable oratory and charismatic personality, which commentators so often remarked on during his long career.

The Socialist Labor Party

Although almost completely forgotten today, the Socialist Labor Party was arguably the largest and most prominent radical formation in the United States in the 1890s. Some background on the culture of the party and its unique world view helps to frame Kingsley's conceptual universe. The party advocated the election of a socialist government that would replace capitalism with a system of social ownership of the means of production under worker control.[6] An understanding of the SLP leader, Daniel De Leon, is also important because it is clear that Kingsley inherited much of his legendary style and politics from him even after Kingsley broke with De Leonism politically and moved to British Columbia. This is particularly true because the post-1917 political left in the western world has been structured primarily around a division between parliamentary social democracy that strives to reform the existing state and Bolshevik communism – an analytical framework that is completely inadequate to capture the originality and distinctiveness of the SLP world view.[7] The early party had branches and newspapers – in English, German, and many other languages – throughout the United States. Originally founded as the Socialistic Labor Party in 1877 in the aftermath of the railway strikes that year, the party was heavily German. It also had branches that operated in Yiddish, Russian, and French.[8] Much of the press was published in German and as a result had great difficulty reaching out to non-immigrant workers. Many members were based in New York City and unable to communicate effectively in English.[9] As many generations of American socialists would discover, a very large proportion of the American working class tended to be more class mobile and oriented toward purchasing consumer goods than fighting for a socialist union movement.[10] The emphasis on consumerism is hardly surprising in an era in which many new technologies became common, including telephones, bicycles, trolley cars, fountain pens, arc lamps, cash registers, phonographs, fire extinguishers, and margarine.[11] Each innovation led to significant changes in working-class life and a real sense of material progress. Nevertheless, this apparently complacent attitude was punctured by intense controversies and moments of class struggle, for example during the Haymarket Affair of 1886 in Chicago, in which nearly a dozen people were killed after a bomb was thrown during a strike.[12]

In 1890, the newly renamed Socialist Labor Party acquired its most prominent and famous member, Daniel De Leon. Hailing from the West Indian island of Curacao and of Jewish background, De Leon was an attorney by training. He graduated from Columbia Law School in 1878 and held a teaching position as a professor of international law at Columbia University in New York City for several years in the 1880s despite the skepticism and hostility of the conservative university administration.[13] Like many of his generation, he was a supporter of the well-known radical Henry George's campaign for mayor of New York in 1886 on whose behalf De Leon publicly spoke. George, a largely self-educated public figure influenced by John Stuart Mill and Herbert Spencer, had become famous nationally for his promotion of the single tax and his 1879 book, *Progress and Poverty*.[14] Although George was no Marxist and his ideas were largely dismissed by Marx as "bourgeois political economy," George saw the appropriation of rents by the state as the way to forestall depressions.[15] Intellectually, De Leon was influenced by Edward Bellamy's futuristic and utopian 1889 novel, *Looking Backward*.[16] Set in the year 2000, it describes a world without economic competition in which the state distributes work to everyone at the same wage and nationalized industry eliminates the massive waste associated with modern industrial trusts – hence, they are looking backward to a better, more prosperous time – in order to promote the common good.[17] One of the bestselling novels in American history at the time and very influential in its day, it convinced De Leon about the merits of transforming capitalism.[18] He first participated in the Nationalist movement in 1889. Inspired by Bellamy, it combined elements of elitist Fabian socialism with theosophy to develop into a remarkable – albeit short-lived – social movement with hundreds of clubs across the United States at its peak.[19] Disillusioned within a year with the failure of the Nationalist movement to move beyond the middle classes, De Leon began to read deeply about Marxism and committed himself to the struggle for socialism from 1890 onward. This provided the impetus for his departure from academia and rapid rise to the leadership of the Socialist Labor Party and editorship of its newspaper, the *People*.[20]

De Leon clearly had considerable skills at debating, organizing, and public speaking. James Young convincingly shows how De Leon's passion for the development of a working-class consciousness for socialism was central to his thought.[21] Both his uncompromising denunciation of reformist socialism and his self-effacing conduct as a leader to minimize his own role are qualities worthy of respect to which many socialist militants would aspire.[22] However, De Leon was also legendary for his dogmatic and sectarian interpretation of Marxism and his willingness to denounce and expel those who deviated from the political line that he developed. As Quint remarks, "in the technique of editorial defamation and coarse personal attack, De Leon had few equals."[23] One typical illustration is his objection to proposals to remove the word *labor* from the name of the party. De Leon commented that the "work [of the party] is serious; its jaws are set; and it moves onward; its every step lighted, not by the penny tallow candles of dilettanteism, but by the steady light of the lamp of science."[24] He went so far as to expel his own son, Solon, from the party for disagreeing with his interpretation of Marx's theory of value.[25] The inflexibility of the Socialist Labor Party became notorious as it sought a policy of constructing its own unions through the Socialist Trade and Labor Alliance rather than "boring from within" to advocate socialist causes in mainstream unions aligned with the American Federation of Labor or the Knights of Labor, as less doctrinaire socialists argued.[26] Even strikes and political protests were frequently regarded as capitulating to the reformist "labour fakirs" betraying the cause of the proletariat. However, what De Leon and his followers regarded as principled and uncompromising was often perceived by socialists and rank-and-file trade unionists outside the party as sectarian.[27] De Leon identified four qualities that he thought were desirable in a genuine revolutionary socialist and that conveyed much of the positive and negative characteristics of the Socialist Labor Party: the ability to work in a socialist organization, the willingness to submit to the will of the majority, the awareness of the need to obey the party's centralized authority, and the ability to be honest and maintain an uncompromising commitment to the final goal.[28]

It is nonetheless true that De Leon demonstrated flexibility in his political intervention and praxis when he thought that it was important. Although a torrent of abuse might rain down on a union leader deemed to be a labour fakir, De Leon genuinely grappled with the question of how to build socialist organizations by tapping into mass movements. He sought relatively respectful and polite engagement with Eugene Debs, the future leader of the Socialist Party, during a prolonged period in the mid-1890s. Debs deeply impressed De Leon through his effective leadership of railway strikes, including the legendary Pullman Strike in 1894, sometimes styled the Debs Rebellion.[29] It is only by appreciating the fact that there was always this desire among the SLP leadership to grow and the fact that SLP members had sharp disagreements with each other that one can understand the context of Kingsley's political life in California. Nonetheless, with the emergence and growth of the more practical and social democratic Socialist Party by 1901 under the leadership of Debs, the Socialist Labor Party had reached its peak.

The Socialist Labor Party in California

Whereas the Socialist Labor Party in New York and other eastern states contained large numbers of ethnic members who frequently organized in separate language federations, often spoke very little to no English, and experienced systemic discrimination as white ethnics in employment by more established immigrants, the pattern of working-class hierarchies was different in California. First, unlike their eastern counterparts, white workers in California were less divided by ethnicity or religion in politically significant ways.[30] Second, although anti-Asian sentiment was widespread, the segmentation of Latino workers into farmwork left urban craft work largely to white workers in California. And third, white workers accorded less deference to political elites, unlike in eastern cities, which had what historian Michael Kazin aptly characterizes as a well-established hereditary governing class. Since the Gold Rush, workers in California were motivated by an egalitarianism that saw the emergence of a relatively powerful labour movement, particularly in San Francisco, a metropolis of 300,000 by 1890 with one-quarter of the state's population.[31] As early as 1886, San Francisco held its first Labor Day parade on the Pacific Coast with some 10,000 workers in attendance, including the Democratic governor, General George Stoneman.[32] Although a relatively high standard of living among American workers still posed a barrier to the development of class consciousness and militancy in California, factors including the relative lack of white ethnic conflict created more propitious circumstances for socialist militants in the Socialist Labor Party.

To understand fully the growth of the party, it is important to appreciate the structure of the San Francisco economy prior to the shattering earthquake of 1906. By 1880, one-third of San Francisco's workforce was in manufacturing and exceeded the output of all other cities in the west combined. Resource processing furnished additional jobs in industries as diverse as sugar, canning, lumber and wood products, metal, clothing, shoes, cigars, leather, and textiles. Not surprisingly, the dynamic synergies unleashed attracted immigration from China and elsewhere since low-wage industries such as cigars and shoes needed a steady flow of unskilled workers.[33]

Populists, a social movement geared to agrarian reform, gained influence among farmers angry about the restrictive credit policies of banks, excessive transportation charges by monopolist railways such as the Southern Pacific Railway, and low commodity prices.[34] In 1892, they nominated General James B. Weaver as their candidate for president on a platform that emphasized the cheap availability of greenbacks.[35] Despite a formal resistance to reformism that sometimes has been interpreted as an unrealistically abstract conception of socialism that ignored day-to-day struggles, the record of the California Socialist Labor Party was in fact far more nuanced. In the 1890s, the party was active on a number of issues, including campaigns for the nationalization of trusts, support for strikes such as the famous Pullman Strike of 1894, and participation in the first national SLP election campaign in 1896.[36]

However, this ideological flexibility went only so far. Despite the existence of a variety of San Francisco craft unions, such as the Furniture Workers Union, that were open to socialist ideas and worked collaboratively with Populist activists, various single tax proponents, and the remnants of the Nationalist Clubs to elect a Populist and anti-railway-interests mayor on the People's Party ticket in 1894, German immigrant and millionaire Adolph Sutro, the Socialist Labor Party stubbornly ran its own candidates in 1896, who won a desultory number of votes.[37] They were also closely related to Coxey's Army, a social movement of the unemployed, helping to feed marchers and signing petitions for submission to the authorities.[38] As Kazin has noted,

> during the severe depression of the 1890s, leading unionists in the two cities [San Francisco and Los Angeles] temporarily joined the People's party, helped to write the state platform, and stood for office as Populists. Despite the party's base among small farmers, even the most class-conscious labor activists were willing to experiment with what, until the fusion campaign of 1896, appeared to be a growing force for basic social change.[39]

There were occasional tensions between socialists and Populists because some Populists perceived that the Socialist Labor Party was simply using their organization opportunistically as a recruiting ground.[40] Nevertheless, as the biographer of De Leon notes, many rank-and-file SLP members disobeyed the leadership's edict against fusion to support Populist candidates for office.[41] The prescribed reading list of the Oakland Branch of the Socialist Labor Party in the 1890s was surprisingly heterodox, featuring Edward Bellamy's *Looking Backward, Fabian Essays on Socialism* by August Bebel, and *The Soul of Man under Socialism* by Oscar Wilde rather than a steady diet of orthodox texts by Marx and Engels.[42] As is well known, Bellamy's iconic vision was deeply influential on many socialists of this generation and cannot simply be conflated with the ideas expounded by Marx and Engels more familiar to current students of socialism.

At the same time, the Socialist Labor Party maintained its own identity. Although apparently less rigid than the SLP branches in other states in its day-to-day practices, the California party opposed outright fusion with the Populist Party to ensure that its own socialist message remained intact and mainly regarded the Populist Party as a potential recruiting ground for new members.[43] The fact that the Populist Party would frequently endorse Democratic candidates for Congress, including the Democrats who ran against Kingsley in both 1896 and 1898, did not help matters.[44] In perhaps a characteristically blustery tone, De Leon ultimately condemned Populism, describing it as a "false movement" that could be saved only by "bluff and blarney."[45] An indicator of theoretical rigidity within the Socialist Labor Party was the requirement for tests on socialism for members of the party (a practice that later would be incorporated into the Socialist Party of Canada, likely as a result of Kingsley's influence). The aggregated result of these tests appears to reveal a degree of departure of Bay Area SLP comrades from Marxian orthodoxy: party activist Edel Hecht informed De Leon in 1898 that the average test score for members in San Francisco was a paltry 18 percent.[46]

The weakness of the trade union movement in California and the high level of unemployment in the aftermath of the 1893 depression rendered the development of political inroads challenging for the Socialist Labor Party. Not surprisingly, many trade union leaders preferred to avoid any discussion of radical politics entirely, opposed aligning with political parties in particular, and preferred to focus on bread-and-butter issues concerning their particular craft while jealously guarding their autonomy.[47] Nevertheless, a decentralized San Francisco Labor Council, with affiliations from some fifty-eight unions, was formed in 1894 to raise broader political issues of the day. They included jobs for the unemployed, municipal ownership of utilities, the eight-hour workday, better safety standards for factories and mines, and opposition to recent legislation attempting to regulate the poor. The Labor Council also endorsed universal suffrage, the use of the referendum, and ballot initiatives to recall irresponsible politicians.[48] Most decision making, however, was left to individual unions.[49] A convention in February 1896 made some progress in overwhelmingly agreeing to create an arm exclusively for political education known as the Central Trades and Labor Alliance of San Francisco.[50] The Socialist Labor Party had several branches in San Francisco, often but not exclusively organized and administered on the basis of language. In the mid-1890s, there were at least six functioning but fractious branches, including units in German, French, and Italian, as well as a Jewish branch that presumably operated in Yiddish. There was also an American branch led by Kingsley plus a Liberty branch, a Karl Marx branch, and a Columbia branch. The last branch was led by Kingsley's rival, Irish American labour activist Robert McIvor, who would eventually abandon the movement. Notoriously, these branches were often in conflict with each other.[51]

During his years in the Socialist Labor Party, Kingsley worked closely with a number of extraordinary union activists and party members in California who became famous in their own right or had been major historical figures in the radical left. Colourful comrades who deserve particular mention are the world-famous novelist Jack London (1876–1916) and the somewhat eccentric socialist lawyer Burnette Haskell (1857–1907). London is well known today for his approximately fifty novels, including the adventure novel *Call of the Wild,* published in 1903, the dystopian novel *Iron Heel,* published in 1908, and the autobiographical novel *John Barleycorn,* published in 1913.

In 1896, a youthful London and Kingsley were members of the Socialist Labor Party in San Francisco. London joined the party in April 1896 at the age of twenty and soon became known as the "Boy Socialist."[52] His massive correspondence includes letters to newspapers such as the *Oakland Times,* such as one letter in 1896 in which he defended the record of the party against the dangers of fusing with larger political organizations such as the Populist Party.[53] In 1897, on Abraham Lincoln's birthday, London was arrested in Oakland for giving a speech on the Bill of Rights at the corner of Tenth and Broadway in violation of a municipal ordinance that prohibited street speaking without the written permission of the mayor. Although ostensibly designed to control noise, the prohibition on street speaking was clearly connected with elite hostility to the socialist message of the De Leonists.[54] This speech was part of the challenges to state restrictions on free speech led by the Socialist Labor Party in the San Francisco Bay Area in the 1890s that resulted in newspaper coverage of London's activism. Although London's De Leonist days have been largely forgotten, London and Kingsley were comrades for a time in the mid-1890s. There is also some evidence suggesting that London might have first encountered the Social Darwinist beliefs that permeate some of his novels through his time in the party.[55] Although there is comparatively little documentation of Kingsley's activities during this time, it is interesting to note that Kingsley later published London's collection of essays, *Revolution,* at the height of Kingsley's influence in two issues of his newspaper, the *Western Clarion,* in February 1908.[56]

Perhaps the most enigmatic of Kingsley's colleagues was Burnette Haskell. A lawyer, a proponent of theories related to the occult (including the Illuminati), and apparently a corrupt huckster, Haskell was born in Downieville, California, in 1857, one year after Kingsley, and passed the bar in 1879 after attempting to obtain a college education.[57] Although never a member of the Socialist Labor Party, he seemed to promote a wide variety of theories during the course of his life. He began his political career as secretary of the Republican Tenth Ward Club and was a member of the Republican Committee that nominated delegates to the 1878 California Constitutional Convention. He resigned his position as deputy tax collector to start his own newspaper, *Truth,* in 1882 after his uncle purchased the four-page weekly for him.[58] Haskell tried to promote labour causes as best he could, including anti-Chinese agitation and the regulation of child labour, but his past support for corporate interests seriously undermined his credibility with the labour movement.[59]

At the same time, Haskell became active in the League of Deliverance, an organization founded to oppose the use of Chinese labour in the aftermath of President Arthur's veto of anti-Chinese legislation, the proposed *Chinese Exclusion Act.*[60] Tensions between Chinese immigrants and native-born Americans were growing significantly, as evidenced a few years later by the landmark decision in 1886 of the United States Supreme Court in *Yick Wo v Hopkins.* In that case, Justice StanleyMatthews for a unanimous court ruled that a neutral rule prohibiting laundries in wooden buildings without a permit was unconstitutional because it was enforced only against Chinese Americans.[61] Haskell also promoted the utopian socialist timber colony of Kaweah in central California, in which a few hundred people lived, many close to the Seamen's Union.[62] Kaweah failed because of internal political conflicts and external economic challenges, including criminal charges against members of the colony for illegal harvesting of timber following the creation of Sequoia National Park (a federal decision allegedly influenced by lobbying efforts of a rival timber company seeking to avoid competition from the cooperative colony).[63]

The anarchist-influenced Haskell began a branch of the International Workmen's Association (IWA) in 1882, complete with secret codes and rituals and, according to some contemporaries, an ultra-left willingness to use dynamite to blast bourgeois employers' and government offices, a rather unusual countenance for an attorney.[64] John Lawrence has described the politics of the International Workmen's Association as "an ideological mixture of Marxism, revolutionary Jacobinism and American reformism."[65] In February 1883, Haskell began to publish articles on the Illuminati, a secret French revolutionary order.[66] Despite the apparent eccentricity, Haskell worked for trade union solidarity between the International Workmen's Association and the Knights of Labor.[67] He later devoted his energies to founding a branch of the Bellamyite Nationalist club in San Francisco in 1889.[68] One of the largest in the country, the club reached beyond the manual working class that was the target of most leftists in the Gilded Age to include physicians, lawyers, authors, artists, and professors.[69] Facing another failed project when the Nationalist clubs declined amid allegations of corruption, Haskell turned to the Populist movement in 1894 and unsuccessfully attempted to win the Populist Party's nomination for superior court judge.[70] During the Free Speech fights of the 1890s detailed below, Haskell acted as legal counsel for some of the SLP members facing criminal charges. Whatever his failings, he can be said to have truly attempted to engage in every form of social movement of his era, from utopian colonies in Kaweah to Bellamyite Nationalism to anarchism and beyond.

Kingsley's Leadership in the California Socialist Labor Party

Eugene Kingsley played a pivotal role in the leadership of the California Socialist Labor Party in the 1890s. Beginning with his first run for city council in 1894 (when he received 1.2 percent of the vote for supervisor in the Tenth Ward, in today's South Beach district), he would run repeatedly for public office in the 1890s, a pattern of political engagement that he would continue once he moved to the "other side of the line" to promote his uncompromising vision of socialism in British Columbia.[71] Although Kingsley typically won only a few hundred votes and failed to win office in both of his runs for the US House of Representatives in 1896 and 1898, he clearly had a significant public profile in San Francisco, as indicated by the consistent newspaper coverage that he garnered. This is hardly surprising when one considers that a newspaper report in 1896 described the Socialist Labor Party as having several thousand members in the city and a permanent headquarters at the Metropolitan Labor Temple, also known as the Socialist Hall, at 115 Turk Street, which later housed the Beth Israel synagogue.[72] Kingsley was listed as its secretary in public documents as early as 1895 (as well as secretary of the SLP branch).[73] In the midst of the municipal election campaign in October 1894, identified as secretary of the SLP State Executive Committee, he challenged Republican, Democratic, and People's Party representatives to a public debate.[74] They do not appear to have accepted the challenge. In March 1895, he railed against a proposed revision to the San Francisco City Charter, the city's governing document, on the ground that it "was framed by men representing property interests."[75] A month later Kingsley was included among the signatories on a call to action to "all labor organizations and reform bodies" for a "grand labor demonstration" on International Workers' Day, 1 May 1895.[76]

Kingsley was acclaimed as the state organizer of the Socialist Labor Party in a California-wide referendum of members in April 1896 and was a keynote speaker at the 1896 San Francisco May Day celebrations, which took place at the Metropolitan Labor Temple, the largest auditorium in the city with seating for 2,000.[77] In his May Day address, Kingsley proclaimed that revolutionary politics "could not mix with mere reform any more than could oil and water."[78] One historian described the Metropolitan Temple as "quite an addition to the city's few auditoriums at that time. Although built of wood, it was commodious and handsome; it had what in theatres is called an orchestra; over this was a horse-shoe balcony; the hall was comfortable, and all could see and hear."[79] Adequate space was important since meetings often featured flower displays and musical performances, including trombone solos and choir singing.[80] At major meetings, such as those commemorating the Paris Commune, it was not uncommon to feature speeches in English, German, and French.[81] Other topics included a discussion of the English socialist William Morris, the exploitative aspects of the discovery of gold in the Klondike, and the rather Darwinian topic "The Survival of the Fittest."[82] Sometimes Stanford University faculty members would be invited to give talks.[83] Although the Socialist Labor Party had only a limited appreciation of feminist issues, some meetings were under the management of women.[84]

As early as 1895, Kingsley was giving speeches in San Francisco venues, explaining the central planks and philosophy of the party, and encouraging citizens to vote for and join the party. In April that year, he offered a lecture as part of the SLP Sunday-evening speakers' series at the Metropolitan

Labor Temple, as noted in the eclectic journal *Twentieth Century*, founded by Hugh Pentecost, an enthusiast of Henry George's single-tax proposal.[85] These Sunday-evening lectures would later become a central tactic of the Socialist Party of Canada under Kingsley's leadership. In a speech at San Francisco's Pythian Hall on 27 October 1895, Kingsley spoke about how his vision of socialism could be realized given the various branches of government in the American form of democracy. He argued that the current form of municipal government was wasteful and ought to be replaced by socialism through the destruction of rent, interest, and property.[86] His legendary orthodoxy and impossibilist beliefs, as well as his sarcastic wit, were evident in his speech even at this early stage of his political career. This was no weak Fabian socialist dream of a mixed economy with capitalist enterprises working side by side with a modest state-owned sector. Rather, the point of an election, in Kingsley's conceptual universe, was for the Socialist Labor Party to gain power to transform the entire economy into a cooperative system and build socialism.

One particularly practical innovation was the use of wagons to allow socialist speakers to travel to more remote communities to spread socialist ideas and literature. Frank Hadsell, an SLP member whose health improved when he lived outside, was to lead this expedition, with two companions, to northern California in a wagon ten feet long and six feet wide on which a small house was mounted. Kingsley was mooted as a possible participant given his capacity as the state organizer, and he would later be described in the *San Francisco Examiner* as a "member of the Socialist wagon campaign."[87] He advised the SLP leadership that "the red van sent out by the State Ex [Executive] is now here and good meetings are being held nightly on the street corners."[88] In its 1896 report to the SLP national convention, the party's National Executive Committee noted that in California "we have made remarkable progress within a very short time," going from having two cities organized (Los Angeles and San Francisco) to adding Oakland, San Jose, San Diego, and Santa Cruz "in rapid succession." A state committee had been organized, and steps were being taken to overcome procedural obstacles for small parties in order to "put an electoral ticket in the field."[89] Ultimately, the party gathered about 15,000 signatures to qualify as a party ticket on the state-wide ballot (far exceeding the required threshold of 9,000 signatures).[90]

Kingsley's legendary oratorical skills were also on display in a speech that Kingsley gave for the Liberty branch of the San Francisco Socialist Labor Party in July 1896 at the Metropolitan Labor Temple. After a reading from a socialist journal by the branch secretary, Theodore Lynch, Kingsley spoke about the state of the economy.[91] Reproducing his remarks gives the reader a flavour of his colourful speaking style:

> If I were to ask your attention to-night to a question that affected money, tariff or some of the other unimportant questions, you would be far from the cause of evils, that infest society. Foolish people, who claim that socialism is a product of a particular nation, are daily receiving an object lesson in the economic field. Every intelligent man to-day in this country knows that socialism is the child of economic conditions.
>
> The workers of America today are face to face to-day with a condition of things that must inevitably end in their complete degradation to abject slavery or revolution if those who love their country and their fellow-beings neglect the advantages that socialism offers to adjust the society we live in on a more harmonious basis. We are living to-day in the heroic age – an age in which the chivalry of youth can again emulate the spirit of liberty that animated the heroes and patriots of days gone by.[92]

It was, however, the Free Speech fights and the associated legal proceedings beginning in 1895 that increased Kingsley's profile. To our knowledge, almost no sustained scholarly attention has been paid to the SLP-led Free Speech fights of the 1890s in San Francisco and Oakland, but they are important precursors to the more widely known Free Speech fights in California, Washington State, British Columbia, and other places in the early twentieth century.[93] The first known report was in October 1895 outlining the arrest of Kingsley at the corner of Seventh Street and Market Street for obstructing a sidewalk and disturbing the peace. A few days later other socialists were arrested.[94] In an era prior to the modern development of First Amendment jurisprudence, the newspaper report noted that the treatment of socialists was not consistent with that of religious supporters of the Salvation Army allowed to make public speeches. It also referred to a previous case decided by Judge James Conlan involving the

FIGURE 7 Market Street in downtown San Francisco, where Kingsley and other socialists made their stand for free speech in 1895 and 1896. | Library of Congress, 2015651519. Photograph by I.W. Taber.

leader of the radical cigar makers' union. The SLP members demanded a trial by jury, likely in conformity with their beliefs on how the justice system should work.[95] After a jury acquitted Kingsley, Anna Smith, and T.E. Zant, the San Francisco Labor Council adopted a resolution in mid-November 1895 declaring that,

> Whereas, The police authorities of this City have in defiance of law, the decision of our courts and our constitutional rights, interfered with and abridged the right of free speech by arresting American citizens without cause or justification while holding meetings on our public streets, therefore be it
>
> Resolved, That the San Francisco Labor Council, in the name of justice and liberty, considers this usurpation of power and violation of our rights as tyrannical, unwarranted and a defiance of rights guaranteed by our constitution.

> Resolved, That we demand that the proper authorities do in future protect and insure [*sic*] to all citizens the right to peaceful utterance in public of their sentiments upon all proper subjects; and be it further

> Resolved, That the council take the necessary steps to see that no interference under the guise of ignorant or arbitrary authority or otherwise be permitted to violate the constitutional rights of American citizens.[96]

After several demonstrations by Kingsley, the Socialist Labor Party, and labour supporters to flout openly the authority of the police, the issue appears to have subsided, and the socialists continued to conduct open-air meetings.[97]

Nearly a year later, Kingsley was again arrested on a charge of obstructing a sidewalk and disturbing the peace while giving a speech at the corner of Seventh Street and Market Street after complaints from the Odd Fellows Association. The incident occurred during his 1896 congressional campaign, when Kingsley was arrested midway through his speech on 15 August by four San Francisco police officers, "public watchdogs of private property," as an SLP member quipped in a letter to the National Executive Committee.[98] A report in the *San Francisco Examiner* described Kingsley's arrest as well as his impairment:

> E.T. Kingsley, candidate for Congress in the Fourth District, lost both his legs in a railroad accident. He walks on two wooden ones and gets about on them fairly well with the aid of a stout cane. He was nicely balanced on his patent rostrum on Saturday night when the police made a rush at him, and had it not been for the outstretched arms of his comrades he would have been tumbled on the paving stones.[99]

Despite informing the police of their rights as American citizens, several others were also arrested before a crowd of some 200, including George Speed and an African American man, William Costley, the chair of the meeting.[100] Again the lawyers for the SLP members, including Burnette Haskell, demanded a trial by jury, confident that the real reason for the arrests was the radical political message.[101] A fine of five dollars or twenty-four hours in jail was imposed.[102] In response to the arrests, the Socialist Labor Party organized a mass meeting, building a coalition with other

FIGURE 8 Political cartoon in the midst of the 1896 San Francisco Free Speech fight. | *San Francisco Chronicle.*

organizations such as the Women's Suffrage Club and trade unions concerned about free speech.[103] They demonstrated remarkable creativity in organizing another protest of some twenty SLP members in complete silence in order to test the police response. Their banners proclaimed slogans such as "Don't make a noise. This is the new way to discuss political economy and public matters." Nevertheless, they faced further arrests, including Charles Sunflower, an African American socialist and cook.[104]

In the end, a jury in Judge Conlan's court convicted Kingsley, Costley, and the other six socialists arrested on 15 August of obstructing the street, but the charges against Sunflower and others arising from subsequent protests were thrown out when the jury failed to reach a verdict.[105] In a surprising departure from the staid socialist orthodoxy, they demonstrated innovation, albeit of a sexist kind, when it was suggested in correspondence that they should arrange in the future to have "a good looking woman arrested and go to jail" because newspapers would cover it to increase

FIGURE 9 Socialist Labor Party of America poster during the 1896 San Francisco Free Speech fight. | Wisconsin Historical Society.

sales.[106] In defiance of the authorities, Kingsley and the socialists continued to convene open-air meetings on the streets of San Francisco, pledging to do so up to the mid-term election.[107] The Socialist Labor Party consequently played a pioneering role in raising the issue of free speech, which would continue for some years, including in Vancouver in 1909 and 1912. At the San Francisco May Day meeting of 1897, Kingsley also condemned the police for arresting a wagon operator advertising the meeting and for restricting free speech by preventing street meetings.[108] As noted earlier, Jack London was arrested for leading his own campaign for free speech that year in Oakland.[109]

Kingsley's Fall from Grace

Although Kingsley clearly was an esteemed member of the Socialist Labor Party as the state organizer and the party's candidate for the Fourth and Fifth Districts of California in the House of Representatives in 1896 and 1898, respectively, at some point he fell out of favour with sections of the

SLP leadership in California.[110] Indeed, in April 1896, he was acclaimed as the state organizer in a referendum vote of the membership of the California branches, and he was re-elected in 1897.[111] Kingsley also continued to lecture regularly on behalf of the party, including at an event commemorating the Paris Commune in March 1897.[112] However, his falling out with the SLP leadership was far from difficult given De Leon's propensity to discipline or expel anyone who seemed to be deviating, even slightly, from his rigid vision of socialism. Kingsley's style of leadership and political views also appear to have contributed to tensions with other members of the California section of the Socialist Labor Party.

Early signs of this dysfunctionality can be seen in a revealing letter dated 15 May 1896 from Edel Hecht of the San Francisco branch to Henry Kuhn, the SLP national secretary in New York.[113] Hecht detailed the deep tensions among the SLP branches over the issue of trade unionism, describing the state of internal party functioning in San Francisco as deplorable. This political dispute inside the party played out in the May Day celebration events of the San Francisco branch and was covered in detail by the *San Francisco Call* the next day. Kingsley, in charge of the American branch that controlled the city-wide central committee, strongly opposed unions as ineffective sops to reformism. Even if they were modestly effective, he would redouble his opposition to trade unionism because he firmly believed that the greater immiseration of the proletariat would lead to working-class revolts.[114] Indeed, Kingsley was so dogmatic in his outlook on the trade union question that he actually boycotted the SLP newspaper, the Santa Cruz *New Charter*, because its staff was unionized.[115]

Robert McIvor, the feisty Irish American business agent of the Painters Union and with support from many immigrant members as well as key leaders such as Hecht, argued that the Socialist Labor Party ought to fight for reforms that enhanced the quality of life for the working class while continuing socialist propaganda for a complete transformation to abolish capitalism. He emphasized that socialists "were not dreamers but practical exponents of the class interests of the working class."[116] In a departure from De Leonist orthodoxy, McIvor acknowledged that incremental reforms might be appropriate in some situations to bring trade unionists together with socialists. He thought that there should be an immediate campaign to end child labour in the factories.[117] Over time, it appears that the SLP national leadership came to prefer the perspective of McIvor to the orthodoxy of Kingsley.

In a dramatic letter from George Benham to Henry Kuhn, dated 20 March 1897, both Kingsley and McIvor garner sustained and critical attention. Benham, a colourful and prolific SLP activist and an author whose diverse works include *Patriotism and Socialism, The Story of the Red Flag,* and *Peru before the Conquest,* wrote to provide the SLP national leadership with an account of the day-to-day dilemmas in the San Francisco branches. In the letter, Benham observes that the quick-to-anger McIvor as well as other trade unionists were no longer willing to attend branch meetings because of Kingsley's perceived dogmatism on the reformist nature of trade unions.[118] Benham remarks that Kingsley "defied anyone to tell him the slightest difference between a boycott and a blacklist" and that Kingsley had stated that the time for dropping all forms of economic organization and focusing solely on political means had arrived.[119] Indeed, in May 1897, McIvor and other SLP leaders such as Hecht established the Columbian branch of the party to promote a socialist philosophy that worked more closely with trade unions.[120] It seems to be clear that this measure was taken to establish a bulwark against Kingsley's perceived dogmatism.

Benham also documents how Kingsley and other SLP leaders such as George Aspden and William Costley were opposed to the editorial line of the Santa Cruz *New Charter* as articulated by Wilkins.[121] Benham dismisses this sentiment and expresses considerable frustration that, despite being elected as the SLP state organizer, Kingsley was taking such an intransigent stance rather than loyally supporting the party's newspaper. Remarkably, the letter goes on to criticize Costley, calling him "a cloudy reflection of Kingsley in the shape of a mulatto coachman, very ignorant, very sympathetic, very garrulous."[122] Benham makes direct reference to Kingsley's impairments and links them to what he regards as Kingsley's financial mismanagement of and improprieties with branch funds: "I hardly think he has the proper sense of 'separation' from any money placed in his hands."[123] Benham notes that the branch voted to provide Kingsley with a salary, since he was behind on his dues, despite being awarded publishing work such as printing the Maguire-Harriman debate.[124] The branch also paid Kingsley eighty dollars for incidentals, a considerable sum in the 1890s, but he refused to itemize his expenses. Benham observes that Kingsley "is badly crippled (both legs off) and seemingly deliberately throws himself into a chance at funds, depending on sympathy to get him out, and up till now, successfully."[125] Benham also makes a point of noting that Kingsley had no occupation and consequently had the time to serve on SLP committees, which he always sought out, but he had been "somewhat expensive" in his services.[126] Benham remarks as well that Kingsley was part of a committee to manage a sizable legacy to the SLP left by a recently deceased supporter named Robert Nagler, a wealthy inventor of trusses, used in this era to treat hernias.[127] Benham's letter clearly demonstrates a disdain for Kingsley's lack of formal employment status and portrays Kingsley as manipulating his comrades to support himself financially. This likely reflected intense ideological differences within the Socialist Labor Party in the heat of class conflict and Benham's comparatively reformist and pragmatic politics given Kingsley's subsequent decades of self-sacrifice on both sides of the international line. At the same time, the letter does suggest a somewhat self-serving side to Kingsley that, coupled with his divorce in 1894 in which cruelty was alleged, perhaps indicates a certain level of egotistical behaviour, certainly not uncommon among otherwise worthy left leaders.

In another letter from Hecht to Kuhn, dated 2 May 1897, generally discussing the quotidian problems in the San Francisco branches, Hecht mentions two troublesome members of the American branch, a comrade by the name of Leffingwell and his understudy, E.T. Kingsley. Hecht denounces the alleged financial improprieties of Leffingwell's management of the Labor Temple and how, as an unemployed man supported by his wife, he spent all his time drinking in the temple saloon and causing political unrest in the branch.[128] Hecht goes on to say that, unlike Leffingwell, Kingsley, though "lame" and also unemployed, had a speaking ability and could be described as having malice, vindictiveness, and a capacity for personal insult.[129] Even at this early stage of his political career, his rivals clearly recognized his formidable intellect and regarded Kingsley as a potential threat.

Interestingly, Hecht specifically references the facts that both Leffingwell and Kingsley were "incapacitated from working" and denounced the unions as "relics."[130] This speaks to the tensions between unionized workers and those unable to perform wage labour, directly related to a moralist conception of the value of work. The slight but tantalizing evidence in the letter suggests that perhaps Kingsley's radical conception of class was at least partly influenced by the fact that the barriers raised by his physical disability prevented Kingsley from doing wage labour. Marginalized by a conception of socialism that privileged wage labourers and facing significant barriers to obtaining most paid work in the 1890s, he was likely more open to a De Leonist theory more dismissive of the potential for trade union struggles to achieve substantive reforms. Yet it is also interesting how the concept of work seems to change significantly depending on the context. It is apparent that Kingsley did a tremendous amount of work as the SLP state organizer in giving speeches, writing correspondence, and even facing arrest. It is hard to square his obvious labour with the complete dismissal of his status as a worker when it was politically convenient for his SLP rivals to do so. This is even more transparent when one considers that De Leon himself spent years as a legal academic at Columbia University.

As Mark Sherry has eloquently argued, a phenomenological approach to understanding impairment and what he calls "the negotiation of embodied health identities" can enrich one's understanding of disablement. In so doing, Sherry stresses the need for an intersectional approach to phenomenological analysis recognizing that gender and impairment are mutually constitutive: gender shapes impairment just as impairment shapes gender.[131] Judith Butler has famously demonstrated that gender is a performance. From an early age, women and girls are socialized to wear skirts and bras, watch their weight, apply makeup, and shave their legs to accord to patriarchal standards of beauty.[132] Sherry suggests that impairment is also a performance. For example, disabled people are expected to ask for help in a certain way and be grateful to medical professionals and the public. This was all the more true in the nineteenth century before the modern disability rights movement shifted attention away from physiological impairment and toward structural barriers such as a lack of wheelchair ramps.

We are forced to speculate about the details because Kingsley did not leave an abundance of personal records, particularly during his American period. In many cases, one can say that male amputees who had symptoms associated with phantom limbs were often perceived, particularly in the nineteenth century, as feminine. To the Victorian mindset, phantom pain was similar to hysteria or malingering associated with women's medical disorders.[133] Moreover, disabling amputations were seen as emasculating because of the link between manliness and the capacity for physical labour. The entire politics of prosthetics discussed in Chapter 2 is underscored by a desire to restore masculinity. Kingsley apparently ambulated with a cane. As Richard Walker has documented, this was likely feasible because, in the late nineteenth century, 80 percent of San Francisco labourers lived within half a mile of their jobs.[134] It seems that Kingsley attempted to redirect any attention that his impairment might have drawn to his superb skills as an organizer and a speaker – and perhaps to his other physical characteristics. Peter Newell noted that Kingsley "was a big man, a 250-pounder, with a rugged physique; and his large bald head made him look bigger and more formidable."[135] His aversion to drawing attention to his impairment might also explain his consistent reluctance to discuss his personal life despite having been a public figure in two countries from 1894 onward. It would have been particularly easy for Kingsley, as a radicalizing injured worker, to view his impairment through the lens of capitalist exploitation and to develop a purely ideological explanation of disablement.

Yet it is likely that Kingsley had to devote significant energy, in a world before automobiles became common, to navigating a large city that contained systemic barriers on a daily basis for those with physical impairments. Indeed, he lived for most of his time in San Francisco near both the Socialist Hall and the intersection of Seventh and Market, where he delivered his contentious street-corner oratory.[136] Kingsley chose to live in the heart of San Francisco – a pattern of city living that would persist when he moved to San Jose and Vancouver – likely to reduce daily travelling distances in light of his impaired mobility; indeed, his original decision to relocate from Minnesota to the West Coast in 1893 – and to remain there for the rest of his life – might have been influenced by the mild climate with its corresponding reduced barriers such as ice and snow. Finally, as Sherry notes, some people manage their impairments through a strategy of passing as able-bodied, similar to gays and lesbians in the closet.[137] As Ryan Sweet has noted, disability studies scholars have long noted the dilemma of passing since it requires constant surveillance by the disabled person to maintain the cloak of able-bodiedness lest the secret be revealed and since it fails to address the struggles imposed by an inaccessible environment not designed to accommodate people with mobility limitations.[138] Although Kingsley might not have undertaken such a strategy consciously, his consistent silence about his impairment, despite his high public profile, suggests that at the least he did not discuss these matters as he focused on his political activism.

Kingsley's Split from the Socialist Labor Party

Throughout the late nineteenth century, Kingsley had a well-established pattern of remaining in one community for only a few years at a time. He departed from San Francisco for San Jose, at the bottom of San Francisco Bay, sometime in 1898. There he was nominated to stand as the SLP candidate for the US House of Representatives for California's Fifth District in the November 1898 election. Although Kingsley finished in third place, losing to a Republican Civil War veteran, Eugene Lourd, he saw an increase in his vote share to 3.9 percent or more than 1,500 votes.[139] Days after the election, Kingsley told a crowd at an SLP meeting during a visit to San Francisco that "the contest was of great benefit to socialists and showed an increase of converts throughout the state."[140] During his time in San Jose, he lived in the city centre (as he did in San Francisco and as he would in Vancouver).[141] In 1900, Kingsley would seek elected office again, standing as a candidate for council in San Jose's Second Ward on a Socialist ticket, receiving 4.7 percent of the popular vote.[142] Despite this public stature, Kingsley was increasingly unpopular with some California members of the Socialist Labor Party, even though he had been loyal in opposing the more pragmatic moderate socialists who left the party in the later 1890s to support the Socialist Party led by Eugene Debs in the so-called revolt of the Kangaroos.[143]

Kingsley continued to make speeches in defence of his impossibilist socialist beliefs, travelling regularly between San Jose and San Francisco. In a speech given at the Metropolitan Labor Temple on 31 May 1899, he did not mince words in his sharp denunciation of the Spanish-American War.[144] The war saw the United States battle with Spain over Cuba and the Philippines. Kingsley commented in dramatic terms that merit reproduction:

FIGURE 10 Socialist Labor Party of America logo. Kingsley was a leading figure in the California section in the second half of the 1890s, serving as state organizer and running twice for the US Congress under the party banner. | Wisconsin Historical Society.

Armed murderers have marched beneath the glorious American flag to deprive people of their liberty. The flag has been sold and resold for profit until the very clothes on Uncle Sam's back smack of the bargain counter. Few wars have been fought with a worthy purpose, and the war against Spain is a capitalistic war which has besmirched the fair name of the United States. The soldiers came mainly from the working classes, and they received death in return for the self-sacrifice, while the officers got a little cheap glory.

Every citizen should protest with his last breath against the brutality of the war and endeavor to overcome the danger which lurks behind the scheme, namely, military despotism. If it be treason, to protest against ruthless murder, rapine, invasion of the rights of people, against the military drilling of our children in our public schools and the other evils that beset our land, then we plead guilty and, in the language of Patrick Henry, "make the most of it."[145]

Interestingly, though Kingsley's anti-war position was unequivocal, there was a measurable degree of confusion in the Socialist Labor Party, and the American left more broadly, on the appropriate stance to take on the war. As late as 1897, Daniel De Leon was skeptical about the cause of Cuban independence, fearing that it would simply facilitate exploitation by large sugar and tobacco conglomerates.[146] Howard Quint suggests that De Leon delayed taking a clear position for some months. Only with the outbreak of war did the Socialist Labor Party grow vocal in its opposition to the conflict. De Leon cursed both houses in the *People,* demonstrating principled opposition to each main imperialist bloc.[147] Unfortunately, this would be Kingsley's last hurrah in the party. His fierce loyalty would not be reciprocated.

Tensions between Kingsley's perspective and rival SLP factions had been evident for some years, notwithstanding his support in suppressing the revolt of the Kangaroos, and they came to a head when the San Francisco section of the party moved to expel Kingsley and two other members, named Low and France, in March 1900.[148] There had been earlier episodes, such as one reported in the *People* in November 1899 regarding an initiative by a Comrade Job, presumably leading SLP member and California 1898 gubernatorial candidate Job Harriman, who eventually sided with the nascent Debsian Socialist Party, to encourage Kingsley, by then the Santa Clara party organizer, to withdraw from the party.[149] Kingsley nonetheless remained loyal to it until 1900. The highly obscure precipitate issue supposedly related to the fact that Kingsley was trying to get himself elected as a city organizer of the San Francisco section. At the same time, Low wished to be elected secretary. It might well have been associated with an honorarium that might have been important to Kingsley, who likely struggled with financial issues since his disablement a decade earlier (the 1900 US Census lists his occupation as "librarian," suggesting a reliance on income from outside the party).[150] In a letter from a comrade named Lambert to the SLP leadership, Low claimed that Kingsley had alienated a large proportion of the San Francisco membership because he had shamelessly exploited the section.[151] It seems that he had attempted a tactical manoeuvre to have the Los Angeles section be made the seat of the state committee so that it would make the organizational decisions while a vote determining the matter had to be repeated to comply with constitutional requirements. The allegation was that Kingsley was manipulating the party because he was less well known in Los Angeles and consequently thought that he would have a better chance of being elected as the city organizer of the San Francisco section. The latter section decided that this constituted grounds to expel Kingsley and suspend Low and France.[152] Commenting on the rift, the secretary of the Kangaroos' renegade San Francisco section noted that "the skunks are disintegrating. They have expelled E.T. Kingsley, the brains of their faction, for exploiting the movement and have laid charges against several others ... We call them ... the Suicide club."[153]

Responding to Kingsley's expulsion by his San Francisco comrades, the De Leonist SLP National Executive Committee observed that Kingsley was by that time a member of the Santa Clara County section of the party and that, under the provisions of the SLP constitution, "sections have jurisdiction over their own members, and ... the expulsion of a member of one section by another section is simply an absurdity" – effectively quashing his supposed expulsion.[154] In the dispute over the location of the state committee, the SLP National Board of Appeals upheld the position of the Los Angeles section and chastised the San Francisco section for failing to conduct a proper referendum, ordering it to hand over the records and finances of the organization and to cease exercising the functions of the state committee.[155] When several executive officers in San Francisco refused to comply, the SLP National Executive Committee responded by suspending and then reorganizing the San Francisco section, a process completed by June 1900.[156]

Kingsley's ongoing stature within the Socialist Labor Party was apparent in June 1900 when the party's tenth annual national convention convened in New York City and the credentials committee anticipated that "California would probably send E.T. Kingsley" as one of its two delegates.[157] However, he does not appear to have attended the convention. The one California delegate who did attend it, H.J. Schade, explained that there had been difficulty raising sufficient funds to send Kingsley to New York.[158] In its report to that convention, the SLP National Executive Committee discussed the strife within the California branches of the party, worth quoting at length because it highlights Kingsley's central role in attempting to reorganize the San Francisco section in the wake of the Kangaroo revolt:

> After the division had taken place, Comrade E.T. Kingsley had been induced to come from San Jose to 'Frisco, because it was felt that a man of recognized ability should take up the fight against the Kangaroos, who were numerically stronger than our section. Kingsley came, certain arrangements were made – not by the section itself, but by a number of members – to subscribe to a fund to be applied to sustain Kingsley and enable him to devote his whole time to the work of building up the organization. But soon all sorts [of] complaints came in. One set against Kingsley, to the effect that he did not want to do any work; that he was

overbearing, wanted to order everybody about, and that they could not get along with him at all. The other set of complaints, also coming from members of the section, sounded different, and were directed against a number of other members, and these set forth that Kingsley, a man of energy and ability, had first tried to get the section down to correct methods of conducting its work, which work had all along been done in hap-hazard fashion, and had resulted in producing a chaotic state of affairs. That in doing so, he had run up against the pet notions of the very men who had called him, and these men, well-meaning enough, but for the most part very old men, incapable and unwilling to adapt themselves to the conditions confronting the section, had blocked every move he proposed, and had, finally, made it impossible for him to accomplish anything. The outcome of it was that Kingsley went back to San Jose.[159]

Although he appears to have survived the attempt to expel him from the Socialist Labor Party in 1900, the victory was short lived, and Kingsley would break from the party within a year. It was around this time that he left California for a propaganda tour of the Pacific Northwest – which became a permanent move – marking a key turning point in both his life and his political career as a revolutionary.

Sojourn in Seattle

In the latter half of 1900, Eugene Kingsley left California on a speaking tour of Washington State and ended up settling in the Puget Sound area, where he established the Revolutionary Socialist League (RSL) of Seattle with some sixty former members of the Socialist Labor Party.[160] Details of this transitional period in his life are sparse, unfortunately, reduced to small fragments of documentary evidence in the socialist press and no known records of his personal life beyond a reference to his place of residence at 502 21st Avenue in Seattle's Central District, where Kingsley lived as a boarder.[161] In September 1900, the *Spokane Chronicle* had reported that "E.T. Kingsley, a well-known socialist leader in California, is at present lecturing on the coast and the local leaders are offering inducements to bring him to this city," anticipating that he would arrive in Spokane by early October.[162] This speaking tour appears to have resulted in his permanent relocation to the Pacific Northwest, though as late as May 1901 the *Advance* newspaper, a socialist organ published in San Francisco, would run an advertisement indicating that a Mr. "A.T. Kingsley" was looking for work.[163] In December 1900, the Seattle *Socialist,* edited by a Baptist minister and physician, Dr. Hermon Titus, published a letter by Kingsley in which he took part in a debate about whether the Minnesota primary law, governing how candidates would be accorded the nomination of political parties, should be adopted in Washington State.[164] This followed a similar letter that Kingsley published days earlier in the mainstream Seattle *Post-Intelligencer.*[165] He was particularly well suited, of course, to write such polemics having lived part of his life in Minnesota, and his brother-in-law had served as a legislator in that state.

In his characteristically bold writing style, Kingsley assailed the alleged anti-corruption proposal for Washington State to adopt Minnesota law because it imposed a fee of ten dollars on each candidate and presumably disadvantaged less wealthy and more independent candidates, it required that candidates demonstrate 10 percent of the vote or signatures to obtain official standing, and it favoured stronger political movements with the capacity to smother smaller ones.[166] This followed an editorial comment in the previous issue of the Seattle *Socialist.*[167] Kingsley wrote that

> the essence of the law is to restrict the franchise. It is strictly in line with the disenfranchising of the negro in certain Southern states: the introduction of property qualifications in various state constitutions and city charters, and the efforts being made in some states to lengthen the period between election for legislative offices. The object of all this is to accomplish covertly and by stealth that which those responsible for it dare not attempt in the open, i.e. the disenfranchising of the working class. As our republic is cornerstoned upon the right of the citizen to freely and frequently express himself at the ballot box, any attempt to thwart such expression is a blow aimed at our liberties, and must be frowned down by every decent citizen. If these encroachments are to go unchallenged, all liberty will be lost.[168]

Here Kingsley demonstrated the ability to analyze the specific political conjuncture in a thoughtful manner, undermining any interpretation of him as unremittingly doctrinaire. Most remarkably, the December 1900 letter appears to be his only surviving direct reference to the question of race in the United States. Despite coming from the De Leonist tradition legendary for focusing primarily on class oppression, Kingsley clearly was aware of the connection between the disenfranchisement of African Americans in the American South and limiting liberty for all. The Seattle *Socialist* continued to polemicize on this topic in subsequent issues.[169] There were also many progressives who endorsed the Minnesota primary law because they saw it as an attempt to break the power of corrupt party machines that had dominated local politics and resulted in fraudulent nomination meetings.[170]

Regarding Kingsley's role as a catalyst for political realignment, the Revolutionary Socialist League formed at a meeting in Seattle on 17 March 1901, attended by sixty socialists, some of whom had been "expelled from the De Leon section here" and others who were "in sympathy with them," according to a report in the Seattle *Socialist*.[171] The following month the newspaper published the RSL manifesto, written by Kingsley, his first act as a leader of his own socialist organization.[172] Interestingly, perhaps foreshadowing what was to come, the editors of the Seattle *Socialist* distanced themselves from his profoundly impossibilist politics, entirely dismissive of the potential for trade unions to reform society.[173] They took particular exception to the dismissal of trade unions as a locus for class struggle, which Kingsley wrote about in dramatic if sexist fashion: "The battles of the workers on the economic field are no more evidence of the class struggle than the quarrels of fishwomen."[174] He also remarked in his characteristic style that "the rapid concentration of the economic forces of human society into the hands of a few powerful capitalistic combinations ... must be viewed with satisfaction by the clear-headed Socialist, who sees in such manifestations the preliminary steps leading up to the emancipation of the workers form [*sic*] the chains of wage slavery."[175]

The circumstances of the formation of the Revolutionary Socialist League and the precipitating break within the local Socialist Labor Party remain unclear. In 1900, the SLP National Executive Committee had reported that the party was in "proper hands" in Washington State, with no "standing room given to muddle-head or traitor." The state committee at Seattle was "well managed" and had "conducted the affairs of the Party with clearness, firmness and tact ... No Kangs."[176] However, less than a year later, in March 1901, Daniel De Leon would author a scathing editorial in the *Daily People* on the expulsion of Seattle members and "the immediate organization of the expellees into a 'Revolutionary Socialist League.'"[177] Calling out Kingsley (though not by name), De Leon attributed the split to "two leaders":

> Both were "intellectuals"; both were rolling stones, without visible means of support; the one rolled from California, the other rolled from the Social Democratic Federation of England. They met in Seattle and mutually recognized their affinity ... Why they did not join the Kangaroos from the start is a mystery to this day. Of course, every other word they utter is "Revolutionary Socialism," or "Class Struggle," or "Scientific Socialism."[178]

According to De Leon, the split arose from the dissidents' confusion about the trade union question and class struggle: "A correct insight in the Class Struggle teaches ... the necessity of the class-conscious economic organization of the wage-slave as an indispensable battering-ram in the arsenal of the militant Proletariat."[179] De Leon, who would help to found the Industrial Workers of the World in 1905, contrasted this approach to the one taken by "the man, unscientifically poised" (presumably a thinly veiled swipe at Kingsley):

> To him the Trade Union Question is a nuisance; he cares naught about it; "let the Unions alone," says he, and he adjusts his conduct to his unscientific blindness ... Like the poltroon, that he is bound to develop into, he ducks to the Labor Fakir, thus leaving the important field of the economic movement, that hot-bed of the Proletariat, in the hands of the Labor Lieutenants of the Capitalist Class; and, like the freak that he is from the start, he proceeds to preach the most vapid sort of stuff which he pleases to call "Scientific Socialism," and gathers his kindred around him.[180]

Kingsley, for his part, would later describe the Socialist Labor Party in blistering terms in a letter in the Seattle *Socialist*: "For heaven's sake don't refer to those S.L.P.'s as 'Socialists on a Socialist platform.' They are ignorant fanatics upon a platform almost as meaningless as that of the S.P. of the United States."[181] According to McCormack, citing the recollection of one of Kingsley's comrades in Canada, Bill Pritchard, the final falling out occurred "after a bitter 'face-to-face' confrontation with De Leon," resulting in Kingsley's departure from the Socialist Labor Party.[182] George Weston Wrigley, an early leader of the Canadian socialist movement who worked with Kingsley in British Columbia shortly after he left Seattle, suggested that the split arose from the party's "interference with the labor movement in forming the S.T. and L. Assemblies."[183]

Tensions emanating from Kingsley's break from De Leon and the Socialist Labor Party would resurface from time to time, including after Kingsley moved to Canada. In 1904, the organizer of the Vancouver section of the party would lambaste the organization that Kingsley led, the Socialist Party of British Columbia (SPBC), as being composed of "grafters and fakirs with a goodly sprinkling of mental misfits, otherwise known as freaks."[184] The Vancouver section's press committee went even further, accusing Kingsley of misappropriating SPBC funds:

> They have had a revolution since the election and split into three, one part holds forth every Sunday night in a 10c play house, after which a collection is taken up (Mr. E.T. Kingsley can tell you what becomes of that, as I understand the rest of the members of this third must not be too inquisitive, or they may not remain in the "Party").[185]

When De Leon addressed a packed meeting in Vancouver City Hall during a tour through the Pacific Northwest in 1907, Kingsley was in attendance, with the *Weekly People* (New York) reporting that "Kingsley behaved well. He didn't even ask 'The Pope' a question."[186]

On the eve of these fissures in the Washington State left, American socialist luminary Eugene Debs lauded efforts of the socialist movement in the Pacific Northwest, noting that the progress of the Social Democratic Party had been "greatest in the states of Massachusetts, Wisconsin, and Washington ... These three states are marked for early conquest."[187] In July 1901, Debs led disparate socialist forces to unify in the Socialist Party of America (SPA), the pre-eminent left-wing organization in the United States in the first two decades of the twentieth century.[188] Hermon Titus, editor of the Seattle *Socialist*, emerged as the leading theoretician of the SPA left wing, and circulation of his newspaper climbed to more than 7,000 copies – the second largest circulation of a socialist organ in the United States.[189] But Kingsley would not be a factor in this new phase of American socialism. His brief foray into political activism in Washington State was merely a transition to the new chapter of his life when he was summoned to Nanaimo, British Columbia, in 1902. He would remain a socialist militant in Canada for the rest of his life.

4

Crossing the Line
Kingsley Arrives in British Columbia

In March 1902, E.T. Kingsley arrived in Nanaimo, on Vancouver Island, enlisted by coal miners in a group called the Nanaimo Socialist Club to assist with their organization and propaganda work. Within a year, he would be attacked by both the bourgeoisie and sections of the working class – demonstrating his rapid ascent to become the leading figure on the socialist left in the province. This mirrored his earlier rise to prominence in the Socialist Labor Party and the California left in the wake of his disablement at Spring Gulch in 1890. In December 1903, socialists in the town of Revelstoke, in the BC Interior, would lambaste Kingsley for his antagonistic attitude toward labour unions, adopting a resolution threatening to withdraw financial support for the party's newspaper, the *Western Clarion*, "if the tactics alluded to are continued."[1] His rapid ascent in the BC socialist movement no doubt reflected his skill and rigour as an orator, organizer, polemicist, and publisher, as well as his forceful personality, which at times gave rise to sharp clashes with friends and foes alike. His achievements are particularly remarkable in light of his lived experience as a disabled person, underscoring his extraordinary personal and political life. This was noted by a delegate at the October 1902 convention of the Socialist Party of British Columbia, held in Vancouver, where Kingsley orchestrated a Marxist takeover of the party program, six months after his arrival in Canada:

Another delegate who is a power in the movement is Comrade Kingsley, of Nanaimo. He learned his lesson well in the Socialist Labor Party but broke from that organization on its interference with the labor movement in forming the S.T. and L. Assemblies. It is doubtful if there is a clearer and more forceful speaker on political questions in Canada to-day than Comrade Kingsley and his presence in BC for several months past has had a clarifying effect on the socialist movement. Never speaking of it himself few know that Comrade Kingsley was robbed of both limbs by a profit-grabbing railway corporation. He has conquered his handicap, however, and it is to be hoped that his growing business in Nanaimo will allow him to make a tour of the province at an early date.[2]

In this chapter, we consider the implications of Kingsley's arrival in British Columbia through the prism of the racist and ableist immigration legal framework of the day. Through a detailed review of immigration statutes of the era, we explore how disabled people were excluded and how his whiteness and remote location might have allowed Kingsley to move easily across the line. We also examine the class dynamics and tensions in Nanaimo, British Columbia, and Canada at this time and the array of socialist and labour organizations that congealed into a renewed Socialist Party of British Columbia shortly after his arrival in Canada.

Canadian Immigration Law at the Dawn of the Twentieth Century

As early as 1859, even before Confederation, colonial statutes restricted immigrants who were regarded as having undesirable physical characteristics. Although it is true that one purpose of such legislation was to prevent the admission of immigrants with infectious diseases, the statutory language indicates that it extended to those with various impairments that the Crown deemed undesirable for admission.[3] For instance, the 1859 statute *An Act Respecting Emigrants and Quarantine* clearly went beyond disease prevention and required medical inspectors to examine all passengers and deport any unaccompanied passenger who was "Lunatic, Idiotic, Deaf or Dumb, Blind or Infirm," and likely to become a permanent public charge.[4] In 1866, another pre-Confederation statute required the master of a vessel to record the names and ages of passengers who were "lunatic, idiotic, deaf and dumb, blind or infirm" and to record whether they were accompanied by relatives able to support them financially.[5] These statutes empowered authorities to deport such burdensome immigrants to the ports from which they had departed.[6] It is apparent that, given his meagre resources, Kingsley could have been excluded and deported as an "infirm" person under these early statutes had they applied to British Columbia.

After Confederation, Canadian immigration statutes continued the ableist exclusion of disabled immigrants perceived to be a drain on the public purse, as Ena Chadha has demonstrated.[7] In the field of immigration law, one sees the unbridled expression of a medical model of disablement in which prospective immigrants were thoroughly inspected from head to toe to ensure that they would provide quality labour to Canada and never be a burden on the Crown.[8] Hence, the first post-Confederation immigration statute, the 1869 *Act Respecting Immigration and Immigrants* adopted by the Dominion Parliament in accordance with the federal powers related to immigration, continued the tradition of barring immigrants who were deemed undesirable because of their impairments and potential risks of becoming public charges.[9] Section 9 of the *Act* imposed a fine of at least twenty dollars per passenger on any master of a vessel who failed to report such a passenger.[10]

The late nineteenth century saw a large wave of immigration as Canadian officials sought to increase rapidly the number of desirable immigrants who could settle the Indigenous lands of the prairie region, establish farms, and build prosperity for Canada's future. The key word, however, is *desirable*. Along with groups who were explicitly deemed unsuitable for permanent settlement on the grounds of race, such as Chinese immigrants and African Americans, disabled people continued to be excluded under further revisions of the statute.[11] As Jay Dolmage and Jen Rinaldi have eloquently demonstrated, eugenic philosophy gained currency among policy makers, leading to a groundswell of opposition to both racially undesirable immigrants deemed incompatible with the vision of a white Canada embraced by many, including a young William Lyon Mackenzie King, and disabled immigrants perceived as being burdens on the public.[12] The rise of eugenic thinking, a toxic brew of ableism, patriarchy, and racism, would eventually lead in the 1930s to calamitous policy interventions such as the sterilization of significant numbers of, *inter alia,* disabled Canadians in Alberta and to a lesser extent British Columbia.[13]

The 1886 *Immigration Act,* the statute in force when Kingsley arrived on Vancouver Island in March 1902, created a structure of exclusion designed to classify immigrants and deport those regarded as potential burdens on society.[14] The statute continued to require masters of vessels to report whether passengers had any of the prohibited impairments, facing financial penalties if they failed to do so. The legislation also imposed analogous reporting responsibilities on the medical superintendent of a quarantine station. The medical superintendent was required to report that information to the port's immigration collector of customs. The vessel owner was required to indemnify the government and relevant charitable organizations for every ineligible immigrant via a bond on the order of $300 per immigrant.[15]

One illustration of the overlapping epistemic communities linking eugenics, disability, and race was embodied in the ideological outlook of Dr. C.K. Clarke, the medical superintendent of the Kingston Asylum, then the Toronto Asylum, and eventually the Toronto General Hospital in the early years of the twentieth century.[16] Clarke, a prolific scholar and passionate proponent of eugenics, tenaciously fought for the exclusion of dangerous immigrants whom he asserted were "reeking with degeneracy, crime and insanity."[17] He even claimed that immigrant communities would foster the same slum communities in Canada that they had left.[18] Constance Backhouse notes that instructions sent to civil servants to prepare for the first Canadian census in 1901 indicated that they were to classify men by race, with coded letters for the white, black, red, and yellow races.[19]

In many ways, Kingsley was incredibly fortunate. He likely had a certain amount of what is now styled privilege in the sense that, as a Caucasian man with an impairment not immediately obvious, he was well placed to avoid detection. Racialized minorities (defined broadly to include white ethnics in this era) were far more likely to face intense scrutiny by authorities. His timing was also fortuitous since Parliament enacted a statute authorizing a comprehensive system of medical inspection to classify and sort prospective immigrants at ports of entry within months of his arrival in the spring of 1902, under the pretext of barring persons "suffering from any loathsome, dangerous or infectious disease or malady."[20] According to Barbara Roberts, immigrants were divided into three categories: the unfit, the fit, and the curable sick whose impairments could be healed with treatment.[21] The legislation received royal assent in May 1902, two months after Kingsley landed at the Port of Victoria from Seattle, and was not actually implemented until at least 1903, after he was safely established in Nanaimo.[22] However, the scholarly literature suggests that, even after the development of a bureaucratic imperative to remove immigrants perceived as medical burdens on the state, relatively few immigrants were actually deported. Fiona Alice Miller observes that in Ontario, between 1908 and 1913, only 1,300 of the 8,000 immigrants investigated were ultimately deported.[23] This likely reflected the fits and starts of a new bureaucracy gradually shifting decision-making power away from the on-the-ground physicians who implemented medical inspections for the Department of Immigration to expanded centralized control in a nascent Canadian state in line with eugenic priorities. Disputes over methods of financial compensation for these physicians and conflicts over the scope of their duties likely exacerbated already deep tensions among highly trained professionals who resented interference with their professional judgments.[24]

Although William Head on Vancouver Island featured a quarantine station designed for medical inspection of prospective immigrants, Kingsley arrived at the Port of Victoria prior to the passage of the 1902 amendments.[25] It is likely that, given the intense bureaucratic battles documented among immigration officials and medical professionals in central Canada, the exclusion mechanisms for disabled immigrants were not fully established in any structured and systematic way on Vancouver Island in 1902. The process was marked instead by a high level of disorganization and ad hoc deportations on a case-by-case basis. We imagine that this would have applied with even more force in Vancouver Island, relatively sparsely populated and far from the federal decision makers in central Canada. From the evidence available, it does not seem to be the case that the fish shop that Kingsley established in Nanaimo was designed by his socialist comrades to subvert surveillance by the state as a preliminary step toward deportation. Rather, it seems that Kingsley, a Caucasian amputee who could be perceived as able-bodied, slipped across the border unnoticed and that the fish shop fit a pattern of entrepreneurship that accommodated his impairments and fiercely independent personality.

The precise circumstances surrounding his decision to immigrate to Canada remain somewhat opaque. In an obituary of Kingsley, socialist comrade and former Member of the Legislative Assembly (MLA) Parker

Williams recalled that Kingsley "first came to British Columbia ... at the invitation of the Vancouver Island miners."[26] In January 1902, the secretary of the Nanaimo Socialist League, a man named Kilby, had written to the Seattle *Socialist* stating that Nanaimo socialists were isolated from most other socialists in British Columbia on account of their Marxist outlook and requested "all the assistance in your power" to arrange speakers.[27] It appears that Kingsley responded favourably to this appeal. The previous summer the editor of the Seattle *Socialist,* Hermon Titus, had completed a speaking tour in the province, giving lectures in Vancouver, Nanaimo, and Victoria. Describing the political conditions in a report following this trip, Titus predicted that Vancouver fishers and Nanaimo miners would soon join forces "in one overwhelming Socialist vote that will stagger the few capitalists in the province." He asserted that "there is no large political unit on the American continent so favorably situated to win the first Socialist victory as the province of British Columbia."[28] Out of this transnational dialogue among leftists in the Pacific Northwest, Kingsley was invited by the Nanaimo Socialist Club to undertake a propaganda tour on Vancouver Island.[29] James Pritchard, a Welsh-born coal miner (and the father of Kingsley protégé Bill Pritchard), was one of the miners who arranged for Kingsley to come to British Columbia: "Pritchard and a few others arranged for him [Kingsley] to come north to Nanaimo for a series of speaking engagements. This came about and Kingsley stayed on for considerable time, where he did valuable work in consolidating a group," Pritchard's obituary noted.[30] On 16 March 1902, the *Victoria Daily Colonist* announced Kingsley's arrival in the city the previous day (presumably by steamer from Seattle): "The Nanaimo Socialist League has secured the services of Mr. Kingsley, a prominent and capable worker in the movement for two months. Mr. Kingsley will put his time in at propaganda work in Nanaimo and district."[31]

Kingsley's Arrival on British Columbia's Corporate Industrial Frontier

Kingsley settled first in Nanaimo, a coal-mining community on Vancouver Island incorporated in 1874 in the territory of the Snuneymuxw First Nation. The city was formed in the context of the coal economy and the "robber-baron" class dynamics of Robert Dunsmuir and his mining interests, following the discovery of ore at Wellington in 1869 and the construction of the Esquimalt and Nanaimo Railway connecting Dunsmuir's coal operations to the British naval base at Esquimalt (and later to the provincial capital in Victoria). Coal was British Columbia's leading export in the second half of the nineteenth century, and its extraction precipitated the attraction of migrant workers to the island, displacing Indigenous communities.[32] Reflecting this economic structure, Nanaimo was the only settlement in British Columbia in the closing decades of the nineteenth century where industrial wage labour predominated.[33] Dunsmuir, granted one-fifth of Vancouver Island and $750,000 in cash in exchange for building seventy-two miles of railway, was notoriously anti-union, believing that control over operations in his mines was his exclusive purview. He rigorously opposed any move toward unionization among his employees, summarily dismissing union organizers, blacklisting "troublemakers," and enlisting the militia on several occasions to break up strikes.[34] Prior to his death in 1889, Dunsmuir would serve as a member of the provincial legislature and cabinet, and his son James (who succeeded him in running the mining operations) served as premier and lieutenant-governor, demonstrating the nexus of economic and political power in early modern British Columbia.[35]

The coal mines of Vancouver Island were regarded as among the most dangerous in the world since the Dunsmuirs and other operators ignored safety measures and regulations in order to maximize profits, resulting in a death rate that far exceeded that in the United States. As McCormack observed, between 1889 and 1908, British Columbia experienced a shocking fatality rate of twenty-three workers per million tons of coal produced – four times the North American average (already the most deadly continent for miners).[36] According to a pamphlet produced by socialist Jack Kavanagh in the midst of the 1912–14 island miners' strike, a total of 373 miners were killed from gas explosions in the island coalfield in the preceding three decades.[37]

Class conflict in the Dunsmuir coalfield shaped the island's political culture and traditions. As Jeremy Mouat notes in his study of the eighteen-month-long Wellington strike of 1890–91, suppressed by the combined might of the Dunsmuirs, the provincial state, and the militia, "the strike

FIGURE 11 Coal miners at the Extension mine, near Nanaimo, British Columbia. The coalfield fuelled a militant and radical working-class culture, attracting Kingsley in 1902 to assist the organizing efforts of a group of socialist coal miners. | British Columbia Archives, E-01189.

forced coal miners on Vancouver Island to come to terms with their weak position in provincial society: at the work place and in the Legislature they had achieved very little. These failures nourished both a heightened sense of class and a radical political tradition."[38] Through organizations such as the Miners' and Mine Laborers' Protective Association (MMLPA), formed on the eve of the 1890 strike, and the Nanaimo (Independent) Labor Party (NILP), the Nanaimo miners elected pro-labour members to the provincial legislature – thereby developing a tradition of independent working-class political action that laid the foundations for the socialist parties of British Columbia and Canada and, later in the twentieth century, social democratic formations that would take power.[39]

Working-class politics on Vancouver Island was diverse in outlook and approach: the moderate miner and MMLPA leader Ralph Smith (who served as president of the Trades and Labor Congress of Canada) was elected as an Independent Labor MLA for Nanaimo in 1898, migrating over his political career toward the "lib-lab" (liberal-labour) philosophy of class compromise and accommodation. In 1900, Smith resigned his provincial seat to run successfully as an Independent Labor Member of Parliament in Vancouver and promptly sat with the Liberal caucus. His successor as the Nanaimo MLA, James Hurst Hawthornthwaite (whom political scientist Ross Johnson credits with originally swinging the miners' vote behind Smith), began his political life in the similarly moderate lib-lab milieu of the NILP, but unlike Smith he followed the opposite trajectory and gravitated toward Marxism. On Labour Day 1901, Hawthornthwaite publicly proclaimed his support for socialism, and in a subsequent *Nanaimo Free Press* interview he disclaimed the existence of a lib-lab group in the legislature, describing the alignment as only a temporary coalition against Dunsmuir.[40]

It was into this political milieu that E.T. Kingsley entered in 1902. His arrival in Nanaimo followed an atypical path compared with the principal pattern of migration and transmission of radical influences to Vancouver Island at that time: economist J.A. Hobson, writing in 1906, attributed socialism in British Columbia more to its British migrants than "to agitators who come up from Washington state."[41] The demography of Nanaimo, "the spring from which the Socialist Party of Canada first drew its inspiration and life force," according to an account in the *Western Clarion,* underlined the British connection: as late as 1921, 43 percent of its residents were British-born, the highest percentage of any Canadian city.[42] This pattern of heavy British migration to, and settlement in, Nanaimo extended back to the late nineteenth century; historian Jeremy Mouat noted the preponderance of British-born miners among the list of casualties from a May 1887 Nanaimo mine explosion, which took the lives of 148 boys and men.[43] In his leading study of working-class culture in the island coalfield, John Douglas Belshaw argued that the immigrant experience and immigrant identity of British miners was integral to shaping class relations and the political trajectory of these communities.[44] The experience of Asian miners, primarily workers from China and Japan subjected to virulent forms of discrimination by British miners and capitalists, also shaped the early settlement history and labour history of Nanaimo and other mining communities.[45]

Kingsley's year-and-a-half-long foray on Vancouver Island remains somewhat obscure, with fragments in the archival record providing glimpses of his life, work, and activism in Nanaimo and surrounding communities. When Kingsley first arrived in British Columbia, he spent a week in Victoria. During his first day in the capital, he met with members of the local branch of the Canadian Socialist League (CSL), and a few days later he gave two public lectures, on the topics "The Labor Question from a Socialist Standpoint" and "The Capitalist and Laborer," at Victoria's Labor Hall. Members of the Legislative Assembly and Victoria's mayor, aldermen, and clergy were invited: the mayor sent regrets on behalf of the city council, citing a previously scheduled meeting, though several legislators attended the socialist meeting, which Labor MLA James Hawthornthwaite chaired.[46] Intriguingly, Kingsley's arrival in Canada was reported in the local press, in the Conservative Party–aligned *Victoria Daily Colonist,* suggesting a degree of notoriety in the Pacific Northwest at the time or perhaps contemporary journalistic conventions regarding ships' passengers combined with a slow news day.[47]

Kingsley reached Nanaimo from Victoria a week after entering Canada, likely by train on the Esquimalt and Nanaimo Railway, and he appears to have developed a quick and positive rapport with his socialist comrades. On 22 March 1902, possibly the evening of his arrival in Nanaimo, he addressed an open-air meeting in the city centre, and the following afternoon he spoke to a "large" and "attentive" crowd in the Free Press Hall. The *Nanaimo Daily News* described him as "a very convincing speaker" who "firmly believes in the principles which he advocates."[48] According to Johnson, Kingsley and the Nanaimo Socialist Club "were highly compatible."[49] His initial two-month stay was extended indefinitely.[50] James Pritchard, a member of the core group that had brought Kingsley to Canada, would tell a meeting of Ladysmith socialists a few months later that it was "men such as Comrade Kingsley that were required as organizers, who, being thoroughly conversant with the economics of Capitalism, were able by inference and contrast to teach [workers] the economics of Socialism."[51]

It is not clear what remuneration if any Kingsley received from his organizing and propaganda work with the Vancouver Island socialists. To support himself, he operated a fish market during his time in Nanaimo.[52] George Weston Wrigley (the former publisher of the Canadian Socialist League's *Citizen and Country* newspaper and based in Victoria at the time) expressed the hope in October 1902 that his "growing business in Nanaimo [would] allow him [Kingsley] to make a tour of the province."[53]

The Nanaimo city directory for 1903 identifies him as the proprietor of the Nanaimo Fish Market, and the *Victoria Daily Colonist* reported in September 1903 that Kingsley, "until recently, was a fishmonger in Nanaimo city."[54] SPBC secretary Ernest Burns (who would frequently cross swords with Kingsley) had informed delegates at the party's annual convention earlier that month that "we have in the person of Comrade Kingsley as able a worker in the Socialist movement as can be found in America, ... but owing to the lack of funds he has been unable to take to the field for constant work until quite recently."[55] Efforts to deploy Kingsley on a full-time basis were aided by the establishment of an "Organizer's Fund" at the beginning of 1903 to keep organizers in the field to address local propaganda meetings and organize party locals in new districts. "If workers ever expect to get socialism they'll have to pay for it!" the *Western Socialist* newspaper (Vancouver) declared, expressing hope that Kingsley would be deployed "very soon."[56]

In the wake of his arrival in Canada, he rapidly emerged as the pre-eminent socialist speaker and organizer in British Columbia.[57] In May 1902, Kingsley was back in Victoria to give six evening lectures in the Labour Hall on a wide range of topics: "The Earth and Man," "Man as Savage and Barbarian," "The History of Civilization," "The Capitalist System," "The Class Struggle," and "The Politics of Labor."[58] The thematic range of these lectures demonstrated Kingsley's breadth of knowledge and political analysis, highlighting themes that would figure prominently in his writings and speeches for the rest of his life, including in his major work, *The Genesis and Evolution of Slavery.*[59] Demonstrating Kingsley's influence on mainland British Columbia, when SPA leader Eugene Debs spoke in Vancouver in June 1902, addressing the topic "Why I Am a Socialist" at a meeting in Vancouver City Hall, Kingsley was elected to chair the meeting – three months after his arrival in Canada.[60] Two months later, on Labour Day, 1 September 1902, Kingsley was among the speakers at a large demonstration in Nanaimo attended by an estimated 1,200 workers who travelled on two special trains from Victoria and a comparable number who sailed aboard the steamers *Joan* and *Yosemite* from Vancouver; a press report described him as "the leader of the revolutionary socialist party."[61] In January 1903, when elections took place for positions on the Socialist Party's executive committee for districts outside Vancouver, Kingsley topped the polls – with seventy-one votes in a field of thirteen nominees (in comparison, MLA James Hawthornthwaite received forty-seven votes, and Parker Williams of Ladysmith, who would be elected to the legislature later that year, received fifteen votes).[62]

Kingsley's legal status in Canada would later become a public controversy – in 1907, when Kingsley first ran for election to the Legislative Assembly, and in 1919, when Canadian state officials examined options for deporting him on account of his pro-Bolshevik views. Like other immigrants at the time, Kingsley never made a formal application for Canadian citizenship (the law on citizenship in Canada would not be formalized until the 1940s), and his initial temporary stay evolved into a lifelong residence. As Isaac Shin Imai notes, in the years immediately following Confederation, there was no such legal concept as deportation. After a period of residency of three years, an alien could obtain the status of British subject by swearing an oath before a judge, commissioner, or justice of the peace provided that the person was of good character.[63] At the time of Kingsley's arrival in Canada (and the subsequent controversies in 1907 and 1919), the provisions of the 1881 *Naturalization and Aliens Act* applied, extending British subject status to any person who had been in the country for three years, provided that certain conditions were met. Persons in the "disability" category included infants, lunatics, idiots, and married women but interestingly not the "infirm people" category that immigration statutes employed and in which Kingsley would fall.[64] Yet the statute was surprisingly generous, and the Crown could deny naturalization only where an immigrant declared alienage, where a British subject had become naturalized as a subject of a foreign state, where a person made false statements to become naturalized, or where the parents of dependants ceased to be British subjects or the husband ceased to be a British subject.[65] Kingsley presumably satisfied the legal test since he would later succeed in having his name added to the voters' list in 1907 (making him eligible to stand for election to public office) and since the state officials who launched the initial inquiry into his possible deportation in 1919 appear to have dropped the matter.

As Imai has shown, "deportation is a powerful tool of social control."[66] Canadian authorities at the turn of the twentieth century gradually sought to restrict those immigrants deemed to be racially undesirable. Yet there was a countervailing pressure to attract more immigrants to farm the prairie region and to work in industry, especially as Canada was losing the battle for desirable immigrants to the United States.[67] Although the 1881 statute authorized deportation in surprisingly few situations, gradually more restrictive legislation was enacted. Two key examples are the *Chinese Immigration Act* and the *Alien Labour Act*. The *Chinese Immigration Act* of 1885 greatly restricted Chinese immigrants, imposed a racist head tax on Chinese immigrants, and subjected them to a variety of registration controls that impeded their mobility.[68] The *Alien Labour Act*, adopted in 1897 after pressure from unions and some employers in response to similar American legislation targeting Canada, imposed a fine of $1,000 on employers who contracted with American workers and permitted the deportation of the workers within a year. In fact, it was rarely used.[69] The 1906 decision of the Privy Council in *AG v Cain*, a rare occasion when the statute was employed, held that the *Alien Labour Act* was *intra vires* the powers of the Dominion Parliament. An American, Everett Cain, brought to work on the Pere Marquette Railway in violation of the statute, was deported without any hearing.[70] Justice Francis Anglin of the Supreme Court of Ontario ruled that a colonial legislature had no authority to deport a person since it concerned enforcement powers beyond the territorial boundaries of the Dominion of Canada and therefore was *ultra vires* the Dominion Parliament.[71] On appeal to the Privy Council, Lord Atkinson ruled that the power of expulsion complemented the power of exclusion. Since the Dominion Parliament had the power to exclude, it could expel a worker in accordance with the *Alien Labour Act*.[72] As an entrepreneur, Kingsley likely would not have been captured by the *Alien Labour Act*, only sporadically enforced in any case, and was thereby likely shielded from these consequences.

Realignment: Forming the Socialist Party of British Columbia

Kingsley's arrival in Canada coincided with a realignment of the Canadian left, which inaugurated a period of expansion and influence that would be unrivalled until the emergence of the Co-operative Commonwealth Federation (CCF) in the 1930s. Prior to 1902, loci of left-wing strength existed in an "alphabet soup" of local labour and socialist parties spread across Canada – in branches of the Canadian Socialist League and the

Canadian Socialist Federation, both based in Ontario, which published, respectively, the journals *Citizen and Country* and *Cotton's Weekly;* in branches of the De Leonist Socialist Labor Party (including a Vancouver branch formed in 1898 and the associated Vancouver Socialist Trade and Labor Alliance); and in local labour parties from Nanaimo to Winnipeg to Montreal. In 1900, a group of Vancouver socialists broke away from the Socialist Labor Party, forming the United Socialist Labor Party, establishing branches in several communities, and adopting the *Lardeau Eagle* as its semi-official publication.[73] They would reconstitute themselves as the Socialist Party of British Columbia in October 1901 when twenty-one locals of the United Socialist Labor Party convened in Vancouver and adopted the revolutionary program of the Socialist Party of America; of the sixty CSL branches, a smattering migrated into the new SPBC.[74] This period of realignment coincided with moves toward greater consolidation of the socialist press – and signalled a shift within the leadership of the Canadian socialist movement toward the West Coast. In 1902, Richard Parmater "Parm" Pettipiece, an Ontario-born printer and former publisher of the *Lardeau Eagle* in the BC mining town of Ferguson, purchased an interest in the CSL newspaper, the *Citizen and Country,* and in collaboration with former publisher George Weston Wrigley (who moved for a short time to the West Coast) relocated the newspaper to Vancouver. It resumed publication as the *Canadian Socialist* in July and (when Pettipiece bought out Wrigley's residual interest) as the *Western Socialist* in September 1902.[75] Commenting on the eclectic structure of the turn-of-the-century Canadian left, political scientist Paul Fox suggested that "a bewildering array of party names and continual changes in relations between groups testified from the first to the highly individualistic, volatile, and confusing nature of Canadian socialism."[76]

Moves toward consolidation of radical working-class forces in the United States influenced events in British Columbia and Canada. As historian Margaret Ormsby noted, political developments in the United States often attracted greater interest in turn-of-the-century British Columbia compared with Canadian events, particularly in mining communities in the BC Interior populated heavily by recent American immigrants who had been radicalized by militant struggles against mine owners in the United States. For example, the American presidential campaign of

William Jennings Bryan in 1896 created more interest in BC mining communities than the Canadian federal election contested by Wilfrid Laurier in the same year.[77] Two speeches by the legendary socialist Eugene Debs to miners in Rossland, British Columbia, helped to cement links between socialist currents in the two countries.[78] In 1902, the progressive American Labor Union, which the Western Federation of Miners had founded that year as an alternative to the American Federation of Labor, endorsed the entire program of the Socialist Party of America at a convention in Denver.[79]

Following the lead of its parent union to embrace socialist political action, District 6 of the Western Federation of Miners, consisting of BC miners' locals, called a convention in Kamloops in April 1902 that brought together sixty-five delegates representing fifty-one organizations, including WFM locals, other unions, local labour councils, and several socialist and labour parties. Kingsley attended the convention as the delegate of the Nanaimo Socialist Party.[80] Based on the published proceedings, he appears to have been the most radical delegate at the convention. However, during a debate on whether to include a plank in favour of women's suffrage in the new party's draft platform (adopted by a large majority), Kingsley said that he considered the plank "irrelevant" and wanted discussion confined to questions directly affecting labour and wages, insisting that the class struggle was the real issue.[81]

Chris Foley, representing the WFM district, who appears to have been the primary force behind the convention, advised delegates that the platform committee had "exercised extreme moderation" in preparing the document, wanting to rebut a widely held view in British Columbia and Canada that violent conflict in the BC Interior had been caused by the labour movement.[82] Disagreement between labourist and socialist factions at the Kamloops convention resulted in a compromise decision to forge a Provincial Progressive Party (PPP), with socialist delegates pushing for a name and a political identity stronger than a straight Labor Party favoured by labourist delegates. Familiar labour demands for the eight-hour day, improved workplace safety, and recognition of the right to organize, negotiate, and strike were supplemented by more far-reaching demands for government ownership of railways, smelters, and refineries and women's suffrage; however, within a year, the Provincial Progressive Party would collapse under the weight of its rival factions.[83]

Dissatisfaction with the relatively moderate course adopted at the Kamloops convention impelled Kingsley and a coterie of Vancouver Island Marxists and coal miners in more radical directions. He delivered a report on the Kamloops convention "from a Socialist standpoint" at a public meeting in Nanaimo after his return, and in May 1902, less than two months after arriving in Canada, Kingsley would spearhead the transformation of the Nanaimo Socialist Club into the Revolutionary Socialist Party of Canada (RSPC), breaking away from the Socialist Party of British Columbia.[84] The new party's "Advanced Programme," which Kingsley drafted, was published in the Seattle *Socialist* and took aim at moderates such as Ernest Burns, president of the Vancouver fishermen's union, for advocating a gradualist "step-at-a-time program," and Ralph Smith, "the Gompers of Canada." The RSPC, in contrast, pledged itself to "uncompromising political warfare against the capitalist class, with no quarter and no surrender," calling on "all wage earners and decent citizens to organize under the banner of the Revolutionary Socialist Party of Canada, with the object of conquering the public powers, for the purpose of setting up ... and enforcing the economic program of the working class."[85] The RSPC established branches in Northfield, Ladysmith, and Vancouver, and in July 1902 it opened a Socialist Hall in Nanaimo. Kingsley addressed the inaugural meeting on the topic of "Lessons for the Workers in the Great Coal Strike and Its Relation to the Class Struggle."[86] According to historian John Hinde, the RSPC "consisted primarily of Nanaimo miners disaffected with the SPBC," a consequence of the reformist/impossibilist split, with Kingsley being the foremost figure associated with the emerging impossibilist strain of BC socialism.[87]

In October 1902, Kingsley would help to broker a rapprochement between the RSPC and the SPBC, or perhaps more accurately a takeover, when delegates at a convention in Vancouver agreed to reconstitute the SPBC on an impossibilist foundation – signalling a lurch of the BC socialist movement to the left (and the migration of moderate SPBC members toward the Provincial Progressive Party, as Thomas Loosmore hypothesized in a graduate thesis in the 1950s).[88] Embracing key elements of the strident RSPC platform in nearly verbatim form, the reconstituted SPBC pledged itself to "conquering the public powers" for the working class and undertaking "the transformation, as rapidly as possible, of capitalist property ...

into the collective property" and "the establishment ... of production for use in lieu of production for profit." Delegates also introduced a benchmark in the platform for evaluating proposed reforms (later imported into the Socialist Party of Canada): "Will this legislation advance the interests of the working class and aid the workers in their class struggle against capitalism? If it does, the Socialist party is for it; if it does not, the Socialist party is absolutely opposed to it."[89] The merger of the SPBC and the RSPC was welcomed by the Seattle *Socialist:* "We can now expect great results in British Columbia, as the field is ripe for a vigorous working-class propaganda."[90]

Growing strength for the Marxists, and waning fortunes for the labourists, were apparent in the immediate aftermath of the Vancouver convention in 1902, when James Hawthornthwaite, recently elected as Labor MLA for Nanaimo, publicly broke from the Nanaimo Labor Party and applied for membership in the Nanaimo Socialist Party. He declared his intention to stand in the next election as a candidate of the Revolutionary Socialist Party, stating that it was the only existing party representing the interests of wage earners.[91] Demonstrating the rapidity of his political transformation, Hawthornthwaite had sent a congratulatory telegram to the founding PPP convention in Kamloops only a few months earlier expressing the hope that delegates would adopt a "moderate" platform.[92] His application for membership in the Revolutionary Socialist Party was considered and approved at a business meeting of members held on 15 October 1902, with Eugene Kingsley and George Weston Wrigley Jr. (previously of the Canadian Socialist League, son of George Weston Wrigley, and living at the time in Victoria) among those in attendance.[93]

Within the SPBC, distinct ideological strains could still be discerned. In contrast to the Marxism of Kingsley and others, Christian socialists from the Canadian Socialist League occupied positions of leadership, including Ernest Burns, president of the Vancouver fishermen's union and operator of a second-hand store with an upper floor that would serve as the party's headquarters for a number of years.[94] In an article in the Seattle *Socialist* in January 1902, Burns explained that

> my socialism is of a more elastic quality than that of some ultra-orthodox
> comrades, who have reduced Socialism from a philosophy to a creed,

and regard the slightest questioning of their tenets and dogmas as heresy of the most outrageous type ... Constructive practical work is of far more service than revolutionary air fanning or unintelligent repetitive stock phrases or revolutionary jargon.[95]

Burns would later advocate for the SPBC to follow the lead of the Socialist Party of America and adopt a "program of immediate legislative activity."[96]

Women also played important roles in the SPBC. Three women were nominated for positions on the party's executive in 1902, shortly after its founding: Ada Clayton of Victoria, Dora Kerr of Phoenix, and Bertha Merrill of Nelson; Merrill was elected, receiving the second highest number of votes, only three votes behind Kingsley.[97] Merrill assisted Pettipiece with the publication of the *Western Socialist* and, later, the *Western Clarion*, authoring a popular advice column for women under the pen name Dorothy Dew; by the end of 1903, she would marry Burns.[98] In that year, on the eve of the provincial election, the prominent socialist Irene Smith of Tacoma, Washington, addressed a Victoria audience alongside Kingsley in a series of speeches on the island and mainland in support of local socialist candidates (the text of which unfortunately was not recorded in the local press).[99]

What does Kingsley's dogmatic stance on suffrage for women indicate about his overall politics and his biographical narrative? There is too little evidence to link his insensitivity on gender politics to his alleged cruelty or vindictiveness in his failed marriage. Yet given his dramatic departure for California, abandoning his wife and children, with whom he seems to have had little contact for the rest of his life, it raises important questions that must be considered in order to have a rounded appreciation of his legacy. One might also remember how his ex-comrades in the California Socialist Labor Party bitterly perceived Kingsley as vindictive and manipulative in his dealings with party finances. Although there might not be a direct correlation between his failed marriage and his traditional stance on suffrage, Kingsley apparently was not advanced in his thinking on gender politics, even for the early twentieth century.

Although the SPBC provided organizational cohesion to the socialist movement in the province, ideological disputes were common, particularly on the questions of reforms and the party's relationship with trade unions. Kingsley was frequently at the centre of these conflicts as the foremost proponent of the impossibilist viewpoint and given his substantial (and growing) influence in the party. When, as SPBC organizer, he told a Victoria crowd in a lecture on "The Labour Problem" in early 1903 that unions were "reactionary products of the present competitive system," and that a replacement worker (a "scab" in union parlance) was "a noble man," an outcry erupted from several sections of the party.[100] A correspondent writing in the *Victoria Daily Colonist* suggested that Kingsley's remarks provided a "note of warning" to the labour movement, and prominent party members, including Burns in Vancouver and Wrigley Jr. in Victoria, objected strongly to Kingsley's remarks. The SPBC's Victoria local went so far as to request that Kingsley be relieved from his position as organizer.[101]

Despite this opposition, his influence in the party grew. By the end of 1903, Kingsley would be appointed as managing editor of the *Western Clarion* (succeeding Pettipiece), securing a platform from which he would continue to lambaste trade unions for attempting to raise wages, on the grounds that these were selfish efforts designed to boost the interests of one group of workers at the expense of the interests of the proletariat as a whole.[102] In a report on the AFL annual convention in December 1903 (the second issue that Kingsley edited), he repeated the argument that unionism and socialism "possess nothing in common," suggesting that those who believed otherwise ascribed to a form of socialism "less than skin deep."[103] Revelstoke Local No. 7 of the SPBC responded with a sharply worded resolution, questioning the appointment of Kingsley as editor, condemning the stance of the newspaper, and threatening to discontinue support for it unless this position changed.[104] In a strongly worded response of his own, which several scholars have cited as exemplifying his impossibilist stance, Kingsley doubled down on the claim that unions, as products of commodity struggles under capitalism, had interests antithetical to the socialist cause. He identified an apparent "antagonism" between the principles of unionism and those of socialism:

The stock in trade of the present working class movement is "Capital and Labor are brothers," "Capital has rights as well as Labor," "A fair day's pay for a fair day's work," "All we demand is justice," "The Right to Organize,"

"Collective Bargaining," "Demand the Union Label," etc. Its stage para-
phernalia consists of the strike accompanied with the privilege of getting
licked, the boycott under which the commodity labor power can strut
the stage and bawl out other offending commodities ...

The Socialist Party cannot depend on the support of members of trade
unions unless they are to go back on union principle. The principles of
unionism and socialism are opposite therefore antagonistic. To support
one is to deny the other. No man can serve two masters ... If the Socialist
Party of the United States or any other country commits folly through
ignorance, that is no reason why the party in British Columbia should
do likewise.[105]

Notwithstanding this avowed antipathy toward unions, Kingsley continued
to attract a following in labour's ranks, delivering dozens of lectures every
year (see Appendix 3).[106] On Labour Day 1904, he was invited to speak at
a mass meeting in Victoria organized by the local trades and labour council
and convened in Victoria City Hall. He appeared on a platform with a
former premier, Joseph Martin, SPBC MLA James Hawthornthwaite, and
local Liberal MLA and trade unionist J.D. McNiven (who had been elected
as the PPP founding secretary-treasurer at the Kamloops convention in
1902 and who would later serve as a provincial deputy minister of labour).[107] As Socialist MLA Parker Williams would note a quarter of a
century later in an obituary of Kingsley, "on Labor matters he had very
definite opinions, and the courage to hold them even if standing alone."[108]

Nanaimo Socialists and Political Action

Kingsley and the Nanaimo socialists pursued the parliamentary road to
socialism – the strategy that workers must "strike at the ballot box," seizing
the reins of state power through constitutional means to pave the way for
working-class emancipation and the peaceful implementation of labour's
economic program. These efforts built on the foundation of independent
political action, including the election of several Labor MLAs to the BC
legislature in the 1890s and Hawthornthwaite's more recent election and
subsequent conversion to socialism. Gains at the federal level also helped
to buoy the socialist cause, including the election to Parliament of Labor
candidates miner Ralph Smith in Vancouver and printer Arthur Puttee in

Winnipeg in 1900 (followed by plumber Alphonse Verville in Montreal in 1906).[109] A respectable showing in Vancouver in the 1900 provincial election by machinist and SLP member Will MacClain – the first overtly Socialist candidate to stand for election to the BC legislature, with the endorsement of the United Socialist Labor Party, the Canadian Socialist League, and the Vancouver Trades and Labor Council – also demonstrated rising support for the socialist point of view.[110]

In December 1902, Kingsley made what the press described as "a red hot Socialistic speech" during a candidates' meeting in Ladysmith's Gould's Hall on the eve of a provincial by-election in the North Nanaimo riding, triggered by the appointment of William Wallace Burns McInnes as provincial secretary. The meeting was attended by McInnes as well as Socialist candidate Parker Williams, Premier of British Columbia Edward G. Prior, and James Hawthornthwaite, the sitting Socialist member for the neighbouring Nanaimo City riding. In his speech, Kingsley adopted a familiar refrain of the day, suggesting – according to a press report – that "the working man must take hold of the country and shut out the Mongolians." He declared that "a deadly fight was on between capital and labor" and predicted that he would "live to see the time when not a voice would be heard in any legislature without the mandate of the working man."[111] When challenged by McInnes to debate socialism in the Nanaimo Opera House, for the benefit of the Nanaimo Hospital, Kingsley immediately accepted the challenge. McInnes defeated Williams in the by-election the following day 263–155 votes (both men would be elected in the general election the following year, with Williams winning in the reconfigured Newcastle riding and McInnes elected as the member for the rural Alberni riding).[112] During the Ladysmith debate, McInnes described Kingsley as "the high priest of Socialism," a philosophy that he assailed as "immoral, unjust and robbery."[113]

In February 1903, Kingsley would join Hawthornthwaite and others in disrupting a meeting in Nanaimo called to promote an extension of the railway to northern Vancouver Island, with Kingsley publicly mocking the secretary of the British Columbia Mining Association to his face and openly disrespecting a town alderman.[114] In the aftermath of this railway drama, a correspondent identified as "A Socialist" offered sarcastic criticism of

Hawthornthwaite's association with Kingsley in a letter to the *Nanaimo Free Press:*

> Pity, if you will, but don't blame. Was it his fault he had never come under the skillful guidance of Comrade Kingsley? Was it his fault that he had never learned to inhale the delicious odors of fish? No, sir. But to his everlasting praise be it said, no sooner had he come under these delightful influences than we see him turning his back upon all that he had previously espoused, and like the cod fish, that lingereth in the sun, he has continued to gain in strength daily. Look at the man then and the saint now ... Then he would make all he could out of real estate, now he would give it to you for nothing. Then his hands were seared by the touch of a corporation's gold, now he holds aloft the poor hands blistered by the pick. Then he believed in working for anybody or anything to earn the bread that perisheth; now he has raised himself above all this, and has set himself upon a pedestal where all men can admire the beauty and grandeur of his unswerving fidelity to himself and Kingsley.[115]

In contrast to these disparaging remarks, a correspondent in the *Nanaimo Daily News* identified only as "Barnacle" nominated Kingsley to head a slate of Socialist candidates for election to Nanaimo City Hall: "For Mayor, Mr. E.T. Kingsley, Fish Merchant, late of the U.S. (Nationalities not recognized among socialists)."[116] There is no evidence that Kingsley considered accepting the nomination and standing for municipal office at that time.

The looming 1903 provincial election campaign took place against the backdrop of major industrial unrest, including a strike of railworkers on the Canadian Pacific Railway that left labour leader Frank Rogers dead and a bitter four-month strike of coal miners that halted production at Dunsmuir's Extension and Cumberland mines.[117] On the eve of the latter strike, the Nanaimo miners had affiliated with the Western Federation of Miners, breaking from a non-socialist Canadian miners' union and demonstrating the evolution of their local away from the conciliatory leadership embodied by Ralph Smith and toward the militancy and radicalism of the federation and the SPBC.[118] James Pritchard, who had brought Kingsley to the island, and Parker Williams were influential in organizing the miners into the Western Federation of Miners and harnessing the Extension miners' grievances into a work stoppage.[119] During the strike, Kingsley embarked on an organizing tour to Courtenay and Cumberland, where he delivered four lectures and organized "an active Local of a substantive nature."[120] George Weston Wrigley, previously critical of Kingsley, credited his "splendid work."[121]

Kingsley and the Socialists played an active role in the provincial election campaign of 1903, fielding candidates in eleven ridings.[122] From spring to autumn that year, Kingsley and fellow SPBC organizers James Hawthornthwaite and Fred Ogle embarked on tours around the province, stumping for Socialist candidates from Vancouver Island to the Cariboo to the east Kootenays.[123] Kingsley described the election as "the most important political campaign thus far fought in British Columbia" because it was "the first time a ticket of the revolutionary proletariat will have appeared on the ballot at a general election."[124] In early July, Kingsley and Hawthornthwaite addressed the Ladysmith Socialist party on the topic of "The Coming Campaign."[125] In August, Kingsley travelled with Pettipiece to Fernie in the southeast corner of the province, speaking at meetings in support of the local Socialist candidate, before venturing to Phoenix, Greenwood, and other mining towns in the Boundary and Kootenay districts on behalf of the SPBC.[126] In Victoria, Kingsley gave outdoor lectures "before a large crowd" at the corner of Yates and Broad Streets on topics such as "The Labour Problem," harking back to the old SLP tactic of the street-corner meeting, and addressed meetings in support of James C. "Jimmy" Watters's candidacy at the local Odd Fellows' Hall.[127] The 1903 election campaign was marked by a minor controversy in the multiple-member Vancouver City riding (which at the time elected five MLAs) when a leaflet endorsing a "fusion" slate of Labor and Socialist candidates inflamed SPBC activists, provoking a flurry of accusations in the socialist press.[128] Of more serious import was an allegation circulated in Liberal Party–leaning newspapers around the province to the effect that Hawthornthwaite had entered into an alliance with McBride's Conservatives – a suggestion that the Socialist MLA strenuously denied.[129]

The 1903 BC provincial election, which returned two Socialist MLAs from Vancouver Island coal-mining districts (Hawthornthwaite in Nanaimo and coal miner Parker Williams in neighbouring Newcastle), as well as a Labor MLA in a hard-rock mining district (William Davidson in Slocan), was the first election in the province contested along partisan lines, and it demonstrated the pressure that a small group could exert in a Westminster parliament.[130] Province wide, the SPBC took a respectable 8 percent of the popular vote.[131] Although the party would lament the defeat of several of its candidates by narrow margins in the BC Interior, including Ernest Mills (who lost by nine votes in Greenwood amid allegations of fraud), a correspondent writing to the *Western Clarion* would later proclaim that Hawthornthwaite had "got more legislation passed in the interest of the workers than any other man in the world with like opportunity."[132] In contrast to the pursuit of reforms by Hawthornthwaite and Williams in the legislature, the SPBC expressly disavowed "palliative" measures at its 1903 convention, which occurred in Vancouver immediately prior to the provincial election, with delegates adopting this uncompromising resolution:

> Resolved that this convention place itself on record as absolutely opposed to the introduction of palliative or immediate demands in propaganda work, as being liable to retard the achievement of our final aims, and that the S.P. of B.C. henceforth stand firmly upon the one issue of the abolition of the present system of wage slavery as the basis for all political propaganda.[133]

It was shortly after the 1903 provincial election that Kingsley left Nanaimo for Vancouver. The precise date and circumstances of his move are not known. Although the proceedings of the SPBC convention in Vancouver on 8 September 1903 identify him as "E.T. Kingsley of Nanaimo," later that month the *Victoria Daily Colonist* reported that Kingsley, "until recently, was a fishmonger in Nanaimo city."[134] He was re-elected to the SPBC's Provincial Executive Committee at that convention, continuing in the position of organizer, and party treasurer Ernest Burns informed delegates of plans to "send Organizer Kingsley on a tour through the eastern provinces in order to 'educate' the inhabitants thereof in the philosophy of real Socialism."[135] It is not clear whether this trip materialized. In early November 1903, the *Victoria Daily Times* and *Victoria Daily Colonist* were still referring to "E.T. Kingsley, of Nanaimo," in reports on meetings that he convened in the south island, including one to organize a Gordon Head branch of the SPBC.[136] By the end of that month, Kingsley would be appointed as the managing editor to rescue the financially beleaguered *Western Clarion,* published in Vancouver, where he would live for the rest of his life.[137]

Kingsley had certainly left his mark on the political climate of Vancouver Island and British Columbia, establishing himself as "the high priest of Socialism," according to his critics.[138] Organizationally, he had been influential in the consolidation of the socialist left into a unified political force, under the aegis of the SPBC, laying a foundation for national growth. At the same time, the Marxist program that Kingsley ingrained in the SPBC, and his own uncompromising views on class struggle, trade unions, and the process of political change, would contribute to centrifugal forces within the party and movement, giving rise to recurring episodes of fragmentation. On the electoral field, Kingsley's rhetorical and organizational prowess played an important role in the doubling of Socialist representation in the legislature at the inception of the party system in 1903 – and contributed to the growth of socialist electoral support in working-class districts around the province – shaping the political culture of British Columbia well beyond his brief flurry of activity in Nanaimo. A little more than a year after arriving in Canada, Kingsley relocated to the emerging Pacific metropolis of Vancouver, where he would establish his printing business and embark on the next defining moment of his political career – his central role in the Socialist Party of Canada.

5

No Compromise
Kingsley and the Socialist Party of Canada

From the moment of his arrival in Vancouver in the autumn of 1903 until his fall from grace with the Socialist Party at the outbreak of the First World War, Eugene Kingsley was the dominant figure on the socialist left in British Columbia and Canada (the leader of the BC school of socialism), serving as editor and publisher of the party's organ, the *Western Clarion,* as dominion organizer of the party until 1908, and as a member of the Dominion Executive Committee until 1912. As his comrade Jack Harrington would recall, Kingsley was "the real founder" of the Socialist Party of Canada, and his friend Wallis Lefeaux suggested that the party's platform, largely authored by Kingsley, was "the most clear-cut and revolutionary, of any Socialist Party, of any country in the world."[1] Historian Ross Johnson described Kingsley as "the fountainhead from which emanated many of the positions of the SPBC and SPC."[2] A contemporary report in the *Victoria Daily Times* identified Kingsley as "the only Red Chamber member of the parent order and head of the Socialist [P]arty of Canada."[3] He stood for public office as an SPC candidate five times – including three runs for MLA for Vancouver and two runs to represent the city as its federal MP. Variously chided by friend and foe alike, Kingsley left his mark on the political culture of the working class during this formative phase of Canadian socialism. Notwithstanding his disablement and lived condition as a double amputee, he displayed a prodigious commitment to the movement and party in his role as a publisher and propagandist and his role as a public speaker and an organizer delivering hundreds of talks in small and large towns across the province and the country. The Victoria *Week* newspaper would attack

Kingsley as "an illogical, irreconcilable, revolutionary demagogue of the worst type" during a 1907 by-election campaign, but he also developed a strong following among a section of the BC and Canadian working class. Their lived experience of class and capitalist exploitation resonated with his uncompromising advocacy for the democratic seizure of the state by workers in order to achieve their emancipation and implement labour's economic program.[4]

This period of Kingsley's life represented the apex of his political influence – forging a party and an ideological approach that shaped the politics of his adopted province and country, both when he was its leader and for decades to come. Given his physical impairments, his frenetic level of activity is all the more remarkable, but it is also true that Kingsley abandoned his wife, Myra, in Minnesota nearly a decade earlier. As we noted earlier, there appears to be no record of future romantic relationships with women. A solitary life of political activism is certainly challenging, yet Kingsley, completely lacking family responsibilities, had the time to devote himself fully to his political and agitational work on behalf of impossibilist socialism.

Interrogating Kingsley's "Impossibilism"

E.T. Kingsley was the most prominent figure in the formative phase of the Socialist Party of Canada and prewar Canadian left, "reputed to be the best exponent of scientific Socialism on the American continent," according to a contemporary report in the Winnipeg *Voice*, and the leader of "the British Columbia School" of socialism, according to Ross McCormack.[5] His ideas extended beyond the Western hemisphere, as evidenced in dozens of articles in the Australian labour press between the 1910s and 1940s expounding his Marxist perspective.[6] But his contribution has hitherto been noted only in passing rather than explored at length. When Kingsley is mentioned at all in the scholarly literature, he usually appears briefly in caricature, his name cited abruptly and dismissively as a synonym for, and personification of, the impossibilist strain of BC socialism: the commitment to "one-plank" Marxism, "abolition of the wage system," and strident opposition to "palliative measures," reforms that would pacify workers and prolong the inevitable collapse of capitalism, postponing the transition to socialism. There is frequently a heavy tone of derision in prevailing scholarly treatment of Kingsley (with a few excep- tions, such as Dorothy Steeves and Ross McCormack), dismissing impossibilism as hopelessly naive, elitist, and otherwordly.[7] Political scientist Paul Fox, for example, takes issue with unnamed members of the Socialist Party of Canada "who conducted its affairs as if it were a semi-private club of Marxist philosophers," identifying a "puritanical obsession" and "a distinct element of intellectual snobbishness and arrogance amongst the brilliant leaders," who had no interest in forming a mass party (an outcome that they achieved, according to Fox, by imposing an examination of scientific socialism on applicants for membership).[8] The SPC decision not to affiliate with the Second International, on the ground that it was too heavily influenced by reformism, is also cited as exemplifying the party's doctrinaire, otherworldly character. Other developments highlighted by Fox include the expulsion of MLA Parker Williams and the suspension of founding member Ernest Burns, the catalyst for the split in 1907 that resulted in the formation of the Social Democratic Party of Canada (SDPC).[9]

The scholarly focus on Kingsley's impossibilism and dogmatism certainly has an evidentiary foundation in his speeches, published writings, and record of activism within the Socialist Party of Canada and other left parties. Indeed, his contemporary and comrade D.G. McKenzie observed half-jokingly that "since Marx died nobody was capable of throwing light on [economic] matters except the editor of the *Clarion*."[10] However, a key factor that previous scholars appear to have missed, and that has become apparent to us only in the preparation of this book-length study of Kingsley's political life, is the centrality of irony, humour, sarcasm, and hyperbole in his rhetorical and polemical style. Indeed, this style was central to his public speeches and published writings during his time in British Columbia, and it would become a defining element of his persona within the party and among the broader public in British Columbia and Canada. His style included outlandish barbs against his audience members (whom Kingsley frequently referred to as "slaves"), cutting similes that would leave opponents speechless (as noted by Bill Pritchard in the epigraph at the beginning of this book), and self-deprecating humour related to his baldness and other qualities (though, importantly, never related to his impairment as a double amputee). A correspondent to the *Western Clarion* noted this style in a friendly letter in 1910, suggesting that the newspaper issue "picture–post cards" as a light-hearted propaganda measure depicting, among other things, "Comrade Kingsley growling."[11] Kingsley himself acknowledged this rhetorical style, admitting at a socialist meeting in Nelson, British Columbia, in 1906 that he had been accused of having a "nasty tongue," conceding that "the charge was true" while explaining that "he had acquired it while working for wages and he intended to keep on using it as long as the wage system lasts."[12] At the same meeting, Socialist MLA James Hawthornthwaite credited Kingsley with being the "greatest authority on economic questions on the whole continent."[13]

Appreciation of his humour and "over the top" rhetorical style appears to have been lost in the years between his political activism in the early twentieth century and the emergence of the new social history in the 1960s and 1970s, which began looking at questions of class and left-wing politics in serious ways. As a result, most scholars, we hypothesize, have applied a literal reading to Kingsley's speeches and writings that was never intended to be applied and would not have been applied by contemporary listeners and readers. Indeed, as Dorothy Steeves (whose period of political activism began just after Kingsley's death) noted, "there was the old maestro, E.T. Kingsley, a man who had had both legs amputated in a railway accident, who delighted his hearers as he analysed capitalism with biting, excoriating acid on his tongue."[14] Charlie O'Brien, Kingsley's SPC comrade who served in the Alberta legislature from 1909 to 1913 (and whom George Weston Wrigley described as resembling Kingsley in appearance and speaking style), also shone light on this dynamic, describing working-class attempts to "rid ourselves of what Com. Kingsley calls Orcharditis – a low down cussedness that slavery, and particularly wage-slavery, has brought into us."[15] A socialist in Fernie, British Columbia, looked forward to being reacquainted with that "cheery old grouser" Kingsley prior to a 1908 convention.[16]

Working-class audiences in prewar British Columbia and Canada, familiar with Kingsley's style, would have taken his words with a proverbially healthy grain of salt, looking to the underlying meanings of the issues that Kingsley was raising while appreciating the light-heartedness, audacity, and fun that he brought to the examination of serious social questions, which likely seemed to them patently absurd. "Kingsley yet stirs in his hearers the very emotions he affects to condemn," a correspondent noted after hearing him speak in Vancouver in 1903. "Shame, anger, self-contempt and sudden hope ... chase each other around the diaphragms of the men who listen to his scathing words, and a rising sense of conscious power makes them long to get their hands on the ballot."[17] This connection between Kingsley's rhetorical wit and intellectual depth of his political analysis was recognized by contemporaries who did not share his uncompromising beliefs. Grace MacInnis, the daughter of J.S. Woodsworth and hardly a member of the Marxist left in British Columbia, recalled half a century later (on the eve of her re-election as the lone woman in the House of Commons in 1968) that Kingsley was a "particular idol" of her deceased husband, former CCF MP Angus MacInnis, "because of his incisive wit and his intellectual abilities."[18] What scholars have interpreted as a lack of depth in Kingsley's political analysis represents, in our opinion, a misreading of speeches and writings never intended to be taken literally, resulting in the erroneous portrayal of Kingsley as an intellectual clown of the early Canadian left – when in fact he was arguably its most serious thinker, as was widely acknowledged inside and outside the party at the time.[19]

An example of Kingsley's supposed intellectual arrogance, emblematic of the attitude of a layer of SPC leaders, is cited by Ian McKay in his groundbreaking work on the early Canadian left, *Reasoning Otherwise*. Writing in the *Western Clarion* in August 1908, on his way home from a propaganda tour across the continent, Kingsley declared that "along the north shore of Lake Superior is rock and muskeg, a combination shunned by every animal in the category, except that brilliant specimen, the wage-slave, who would cheerfully go to hell itself, if its brimstone deposits could be used as a means of squeezing a little profit out of his foul carcass for his capitalist masters."[20] A literal reading of this passage leads McKay to conclude, like many other scholars before him, that the Socialist Party of Canada "sheltered a number of hard-core individualists, self-made mavericks who prided themselves on their freedom to decide on a whole spectrum of issues. They were possessed not only of themselves but also of a substantial cultural capital attesting to their individual attainments. The SPC thus mirrored basic elements of the liberal order it was sworn to critique."[21] We do not reject the proposition that the Socialist Party of Canada – like socialist groups the world over – probably included a disproportionate share of individualists and mavericks given that it was a primary locus of dissent in the prewar era. We also accept that these qualities of individualism, which Kingsley possessed, were part of the cultural fabric of an order that he was pledged to destroy. However, we believe that a more nuanced approach is warranted, both to illuminate properly Kingsley's life and contribution and to provide for an accurate understanding of the dynamics, motivations, and developments of the early Canadian left.

The scholarly trend toward derision and caricature of Kingsley impedes, in our view, a rigorous analysis and critical appreciation of his approach to the complex issues that he and other socialists confronted in the opening decades of the twentieth century. In this chapter, we therefore aim to avoid the common approach of conflating his entire contribution into a simplistic impossibilist and doctrinaire box, instead favouring a more nuanced look at his speeches, writings, and activism on specific issues – without ignoring patterns that potentially emerge in his words and deeds.

There is another aspect of Kingsley's political thought worthy of mention. His impossibilism has been characterized as being hopelessly unrealistic, even elitist and unhelpful, by undermining efforts to improve conditions for workers in the near term either through trade union bargaining or through legislative changes and state programs. But there is an alternative interpretation that we would put forward. Kingsley's unwavering focus on the "one-plank" Marxist demand to overthrow the capitalist system can be interpreted as extraordinarily hopeful. In the face of sharp opposition within every organization to which he belonged, from the Great Panic of the 1890s in the western United States to the period of "capitalist consolidation" in the 1920s in British Columbia, Kingsley refused to accept that capitalism was the natural order of human relations. He displayed an enduring and unwavering optimism in the capacity of working-class people to transform their social relations of life and work by ending the economic and political primacy of private property. The political objective of "conquering the public powers, for the purpose of setting up ... and enforcing the economic program of the working class," which traced its lineage to the revolutionary turn of American socialists at the convention in 1901 that gave birth to the Socialist Party of America, would be incorporated under Kingsley's leadership into the political platforms of the

Revolutionary Socialist Party of Canada, the Socialist Party of British Columbia, and the Socialist Party of Canada.[22] Kingsley's fundamental hope in the possibility of the socialist transformation of human society was evident in his first speech in Vancouver after the bloody suppression of the Winnipeg General Strike and police raids against his comrades that ended sympathetic strikes in Vancouver and other cities: "Nothing except temporary gains ... had ever been won by the workers in a fight for better conditions," Kingsley declared, asserting that the only lasting solution available to the working class was "political action ... to strip the ruling class of power."[23]

Kingsley's Class Location

Kingsley's approach to socialism, variously described in previous studies as "extreme," "doctrinaire," or "impossibilist," was a reflection of his life circumstances as a double amputee as well as his class location removed from the material relations and conditions of the wage-earning working class. There is no record that Kingsley was employed in what could be described as "ordinary" wage labour following his fateful service with the Northern Pacific Railroad Company up to 1890, beyond an elusive reference to his occupation as a "librarian" in the 1900 US Census for San Jose (which could have referred to employment in a library operated by the Socialist Labor Party).[24] In his work as an organizer for that party, and in his later work with the Nanaimo Socialist Club, the SPBC, the Socialist Party of Canada, and the Federated Labor Party (FLP), Kingsley earned income, but from entities that he led to various extents, frequently as a member of the organizations' governing committees. As a result, his material relations of life and work – and his relationship with the means of production – were distinct from those of a wage-earning worker employed in a capitalist industry.

This has led historian Ian McKay to remark that these "SPC cadres might be described as self-employed men," and Mark Leier defines Kingsley and other SPC intellectuals as petit bourgeois, rather than proletarian, exercising a large degree of control over their labour power: "Collective bargaining and reforms to ease relations between employers and employees [were] equally irrelevant to them."[25] Yet it might well be that Kingsley sought out a role as a proprietor as an innovative form of self-accommodation for his impairments in a British Columbia that restricted employment opportunities for disabled men. This seems to be a common thread from his publishing work in the San Francisco SLP branch to his fishmonger business in Nanaimo and finally to his successful printing business in Vancouver. As the manager dispensing work assignments and overseeing sales and relations with customers, Kingsley would not have faced the kind of physical pressures that wage labourers experienced to meet daily Taylorist production standards and that he likely would not have been able to achieve.[26] In a patriarchal world where dignity and self-respect for men were closely tied to remunerated wage labour, Kingsley might have turned to entrepreneurship as a way of levelling the field in a structurally ableist world.[27] Although one cannot anachronistically say that Kingsley was consciously articulating entrepreneurship as an explicit strategy to craft accommodations, he nevertheless was a highly talented man who wanted to make a contribution.

We can also find critical scholarly commentary on Kingsley's class location as an employer of labour at his printshop. Leier points out that Kingsley, like Pettipiece, owned the means of production and hired others. Although the printshop was unionized (and though Kingsley advertised being the only shop in Vancouver that used paper bearing the watermark of the papermakers' union), Leier suggests that, "as an employer, Kingsley may have left much to be desired."[28] He cites an interview with Kingsley's friend and SPC comrade Wallis Lefeaux, whose brother Stan worked as an accountant at Kingsley's printshop, to the effect that Kingsley was "selfish, always collecting a generous salary every week, before paying anyone else."[29] Although impossible to determine at a temporal distance of a century, the repeated references by comrades in both California and British Columbia to financial management raises questions about whether Kingsley was unfairly maligned largely because of his impairments and stereotypical reactions to them. Shedding light on Kingsley's income, Pritchard recalled that his own compensation as *Western Clarion* editor ranged from eleven dollars to fifteen dollars per week, and McKay suggests that *Western Clarion* editors earned about sixty dollars per month and that organizers were paid two dollars per day.[30] Pritchard recalled that the Socialist Party of Canada had "very little money" in those years: "You were biting your fingernails financially. I think it's healthy for a working-class party. When they get legacies, they get lazy, and they also get dependent upon the donor."[31]

In addition to remuneration for his work with the Socialist Party of Canada, Kingsley maintained other sources of income throughout his time in British Columbia. During his initial foray in Nanaimo, he supported himself as a fish merchant.[32] In Vancouver, he went into the printing business and occasionally dabbled in speculative ventures in timber and real estate (which do not appear to have taken off). Publishing appears to have been the mainstay of his income for the first two decades of the twentieth century. Kingsley's move from Nanaimo to Vancouver occurred on the eve of the most rapid population growth in the history of both the city and the province: the population of Vancouver increased by a staggering 284 percent in the decade from 1901 to 1911 – from 26,000 to more than 100,000 people – and the population of British Columbia more than doubled from 179,000 to 392,000 people.[33] This was the economic climate in which Kingsley established the firm of E.T. Kingsley Printing, moving into a sector that grew from fewer than a dozen firms when he arrived in the city in 1903 to more than sixty at the outbreak of the First World War.[34]

In 1905, Kingsley secured control of the *Western Clarion*'s printing plant from Richard Parmater "Parm" Pettipiece, amid tensions between the men, but despite the apparent rift they would emerge as confidants and allies.[35] The printing press itself had been used in the 1890s to publish the *Daily Ledger* in New Westminster before being relocated to Vancouver.[36] Kingsley operated the business for a time in partnership with several socialist comrades, first Leo English and then Annie Arnason and John Stow (who moved from Victoria to join the business); from 1908 on, Kingsley appears to have run it as a sole proprietorship, incorporating the business in 1911, with a capitalization of $50,000 and the object of doing "business as printers and publishers of newspapers, journals, magazines, books, dealers in stationary [*sic*], etc."[37] The business was located in the basement of the Flack Block at 165 West Hastings Street in downtown Vancouver until the end of 1911, when it moved into a location off Richards lane in the basement of the Vancouver Labor Temple at 411 Dunsmuir Street.[38] Around 1914, there appears to have been a restructuring, with the business operating briefly as Lefeaux Bros. (E.T. Kingsley) before being sold to a

FIGURE 12   Advertisement for Kingsley's printing company, 1911. | *Western Clarion.*

competitor, Cowan & Brookhouse, which merged its operations with Kingsley's and moved into the Labor Temple (where it would continue to operate until 1920).[39]

Kingsley's roles as a commercial printer and the editor and publisher of the *Western Clarion* and subsequent working-class publications were intertwined throughout his time in Vancouver. In 1903, Kingsley referred to the *Western Clarion* office as "a job office" that printed "much stuff that would fail to pass muster before an 'International Censor,'" suggesting that there was a commercial component to the publishing venture from the outset.[40] In 1905, an advertisement announced the expansion of the Job Printing Department with the purchase of a new press and other materials.[41] A retrospective article in the newspaper in 1907 noted that the paper had succeeded in "keeping afloat" with "the assistance of the job plant."[42] Unlike Pettipiece and English, Kingsley does not appear to have completed an apprenticeship as a printer or belonged to the International Typographical Union.[43] Even so, labour organizations were a mainstay of Kingsley's printing business, notwithstanding his political aversion to their activities. In 1909, an advertisement for his company in the Vancouver Trades and Labor

Council's short-lived organ, the *Western Wage-Earner,* proclaimed that "nearly all the Labor Organizations in BC secure their printing from E.T. Kingsley (Publisher of the *Western Clarion*). All of it could be done here as we make a specialty of this work."[44] Kingsley subsidized the newspaper from the profits of his printing business until 1912, contributing "considerably over one hundred dollars per month" by his own estimate (approximately $2,500 in 2021 dollars).[45]

Following his fall from grace with the *Western Clarion,* Kingsley would remain active in the working-class publishing world in western Canada. During the First World War, he served as an associate editor with the BC Federation of Labor's *British Columbia Federationist* newspaper (and, briefly, as the editor), and he launched the short-lived *Labor Star* with Pettipiece during the turbulent period following the First World War.[46]

Beyond his printing business, Kingsley ventured into other fields of private enterprise from time to time. He appears to have sought to leverage his close association with Socialist MLA James Hawthornthwaite to advance his private business pursuits, often under the guise of ensuring the financial health of the *Western Clarion* and the Socialist Party of Canada. In 1904, Kingsley introduced Hawthornthwaite to Vancouver lawyer and SPBC member J. Edward Bird via letter, indicating that the Socialist MLA "may be able to do Mr. Bird a favor" and that in doing so he would be doing Kingsley "a favor as well."[47] A year later, in May 1905, Kingsley asked Hawthornthwaite to keep him informed about the location of the terminus of the new Grand Trunk Pacific Railway on British Columbia's north coast, as a boatload of land speculators made their way through Vancouver to Port Essington on the Skeena River, a rumoured location for the western terminus of Canada's second transcontinental line. Kingsley advised Hawthornthwaite that his business partner and socialist comrade Leo English had "some one on the string who will finance him in locating if he can know when and where": "If you can furnish any definite information at any time send it to me and I'll put it where it will do the most good."[48]

In 1907, Kingsley's business interests shifted toward the timber resources of Vancouver Island as Kingsley pursued distinct ventures with Hawthornthwaite and with a consortium of Vancouver businessmen. In May that year, Kingsley wrote optimistically to Hawthornthwaite (who had drawn his attention to a tract of timber near Cowichan Lake) on the opportunity for a profitable venture: "There is a tremendous bustle for timber here now. I am in touch with parties here who are commissioned to buy for US capitalists. They assure me they can twice over any amount that can be gotten hold of, and more especially if it be fir timber."[49] Kingsley warned that time was of the essence in light of rival interests in the area: "If there be anything there worthwhile we should be too late if we do not move soon ... [T]here is evidence of a considerable move after timber on the west coast of the island at present. That territory toward the north end that I was speaking to you about is being invaded from all sides."[50] He predicted that "with a little energy on our part we can even manage to pick up a few dollars through some such scheme this summer." Pressing the Socialist MLA to provide details on the location of the tract, Kingsley wrote that

> I do not think it would hurt either of us to get hold of at least enough to enable us to square up with the world. I have some prospect of securing options (in connection with others) on some good sized tracts of timber with a view to making a profitable turn. In fact I should have to do something or eventually I should go under in carrying the *Western Clarion*.[51]

Kingsley appears to have placed considerable weight on the potential for financing the operations of the *Western Clarion* and the Socialist Party of Canada through a stake in the wealth generated from the timber resources of Vancouver Island. The proposed timber venture with Hawthornthwaite was not pursued, and Kingsley entered into a separate syndicate agreement in July 1907 with a group of Vancouver businessmen "for the purpose of cruising and staking for timber" in the vicinity of the Alberni Inlet on Vancouver Island.[52] His partners in that enterprise (which might have operated as the Herron Timber Company but does not appear to have progressed to the point of harvesting operations) were lawyer J. Edward Bird, the SPC member who famously defended the passengers of the *Komagata Maru*; Malcolm McBeath, a printer and real estate broker (and future Vancouver mayor); Herbert W. Baker, an insurance and real estate broker; Thomas R. Pearson, a publisher and bookseller who moved into the insurance and real estate business; and John McLarty Macmillan, a businessman in the fishing industry who also dabbled in real estate. The new timber venture quickly ran into trouble as a result of the rival interests about which Kingsley had warned Hawthornthwaite. A competing company involving two Americans, the Chippewa Farm Lands Company, had sought to register timber rights to the same Alberni lands as the Kingsley group. In December 1907, Bird wrote to Hawthornthwaite requesting that the Socialist MLA intervene with the commissioner of lands and works, Frederick Fulton, "not to make any pull on my behalf but just to see that I am going to get a square deal" with respect to thirty-seven claims in the vicinity of Coleman Creek and Tuck Lake in the Barclay District.[53] Bird shed light on details of the dispute, insisting that "we were first in this country" but that "our own first cruiser played sharp on us and went and tipped the matter to my opponents."[54] In a follow-up letter to Hawthornthwaite tying the dispute to SPC finances, Kingsley expressed the hope that "the matter can be pushed to a favourable conclusion as the proposed trip east largely depends on it."[55]

A year later, in February 1909, with the Kingsley syndicate's claim to the Alberni timber rights still unresolved, another member of the syndicate, McLarty, filed a petition in the BC legislature requesting that a select committee be established to investigate the matter amid allegations of fraud in the staking and registration of timber rights by the rival American party. However, the response from the provincial attorney general suggested that nothing was amiss, and no further action appears to have been taken on the petition.[56] With an air of desperation, Kingsley wrote a short, sharp, and vague letter to Hawthornthwaite in May 1909 that is worth reproducing in full: "Dear Comrade: What are the prospects? I am hard pushed – no one here knows how hard – and I fear for the safety of the *Clarion* and other Party interests. As far as I am concerned I give not a d–n. Guess you know that, Eh?"[57] The syndicate apparently dissolved a short time later.

In 1911, Kingsley became involved in yet another speculative business venture, the Prince Rupert–Nanaimo Collieries, Ltd., with mineral rights to an estimated "hundred million tons of coal" on Graham Island in Haida Gwaii on British Columbia's remote north coast. Kingsley served on the board of directors of the company, which like the earlier ventures apparently did not get off the ground.[58]

His involvement in private enterprise and his distance from the wage-earning working class led to some conjecture when the Victoria

Board of Trade met after the First World War to discuss potential responses to a fiery lecture that Kingsley had delivered defending the Russian Bolsheviks. Potential responses ranged from suppression of radical meetings to deportation. During that meeting, a member of the Board of Trade indicated that he had known Kingsley personally when he was based in Nanaimo two decades earlier and that Kingsley ran his business "along the most capitalistic lines." According to the businessman, Kingsley "went over to the bigger field in Vancouver" and for a long time "had not done a stroke of real work, although he claimed to be spokesman for the workingman."[59] Again it might well be that his expressed and repeated interest in entrepreneurship was an attempt to retain a sense of masculinity and accomplishment in an ableist world. Of considerable intelligence, he arguably sought to transcend his physical impairments through business dealings that he could then channel effectively into finance and further the socialist cause to which he was deeply committed.

We know little about his personal life during the quarter of a century that Kingsley lived in Vancouver. He appears to have been missed by the enumerators for the 1911 and 1921 federal censuses, perhaps because he was out of town on organizing tours for the socialist cause, perhaps because he avoided the watchful eye of the bourgeois state. City directories beginning in 1906 list his places of residence at rooming houses in downtown Vancouver – West Cordova, Richards, Seymour, Water, and West Pender, clustered around the offices of the *Western Clarion,* the *Federationist,* and his printshop at the Flack Block and the Dunsmuir Street Labor Temple.[60] Mirroring the earlier pattern in San Francisco and San Jose, Kingsley usually lived within one or two blocks of his workplace – suggesting a rational adaptation to life as a double amputee by limiting daily travel distances (as well as hills and stairs). Until 1908, he appears to have ambulated on wooden legs before acquiring a pair of more modern prosthetic limbs.[61] Kingsley is recorded as being retired in the 1928 city directory, and he died in December 1929 in his apartment at 309 West Pender Street – one block from the *Western Clarion*'s long-standing headquarters.[62] There is no record of any romantic relationship following his divorce from his wife in the early 1890s, and he appears to have had little contact with his two sons, with the exception of a possible visit in 1913 with Percy.[63] Kingsley appears to have devoted his life to the socialist cause that he had advanced since at least 1894, apparently forging close friendships with several comrades, including socialist lawyer Wallis Lefeaux, recorded as the personal contact on his death certificate, and Parm Pettipiece, with whom Kingsley established a long-standing publishing relationship in relation to the *Western Clarion* and later the *Federationist* and *Labor Star*.[64] He also appears to have had an affinity with long-standing SPC MLA James Hawthornthwaite of Nanaimo. We can also make inferences about Kingsley's personal network from the identities of his business associates, for example in the Alberni timber venture.[65]

Regarding his disablement and physical appearance, Kingsley appears to have passed at times as able-bodied through the use of the prosthetic limbs and a cane. For example, a detailed description of his personal characteristics by a *Vancouver Daily Province* reporter in 1908 gave no hint of Kingsley's disablement:

> He is a typical American, whose fifteen [*sic*] years' residence in Canada has not spoilt his accent. He speaks in short sentences, and drives them at his audience with sharp forward jerks of his head. But the most curious of his mannerisms is the way, when wishing to make a point, he licks his first finger, for all the world like a baseball pitcher preparing the famous spit ball. Tall, and inclined to be stout, with keen small eyes, that seem to be continually raking his audience for possible hecklers, he is a good speaker with a forceful manner.[66]

However, Kingsley's disablement also appears to have been common knowledge to many of his Socialist Party comrades and to sections of the press and the public in British Columbia, as evidenced by his description in the *Victoria Daily Colonist* in 1903 as "the legless wonder of Social Economics."[67] Ronald Grantham, writing a graduate thesis less than fifteen years after the death of Kingsley, described him as "a crippled printer."[68] In an article and a radio address three decades after his death, former SPC member Roy Devore described his physical appearance: "Due to a railway accident in his young days Kingsley was minus both feet. But he was a big man, a 250 pounder[,] and his rugged physique coupled with an indomitable will kept him going. He was a masterly lecturer and deadly debater."[69]

An important side note is Kingsley's apparent silence on issues related to workplace safety, injury, disablement, and compensation. Although BC labour unions and socialist parties would advocate consistently in the first two decades of the twentieth century for laws and programs to improve safety for workers and provide security for those who had been injured on the job, Kingsley's name was never associated with these efforts in hundreds of documents that we have consulted. For example, in a speakers' series hosted by the Vancouver Trades and Labor Council (VTLC) toward the end of the First World War, it was VTLC president James McVety, rather than Kingsley, who spoke on the topic "Industrial Accidents and Workmen's Compensation." Kingsley stuck to more familiar ground in an address on "Capital, Labor, and the State."[70] Of course, this might have related to his strident adherence to "one-plank" Marxism, rejecting advocacy for workplace safety laws and compensation programs as "palliative" measures that would only prolong the demise of capitalism. However, given his personal experience of workplace injury and disablement, it seems to be peculiar that Kingsley – the foremost orator and propagandist of British Columbia's working-class movement in this era – would have avoided any association with issues so immediately connected to his personal experience. This perhaps suggests that Kingsley sought strenuously to avoid drawing attention to his disablement, avoiding advocacy on issues that would draw the attention of comrades, the public, and opponents to his lived reality as a double amputee.

Although Kingsley himself never advocated publicly for workplace safety measures or programs to help workers who had been injured or disabled on the job, these themes figured prominently in the *Western Clarion*. Especially during his term as the editor, the paper frequently reported on industrial accidents in Canada and the United States. Many of these reports included some sardonic remark about the fact that no capitalist had been injured, and they suggested that mine explosions, railway accidents, and all manner of other hazards were inherent to the capitalist system, in which workers' lives were expendable.[71] When twenty-three coal miners were killed in an explosion in West Virginia in 1905, an unsigned article in the newspaper commented that the cause of the explosion "was, of course, not due to any negligence of the company. Such affairs never are as capitalist concerns are proverbially more zealous in providing for the safety of employes [*sic*] than in making profit."[72] Another article, discussing statistics on the deaths of railworkers involved in the coupling and uncoupling of cars (a task with which Kingsley was intimately familiar), noted that the "property loss was the same" regardless of how many workers died, "as fortunately none of the cars or engines were injured."[73] When the Canadian Department of Labor released figures for industrial accidents in August 1906, showing that 111 workers had been killed and 280 seriously injured, the *Western Clarion* commented bitterly on "Canada's Slave Market" in which "Lives [Are] Cheaper than Safety Appliances."[74] "The list of capitalists killed and injured has been omitted, probably through an oversight," the paper noted sarcastically.[75] The *Western Clarion* regularly took aim at the disregard of state officials for workers' well-being, for example when two miners were killed in an explosion at the Sullivan Mine near Cranbrook: "The coroner decided that no inquest was necessary. Of course not. Only two working-men killed, anyway."[76]

Workplace safety was also an important legislative preoccupation for prewar Socialists in British Columbia, with MLAs James Hawthornthwaite and Parker Williams forging the *Workmen's Compensation Act* and revising the *Coal Mines Regulation Act*. This likely had more to do with the hazards facing coal miners in the Vancouver Island districts of Hawthornthwaite and Williams, however, rather than any personal intervention by Kingsley.

The *Western Clarion* also contained occasional references to disability and dismemberment, though none was authored openly by Kingsley. In 1905, the newspaper carried a report on the death of a Winnipeg worker who had been crippled after having his feet frozen. Connecting a critical analysis of disability to capitalism and organized religion, the newspaper commented that "able-bodied men are walking the streets of Winnipeg by the score, unable to obtain a job; among these the poor cripple had no chance. It is these conditions that the church helps to perpetuate. The church must go."[77] Years later, in February 1919, in an article in the short-lived *Labor Star,* which he edited, Kingsley provided the one published reference that we have found under his byline that explicitly relates to disability. In an article on "Reconstruction," Kingsley made the sharp observation that "pensions for disabled soldiers, homes and sustenance for cripples[,] ... will settle nothing, will change nothing ... The slaves will still be slaves, and the masters will still be masters, in spite of all the 're-construction' that stops short of revolution ... Though that may smack of 'Bolshevism' it may nevertheless be true."[78]

Publishing the *Western Clarion*

Kingsley's move from Nanaimo to Vancouver in the autumn of 1903 coincided with his appointment as manager-editor to rescue the financially beleaguered *Western Clarion* newspaper. Reflecting his pre-eminent status within the Socialist Party and his commitment to a socialist press, Kingsley would serve as the editor of the newspaper until 1908 (and again in 1912), as the publisher from 1905 to 1912, and as an editorial writer until the outbreak of the First World War (when an editorial that he wrote on the causes of the war erupted into a major controversy in the party, resulting in the end of his association with the *Western Clarion* and the party). As editor and publisher of the newspaper, Kingsley played a key role in shaping political thought in British Columbia and Canada in the crucial first decade of the twentieth century. When combined with his duties as dominion organizer of the Socialist Party of Canada (until 1908) and member of the Dominion Executive Committee (until 1912), Kingsley was the dominant personality on the socialist left throughout this period.

The *Western Clarion* was founded in May 1903 when the publisher, Ontario-born printer Richard Parmater "Parm" Pettipiece merged his *Western Socialist* (published since September 1902) with the *Nanaimo Clarion* and the United Brotherhood of Railway Employees' *Strike Bulletin*. The *Western Clarion* was privately owned by the Western Socialist Publishing Company, which Pettipiece controlled, but served as the official SPBC organ, with the endorsement of the Socialist Party of Manitoba, the American Labor Union, the Western Federation of Miners, and the Vancouver Trades and Labor Council.[79] However, despite investing some $1,600 of his personal funds in the paper, Pettipiece declared in October 1903 that he was unable to put it on a firm financial footing, reporting a monthly deficit of between $30 and $50. With his personal savings exhausted, he relinquished the editorship to find other work, and the board of the publishing company, including Kingsley as vice-president, decided to suspend publication in early November.[80]

Published in the basement of the Flack Block at 165 West Hastings Street in downtown Vancouver until the end of 1911 (and then in the new Labor Temple at 411 Dunsmuir Street when Kingsley's printshop and the newspaper relocated there), the *Western Clarion* was the leading publication on the BC and Canadian left in the decade leading up to the First World War.[81] Dorothy Steeves recalled in her biography of Ernest Winch that "socialist friends were often to be found in the paper's lair, 'the bear-pit' in the basement of the Flack Building of Vancouver."[82] Insight into the working environment at the newspaper can also be gleaned from the fictionalized account in A.M. Stephen's novel *The Gleaming Archway* (1929), which has a strong factual foundation, including the character Tacey modelled on Kingsley:

> The cubby-hole which they called their office was built in at the end of the printing shop, which was itself but a tiny room facing upon Pender Street. The light from the large window at the front was not sufficient for the whole place, so that a green-shaded lamp hung above the flat-topped desk at which the men were seated. Files of exchanges bulged upon the wooden walls, and a shelf above Tacey's head supported a dictionary, *Wage, Labour, and Capital,* by Karl Marx, and a miscellany of Socialist books and pamphlets.[83]

Kingsley's appointment as managing editor of the *Western Clarion* was announced in a special issue on 28 November 1903, following a three-week hiatus in publication. Kingsley apologized for the "temporary stoppage of publication," which had "caused a break in the revenue for the paper, through ads. and subs. falling off," but he promised subscribers that "publication will be resumed at the earliest possible date."[84] Kingsley made good on this promise, printing the next issue a week later (while pruning Pettipiece's previous ambitious and costly printing schedule of three issues per week down to a single issue published on Saturday mornings).[85] Kingsley would suspend publication again at the end of December, to allow "the collection of advertising accounts for the current month" and to "square all expense[s] incurred since the present manager took charge," expressing the hope that party members "would guarantee a small sum per month to provide against any deficit that might occur" (with Kingsley estimating that a guarantee of fifty dollars per month would be sufficient).[86] He appealed to Hawthornthwaite to use his influence to keep the newspaper alive: "The *Clarion* goes under for 30 days, and unless the comrades come to their senses, for good ... It is the d___est [*sic*, damnedest] stupidity that ever happened to let her go down now. $200 in hand and a small monthly guarantee for a short time would put her on her feet."[87] George Weston Wrigley, living at the time in Victoria and intimately familiar with the financial challenges of the socialist press as the former publisher of *Citizen and Country,* publicly pledged financial support for the newspaper, drawing particular attention to the efforts of Kingsley, "crippled physically and financially as he is."[88] By June 1904, the SPBC executive would express appreciation of "the efforts of Comrades Kingsley and English to resuscitate the *Western Clarion.*"[89]

However, financial difficulties would persist for the duration of Kingsley's tenure as editor and publisher, at the same time that Kingsley stood out as its most vocal defender. He had refused to "contract any indebtedness" when he had assumed the duties of editor, but by 1912 he would inform readers that he had absorbed an operating deficit of "considerably over one hundred dollars per month" in the previous eight years (no small sum – about $2,500 per month in 2021 dollars).[90] On the eve of the transformation of the SPBC into the SPC in November 1904, Kingsley reported to Hawthornthwaite on financial intrigue surrounding the *Western Clarion*'s printing plant and a power play that he had under way to assume total control of the operation. A.R. Stebbings "bought Bird's mortgages on the *Clarion* plant and expect[ed] to put in press and monoline. The *Clarion* will then be safe," Kingsley declared. He asked Hawthornthwaite for assistance in tracking down back issues of the newspaper to assist the party in a manoeuvre to "force the ... Pettipiece outfit off the premises."[91] (Pettipiece had earlier resumed the role as manager of the *Western Clarion,* with Kingsley serving as editor.[92]) How the specific mechanics of this manoeuvre played out are unclear, but by January 1905 Kingsley had secured control of the printing plant from Pettipiece, assuming the role of publisher and a subscriber list of 2,500.[93] Kingsley had earlier pledged to Hawthornthwaite to devote his "time and energy" to the success of the newspaper as soon as he returned from an organizing tour in the "upper country."[94]

There were ebbs and flows in the fortunes of the *Western Clarion,* with circulation ranging between 2,500 and 5,000 copies per week during Kingsley's years as editor and publisher before reaching an estimated peak distribution of 10,000 copies after the lifting of the wartime ban, according to Johnson.[95] In September 1905, the party printed 14,000 copies of a special Labour Day edition – at a time when the population of Vancouver was 45,000.[96] Later that year a party member named Leeds urged "all comrades ... to make the audience who hears Com. Kingsley each week ... as large as possible," describing the *Western Clarion's* hard-hitting class analysis as "like getting to a good big beef steak, after having been obliged to exist for a week on snowballs."[97] However, centrifugal pressures facing the Socialist Party of Canada, such as the split of the Social Democrats in 1907, affected subscriptions, advertising, and finances. Beginning in November 1908, and continuing until the end of 1911, the Dominion Executive Committee "indulged" in "the fiction of party ownership and maintenance," Kingsley would later recount, in the hope that it would "spur the comrades on to extra efforts toward financial success" while he continued to subsidize the operations of the newspaper from his personal finances.[98] In 1912, he briefly reassumed a direct role in the operations of the paper when the Dominion Executive Committee appointed him editor and dominion secretary (after the resignation of R.I. Matthews), and Kingsley agreed to forgo a sixty-dollar monthly stipend in the hope that the paper's revenues would cover its printing costs. "The task involved, I confess, is not to my liking," he advised readers. "I have, however, undertaken to fulfill it until such time as other and more suitable arrangements can be made."[99] The offices of the newspaper and party were also moved into Kingsley's printing press space at the Labor Temple on Dunsmuir Street at that time in this bid to contain costs.[100] Earlier, between July and November 1911, the publication had been pared down to a monthly pamphlet.[101]

The fortunes of the *Western Clarion* were also affected by the tendency of labour unions to strike out on their own, initiating publications under their control rather than delegating communications to that paper (decisions no doubt influenced by Kingsley's and the Socialist Party of Canada's strong antipathy to trade union issues). In 1909, the Vancouver Trades and Labor Council started its own paper, the *Western Wage-Earner* (building on an earlier private concern, the *BC Trades Unionist*), with an editorial line similar to the SPC line, emphasizing the "necessity of securing control of the state by constitutional means – the ballot box."[102] Indeed, the founding issue of the *Western Wage-Earner* included a prominent ad for Kingsley's printing business.[103] In 1911, the recently formed British Columbia Federation of Labor (BCFL) initiated its own newspaper, the *British Columbia Federationist*, edited by Pettipiece, cutting further into the *Western Clarion*'s subscriber and advertising base (the *Federationist* would publish continuously until 1925, with Kingsley serving for a time as an editor after his falling out with the *Clarion*).[104]

In November 1912, Kingsley made the decision to cease subsidizing the *Western Clarion*.[105] Publication was suspended for the next four months, until March 1913. "No wonder Marx died in poverty," a writer, presumably Wallis Lefeaux, quipped in the *Federationist*. "We have a long line of propagandists, well posted in the material conception, hovering on the border line of financial overdraft, down to our own immediate vicinity and days of Kingsley, McKenzie, Vancouver Local No. 1, et al."[106] Kingsley, for his part, wrote that he had "patiently and hopefully" looked forward to the time when, through the zeal of comrades across the country, the subscription list would "reach such proportions as would not only pay the cost of publication but bring a revenue to the Party treasury." However, circulation had "been falling off" for some time, "not rapidly it is true, but rapidly enough to be seriously threatening." He could not personally absorb the newspaper's deficit indefinitely and therefore had been "compelled to call a halt": "No individual could be expected to carry this sort of thing forever."[107] To fulfill obligations to existing subscribers, Kingsley arranged for the *Federationist* to assume responsibility for the *Western Clarion*'s mailing list, with a circulation of 5,200, each subscriber receiving a copy of the *Federationist* for the duration of his or her subscription.[108] Kingsley also agreed to contribute two editorial columns for each issue of the *Federationist*, and the Socialist Party of Canada was to be allotted three columns. Demonstrating this continuity, subsequent issues of the *Federationist* carried a detailed listing of the twenty-four SPC locals across the country and other party news.[109]

Although the *Western Clarion* would be revived four months later, with the Socialist Party of Canada assuming direct responsibility for its costs and operations, Kingsley would no longer be the driving force (though he would contribute editorial content until the autumn of 1914); negotiations also unfolded between Kingsley and the SPC Dominion Executive Committee over payment of a debt of $440, with Kingsley holding literature and supplies as collateral before settling for a cheque of $140.[110] As editor and publisher, he had played a central role in policy making and communications within the party, but it was not a highly coveted position according to Bill Pritchard (who served as editor from 1914 to 1917, assuming the role as a result of the controversy over Kingsley's editorial on the causes of the war). "It wasn't a job that people were looking for particularly," Pritchard recalled.[111] SPC members closely monitored the *Western Clarion* and its editorial line, not surprising in light of the importance of policy and ideology in the life of the prewar Socialist Party of Canada. "If you made a slip even in terminology in the articles in the *Clarion,* particularly in the editorials, you'd hear from some local with a blast," Pritchard recalled. However, he suggested that the Dominion Executive Committee took a fairly hands-off approach to the paper's daily operations, providing only "a watchful eye": "The editor, it was assumed, knew what he was doing and what he was writing about. But if he ever made a slip, he got a crack on the head, and sometimes unjustifiably so."[112]

In addition to the *Western Clarion,* the Socialist Party of Canada distributed extensive socialist literature to its members and supporters. This literature consisted of Marxist texts that it published under its own imprint, such as a "nice, stiff-backed" edition of the first nine chapters of *Das Kapital* for use as the textbook in SPC economics classes, according to Pritchard, as well as 2,000 copies of Marx's *Wage-Labour and Capital* sold for two and a half cents apiece in 1905.[113] The party also distributed pamphlets by North American writers examining a range of social, economic, and political questions through a Marxist lens – "everything from three volumes of *Capital* all the way through," Pritchard recalled. At one point, the Socialist Party of Canada was ordering $200 worth of literature each week from Charles H. Kerr & Company of Chicago, a leading North American left-wing publishing house – a sizable sum in the currency of the day.[114] One specific piece of literature in the SPC catalogue harked back to an earlier phase in Kingsley's political life, written by an old comrade from San Francisco: Jack London's *Revolution,* a pamphlet published by E.T. Kingsley Printing, Vancouver.[115]

Leading the Socialist Party of Canada

Virtually from the moment of his arrival in British Columbia to about 1912, Kingsley was the dominant force in the socialist movement in the province. The primary vehicle for this political activism and propaganda was the Socialist Party of Canada. The party came into being at a convention in Vancouver on 31 December 1904 attended by thirty-seven delegates representing all branches of the SPBC, and they approved a resolution moved by J.G. Morgan and seconded by Kingsley "that the party name be changed to the Socialist Party of Canada, and that the party proceed with organization."[116] This decision was prompted by a report to the convention indicating that local socialist groups from Winnipeg to Toronto to Fredericton had applied for affiliation with the SPBC, prompting the delegates to expand the geographic mandate of their organization to make it national: "In consequence, the field of hitherto purely provincial organization had been expanded and the Socialist Party of Canada given birth."[117] Kingsley was "engaged as organizer" and prepared to embark on a recruiting tour of eastern Canada; he was also appointed to continue serving as editor of the *Western Clarion* and to sit on a three-person committee with Hawthornthwaite and Williams tasked with drafting amendments to the party's constitution to reflect the new national scope.[118] The *Victoria Daily Colonist* reported that affiliation with the Second International would come "in the natural course of events" (a matter later subjected to rigorous debate within the Socialist Party of Canada before ultimately being dropped).[119] Ideologically, the party maintained the same aggressive stance of the SPBC (like the RSPC before it), inviting workers to organize under its banner "with the object of conquering the public powers, for the purpose of setting up ... and enforcing the economic program of the working class."[120] Reflecting the emphasis on political action from the inception of the Socialist Party of Canada, delegates adopted a resolution urging the BC government to amend the *Elections Act* to remove the $200 deposit for candidates standing for election to provincial office.[121]

Organizationally, the Socialist Party of Canada was led by the Dominion Executive Committee, which, despite the party's national aspirations, remained firmly based in Vancouver because of a decision at the December 1904 convention that the SPBC's Provincial Executive Committee would act as the Dominion Executive Committee until such time as a national convention was called, but that convention never took place.[122] Bill Pritchard (who met Kingsley the day of his arrival from England in May 1911 and would serve with him briefly on the Dominion Executive Committee) attributed the party's Vancouver-centric power structure to geography and the rudimentary means of communication available at the time:

> We didn't have the lines of communication then that we have now. You can get one of these ferries, go right from here on a bus and be in Victoria in no time. That used to be an all-night trip ... to go to Victoria. You can go over and come back the same day if you have to. So it would be possible now to have an executive in Vancouver and have representatives come in from Victoria or Nanaimo, any place. They can fly in. We didn't have it then.[123]

Other than a Toronto branch (which had affiliated with the Socialist Party of Canada following an earlier incarnation as the Toronto Socialist League) and a smattering of other locals, British Columbia was the primary base of operations of the party for most of its existence. Although no membership figures were ever published by the party, and reliable membership records do not exist, according to interviews with Kingsley's former comrades Jack Harrington and Wallis Lefeaux the party had somewhere between 500 and 3,000 dues-paying members in the prewar period; Harrington recalled that about 150 of the party's 500–600 members lived in Vancouver.[124]

Kingsley served in various roles on the Dominion Executive Committee from the party's inception until 1912.[125] He also served as SPC dominion organizer until 1908.[126] It is noteworthy that Kingsley's attendance at meetings of the executive dropped sharply in 1909, coinciding with the end of his term as dominion organizer and *Western Clarion* editor.[127] Apart from Kingsley as an American, British Canadians dominated the leadership

FIGURE 13   Socialist Party of Canada activists, Vancouver, c. 1913. | Socialist Party of Canada.

of the group prior to the First World War, though there were a few "language branches," foreshadowing the expansion of ethnocultural organization by the Social Democratic Party of Canada and, after 1921, the Communist Party of Canada. A Finnish local based in remote Sointula (a fishing community and the site of a former utopian socialist cooperative colony) and a Latvian local based in Vancouver lent some ethnocultural diversity to the heavily British composition of the Socialist Party of Canada. In 1910, delegates at a convention of Ukrainian socialist organizations in western Canada debated whether to join the SPC or SDPC.[128]

The Socialist Party of Canada less actively embraced Asian workers, particularly those from China and Japan, reflecting the historical antipathy of white settlers in British Columbia toward immigrants from Asia, disparagingly viewed as a pool of low-wage workers exploited by employers to drive down working conditions.[129] However, demonstrating an exception to this discriminatory approach (and foreshadowing a more robust embrace of racial equality among sections of the left after the First World War), Kingsley and the Socialist Party of Canada spoke out against the ugly and racially motivated violence that erupted in Vancouver in the race riot of September 1907, when white mobs riled up by a group called the Asiatic Exclusion League rampaged through Chinatown and Japantown:

The working class mind is being inflamed with the idea that the Japanese, Hindu or Chinese workingman coming to Canada ... comes as an enemy to the white worker. As racial prejudice is one of the meanest in the category and the least found[ed] upon reason, it is one of the easiest to stir up. When stirred up it is virulent and bestial in the extreme and capable of being used to carry out the purpose, however vile, of those who know how to manipulate it and turn it to account ...

Whatever steps were taken by the political tools of the business interests to bring about the senseless attack upon Chinatown and the Japanese quarter it is evident they were successful in inducing the most ignorant, hoodlum element of Vancouver to do the job, while the working class of the city get credit for it.[130]

The *Western Clarion* (and presumably Kingsley as its editor) connected deliberate efforts to stir up race hatred with the growing strength of the socialist movement in British Columbia – and a corresponding political imperative for the bourgeoisie to distract workers – warning workers not to be duped: "Keep your eye open for fake issues. Be not misled by them."[131] In contrast to this strong statement against racism, the *Vancouver World* would later claim that Kingsley (along with the three other candidates in the 1908 federal election for Vancouver City) supported Asiatic exclusion.[132] However, he advised the *Winnipeg Tribune* during a visit to the city in 1908 that "the question of yellow immigration was not troubling to him and his friends ... What they were concentrating their energies upon was filling the lower house at Ottawa and provincial houses with their men."[133]

On the question of race, Kingsley had a contradictory record, perhaps reflecting the incoherent politics of his tradition. The impossibilist politics that he embraced, from the De Leonist Socialist Labor Party to the Socialist Party of Canada, frequently saw class struggle as the motor of history, to the exclusion of other identities. The first significant reference to race came from his political activism in Washington State when he wrote about racist policies that disenfranchised blacks in parts of the American South in the context of a dispute about the Washington State primary law. Yet Kingsley largely abided by the class-centred focus of socialist politics common in this era. His xenophobic attack on "the Mongolians" in 1902 was disappointingly exclusionary and racist. At the outbreak of the First World

War, he would express virulent anti-German sentiment. This is in contrast to his support for South Asians and blacks and his general commitment to international working-class solidarity.

Demonstrating its commitment to internationalism, and emerging connections to the local Asian community, the Socialist Party of Canada convened a mass meeting in January 1911 to protest the execution of Japanese anarchist journalist Kōtoku Denjirō and eleven comrades attended by an estimated 1,500 people, "of both sexes, and various colors, an international audience, in fact."[134] The party also began to develop linkages with the local South Asian population, as Peter Campbell and Sunit Singh have demonstrated, particularly Sikh people through the revolutionary Ghadar movement.[135] In the wake of the *Komagata Maru* incident in 1914, which saw the government of Canada deny entry to a ship from India carrying 376 British subjects, Kingsley defended the Sikh, Hindu, and Muslim passengers and the local Sikh population in a speech in Vancouver's Empress Theatre, condemning efforts "to incite the populace to violence against the Hindus on the *Komagata Maru* and also against the shore Hindus."[136] As early as 1903, he had declared in a speech in Victoria that the "labour problem" was "not a matter of excluding the Chinese, negroes, etc." but a problem of "securing for labor all the wealth it creates."[137]

Kingsley and a coterie of British-born men dominated the Socialist Party of Canada throughout this period, but as historian Linda Kealey and others have demonstrated there were examples of women who exercised leadership within the party, building on the foundation established in the SPBC. Bertha Burns (née Merrill) had served on the party's executive in its formative years, and Ada Clayton served as secretary of the party's Victoria local.[138] In an article entitled "Why Women Should Be Socialists" in the journal of the American Labor Union, Burns discussed why women were less involved than men: "The fault, if fault there be, does not lie directly with the women themselves but is rather the natural result of education and environment."[139] Joan Sangster suggests that the "rigid class perspective" of the Socialist Party of Canada prevented it from acknowledging "the special oppression of women."[140] Commenting on the attitude of men in the party toward women and their interests, Ian McKay notes that the "one-plank Marxism" advocated by Kingsley and others – with its explicit opposition to "palliative" measures designed to improve conditions under capitalism – foreclosed rigorous support for women's suffrage, serving as an example of "the arrogance of male socialists and their indifference to such a basic democratic demand."[141] Although the *Western Clarion* proclaimed SPC support for "political equality of the sexes," when a "Women's Column" was proposed for the newspaper, the new editor, D.G. McKenzie, deferred judgment on the matter "to the Old Man" Kingsley, and no action appears to have been taken.[142] Occasionally, there were glimmers of recognition of the particular oppression facing working-class women. In 1910, the newspaper observed that, whereas a man was free in the evening after he had delivered "his quota of labour-power" to the boss, a woman "is free only when she sleeps and is free then only to store up energy for the next day's slavery," suggesting that the destruction of capitalism and the capitalist "home" would liberate the "wife-slaves."[143]

One area where Kingsley and the socialists demonstrated little concern was the interests of Indigenous people. John Belshaw has explored the connection between the British immigrant identity of working-class settlers on Vancouver Island and the process of colonization of Indigenous lands (as well as attitudes toward workers from Asia), suggesting that, "as in many colonies, definitions of belonging to the Vancouver Island white community depended on the simultaneous exclusion of these other two 'races.'"[144] There is little evidence to suggest that Kingsley and the Socialist Party of Canada lent active support to demands for Indigenous rights to land or for relief from the repressive shackles of the *Indian Act* and residential school system. This was despite the fact that Indigenous people occupied an important place within the industrial working class of Vancouver in the first decade of the twentieth century, as Andrew Parnaby demonstrated in his research on Indigenous longshore workers in the city.[145] To be sure, there were moments of socialist intervention in defence of Indigenous rights. When a member of the Legislative Assembly proposed in 1906 to "open up the Indian Reserves" to development, SPC MLA Parker Williams forcefully challenged this view, suggesting that Indigenous people were being "trespassed on and put off the land they occupy" because they were "not imbued with the speculative spirit," noting that thousands of acres of land were available in the Fraser Valley and elsewhere in the province if they were "taken out [of] the hands of the speculators."[146] However, interventions of this sort were few and far between. When a delegation of

Salish chiefs led by Chief Joe Capilano of the Squamish Nation in the Vancouver area travelled to London in 1906 to bring Indigenous grievances directly to King Edward VII, the Socialist Party of Canada remained silent.[147] As McKay noted, comments by Kingsley such as his suggestion that the territory north of Lake Superior was "worthless," offering nothing more than rock and muskeg, erased thousands of years of Indigenous use of, and connection to, these lands, revealing an inherently Eurocentric view.[148] Moreover, the same cultural superiority (which could also be discerned in the writings of other socialists from Karl Marx to J.S. Woodsworth) was manifested in Kingsley's principal published work, *The Genesis and Evolution of Slavery,* in which Kingsley adopted a familiar trope in European and leftist thinking and writing around this time – describing an "evolution" of the human species from "savagery" to "barbarism" to "civilization."[149]

Although the Socialist Party of Canada might have been narrow in its social composition and political orientation, it nurtured a vibrant educational and social life for its members. The centrepiece of the party's work was its mission of political education – winning over a majority of the ethnically European working class to socialism – through publication of the *Western Clarion,* distribution of associated left-wing literature, electoral campaigns, and the convening of frequent public lectures and smaller reading groups, centring on weekly educational meetings on Sunday evenings on topics ranging from Marxist economics to contemporary proposals such as the single tax from a Marxist standpoint.[150]

Like the Socialist Labor Party before it, the Socialist Party of Canada imposed an examination on scientific socialism as a condition of party membership, demonstrating the centrality of ideology in its work.[151] George Hardy, who would later grow intensely critical of the dogmatism of the party, credited it and Kingsley with playing an integral role in his conversion to revolutionary socialism after attending one of the party's Sunday-evening meetings in Victoria, which were "always packed," and purchasing a copy of Marx's *Value, Price, and Profit.* "I went to hear E.T. Kingsley, of Vancouver, lecture on Marxist economics. That was a real eye-opener. I believe my real education began in this period."[152]

The party would also host annual events tied to the history of class struggle – notably, commemorating the anniversary of the Paris Commune,

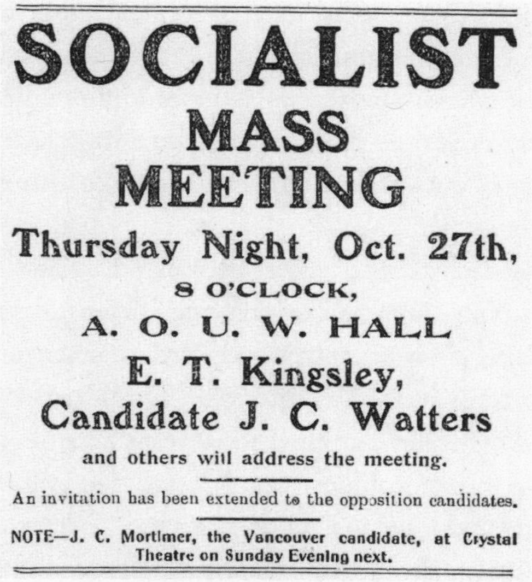

SOCIALIST

MASS
MEETING

Thursday Night, Oct. 27th,

8 O'CLOCK,

A. O. U. W. HALL

E. T. Kingsley,
Candidate J. C. Watters

and others will address the meeting.

An invitation has been extended to the opposition candidates.

NOTE—J. C. Mortimer, the Vancouver candidate, at Crystal Theatre on Sunday Evening next.

FIGURE 14   Advertisement for a Kingsley speaking engagement in Victoria during the 1904 federal election. | *Victoria Daily Colonist.*

International Workers' Day, and revolutionary events in Russia. In a meeting in Vancouver City Hall in January 1906, commemorating workers and peasants massacred in St. Petersburg a year earlier during the "Bloody Sunday" repression by Czarist forces that triggered the Russian Revolution of 1905, Kingsley declared that "this century belongs to the man in overalls" and that "the day has come when the rule of capital shall be broken." A collection was taken at the meeting, totalling $32.65, to be sent to the Russian workers "to aid them in their struggle for freedom."[153]

Alongside this educational and propaganda work, the Socialist Party of Canada provided a distinct social milieu for its members. As Pritchard recalled, in the winter months, the party hosted weekly "smokers" on Saturday nights – social nights in community halls – with music, comedy, and conversation for entertainment, fuelled with sandwiches, coffee, and a free barrel of beer provided every week by the Vancouver Brewery. "I guess they figured it was a good advertisement," Pritchard said.[154] In the summer months, the party hosted weekly picnics on Sunday afternoons on beaches at English Bay, Stanley Park, Kitsilano, Jericho, and Spanish Banks in Vancouver.[155] Similar social events took place in all of the communities where SPC locals took root, demonstrating a focus on working-class culture common to the North American left at this time. The party also demonstrated a commitment to mutual aid characteristic of other working-class organizations in this era. In 1913, Kingsley donated 500 tickets for a benefit concert for the widow and children of a Vancouver carpenter who had died.[156]

To extend its reach beyond its base on the Pacific Coast, and to maintain connections with far-flung party locals, the Socialist Party of Canada deployed Kingsley as party organizer and other speakers on regular lecture and organizing tours in the BC Interior.[157] On the eve of the party's formation in 1904, Kingsley travelled to Revelstoke and Nelson, where he purportedly said that a revolution was coming either by the franchise power or by force of arms, adding "and I don't care which" – for which the *Kootenay Mail* assailed him as "the revolutionary type of Socialist whose next stepping stone is nihilism and anarchy."[158] The party had earlier considered plans to "send Organizer Kingsley on a tour through the eastern provinces in order to 'educate' the inhabitants thereof in the philosophy of real Socialism."[159] In September 1905, he returned briefly to the United States at the invitation of an SLP local in Seattle, travelling by steamer via Victoria and delivering two lectures at the party headquarters attended by 200 and 450 people. Kingsley provided a colourful account of the trip in the *Western Clarion,* including seeing salmon and whales at the mouth of the Fraser River and enjoying the "pleasing sight" of "the brilliant illumination of the leading hotels and other prominent buildings" as the vessel approached Seattle – a rare uncritical observation of what otherwise could have been described as a garish display of bourgeois opulence. Emphasizing thrift during the trip, Kingsley described conditions in the hotel room that he secured for one dollar, with the bed linen looking as though "it might have served as bandages at the Battle of Mukden" (a recent bloody clash in Manchuria between Russian and Japanese forces). After his return to Vancouver, Kingsley was optimistic that "the movement of the proletariat along the pathway leading to labor's emancipation is forging ahead in other lands as well as in British Columbia."[160] He was invited to return to Seattle to give another talk in December 1905.[161]

In May 1908, Kingsley embarked on what appears to have been his most ambitious journey after delegates at an interprovincial SPC convention in

1st D.E.C. of The SOCIALIST PARTY of CANADA

Peterson   Steadman   1904   Kingsley   MacKenzie
Morgan   Pritchard   S   Lambert

FIGURE 15   Inaugural Dominion Executive Committee of the Socialist Party of Canada, c. 1904. | Library and Archives Canada, C-038687.

Fernie (representing BC and Alberta locals) approved a recommendation from the Dominion Executive Committee to send him on a speaking tour of eastern Canada, coinciding with a provincial election campaign in Ontario.[162] The costs of the trip were defrayed through the establishment by the party of a "Dominion Organization Fund," with a special appeal issued to members to contribute what they could to keep Kingsley "in the field as long as circumstances will allow."[163] He travelled from Fernie to Calgary, Winnipeg, Port Arthur, Toronto, Hamilton, Guelph, Berlin, Cobalt, Montreal, and other points, delivering dozens of lectures while riding "night after night in the day coaches without taking a sleeper" because "funds [were] running short."[164] Sailing back up Lakes Huron and Superior from Sarnia to Port Arthur, Kingsley travelled on a "rough" and "crowded" boat, standing in line for over an hour to get his meals and being confined to a top bunk after the passenger in the lower bunk refused to switch places. Despite travelling on a boat not designed for physically disabled passengers and facing hostility from ignorant travellers, Kingsley completed this epic journey devoted to socialist propaganda.

A detailed account of his journey was provided in a *Western Clarion* report by George Weston Wrigley, who contrasted the Old Man's frugality with the opulent global travels of British socialist luminaries Keir Hardie, Ramsay MacDonald, and Victor Grayson. Wrigley also provided a rare glimpse of Kingsley's life circumstances as a disabled person, prefacing the account as follows:

> It isn't generally known that some years ago Comrade Kingsley, in his calling as a railway worker, lost his two limbs and for years put his earnings which should have gone toward modern artificial limbs ... into the party propaganda. Just before beginning his present tour, however, he got a new pair and had to break them in while on the road. I may be telling tales out of school, but some need to be told.[165]

His resilience and dedication to the socialist cause as a field organizer are particularly remarkable in light of how Kingsley lived his day-to-day life: in both San Francisco and Vancouver, he lived within a block of his place of work, in all likelihood because of his impaired mobility on account of his disablement. As Ross Johnson noted, "in spite of his handicap he managed to travel thousands of miles on speaking and organizing tours, sometimes under the most adverse conditions."[166]

After the cross-Canada trip in 1908, Kingsley stepped down as dominion organizer for the Socialist Party of Canada, perhaps reflecting the toil of the journey and the feverish pace of work that he had sustained in the years leading up it, perhaps to make room for other comrades. However, even after he stepped back from this role, his influence continued across the country, even in places that he had not reached in person. In 1909, a supporter in Saint John, New Brunswick, writing in the business-aligned *Saint John Sun,* defended socialism and located Kingsley among a cohort of "socialist writers and speakers" that included international luminaries Debs, London, Haywood, Berger, De Leon, Hyndman, Babel, and Jaures.[167] SPC support peaked in the Maritimes in 1909 – with the party expanding to fifteen locals in the region, building on traditional beachheads in Fredericton and Cape Breton.[168]

Closer to home, Kingsley continued to engage working-class audiences on the Pacific Coast on a broad range of topics, examined as always through his lens of class struggle.[169] This engagement included a lecture on religion and its connection to the struggle for working-class emancipation in Victoria's Grand Theatre in 1910, where he asserted that Christianity and socialism were identical.[170] He based this argument on recently unearthed archaeological records that, according to Kingsley, proved that Jesus Christ had indeed existed, coming into the world shortly after the suppression of slave revolts by Roman military authorities. According to Kingsley, Jesus responded by teaching the "doctrine of passive resistance" – turning the cheek to a person who is smiting you while preserving and strengthening the communal life within your organization – which Kingsley identified as the main feature of these early working-class movements led by Spartacus and others. According to Kingsley, the threat that this communal impulse posed to the priestly class resulted in a perversion of Christ's teachings, with "the common table" for eating being banned and "communal houses" being converted into churches.[171] Earlier, during a public meeting in Vancouver City Hall during his candidacy in the 1907 provincial election, Kingsley revealed his disdain for both organized Christianity and monarchy: "There never was a King on this earth who ruled by the grace of God – he rules by the ignorance of his subjects. You can't stuff that grace of God business down me – because too many of my ancestors had their ears lopped off by Kings by the grace of God."[172]

The pace of his propaganda and organizational work on behalf of the Socialist Party of Canada slowed after his departure from the *Western Clarion* and the Dominion Executive Committee in 1912, but Kingsley continued to make contributions. In May of that year, he addressed a May Day gathering in Nanaimo as well as a number of meetings in the Vancouver area.[173] When a strike broke out at Cumberland in September 1912, mushrooming that winter into the epic Vancouver Island coal miners' strike (which Kingsley's socialist comrade Jack Kavanagh would describe as "the Vancouver Island War" as 1,000 militiamen occupied the island coalfield and arrested more than 200 miners to aid the mine owners' campaign to keep the United Mine Workers union off the island), Kingsley and the Socialist Party of Canada lent their support. At the outbreak of the strike, he declared that "the newspapers lie[d] like horse thieves" when they suggested that the miners had made no attempt to settle the dispute short of a strike.[174] A year later, in the autumn of 1913, as the arrested miners (including SDPC MLA John "Jack" Place) awaited trial, and mining families were on the brink of starvation, Kingsley and the Socialist Party of Canada joined forces with erstwhile left-wing rivals in a coalition called the Miners' Liberation League (MLL). A defence committee formed in the wake of the arrests that included the United Mine Workers of America, the Socialist Party of Canada, the SDPC, the Industrial Workers of the World, and the BC Federation of Labor, and the Miners' Liberation League demanded that the provincial minister of justice intervene to release the imprisoned miners while unions contemplated a forty-eight-hour general strike to force their release.[175]

Notwithstanding his long aversion to trade unionism and "palliative measures" that would ameliorate conditions for the working class under capitalism, the scale of state violence directed toward the miners and the degree of class solidarity in the island coal communities appear to have impelled Kingsley to act. In November and December 1913, he spoke on behalf of the Socialist Party of Canada at a series of mass protest meetings in Vancouver organized under the auspices of the Miners' Liberation League, declaring on 8 December that "corporation tools and thugs were always on hand to suppress slaves in rebellion." He expressed the hope that "the working class would arise some day and knock the 'block' off every ruler that lived."[176] In the spring of 1914, Kingsley undertook a speaking tour among the striking miners at Cumberland, Nanaimo, and other points.[177] Despite these efforts, left-wing militant George Hardy would lambaste the "spitoon [*sic*] philosophers" of the Socialist Party of Canada who "stood aloof" and "fiddled while the armed forces of the State suppressed the miners and locked up resisters."[178] In August 1914, following the outbreak of world war, the United Mine Workers of America called off the strike as miners drifted back to work, with the island "war" ending in an unqualified defeat for the workers.[179]

Fissures and Splits

The growth of the Socialist Party of Canada and Kingsley's influence among BC and Canadian workers were impeded by periodic splits, notably after 1907, when the suspension of party founder Ernest Burns prompted the resignation of Bertha Merrill Burns and sixty other members, who reconstituted themselves as the Social Democratic Party of Canada.[180] In a column in the *Western Socialist* four years earlier (writing under the pen name Dorothy Drew), Bertha Burns had highlighted the tension between the "doctrinaires" and the "pragmatists," distinguishing herself from the Marxist orthodoxy associated with Kingsley: "It may not smack of 'scientific socialism' to say so, but I believe more men and women are attracted to socialism by the divine reaching-out-for-others spirit that is its basic principle than come to it from any other motive of self-help or expediency."[181] The suspension of Ernest Burns was prompted by a controversial meeting that he and his wife hosted in Vancouver City Hall in March 1907 featuring a lecture by a prominent American socialist, Walter Thomas Mills, a political moderate who advocated the electoral "fusion" of socialists with other progressive forces.[182] When the Burnses persisted in hosting the meeting, despite a vote of SPC Vancouver Local No. 1 against endorsing the event, Kingsley and party member J.T. Mortimer shepherded a resolution through the local to suspend Burns (an earlier attempt to expel him had failed).[183] The wider context of the split was the long-standing grievance of reformists against the impossibilism of the party, which they viewed as the primary cause of the lacklustre performance of the party in the provincial election in February 1907 (the party retained three legislative seats but achieved no appreciable increase in votes despite massive population growth in the province: in Vancouver, SPC support dropped from 1,333 votes in the 1903 election to a meagre 617 votes in the 1907 election).[184] Bertha Burns had earlier noted in a letter to Margaret MacDonald, a British socialist (and the wife of Ramsay MacDonald, a Labour Party MP) that "the Impossibilist element [was] in full control" but that there was a movement among Finnish members of the Socialist Party of Canada, who outnumbered English speakers, "for a reconstruction of the constitution along more rational lines, and for a platform of Immediate Demands."[185]

In April 1907, the Burnses and other SPC dissidents convened a meeting in Vancouver in O'Brien's Hall, where they formed the SDPC, pledging to establish themselves "on a wider basis" than "the Kingsley party," which wanted "a complete overthrow of power."[186] In a petition announcing the formation of the new party, the dissidents lambasted the "purely ... negative" SPC propaganda, which did not "appeal to the average working elector as practical," and they described the condemnation of all labour union activity as "entirely unnecessary" (highlighting a long-standing grievance of Ernest

Burns, who had led the Vancouver Fishermen's Union).[187] The dissidents also criticized the "centralization of power" in the hands of the SPC's Provincial Executive Committee.[188] Contrasting their new party to the impossibilism of the Socialist Party of Canada, the SDPC enthusiastically embraced reforms:

> As a means of preparing the minds of the working class for the inaugur-
> ation of the co-operative Commonwealth, the Social-Democratic Party
> of Canada will support any measure that will tend to better conditions
> under capitalism, such as: (1) reduction of hours of labour, (2) the elim-
> ination of child labour, (3) universal adult suffrage without distinction
> of sex or regard to property qualifications, and (4) the Initiative, Refer-
> endum, and right of Recall.[189]

In the wake of this split, Bertha Burns observed that Kingsley was "left with only a few ranters to support him – lip revolutionists but utterly incapable of any organized activity."[190] The Kingsley group, for their part, declared in the *Western Clarion* that "these free lancers of the Mills type are merely nuisances to the proletarian movement."[191] Daniel De Leon, who undertook a speaking tour in the Pacific Northwest at the time, including a lecture at Vancouver City Hall that Kingsley attended, denied accusations that he had sent Mills into the region to "bust up the S.P.," speculating that Kingsley feared the impact that the presence of Mills would have on the "dwindling subscription list" of the *Western Clarion*.[192]

The growth of the SDPC was slow initially, but over time it would emerge as a major alternative to the influence of Kingsley and the Socialist Party of Canada in British Columbia and Canada, ultimately joining forces with a party of the same name based in Winnipeg. Harnessing radicalization within working-class communities experiencing strains associated with industrialization, urbanization, and the deepening structural inequality of capitalism, the SDPC put down roots from Vancouver Island to Port Arthur to Toronto to the Maritimes.[193] In 1912, the SPC Nanaimo local defected as a block to join the SDPC, as did its MLA, Parker Williams.[194] The emerging rift within the Nanaimo local had resulted earlier in the resignation of the party's de facto leader in the legislature, James Hawthornthwaite (succeeded by an SDPC MLA, John "Jack" Place), and torn apart the annual SPC convention in the autumn of 1911, with "fully thirty percent of the delegates" walking out. Party stalwart D.G. McKenzie responded to the convention debacle by resigning as *Western Clarion* editor and dominion secretary, railing against the "vapidity and futility" of the convention.[195] Earlier that year a number of disaffected SPC locals in eastern Canada left that party, including the Finnish sections, affiliating at first with one another as the Canadian Socialist Federation before joining the SDPC at a convention in Port Arthur.[196]

Kingsley's Socialist Party of Canada entered a period of decline with the split of the SDPC and the Nanaimo and eastern Canadian locals, one from which it would never fully recover. According to McCormack, "the party reached its nadir in 1912."[197] An editorial writer, presumably Kingsley, admitted frankly in March of that year that "the Locals ... are either semi-defunct, or in a state of philosophical dry-rot."[198] When questioned by McCormack on democracy within the Socialist Party of Canada and whether the Dominion Executive Committee functioned in dictatorial ways, Pritchard (who joined the committee shortly after his arrival in Vancouver from England in 1911) described the committee's functioning as follows: "They would set down a position according to the accepted principles of the party when a question came up. They'd make that decision. Now that decision was subject to appeal, subject to referendum."[199]

Criticism of the doctrinaire stance of Kingsley and the SPC leadership was not confined to Canada. Tension was apparent between the British Labour Party leadership and Kingsley and other theoreticians of the BC school of socialism. In 1906, Margaret MacDonald, the British socialist and wife of Ramsay MacDonald, noted in a letter from Victoria that she and her husband "were not Marxian enough" for Kingsley – after he told the MacDonalds in a conversation during their Canadian speaking tour that Canadian socialism was "built up on Marxianism."[200] A year later Kingsley shared a platform in Vancouver's Recreation Park with Keir Hardie, who commanded at the time a caucus of twenty-nine Labour MPs in the UK Parliament. Although Kingsley said in his remarks that "socialism, in its fundamental conceptions, is the same in the new world as in the old," Hardie would later lambaste the "impossibilist element" that dominated the Canadian movement and that had "to be downed everywhere – including in the United States of America – as a preliminary to

Socialism becoming a living, vitalising power."[201] Although not naming Kingsley, Hardie criticized "American speakers ... imbued with the De Leon spirit" whose talk was "spiced with all the crudities and absurdities which Marx and Engels trounced so roundly in their day, but which these men believe to be the very essence of Socialist faith." Nonetheless, Hardie expressed the view that the political situation in Canada was "distinctly hopeful" and that in time "the movement will grow out of this dogmatic, arid, blighting creed of withering materialism."[202]

The Socialist Party of Canada also faced strains associated with the rise of militant industrial unionism, as embodied in the Industrial Workers of the World, formed at a conference in Chicago in 1905 with leading American socialists, including Eugene Debs and Daniel De Leon, playing an active role, but within a few years rifts would emerge between the "political" and "industrial" arms of the American working class. In 1906, shortly after the establishment of the first IWW local in Vancouver, two "wobblies" challenged Kingsley at an SPC mass meeting in the Grand Theatre, asking him how the working class could be emancipated without an economic organization of workers. Kingsley responded that workers were already "rigidly and automatically" organized by the character of industry itself and would remain thus "so long as capitalist control lasts." The *Western Clarion* suggested in its next issue that, rather than "obtruding themselves" as speakers and organizers on platforms that they did not hire, the "advocates of the new unionism" should rent a hall and convene an audience of their own to discuss "the folly of 'putting your Socialist ballot in a capitalist ballot box.'"[203] However, criticism from proponents of industrial unionism would persist, with a correspondent to the *Western Clarion* in 1910 suggesting that "E.T.K. and the other S.P.C. giants have formed your ideas of unionism under the old craft regime, and you seem incapable of reaching beyond it."[204]

Kingsley and the Socialist Party of Canada also attracted criticism from individual workers and party members about the party's strategic and tactical approach. A critic writing to the *Western Clarion* named Charles MacDonald suggested that the party's favoured strategy of putting a socialist speaker on a platform – a Kingsley – to hurl "economic thunderbolts into a dazed audience" had failed to achieve any appreciable results. Although the party had succeeded in organizing the "abnormal worker," the "normal worker" continued to be captivated by "the idea that riches will cure their ills." MacDonald proposed that the Socialist Party of Canada needed to evaluate and revise its approach, showing workers "the misery in the homes of the rich" to "break the magnetic force of the fetishism of gold."[205]

Even in the face of these challenges, Kingsley and the impossibilist position maintained a degree of support. W.H. Stebbings, an SPC member from Winnipeg, lauded Kingsley's role in transforming the Canadian socialist movement in a letter to the *Western Clarion* in 1910, debunking his detractors' claims with a healthy dose of sarcasm, worth quoting at length:

> Approximately a decade ago Kingsley formed the nucleus of what is now the Socialist Party of Canada. Could or would the party have been formed at that psychological moment if Kingsley had remained in California or gone to heaven? The enquiry cannot be answered. What we do know is this: that when Kingsley made his debut in Vancouver society (proletarian) he found many Socialists, so called, with ideas ranging from Pettipiece's "Socialist post office" to Watters' "Socialist policeman" ... From Halifax to Victoria similar sloppy ideas were promulgated, in fact they had everything that any Socialist platform ever had from the "exportation of dilapidated old maids to Utah," to the institution for the humanitarian method of asphyxiating cockroaches.
>
> What a protoplasmic mass of ideas to be operated on! All that was needed was an economist, and one acquainted with the futility of utopian idealism as a means of educating the working class to their helpless condition under capitalism. Kingsley was there, so was the job ... Whether by reason of the eternal fitness of things or the "will of the Almighty," the *Western Clarion* (Pettipiece's organ) contracted the malignant disease known so well to the working class, brokitis (from which, thanks to the reds of the party it has never recovered). Parm being unable to negotiate a loan from his Socialist post office savings bank, and although not entirely broke, was sufficiently bent to induce him to relegate the blue pencil to the old man.
>
> From the moment the paper changed hands revolutionary ideas emanated from the editorial chair, and trouble began. Not only was it necessary that a fight be carried on against our common enemy, but also against

the reactionaries inside the party who were bent on a plan of making the movement attractive, above all, respectable ... Is it any wonder then, that Kingsley, coming from fields where reform had being weighed in the balance and found wanting, should use his position as editor to inculcate into the new movement revolutionary ideas?

The movement today in Canada is the result of one man's interpretation of Marx. He nursed a child that has grown independent of any man or set of men and that "despotic" and "domineering" bunch in BC, known as the Dominion Executive, exists solely because its rulings are in harmony with the majority of the party.[206]

Throughout this period, from Kingsley's arrival in Vancouver in 1903 to the outbreak of the First World War, the Old Man was the guiding force within the Socialist Party of British Columbia and the Socialist Party of Canada, nurturing a radical, oppositional, working-class political culture and organization, pledged to dismantle capitalism and break its hold on state power. Although constrained by the sexist, racist, and ableist biases of Kingsley and his times, this contribution is remarkable in light of his impairment as a double amputee. The political culture and world view that he helped to nurture left their imprints in British Columbia and places farther afield for decades to come. Kingsley's leadership role as the foremost SPBC and SPC polemicist, orator, and publisher also attracted the interest of the emerging personnel and apparatus of the Canadian security state, which we examine in the next chapter.

6

Kingsley and the State
Clashes with Authority
in Early-Twentieth-Century Canada

When the Royal North West Mounted Police opened security files on Canadians in 1919 – in the midst of the postwar Canadian labour revolt and on the eve of the RNWMP's transition into a national force, the Royal Canadian Mounted Police (RCMP) – E.T. Kingsley was among the first thirty "persons of interest" to be identified in the security service register.[1] He was assigned personal file number 15 in the RCMP's register of nearly 5,000 radicals who would be identified over the ensuing decade (the file numbers for the first thirty subjects, including Kingsley, were assigned alphabetically by surname, so we do not know where he ranked in terms of risk level among this initial cohort). However, the fact that Kingsley was among the first group of Canadians targeted for surveillance by the emerging security state indicates the threat that he was perceived to pose to capitalism and the Canadian state. Indeed, Chief Press Censor of Canada Colonel Ernest Chambers described Kingsley in a confidential letter to his superiors in April 1919 as "unquestionably one of the most dangerous men in Canada" who "would unquestionably do anything he possibly could to undermine the constituted authority."[2]

Through an analysis of Kingsley's political activities in the first two decades of the twentieth century, we gain a deep understanding of the world in which Kingsley lived and how the law regulated and shaped his activities and those of other leftists in early-twentieth-century Canada. This chapter includes an examination of Kingsley's electoral activism within the Socialist Party of Canada prior to the First World War as well as a legal analysis of the emergence and limitations of the national security state in this period. From the discussion of Kingsley's campaigns for political office in the early 1900s, we turn to the ways in which state power was deployed in response to Kingsley and fellow dissidents – during a period marked by Free Speech fights in Vancouver in 1909 and 1912, intense political conflicts over the introduction of conscription during the war, and tumultuous labour relations culminating in the Vancouver and Winnipeg General Strikes and the One Big Union movement in 1919. Canada enlisted new personnel, apparatus, and institutions to meet the challenge of labour and the left, infiltrating labour unions and socialist organizations with state agents and introducing surveillance of a broad range of English- and foreign-language publications, including the short-lived newspaper *Labor Star,* which Kingsley coedited in 1919 with Parmater Pettipiece. Understanding the evolution of the national security state not only helps us to appreciate the political and legal contexts of Kingsley's decisions but also is insightful in its own right, especially as civil liberties increasingly have been challenged in Canada in a post-9/11 environment.

Contesting Elections

Although largely shunning reforms as "palliative" measures that would only prolong the demise of capitalism, Kingsley and his comrades in the Socialist Party of Canada pursued with rigour the "parliamentary road to socialism," seeking to seize state power by electoral methods by challenging capitalist candidates and parties in every provincial and federal election. This built on the tradition established by its predecessor parties and Kingsley's own history running for the San Francisco Board of Supervisors, San Jose City Council, and US House of Representatives as an SLP standard-bearer in California in the 1890s. Kingsley anticipated in a column in the *Western Clarion* in 1910 that, "when their miseries become no longer bearable, and they are rapidly becoming so, the slaves will take the necessary action to strike the fetters from their limbs," marshalling for "the conquest of the capitalist state that they may turn that instrument of repression into the means of their own deliverance, by using its organised powers to sweep the field of industry clear of the polluting influence of master and slave."[3] Although the Socialist Party of Canada never approached political power (and though Kingsley himself fell far short of winning a legislative seat in the six elections that he contested in Canada), the party maintained continuous representation in the BC legislature throughout the period that Kingsley served as its driving force – electing between one and three Members of the Legislative Assembly with approximately 10 percent of the popular vote in each election.

Kingsley ran five times for public office under the SPC banner: twice for federal Member of Parliament for Vancouver (in 1908 and 1911) and three times for provincial Member of the Legislative Assembly for Vancouver (in the 1907 and 1909 general elections and in a 1907 by-election). He was roundly defeated all five times, mirroring the results in his past campaigns in California as well as his final run for MP as an independent labour candidate for Vancouver in 1926. However, his greatest success as a political candidate occurred during these years with the Socialist Party of Canada when Kingsley received 18 percent of the popular vote in the 1907 provincial by-election (a two-way race against a Conservative cabinet minister) and 11 percent of the popular vote in the 1908 federal election (for full results in all ten campaigns, see Appendix 2).[4] This reflected a durable, albeit minority, base that the Socialist Party of Canada as an organization, and Kingsley as its pre-eminent figure, established among a section of Vancouver's working class in the turbulent opening years of the twentieth century.

When the party was formed out of the SPBC in 1904, there were two elected Socialists in the BC legislature and one allied Labor member, all representing mining districts (and all hailing from different corners of the British Isles): Irishman and coal company clerk James Hurst Hawthornthwaite in Nanaimo, Welsh coal miner Parker Williams in neighbouring Newcastle, and Scottish miner William Davidson in Slocan (who had been elected as a Labor candidate and would run in the next election under the Socialist banner). In a political period dominated by the Conservative Party of Richard McBride (and beginning with the introduction of the party system in the 1903 election), the socialists exerted a concentrated impulse within provincial politics and nurtured a political culture of working-class representation independent of the bosses and "old line" parties. According to historian Allen Seager, Hawthornthwaite enjoyed considerable influence during McBride's first term because of the Conservatives' small majority, pushing through improved safety standards

8-HOUR BILL FOR COAL MINERS

Has Passed Its Third Reading in the Legislature.

As we go to press the following telegram comes to us :

Victoria, B. C., April 6, 1905.

E. T. Kingsley, Editor Western Clarion :

Eight-hours, bank to bank, passed third reading successfully after biggest fight on record.   The Dunsmuir-Stockett combine worsted.   Small majority.

J. H. HAWTHORNTHWAITE.

Note.—Next week' issue of the CLARION will contain a report in full.

FIGURE 16   Telegram announcing the passage of legislation enshrining the eight-hour workday for coal miners, which Kingsley published on the front page of the *Western Clarion* in April 1905. | *Western Clarion.*

and labour reforms in the mining industry and developing a personal relationship with the premier.[5] On 6 April 1905, Hawthornthwaite wired a triumphant telegram to Kingsley, who promptly published it on the front page of the *Western Clarion,* announcing that the Eight-Hour Bill for coal miners had "passed third reading successfully after biggest fight on record. The Dunsmuir-Stockett combine worsted. Small majority."[6] As we noted in Chapter 4, a correspondent writing to the newspaper from Boundary Falls, a mining town in the southern BC Interior, would later proclaim that Hawthornthwaite had "got more legislation passed in the interest of the workers than any other man in the world with like opportunity."[7]

As several scholars have noted, a tension existed within the Socialist Party of Canada between vying for electoral success and adhering to an overtly Marxist platform. Peter Campbell described the debate in terms of "catching votes" or "making socialists" (converting a majority of the electorate to socialism), whereas an older literature discerned fault lines "between the doctrinaires and pragmatists."[8] According to Paul Fox, "the

S.P. of C. never quite decided why it was running candidates." Citing interviews with surviving members of the party (whom he did not identify by name), Fox suggested that some members believed that the party could win power constitutionally by contesting elections, whereas others approached elections more narrowly as opportunities to spread propaganda and promote socialist ideals among the electorate, preparing for the inevitable transition to socialism. One candidate (not named by Fox but potentially Kingsley) "occasionally concluded his campaign addresses by telling his listeners that it did not really matter whether or not they voted for him since the revolution was coming anyway."[9] Reflecting earlier debates in the MMLPA and the SPBC, the Socialist Party of Canada was not unilaterally opposed to all reforms, but it applied an impossibilist lens to its electoral approach, measuring each proposed reform against the question first laid down in the platform of the SPBC: "Will this legislation advance the interests of the working class and aid the workers in their class struggle against capitalism?"[10] In 1906, socialist trade unionists defeated an attempt to form a BC section of the Canadian Labor Party, rejecting reformism with a resolution pledging support for the Socialist Party of Canada at a convention in Vancouver.[11] In January 1907, members of the party's Vancouver Local No. 1 reaffirmed their "allegiance to the unequivocally revolutionary attitude of the party" at a convention called for the purpose of nominating candidates for the upcoming provincial election.[12] The party appears to have departed at times from the constitutional approach to accept philosophically violent revolution. A primer that Ross McCormack attributes to Kingsley described an apocalyptic final battle between capital and labour: "The earth will tremble from the shock as slaves and masters meet in the death grapple in that supreme hour; ... there will be a smell of blood in the air and the torch will light the heavens with the glare of destruction."[13]

Municipal politics was not a priority for Socialist Party members, notwithstanding Kingsley's initial forays in San Francisco and San Jose before moving to Canada. To be sure, party members would contest and at times win elected local office (e.g., Vancouver lawyer and Kingsley confidant J. Edward Bird in 1908 and, in the years following their involvement with the Socialist Party of Canada, Parm Pettipiece, Helena Gutteridge, Bill Pritchard, and Angus MacInnis, among others). But, as political scientist

Martin Robin notes, the systematic nomination and campaigning of municipal candidates were not ordinary features of the party's work.[14] This perhaps reflected a strategic choice in light of a local government's diminished role in Canada's constitutional framework as well as the practical realities of mounting sustained municipal campaigns in far-flung communities at a time when municipal elections were held every year. On the eve of the 1904 Vancouver municipal election, Kingsley asked in a letter to Hawthornthwaite "why do the comrades not put up a candidate?"[15] Kingsley believed that a local resident, Thomas Hardy, "would win hands down. It would give the boys something to do for a couple of weeks thus keeping 'em out of mischief. A municipal victory would tend to influence the vote at [the] Dominion election. This should not be allowed to go by default."[16] However, the SPBC Vancouver local does not appear to have acted on Kingsley's suggestion.

It was labour, rather than socialist formations, that demonstrated a stronger commitment to involvement at the municipal level, perhaps reflecting a greater openness to political reforms as well as the material interests of municipal workers. In 1908, Pettipiece, acting in his capacity as an officer of the Vancouver Trades and Labor Council, told a meeting in the city's Ward Five that the aldermen should be "fired" for failing to implement the results of a plebiscite endorsing the eight-hour working day for civic employees with nine hours of pay.[17] In 1912, Kingsley would again advocate for socialists to play an active role in the municipal field after the VTLC sent a deputation to request formally that the Socialist Party of Canada take a position, suggesting that "actual experience in administration was a prime necessity for the workers, and the sooner they set about acquiring domination in social administration, the sooner would their ultimate object be attained."[18] Although members of Vancouver Local No. 1 initially wavered, it appears that Kingsley ultimately succeeded in convincing a majority of his comrades to support a resolution placing the local on record "in favor of entering municipal politics" and striking a three-member committee to draft a manifesto.[19] A writer in the *Western Clarion*, potentially Kingsley, would state two weeks later that "much good can be done by entering a municipal campaign" but advised that "in every campaign the workers must ever be directed towards the one goal – Socialism. To go on advocating the municipal ownership of soup kitchens and other such silly nostrums is to confuse the issue and is worse than wasted energy."[20] A few years earlier another letter writer paraphrased Kingsley in advocating against municipal electoral action: "As Comrade Kingsley says, 'Your mansions are in the skies,' so it is no concern of the wage plugs how their masters spend the money to build their own sewers, sidewalks, boulevards or buy policemen's clubs."[21]

In provincial and federal politics, the Socialist Party of Canada conducted internal nomination processes to determine its candidates in the various ridings and elections, focusing heavily on the mining districts where SPC support was strongest (and where a smattering of labourist and socialist candidates had been elected over the years) and in Vancouver, where the party had its base of operations. At times, these nominations were controversial. Prior to the federal election in 1908, Kingsley's candidacy was rigorously opposed by members of other socialist parties. In Vancouver in particular, where the party's prospects for electoral success were remote (at the time, the city's electorate heavily favoured the Conservatives in provincial and federal politics), SPC nomination races often had less to do with securing a viable chance of winning election and more to do with determining positions of leadership and authority within the party and the left-wing and labour movements.

In the 1904 federal election, on the eve of the transformation of the SPBC into the Socialist Party of Canada, the party fielded four candidates in British Columbia (none of whom was elected).[22] Kingsley did not contest that election but actively promoted Socialist Party candidates. At a meeting in Victoria on 27 October 1904 – "the largest gathering of socialists held in Victoria," with "a good sprinkling of ladies in attendance," according to the *Victoria Daily Colonist* – Kingsley spoke in support of SPBC candidate James C. "Jimmy" Watters, a member of the carpenters' union. Kingsley began his remarks by telling all of the reporters in the room that they should "save their elbow grease" because, if they bothered to report on his remarks, their editors would not publish their reports anyway. He then proceeded to "rattle off, at a great rate, a tirade of abuse at 'capitalists,' and also got in some hard rubs at labor, slaves, suckers, political henchmen, packages of labor power walking on two legs, dirty labor skates, labor-skinners, grasshoppers, etc." To loud cheering, Kingsley described the Senate of Canada as a "blasted lot of humbugs – an old man's home" – and said that he was ashamed of himself for having supported capitalist candidates in the past. "Mr. Kingsley's cutting sarcasm and humorous bits proved very effective and in turn elicited the laughter and hearty applause of his auditors," the paper reported.[23]

In the first provincial election following the inception of the Socialist Party of Canada, in February 1907, the party nominated candidates to run in ten ridings – including Kingsley in the multiple-member riding of Vancouver City.[24] However, three weeks before voting day, his candidacy was cast into doubt when it was discovered that his name did not appear on the provincial voters list for Vancouver City, a statutory requirement at the time. According to a front-page article in the *Vancouver Province*, Kingsley, as a naturalized American citizen, had not voted in a provincial election since his arrival in Canada five years earlier and had failed to meet the deadline for having his name added to the list.[25] He presumably responded by successfully petitioning the court of revision to add his name to the list, for a week later his nomination papers were accepted "without question" at City Hall, and he was duly included as a Socialist Party candidate in Vancouver City.[26] He declared at a campaign meeting that "the Conservatives are in control of this province at the present time – that is, they are next to the pie counter, and it is no wonder that they heap abuse on men who are attempting to stand between them and the pie counter."[27] In another meeting on the eve of the election, in remarks laced with "profanities," Kingsley said that he sometimes had difficulty "expressing himself as he should in the presence of ladies," to laughter from the crowd.[28] Controversy also arose during the 1907 campaign over attempts to split the working-class vote, with Kingsley's comrade Parm Pettipiece noting in a letter in the *Vancouver Daily Province* that the "growth and development of the Socialist movement" in Vancouver had "been the cause of much alarm and uneasiness among that portion of the community which profits by the present economic system, and form of property ownership."[29] Another *Province* correspondent responded with a scathing attack on Kingsley:

> A Socialist "seeker of the spoils of office," one of the aliens mentioned above, ... thinks he can secure a portion of said spoils, hastens to comply with the law he is so desirous of destroying, takes out his citizen's papers,

declares his oath of allegiance to King Edward, etc., and in the next breath denounces loyalty and patriotism, and declares the flag of the country and Empire an old rag unworthy of respect, and by every means in his power endeavours to overthrow the bulwark of personal and religious liberty. Thank God the majority of the working men possess the intelligence to know that Socialism never helped the working man to obtain the remuneration for their labor that they now enjoy.[30]

Along with his duties as candidate, Kingsley served as one of three party organizers for the provincial campaign, focusing on ridings in the Vancouver area and BC Interior.[31]

On voting day, 2 February 1907, Kingsley received 617 votes (compared with about 3,000 votes for the five successful Conservative candidates in Vancouver City), which the *Western Clarion* described as a "triumph of capitalism."[32] Province wide, SPC candidates captured 24 percent of the popular vote in the ten ridings that they contested (and nearly 9 percent of the popular vote province wide). Hawthornthwaite and Williams were re-elected in Nanaimo and Newcastle, respectively, and William Davidson, running this time under the SPC banner, was defeated with 30 percent of the popular vote in Slocan (compared with 49 percent for the Conservative victor). However, SPC representation in the legislature held at three seats, with carpenter and miner John McInnis winning the election in Grand Forks, a mining community in the southern BC Interior. Conservative Richard McBride was handily re-elected as premier, his party holding twenty-six seats to thirteen seats for the opposition Liberals.[33]

Kingsley would stand again for provincial office six months later, in August 1907, when a by-election was called for one of the Vancouver City seats following Conservative William Bowser's appointment to McBride's cabinet (a procedure then in place in Canadian federal and provincial politics to test public support for newly appointed ministers of the Crown).[34] Whereas the Liberal candidate, former premier Joseph Martin, dropped out at the last minute, citing a lack of support, Kingsley remained in the race. He predicted on the eve of the by-election that the people "would vote for Mr. Bowser and the perpetuation of the capitalist system" at a mass meeting at which British Labour Party leader Keir Hardie gave the keynote address.[35] Kingsley was proven correct, with Bowser taking

82 percent of the vote to 18 percent for Kingsley.[36] Although he was roundly defeated, demonstrating minority support for the socialist viewpoint among the electorate, his nomination as the socialist standard bearer indicated his pre-eminent place in the Vancouver Socialist Party of Canada.

This was confirmed in the lead up to the federal election the following summer, in July 1908, when Kingsley captured the SPC nomination for Vancouver City, taking "the large majority of the votes" in a nomination contest against the "red dentist," Dr. W.J. Curry.[37] Prior to the nomination meeting, the *Victoria Daily Colonist* reported that Kingsley "was looked upon by the Socialists as the strongest man they could put in the field."[38] Beyond SPC circles, however, there was strong opposition to him, as evidenced in a subsequent nomination meeting called by the "three other branches" of the socialist movement (the Social Democratic Party of Canada, Industrial Workers of the World, and Socialist Labor Party of Canada) in September 1908 to consider whether or not to endorse Kingsley. Attendees at the meeting, which took place in Vancouver City Hall, expressed concern about the SPC decision to nominate a candidate unilaterally without involving the other parties, suggesting that the "Liberal and Conservative parties represented one party in their bolstering up of existing economic conditions, and it was an obligation on the different branches of the Socialist and labor movement to show unity in their attack upon that system."[39] The chair of the meeting, a man by the name of MacLean, suggested that a substantial number of workers thought that Kingsley was not representative of the broader socialist movement and lacked sufficient popularity to win the election. However, after a rigorous debate, a resolution endorsing his candidacy and calling on the Socialist Party of Canada to cooperate with the other parties in the future carried with fifty-five votes in favour and thirty-five votes opposed.[40]

Kingsley adhered stridently to the "one-plank" Marxist position in the 1908 federal election. At a candidates' meeting organized by the Socialist Party of Canada in Vancouver City Hall on 30 September 1908, he articulated the party's political approach: "You have to conquer the reins of public legislation, by which the capitalist classes enslave you. Then proceed to strike down the capitalist power and become free men." Predicting "the greatest upheaval on this continent the world has even seen" within eight years, Kingsley warned that "if necessary the working classes will go forward with clubs in their hands to emphasize their needs. I hope not. But if it be necessary, then let them use clubs. The community as a whole must get control of the tools of production."[41] Reporting on another candidates' meeting a few weeks later, the *Victoria Daily Colonist* noted that Kingsley "dealt as usual with the iniquities of the capitalistic system because of its control of the means of production."[42] Greater detail was provided in a report in the *Vancouver Daily Province,* which quoted Kingsley as saying that the working class of Vancouver was at the mercy of the Canadian Pacific Railway, and if the workers had the sense to use their votes for their own benefit they could swamp the capitalist class, because the capitalist class did not have enough votes "to elect a dog-catcher."[43] In the midst of the campaign, Kingsley appeared in a series of editorial cartoons by James Fitzmaurice in the *Vancouver Daily Province* alongside the other candidates often with his nose deep in a book entitled *Socialism* or *Karl Marx.* Of note, Kingsley was depicted in four of the five cartoons standing in full form, with no hint of being a double amputee, perhaps reflecting the fact that his artificial limbs made his impairments difficult for the casual observer to detect.[44] When the ballots were cast and counted on 26 October 1908, Kingsley was once again defeated, receiving 11 percent of the vote and finishing fourth out of four candidates, with Conservative lawyer George Henry Cowan taking the seat. In the aftermath, Kingsley publicly accused the Liberal Party of vote buying – "the Liberals bought hundreds of votes at the rate of $5 apiece" – and was thankful that there were "1,135 men in this town who did not have to be dragged up to the polls and told how to vote."[45]

This flurry of election activity continued in 1909 when Kingsley ran again for the Socialists in the provincial election in the five-member Vancouver City riding. This proved to be his strongest result in terms of total votes as well as proximity to victory. Kingsley captured 1,883 votes, about half the votes received by the nearest successful Conservative candidate. Although this was a respectable showing, it still fell far short of the threshold necessary to secure a legislative seat.[46] Even so, his comrades urged Kingsley to consider running for mayor of Vancouver on account of his "excellent showing."[47] During the campaign, the *Vancouver Daily Province* lobbed a familiar barb at Kingsley, reporting that he was "grinding out socialist axioms to an audience that filled the city hall last night"; he

FIGURE 17 Editorial cartoon published during the 1908 Canadian federal election campaign, with Kingsley depicted standing on the right, holding his share of the "equal distribution of wealth." There was no indication of his impairment in any of the cartoons in this series. | *Vancouver Daily Province.* Cartoon by James Fitzmaurice.

FIGURE 18 Editorial cartoon, with Kingsley depicted seated on the right reading Marx. | *Vancouver Daily Province.* Cartoon by James Fitzmaurice.

FIGURE 19 Editorial cartoon, with Kingsley (at bottom right) once again displayed standing in full form, with no indication of his disability. | *Vancouver Daily Province.* Cartoon by James Fitzmaurice.

FIGURE 20 Editorial cartoon, with Kingsley on the right with his nose in a socialist text. | *Vancouver Daily Province.* Cartoon by James Fitzmaurice.

also faced criticism from several SDPC members in the crowd.[48] Province wide, the Socialist Party of Canada also reached the apex of its popular support in the 1909 election, won by McBride, with the twenty Socialist candidates collectively receiving a total of 11,665 votes – 11.5 percent of the popular vote – though only two Socialist MLAs, incumbents Hawthornthwaite and Williams, were elected (the third incumbent, McInnis, lost Grand Forks with 33 percent of the vote to 52 percent for the Conservative victor, mirroring the party's earlier defeat in Slocan after holding the seat for a single term).[49]

Kingsley's final contest as an SPC candidate was in the 1911 federal election when he ran again in Vancouver City. Press reports had hinted that Kingsley might withdraw in light of a debate within the party about whether to field any candidates at all, but he stayed in the race.[50] Seeking to improve its prospects, the party had organized a branch in South Vancouver prior to the election to build support for Kingsley's candidacy.[51] Bill Pritchard reflected on a speech that Kingsley delivered during that campaign, shortly after Pritchard's arrival in Vancouver from England. Pritchard's recollection is worth quoting at length for the insight that it provides on Kingsley's rhetorical style:

Oh, he had similes and figures of speech. But the election was, I think, in 1911, the first year I was in town here. The local put him up. It was Vancouver Centre [*sic*]. I think he took about 1,100 votes. It was a small town. The fight was between the Conservative Party who stressed its ties with the Crown, and they wanted a railroad policy that would build railroads east and west. The Liberal Party was talking about reciprocity with the United States.

Well, on the walls there were big pictures, ... beautiful pictures of full market baskets overflowing with vegetables. Kingsley referred to this, and he says "this thing is the first cousin to what we saw in the States called the 'full dinner pail' but it's only a picture. The market basket that you're looking at is just a picture. That's the promise. That's all you'll get is a picture. Now you tell me of any sensible, four-footed donkey that could be fooled with a painted picture of a haystack!"

He'd grind it out, you know, and shake his head. He was very forceful – a very forceful fellow. That was his line – simple propaganda laced with these similes of his. They'd come out quick, right in the middle of things. There'd always be a good crowd when he spoke in those early days.[52]

On voting day in September 1911, Kingsley took 1,056 votes (9 percent of the popular vote) to 3,796 votes (32 percent) for the Liberal candidate and 6,902 votes (59 percent) for the Conservative victor, newspaper publisher and future cabinet minister H.H. Stevens (whom Kingsley would challenge again as an independent Labor candidate in 1926).[53] He spent a total of $652 on the campaign (about $17,000 in 2021 dollars), nearly half on hall rentals and about one-third on the $200 candidate deposit (which

GET OFF THE TRACK

FIGURE 21　Editorial cartoon during the 1911 Canadian federal election, depicting the locomotive of socialism with "Labor" at the controls dispersing a capitalist, a king, a clergyman, and a soldier. | *Western Clarion.*

he lost after failing to achieve the required share of the vote – as would occur in all of his runs for office). Records do not indicate how these funds were raised – whether financed by Kingsley personally or through contributions from party members.[54]

The 1911 federal campaign proved to be Kingsley's final contest as an SPC candidate. Perhaps reflecting his diminished influence in the party after his departure from the Dominion Executive Committee, Kingsley did not contest the provincial election in 1912. In that election, the SPC share of the vote held at 11 percent, but its total votes dropped by nearly 2,000 since voter turnout declined amid turmoil in the opposition Liberal Party. The Conservatives surged to victory once again with thirty-eight of forty-two legislative seats. The Socialist Party of Canada fell to only one elected seat, that of Parker Williams in Newcastle; James Hawthornthwaite decided not to seek re-election and was succeeded in Nanaimo by John "Jack" Place, running as an SDPC candidate. Shortly after the election, Williams was expelled from the Socialist Party of Canada for refusing to relinquish his membership in the SDPC (the Nanaimo SPC local had switched its affiliation to the SDPC, and the MLA had followed suit), leaving the Socialist Party of Canada without an MLA for the first time since its founding.[55]

In addition to this sustained political activity in British Columbia, SPC electoral strength extended beyond the BC borders in the prewar period, notably with the election of miner and logger Charlie O'Brien in Alberta's Rocky Mountain district in 1909 – the first Socialist elected to that province's legislature.[56] Reflecting the same social structure that provided the base for SPC electoral strength in British Columbia, O'Brien's district in the Crow's Nest Pass in the southwestern corner of Alberta was heavily populated by coal miners. O'Brien had worked as an SPC organizer prior to his election to public office, and (according to at least one account in the *Western Clarion*) he resembled Kingsley is physical appearance and speaking style: "Comrade O'Brien proved himself a forceful speaker along scientific and revolutionary lines, his style of speaking, of actions and even his appearance being a reminder of Comrade Kingsley, to whom Comrade O'Brien gives credit for clearing the utopian cobwebs from his upper stopes."[57] O'Brien served in the Alberta legislature for one term, until 1913, advocating for workers' rights and helping to expand the national reach of the Socialist Party of Canada. During an organizing tour to Regina shortly after his election, O'Brien was arrested and charged with obstructing a public roadway while addressing a crowd of 500 people.[58] In 1911, he embarked on an extensive speaking and organizing tour in the Prairies, Ontario, Quebec, and the Maritimes, addressing more than thirty meetings from Saskatchewan to Cape Breton Island. As he prepared to return to the west, O'Brien expressed appreciation in a *Western Clarion* column to "the many comrades for comfortable accommodations and the many other kind acts that go to make life worth while for a Socialist agitator."[59]

In July 1914, days before the outbreak of the First World War, O'Brien issued an appeal in the *Western Clarion* for funds in the amount of $500 (about $11,000 in 2021 dollars) to allow Kingsley – "our oldest and best equipped propagandist ... without a peer in the English language" – to undertake another propaganda tour "throughout Canada" to revitalize the Socialist Party of Canada. O'Brien pointed out that Kingsley was "no longer a young man" and that his serious accident for many years had "made it painful for him to do much travelling." Although Kingsley himself strongly objected to drawing attention to his well-being, O'Brien insisted that "the welfare of the man" had to be considered if he were to undertake this important propaganda work on behalf of the party – a trip that never took place because of intervening events.[60]

The War Crisis and Shifting Socialist Alignments

Following the outbreak of the First World War in August 1914, Kingsley adopted a position that set him apart from many of his comrades in the Socialist Party of Canada – ending his influence in the party that he had founded, led, and shaped in its formative decade. The context of the falling out was an international debate among socialists about the correct position to take in response to the war crisis – and specifically the degree of fault that should be assigned to the various belligerent nations in the war. As the Second International imploded in the face of the "national chauvinism" of various socialist parties, Kingsley penned an editorial for the *Western Clarion* entitled "The Affirmation of 'German Culture.'"[61] Although he was no longer editor of the *Western Clarion,* a role occupied by J.H. Burrough at the time, Kingsley remained one of the party's driving intellectual forces and maintained a close association with the newspaper, writing much of its editorial copy. In the editorial, he argued that Germany was responsible for the war, citing the ruthlessness of its occupation of Belgium as evidence of a particularly aggressive, militaristic quality of German culture while ignoring any culpability of Britain and other belligerent nations. "German militarism cannot exist except by and with the approval of the German people," Kingsley asserted, describing the German working class ("some four millions of them being Socialists") as "traitors to the international working class"; Germany "should be exterminated the same as any other enemy," and he expressed the hope that "the Allies will succeed in crushing Germany speedily" or that neutral countries would intervene and persuade Germany to retreat.[62]

The response of Kingsley's comrades in the Socialist Party of Canada was swift. They emphasized his apparent abandonment of internationalism and a class-struggle perspective and his perceived alignment with the war aims of the Canadian and Allied bourgeoisie. (The editorial also diverged sharply from his previously expressed views on war, for example in a *Western Clarion* editorial in 1909 in which Kingsley wrote "let no workingman shed the blood of his fellow in such an inglorious cause."[63]) Vancouver Local No. 1 registered "a most emphatic objection" to Kingsley's editorial, recommending "that steps be immediately taken that will prevent the repetition of such an obnoxious tirade."[64] Cumberland Local No. 70 forwarded a similar resolution, describing the editorial as "unbecoming a revolutionary Socialist organ such as the *Western Clarion*."[65] The party's Edmonton local also went on record opposing the editorial, as did members from Nelson to Enderby to Brandon.[66] The response from the SPC Dominion Executive Committee was similarly swift, adopting a resolution at its meeting on 23 October expressing disapproval with the editorial and establishing a three-member editorial board consisting of Bill Pritchard, J.H. Burrough, and John Sidaway to oversee the content of the *Western Clarion*.[67] Although a "secretarial note" in the same issue of the paper (presumably written by Kingsley or Burrough) suggested that "no hard feelings have been engendered by the change," the controversy marked the end of Kingsley's active role in both the paper and the party – effectively ending his association with the closest community that Kingsley had ever known.[68] In the midst of the controversy, Burrough resigned as editor and party secretary, suggesting that the "severe criticism" from active locals demonstrated a want of confidence; Pritchard was appointed by the Dominion Executive Committee to replace him.[69]

Reflecting on the controversy six decades later, Pritchard suggested that Kingsley's commentary was justified (particularly in light of the later rise of Nazism): "The editorials were then written by Kingsley. He wrote an editorial which today I wouldn't question in the light of experience of history on the affirmation of German culture. He was jumped on because it would appear that he was slamming Germany in the early days of the war without referring to Britain's part in it." Pritchard confirmed that Kingsley ceased to write editorials for the *Western Clarion* following the controversy: "Not after that. Now looking back again, I think it was a mistake to say that he couldn't. But no one asked him to. If you didn't ask the Old Man at that time – he was getting along in years – he didn't do it. There was a lot of value in the old fellow. But he'd committed the error."[70] Two years later a writer in the *Federationist* would sarcastically lament the loss of "dangerous agitators such as Kingsley" as the Socialist Party of Canada reduced itself to a "residue of purity fanaticism," suggesting that there was only "one kind of a man who never makes mistakes" – "a dead one."[71]

This marked the final break between Kingsley and the party that he had helped to found and the group of comrades with whom he had worked intensively for more than a decade. The Socialist Party of Canada appears to have been the closest thing to a home and a community in his itinerant life. Kingsley moved frequently around the American Midwest as a child and young man and then later to the Pacific Coast following his disablement. His first decade in Vancouver represented a time of unequalled stability and familiarity, even with the intense flurry of political activity and economic stresses associated with the *Western Clarion,* the party, and his printing business. There is no evidence of any personal association, romantic or otherwise, outside the party. It was his life, his community, his passion, and his home. And by the end of 1914, when Kingsley was fifty-eight, it had come to an abrupt end. His personal world shifted abruptly, mirroring the larger global pattern of rupture that the war crisis precipitated for the international left. There is virtually no mention of Kingsley in SPC publications or records after the autumn of 1914. Although we cannot find evidence of a formal resignation from the Socialist Party of Canada, Kingsley ceased to be a leading member, and in December 1915 he would publicly lambaste the "little pin-head bunch in Vancouver" in comments to the *Vancouver World* following former Alberta MLA Charlie O'Brien's resignation from the party to organize with the Socialist Party in the United States.[72] Several months later, in July 1916, the *Vancouver Daily Province* would report that "Mr. Kingsley is not now a member of the Socialist Party" because of the controversy over the editorial, "much to the regret of many of his former supporters."[73] Despite this break from the party, Kingsley remained active within the broader socialist movement in Vancouver and beyond – particularly in the late stages of the war, when he would help to found and lead a new political formation, the Federated Labor Party – and contribute to the left-wing publishing world through the *BC Federationist* and the short-lived *Labor Star.* His ongoing outspoken role as a propagandist, speaker, publisher, and organizer with an uncompromising Marxist viewpoint set him on a collision path with the Canadian state.

Origins of Political Policing and Free Speech Fights

In the opening years of the twentieth century, political policing transitioned in Canada from external threats and suppression of Indigenous militancy in the North-West Territories to monitoring and controlling labour and left-wing social movements in the industrializing nation. As Whitaker, Kealey, Parnaby, and others have observed, the origins of political policing in Canada can be traced to the government's response to Fenian organizations of the mid-nineteenth century, which sought to promote violence and rebellion in what was then Canada West and Canada East to further the cause of Irish independence.[74] By the late nineteenth century and early twentieth century, foreign-born workers had emerged as a central preoccupation of Canadian security forces, as Donald Avery demonstrated, particularly the activities of immigrant and ethnocultural minority communities in the socialist and labour movements.[75] The perceived threat of external forces continued to motivate domestic responses to labour and left-wing radicalism in Canada. The Socialist Party of Canada increasingly became a central focus of state surveillance in Canada in the decade prior to the First World War.

In 1906, after *Appeal to Reason* – the weekly newspaper of Eugene Debs's Socialist Party of America published in Girard, Kansas – ran an article by Debs entitled "Arouse Ye Slaves" (threatening a general strike or armed revolution "from Canada to the Gulf" if the American state persisted with trumped-up murder charges against leaders of the Western Federation of Miners), the postmaster general of Canada issued an order prohibiting the distribution of the American newspaper by mail in Canada.[76] *Appeal to Reason* was deemed "seditious, scurrilous, immoral and indecent," and thousands of copies of the newspaper were confiscated by Canadian customs officers, "aided and abetted by United States officials."[77] Even distribution of the paper by sealed envelope under first-class postage was proscribed, and those caught with copies could be held liable for smuggling. According to the Winnipeg *Voice*, the Canadian action might have been motivated by a request from American authorities, for the same article appearing in the *Western Clarion* had not been banned, prompting *Appeal to Reason* to describe the censorship as "another move in a determined effort of the capitalist class of the United States to put this gigantic propaganda machine out of commission."[78]

The Socialist Party of Canada responded to the suppression of the American socialist newspaper by launching a petition in communities across the country calling for the ban to be lifted. Mass meetings in Vancouver, Fernie, and other points adopted resolutions condemning the Canadian government's move as an "assumption of autocratic power" and an "attempt to establish a censorship of the press in Canada."[79] A protest meeting was convened in Berlin (now Kitchener), Ontario, attended by businessmen and other prominent community members, and the Toronto Socialist League was designated as a depot for the collection of signed petitions for delivery by hand to Ottawa. Writing from Vancouver, Parm Pettipiece, provincial SPC secretary, pledged in a letter published on the front page of *Appeal to Reason* to distribute 20,000 or 30,000 leaflets reprinting Debs's article free of charge across Canada, while Eugene Kingsley, as editor of the *Western Clarion,* was preparing an appeal on behalf of the Socialist Party of Canada to the postmaster general protesting the ban. "We will flood Canada with them," Pettipiece pledged, "and demonstrate beyond doubt that such action by the slave owning class will promote rather than retard the proletarian revolution."[80] Years later Kingsley would recall that the SPC campaign had caused the censor's office to be "smothered with communications."[81]

Another notable chapter in political policing in Canada prior to the First World War occurred in the Free Speech fights of 1909 and 1912 in Vancouver and Victoria. These upheavals over control of public space had antecedents in Canada and the United States as well as parallels in other cities across the Pacific Northwest, including Seattle, Everett, Wenatchee, and Spokane – clashes among leftists, municipal authorities, and police that extended down the coast to Los Angeles.[82] This was not intelligence gathering in the conventional sense but the use of police powers to regulate political speech and protest. In many respects, the Free Speech fights of Vancouver bear an uncanny resemblance to the Free Speech fights led by Kingsley and his SLP comrades in San Francisco in 1895 and 1896. Both instances involved municipalities intolerant of radical political speech at street corners while ignoring religious organizations such as the Salvation Army engaged in the same behaviour. It is likely that Kingsley's direct experience in the San Francisco Socialist Labor Party greatly facilitated his ability to advise the SPC leadership on effective tactics. Mark Leier has documented how members of the Socialist Party of Canada and Industrial Workers of the World, though certainly not identical in their political ideology or tactics, made speeches on 4 April 1909 on Carrall Street in downtown Vancouver but were ordered by the police to disperse. When they refused, they were given summons to appear before a police magistrate.[83] Denounced in the Vancouver press, the soapbox orators were defended by J. Edward Bird, an SPC member, local lawyer, one-time alderman, and future legal counsel for the One Big Union (OBU).[84]

The legal arguments made by Bird are intriguing. Although the VTLC organized a rally in defence of free speech in defiance of the magistrate's wishes that the accused men refrain from further street speeches pending their trial, Bird pursued modest legal arguments that operated within the framework of the liberal conception of the rule of law. He suggested that the speakers in fact had not obstructed the road because they were twelve feet away from the street line and had arranged for wardens to prevent any obstruction to the general public. Interestingly, he also raised the argument, in a pre-*Charter* world, that it was wrong to distinguish between the political speech of the Salvation Army street preachers, tolerated by the authorities, and that of the socialists.[85] On 19 April, the magistrate found one speaker guilty and fined him $5.00 plus $2.50 in costs or ten days in jail with hard labour. An appeal by Bird was unsuccessful.[86]

The left continued to mobilize in Vancouver to defend the right to free speech regardless of the conviction. In the midst of the legal proceedings, the SPC local announced publicly on 7 April that ten socialists would "descend on Carrall street, the 'People's Forum,'" speaking "at once in order to give the police opportunity to arrest them" as a test of "the right of police to arrest men or women who engage in street speaking."[87] Following a subsequent demonstration, T.M. Beamish, a socialist real estate broker, was convicted of obstructing a thoroughfare in May. He was sentenced to thirty days in jail with hard labour or a fine of $100. A few days later the Socialist Party of Canada organized a meeting at Vancouver City Hall to protest the sentence. The speakers included Beamish, VTLC president and SPC member J.H. McVety, Leo T. English, a printer and member of the International Typographical Union, and Kingsley. Nearly 1,000 people attended a mass meeting the following night to hear more speakers.[88] Eventually, the police backed down in the face of constant protests.[89] In the midst of the controversy, Kingsley wryly observed that the actions of city officials had actually aided the socialist cause, describing the municipal crackdown as an example of "propaganda of the deed" that would "clinch the arguments of the soapbox orator and drive his truths home in the mind of the wage animal."[90]

The issue resurfaced in January 1912 when a protest was organized to attack a municipal bylaw prohibiting all outdoor meetings. The protesters were arrested. Subsequent meetings were broken up by the police, sometimes using the vague offence of vagrancy as a ground for arrest, including a clash on 28 January 1912 that the local left described as "Bloody Sunday." Parm Pettipiece was among those arrested (for unlawful assembly, subsequently acquitted in a jury trial), but press reports do not mention Kingsley's involvement. Several of the accused pleaded guilty and served sentences of between two and three months in the provincial jail in New Westminster.[91] In a demonstration of creativity, some SPC and IWW members constructed rafts to address the public via a megaphone off Stanley Park and thereby to avoid the police.[92] When this tactic failed, partly because of strong ocean currents, the latter members contemplated acquiring a hot air balloon, but this appears not to have materialized.[93] The party and the union also cooperated in hosting several raucous joint meetings to protest the "Bloody Sunday" attacks and the incursions on free speech. At a mass meeting in Vancouver's Dominion Hall on 1 February, where the Union Jack was "torn from the walls and thrown on the floor," Kingsley advised the crowd against going out to "tear down the city," saying that he did not think anything would be gained by it, urging political action instead.[94] Two days later he was among the speakers addressing a crowd estimated at 2,500 strong in Vancouver's Horse Show Building, where those gathered adopted a resolution demanding intervention by the provincial attorney general against the "treatment accorded citizens" on "Bloody Sunday."[95]

The reaction from conservative newspapers against the demonstrators was predictably rapid and tremendous. A February 1912 front-page story in the *Western Call,* edited by Conservative MP H.H. Stevens, effectively a pointed editorial written as if it were a news story, denounced in the sharpest possible terms the "aliens, anarchists and extreme, ignorant socialists and I.W.W.'s" attempting to "teach treason, political disruption and *economic assassination.*"[96] However, after meetings between a joint delegation of the SPC and the VTLC with the mayor and then, a few days later, Premier McBride and his cabinet, this second wave of police heavy-handedness came to a negotiated end.[97]

Kingsley at War

Kingsley's falling out with his SPC comrades over the contentious *Western Clarion* editorial on the causes of the war in October 1914 inaugurated a period of diminished political activity, but Kingsley did not disappear from the BC political landscape. He soon assumed an editorial role with the BC Federation of Labor's weekly *British Columbia Federationist* newspaper, published by his long-time collaborator Parm Pettipiece through the Federationist Publishing Company and printed at Kingsley's (and, after 1914, Cowan & Brookhouse's) plant in the Labor Temple at 411 Dunsmuir Street, "Vancouver unionists' quarter-of-a-million dollar building."[98] The *Federationist* was the "largest labour journal in the West," according to historian Gerald Friesen, with circulation climbing from 6,300 to 15,000 copies during 1918.[99] Kingsley worked with the editorial staff at the paper during a high point of activity in the late stages of the war, serving as associate editor.[100] Some sources even identify him as editor of the paper, though corroborating sources are sparse; Canada's chief press censor suggested that Kingsley resigned as editor when "the Directors were compelled to agree to observe the requirements of the Press Censorship."[101] Pettipiece also left amid controversy in 1918, according to historian Dale McCartney, when the directors of the publishing company (controlled by the BCFL and VTLC) discovered that he had been embezzling funds and removed him as managing editor; he was replaced by Albert Wells of Victoria, who appears to have moved to Vancouver to assume the job.[102]

It was also during the war, in 1916, that Kingsley published the only official collection of his political thought, a booklet published by Pettipiece and the Federationist Publishing Company.[103] Originating as an essay in a special Labour Day issue of the *Federationist* in September 1916, *The Genesis and Evolution of Slavery* was subsequently published in booklet form "in response to widespread demand."[104] Even Kingsley's erstwhile SPC comrades acknowledged the value of the work, with Bill Pritchard (who had succeeded Kingsley as the *Western Clarion*'s main editorial writer) describing the booklet as "short, pungent, very good."[105] The Winnipeg *Voice* suggested that the pamphlet cleared up "much that has long confused, not only the workers themselves, but many others who have given thought to the vexations and anomalies of modern civilization."[106] To George Casey, a worker in Prince Rupert who wrote a letter to the *Federationist* lauding the pamphlet, it was "truly the best pamphlet that has yet found its way to my hands, and in my opinion you cannot push this work too strongly." Casey had already "sold 100 to date," during two evenings selling "the pamphlets around town," and he expected to order an additional batch and try to "cover about a thousand square miles of this country with them."[107] The miners' union in Phoenix, in the southern BC Interior, ordered 500 copies, and a writer from Berkeley, California, described the booklet as "a classic of proletarian philosophy," emerging as society halted between "despotism" and "democracy," pledging to distribute 100 copies.[108]

The frontispiece of the pamphlet features a prominent photograph of Kingsley between biographical descriptions as "An Uncompromising

Have You Read the Little Booklet, Printed by The Federationist?

It's a cracker-jack, and should be read by every man and woman interested in the Labor movement.

It is entitled "THE GENESIS AND EVOLUTION OF SLAVERY," written by the Grand Old Man of the Labor Movement in British Columbia, Mr. E. T. Kingsley, and compiled by R. P. Pettipiece, who has for more than 20 years been identified with the organized labor movement of the province.

In a clear-cut and concise style this booklet goes thoroughly into the question of the economic position of capitalist society and the position of the working classes in relation to it.

The troublesome phases of the relations between the capitalist and the worker are dealt with in a manner which solves in plain and forceful logic many points on which the worker of today is often "at sea" when meeting arguments.

THE BOOKLET FORMS A VALUABLE TEXT BOOK AND WORK OF REFERENCE FOR WORKERS AND STUDENTS OF ECONOMIC PROBLEMS

Packages of 100 copies or more, 5 cents per copy (carriage paid).

Single copies, or in any number up to 100 copies, 10 cents each (postpaid).

E. T. KINGSLEY

The Biggest Ten Cents' Worth of Reading Ever Offered in Literature

Send along a dime for a copy today. Try it out on your friends. It's worth while.

ADDRESS:

The B. C. Federationist

LABOR TEMPLE.   R. PARM. PETTIPIECE, Mgr.   VANCOUVER.

FIGURE 22   Advertisement for *The Genesis and Evolution of Slavery*, Kingsley's 1916 pamphlet. | *British Columbia Federationist.*

Enemy of Class Rule and Class Robbery" and "one of the most widely known political economists and socialists in Canada."[109] In the preface, Kingsley offers stinging commentary on the war effort, as well as on the apparent docility of workers, claiming that "the rulers of the world have frequently been siezed [*sic*] with fits of blood madness, that nothing could quell but a plentiful spilling of blood upon the part of their slaves. The slaves have always loyally come through with the goods when called upon."[110] Kingsley then shifts to the solution for resolving the war crisis and the larger structural crisis of capitalism:

> Whether the present blood letting results in the suicide of capitalism or merely forces its development to the culminating stage of state capitalism, matters not. That which does matter is that the working class is the only factor in human society that has either the numerical strength or the justification to bring order out of chaos, by the abolition of its own slavery and the placing of the affairs of human society upon a basis that will make it possible for all people to live in fraternal peace, plenty and decency, in the common enjoyment of the fruits of their common labor.[111]

Harking back to the Marxist doctrine that the emancipation of the working class must be the act of the working class itself, Kingsley declares that "the requisite knowledge to enable the workers to act intelligently in the coming crisis in human affairs, which ruling class madness and ambition is forcing upon us, must be gathered by the workers themselves against all of the intellectual forces marshaled in the service of the ruling class."[112] It was to this intellectual battle – the battle of ideas to advance the interests of workers and the ideal of working-class emancipation against the intellectual armour and apparatus of capitalist exploitation – that Kingsley devoted his life's work from the time of his disablement in 1890 to his death on the eve of the economic crisis in 1929.

His sixty-page pamphlet begins with a lengthy description of the labour theory of value (the classic Marxist notion that human labour is the source of all wealth and capitalist property), from hunter-gatherer societies through slave societies of antiquity and serfdom of feudal times to capitalist wage labour of the industrial age, arriving at the stark conclusion that capitalist property consists of human slaves and that capitalist trade – "the fetich [*sic*] of the whole civilized world" – is nothing more than "the traffic in their flesh."[113] Kingsley calls on workers to focus the class struggle against their masters on "destroying the right of those masters to rule and rob" by attacking their "property rights in the means of production," suggesting that the only approach was a political one:

The class struggle is purely a political struggle. To gain control of the capitalist state is the goal aimed at, so that its guns, which are now trained upon the working class, may be spiked, as against that class. The state, with its terrific repressive powers, is the sole instrument upon which the capitalists rely for the continuation of their golden regime.[114]

In countries where workers had attained the franchise, such as Canada and the United States, "they have the legal right to conquer the state for their own purposes." In countries without the franchise, "or where there are such restrictions placed upon it as to nullify their superiority of numbers," workers are "justified in exercising their political power in any manner they choose," Kingsley asserted, opening the door for extraparliamentary, revolutionary change.[115]

The only barrier standing between the working class in Canada and their emancipation was their docility, Kingsley claimed, a characteristic common to slaves, which manifested itself politically in workers' ability to discern their masters' interests and their corresponding blindness to their own interests.[116] In a familiar swipe at what he perceived to be the distraction of reformism, Kingsley railed against labour's "long struggle to obtain an amelioration of its conditions under slavery," insisting that labour's victory in the class struggle against capitalist exploitation would not be achieved through "petty squabbles over the amount of rations that shall be measured out to the slaves, or the length of time they shall tug in harness for their stipend."[117] Connecting "ten thousand years" of human slavery (which he described as a "hideous nightmare to the working class") with present-day suffering by "millions ... now being ground ruthlessly and recklessly into profit in the industrial torture chambers of modern slavery in order that a few already hog-fat capitalists may still further increase their fat," Kingsley concluded with an expression of hope: "The only rainbow of promise on the social horizon presaging the coming of a better day is seen in the slowly but surely awakening of consciousness of the workers to the hideous wrongs that slavery has heaped upon them; and their stubborn determination to wipe it out."[118]

In addition to his publishing activities, Kingsley continued to play an active role as a public speaker and political organizer during the wartime crisis. At a public meeting in Vancouver's Labor Temple in September 1916, he banged his large cane against a table in an attempt to maintain order as labour agitator and sometime-spy Robert Gosden discussed corruption and vote buying related to the upcoming provincial election.[119] In that election, the Socialist Party of Canada registered its worst showing since its formation, nominating only four candidates and receiving 1.2 percent of the vote; the SDPC fielded three candidates of its own (and took about 0.6 percent of the vote), alongside a smattering of independent socialist and independent labour candidates. In those ridings contested by the Socialist Party of Canada, the candidates received between 10 and 20 percent of the vote, with Albert "Ginger" Goodwin – who would die from a federal policeman's bullet nineteen months later while evading the draft – leading the group with 19 percent in Trail. One bright spot in that election was the re-election of Parker Williams as an independent socialist candidate in Newcastle; former SPC MLA John McInnis also came within seven votes of winning as an independent socialist candidate in Fort George; Nanaimo was lost to the Liberals for the first time in two decades.[120] Kingsley had been touted as a candidate in the Vancouver and Slocan districts, including a nomination from the VTLC, but after being rebuffed by the SPC Vancouver local he declined to run.[121] The *Vancouver Daily Province,* reporting on Kingsley's estrangement from the Socialist Party of Canada, noted the "regret of many of his former supporters, who would have liked to have seen him in his old role as a candidate at the coming election."[122]

The First World War triggered a process of realignment on the BC and Canadian left as SPC electoral fortunes waned and other political formations emerged to harness, and help to direct, mounting working-class grievances and radicalization. The Russian Revolution emerged as a focal point for the workers' movement in British Columbia and everywhere. It was viewed through the lens of workers' own class position in Canada and in turn provided a lens through which workers increasingly came to interpret their own class position and potential role as historical agents. The war crisis also produced a degree of rapprochement among rival factions and individuals on the BC left as the threat to workers posed by the war in Europe and repression on the home front underscored the need for common action notwithstanding organizational and personal jealousies and disagreements over tactics, strategies, policies, and ideologies. In June 1916, Kingsley highlighted the ongoing threat to workers posed by the ordinary operation of capitalism in a *Federationist* article that cannot be read in isolation from his own experience of disablement:

> Figures recently made public by the Interstate Commerce Commission at Washington ... show that 2,581 persons were killed and 43,618 injured by railroad accidents during the three months ending September 30, 1915. It must be remembered that this did not happen "somewhere in France" during times of war, but in the United States during times of peace. And this killing and maiming has been a result of railway operation alone. Just what the grand total of killed and crippled would be if all other branches of industry had made returns, is not known.[123]

In May 1917, Kingsley, as associate editor of the *Federationist,* was invited to address a May Day gathering at South Wellington near Nanaimo, demonstrating his ongoing influence within the working-class movement in British Columbia. His renewed position of leadership within the left occurred against the backdrop of an unprecedented upturn in union organizing and industrial militancy between 1917 and 1919, which socialist pioneer Bill Bennett would later describe as "one long continued strike in BC, breaking out in one place now, another place next."[124]

Demonstrating rapprochement on the left, Kingsley returned to a familiar role on the Vancouver socialist speaking circuit in mid-1917, sharing a common platform with Pritchard and other SPC leaders in a series of public meetings jointly hosted by the BCFL and the VTLC. Seeking to harness working-class opposition to compulsory military service, as mandated in the *Military Service Act, 1917,* the mass meetings were organized under the slogan "no conscription, no compromise" and reflected the new-found spirit of cooperation. The inaugural joint meeting took place in Vancouver's Orpheum Theatre on 3 June 1917 featuring Kingsley and Pettipiece as speakers, followed by another meeting at the Empress Theatre on 13 June, featuring speeches by Lefeaux and Pritchard representing the Socialist Party of Canada, Pettipiece representing the *Federationist,* and Kingsley apparently speaking on his own behalf, though possibly there on behalf of the *Federationist* as well. The meeting was chaired by VTLC president McVety, a machinist.

In his remarks, Kingsley told the audience that every war in history had sprung from economic sources and that the only purpose of the military was "to protect the master." He displayed none of the ideological ambiguity that had inflamed his comrades at the outset of the war, applying a rigorous class-struggle lens to conditions in Canada and globally. Anticipating the deployment of Allied and Canadian forces to Russia the following year, in the wake of the Bolshevik seizure of state power in that country, Kingsley commented on the docility of British troops, predicting that, "if sent to Russia, in case of a rebellion of workers, I should be greatly surprised if they did not fire on their kind at the word of command."[125] As noted by McCartney in a graduate thesis examining working-class responses to the war in British Columbia, Kingsley's position had shifted closer to the internationalism of his SPC comrades by 1917.[126] In an article on war finance, Kingsley noted that the "rulers still rule and rob after the smoke of battle clears away, just as they did before."[127]

This new-found spirit of cooperation can be interpreted as displaying the phenomenon of *solidarity by necessity,* in which otherwise opposing factions within the working-class movement demonstrated a predilection to work together in response to the threat posed to workers and working-class interests by the war crisis in general and Canada's conscription law in particular. A similar spirit of solidarity was manifested the following summer when Goodwin – the SPC candidate for Trail in the 1916 provincial election and vice-president of the BCFL for the Kootenay region – was shot dead by a special federal police constable while evading the draft near a remote camp above Comox Lake on Vancouver Island, resulting in a twenty-four-hour general strike called by the VTLC, among the first city-wide work stoppages in Canadian history up to that time.[128]

Organizing the Federated Labor Party

On the political field, Kingsley and other working-class activists responded to the war crisis with a renewed drive toward consolidation, organization, and cooperation. In the wake of the disastrous 1917 federal "Conscription Election," which saw a coalition of Conservatives and pro-war Liberals capture a large majority amid a routing of independent labour candidates opposing conscription (aided by a controversial extension of the franchise to the wives, mothers, and sisters of soldiers serving over-seas under the aegis of the *War-Time Elections Act, 1917*), BC trade union-ists and socialists forged a new political party.[129] Kingsley had declined to stand as a candidate in the "Conscription Election" (despite his name being put forward at a VTLC meeting), but he actively promoted Labor candidates in the Lower Mainland and on Vancouver Island.[130] The *Federationist* provided a glowing review of Kingsley's role in whipping up public support for the campaign in Victoria: "Our meetings have been altogether success-ful. The effective work of E.T. Kingsley, during the two visits he made here, has certainly proved a mental awakening for many who had lethargic tendencies, resulting, too, in the dispelling of many illusions hitherto existent in this city."[131] Described as "the veteran exponent of the working people of this coast," Kingsley had renewed political stature during the war, as evident when he served as keynote speaker at the Labor candidates' closing rally in Vancouver.[132] A few months later a correspondent from Stewart, a mining town in northern British Columbia, celebrated "the return to active service of so many old warhorses in the Labor movement of this province, such as 'Old Man Kingsley.'"[133] Another correspondent, writing from North Vancouver, following a speech by Kingsley in the autumn of 1918, noted that he "said more in one hour than all the so-called statesmen of Canada did since the days of Confederation."[134]

At the BCFL annual convention in Vancouver in February 1918, dele-gates voted 82–11 in favour of establishing a new political party, the Federated Labor Party, "for the purpose of securing industrial legislation for the collective ownership and democratic operation of the means of wealth production."[135] The formation of the party was also spurred by an electoral victory for the BC socialist movement when James Hawthorn-thwaite returned to provincial politics, winning a January 1918 by-election in the Newcastle riding, precipitated by the appointment of former MLA Parker Williams to the Workmen's Compensation Board (a move lam-basted by former SPC comrades as traitorous accommodation with the employer class). Hawthornthwaite contested the by-election as an in-dependent socialist/labour candidate with the endorsement of the United Mine Workers of America local in Nanaimo and support from Vancouver socialists, including Kingsley and garment workers' leader Helena Gutter-idge, who spoke at campaign events.[136] Another by-election in January

1918 also demonstrated a renewed appetite for independent political action. Mary Ellen Smith, the widow of Ralph Smith (the former Nanaimo coal miner, Trades and Labor Congress of Canada president, MLA, MP, and BC finance minister), was elected as an independent people's candidate for MLA for Vancouver City, filling a seat vacated as a result of her husband's death. Smith was supported by the Liberals, and ultimately sat with the Liberal caucus, serving as the first woman legislator in British Columbia and the first woman cabinet minister in the British Empire (when she was appointed as a minister without a portfolio in the government of John Oliver in 1921). During her initial by-election run, the *Federationist* reported favourably on her candidacy.[137] Kingsley was also touted as a candidate in that by-election by an anonymous letter writer in the *Federationist*: "I know of no man who could better advocate Labor's cause or who has done more for the Labor movement in this province than the same E.T. He is the strongest candidate we could possibly put up and would stand a better show of going to Victoria than any other I know of."[138]

Although some leading SPC members opposed the formation of the Federated Labor Party at the Vancouver convention – notably Cumberland coal miner (and outgoing BCFL president) Joe Naylor, smelterworkers' business agent (and outgoing BCFL vice-president) Ginger Goodwin of Trail, and bricklayer Ernest Winch – an overwhelming majority of the labour delegates favoured establishment of the new party.[139] Kingsley was elected as vice-president at the party's founding meeting, immediately following the BCFL convention, and later assumed the role of president, serving alongside Gutteridge while presiding over the party's Vancouver local.[140] Kingsley was also appointed to serve on a committee to formulate plans for the establishment of the party.[141] "The psychological moment has evidently arrived and the working people and other progressive elements are responding to the call of the Bolsheviki spirit, throughout the world," Kingsley declared.[142] Bill Pritchard commented on the participation of Kingsley in the Federated Labor Party in an interview decades later: "He kind of went into what was called the Federated Labor Party, but he didn't belong there."[143] Historian Allen Seager identifies Kingsley as the chief author of the FLP political platform; an attempt to water it down in April 1919 was rebuffed, with delegates retaining language in the preamble calling for the "complete overthrow of the present system" and asserting "solidarity with the revolutionary working class of the world."[144] In addition to his duties as vice-president and president, Kingsley worked as an FLP organizer and propagandist, addressing dozens of meetings from Nanaimo to New Westminster, the Okanagan Valley, the Kootenays, the Crow's Nest Pass, and Alberta between 1918 and 1920.[145] At the party's first public meeting in Vancouver in February 1918, he conveyed the radical mood, predicting that the spirit embodied in the Russian Bolsheviki would "sweep the whole earth and second-hand shops from that day on will be ramful of thrones and crowns."[146] The following month Kingsley returned to a familiar theme of the battle for political power between the classes: "Without the law the master class cannot exist, hence their efforts to retain their henchmen in office."[147] The Federated Labor Party recruited more than 700 members in its first two and a half months in operation and developed an extensive organizational structure, including branches around the province and a youth wing – the Junior Labor League – and, by 1920, had acquired a hall and library to serve as the party's headquarters on Cordova Street in Vancouver.[148]

Alongside political organizing and propaganda work on behalf of the party, Kingsley intensified his role in the left-wing press in early 1919 as the postwar working-class revolt gathered steam in British Columbia and beyond (in the midst of strikes by laundry workers in Vancouver and shipyard workers in Seattle, which triggered that city's epic 60,000-strong general strike, foreshadowing the sympathetic strike wave that would paralyze Winnipeg, Vancouver, Victoria, and other cities the following spring). In January 1919, Kingsley and Pettipiece founded a new publication, the *Labor Star,* a weekly published in Vancouver oriented toward "that portion of the working class believing primarily in independent political action."[149] Ads for the Federated Labor Party and subjects aligned with its program and objectives figured prominently in the newspaper.

The first issue featured a ringing front-page call to action by Kingsley, alongside photographs of him and Hawthornthwaite, advocating the familiar strategy of seizing control of the capitalist state through electoral means:

> The modern state is the instrument of the ruling class. It is the instrument designed, developed and brought to its present high state of efficiency, solely for the purpose of holding the slaves in subjection to their masters

and owners and rendering them docile and tame to the exactions and schemes of their rulers ...

We still have the franchise in Canada and the United States. Let us use that franchise in our own behalf and that of our class. When we have been deprived of the franchise it will then be time to consider the advisability of using some other equally legal weapon wherewith to effect the deliverance of our class from its age long bondage. In such case even the club would be legal ... The tactics and methods forced up the workers and peasants of Russia are not yet necessary here. Let us hope they never will be necessary.[150]

Kingsley served as editor of the *Labor Star,* with Pettipiece serving as manager. According to Pritchard, "he [Kingsley] didn't publish it. I think he wrote for it. He was getting along in years then too, was the Old Man."[151] Published by an entity known as the Star Publishing Company at the Dominion Building, 207 West Hastings Street, the *Labor Star* unfortunately

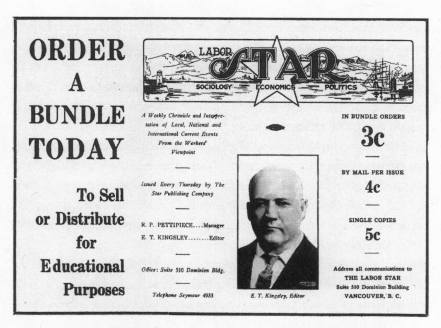

FIGURE 23 Advertisement in the *Labor Star,* a newspaper that Kingsley founded with Richard Parmater "Parm" Pettipiece in 1919. Kingsley served as editor. The paper published only from January to March 1919. | *Labor Star.*

would not last. Plagued by what seemed to be circulation and sales problems, the newspaper ended its run in March 1919 after only two months and was Kingsley's last major publishing endeavour.[152]

Most issues of the *Labor Star* featured a lengthy front-page article signed by Kingsley examining different aspects of the postwar crisis from a Marxist viewpoint. The paper also featured several columns authored by J.S. Woodsworth, based in British Columbia at the time, during his "proletarian apprenticeship" as an auxiliary longshore worker on the docks of Vancouver following his resignation from the Methodist Church. Woodsworth would contest the 1920 BC election as an FLP candidate for Vancouver (before moving back to Winnipeg, where he would embark on his successful career as a Labor and later CCF MP).[153] In contrast to Woodsworth's social gospel message, Kingsley published Lenin's "A Letter to American Workingmen," providing a direct platform for the leader of Russia's unorthodox new socialist republic among the BC working class.[154] In one of his own unsigned columns in the *Labor Star* in February 1919, Kingsley lambasted the Seattle general strike ("the most complete tie-up of a big city that has yet occurred in American history") as a misplaced example of trade unionism "with no evidence of these striking workmen having any vision beyond the narrow confines of their daily allowance of grub."[155] In another article, he signalled an important retreat from BC labour's prewar xenophobic attitude, condemning the misplaced rage of workers who blamed "enemy aliens" for the lack of jobs rather than questioning why they even had to look for jobs.[156]

In March 1919, in what would become the final issue of the *Labor Star,* Kingsley triumphantly declared in a front-page headline that "The Class War Is Now On!"[157] Days earlier delegates at the Western Labor Conference in Calgary had decided to form One Big Union as the primary vehicle for the working-class challenge against capitalist interests in Canada.[158] However, Kingsley urged caution:

> Let no misguided disciple of "One Big Union" or other similar conception delude himself into fancying that the hold of the ruling class can be broken without first stripping from its hands the control of that instrument (the state) solely by means of which it maintains its mastery over the working class and its products ...

Use the legal weapon of the franchise where and when ye still possess it. Where you have it not, struggle to get it. If that be denied you, then take whatever weapons the occasion may warrant and circumstances place within your reach.

But remember the class war is now on.[159]

These were the final words published in the *Labor Star*. Coming on the eve of the Winnipeg General Strike, and in the opening volley of Canadian workers' postwar revolt, Kingsley's advice appears to have provided a prescient warning – confirmed with the benefit of hindsight by the Canadian state's violent suppression of the historical expression of working-class solidarity that manifested itself in Winnipeg and other communities in the spring of 1919. Although Kingsley would never again spearhead a working-class publication, his political analysis remained astutely aligned with the conditions confronting the Canadian working class at this high-water mark in its history.

Unlike many BC socialists in 1919, Kingsley was not receptive to the emergence of the One Big Union. It was led by Pritchard and other members of the Vancouver, Cumberland, Edmonton, and Winnipeg SPC locals and captured the imaginations of workers in a matter of weeks from the Pacific Coast to the Atlantic Coast (24,000 of whom voted in a referendum to sever ties with their existing unions and join the new revolutionary union).[160] Whereas Kingsley had welcomed the 60,000-strong Belfast General Strike of January 1919, declaring in a meeting in Vancouver that it was "pretty near time the people of this town did the same as the people of Belfast," he did not support the emergence of militant industrial unionism in Canada.[161] In April 1919, he declared that "I stand for one big union – for the specific purpose of conquering the reins of power, by peaceful means if possible, and if not, by some other means." He also stated his belief in favour of "mass action with a purpose that can appeal to all," suggesting that the Ginger Goodwin strike of the previous August was "purely a political strike, a protest against the persecution of draft evaders."[162] This provoked a sharp response from George Hardy, who argued that Kingsley's strategy of urging "the slow penetration of the capitalist legislative halls" was "misleading" and "a distortion of all historic change" and represented a "hollow" reading of Marx; Hardy insisted that "we have the nucleus of organizations, which properly managed can form the basis of administration in the new social system," and that "the capitalist state will lose its power in proportion to our growing strength."[163] Kingsley's "wait and vote them out of power" strategy was also criticized by another *Federationist* correspondent, citing the "great deal of death and destruction to individuals" while the working class waited.[164]

Later that spring, in June 1919, in the midst of the Winnipeg General Strike, with cities from Vancouver to Amherst, Nova Scotia, tied up in the biggest sympathetic strike wave that Canada had ever known, Kingsley adhered to his message of caution in a speech on the topic of "Capitalism" in Vancouver's Columbia Theatre. He reminded attendees that, "in spite of the OBU, collective bargaining, etc, the other fellow still owns the shop." He sought to elevate the level of analysis, warning that "a sudden collapse of the system" would result in the deaths of "countless thousands" of workers in the cities, cut off from the food supply in rural areas. His prognosis was that "the workers of the city and country had got to act together; then they could conquer this whole western continent and undo that which the ruling-class had been fastening on them for 10,000 years," wiping out the wage system and becoming free men and women.[165] At that meeting, a woman identified as E. Robb criticized organized labour for confining its protests to "resolutions," asking the crowd what action labour was prepared to take to compel various governments, including that of Canada, to withdraw troops from Russia to prevent them from "slaughtering our helpless, suffering comrades."[166]

As the postwar industrial challenge of the Canadian working class reached its tragic peak in June 1919, Kingsley embarked on a propaganda tour of the Okanagan Valley, the Kootenays, the Crow's Nest Pass, and Alberta, presumably under the auspices of the Federated Labor Party. On 20 June, the *Federationist* reported on his trip, the day before the "Bloody Saturday" police riot, when the Canadian state broke the back of the Winnipeg strike, killing two workers and injuring a hundred more, after arresting its leaders on charges of sedition and on the eve of a wider crackdown against socialist leaders and organizations from Victoria to Saint John:

Probably no one will be more amused than the "old man" himself when he learns that the Dominion authorities have included among their up-to-date activities an investigation into his "antecedents" ... Perhaps when the Dominion honor roll is complete and the "deportations" ended, it may be the intention of the Ottawa people to move over "E.T." as the first president of their new Botany Bay. On the other hand it may be that his continued insistence upon constitutional methods is displeasing to a class whose only argument is force and whose only propaganda is incitement to riot through "Citizen's Leagues."[167]

Alluding to the British penal colony at Botany Bay, established in Australia a century and a quarter earlier, the *Federationist* emphasized his adherence to constitutional methods, which placed Kingsley out of step with the predominant mood and tactical predilection of workers and leaders at this tense moment in Canadian working-class history.

On his return to Vancouver in July 1919, Kingsley humorously admonished his audience for "getting into trouble while he was away, e.g. going on strike about 24 hours after his back was turned."[168] Invoking Marx's "Iron Law" of wages (which held that wages under capitalism would always tend in the long run toward the minimum wage required to sustain the life of a worker), Kingsley suggested that "nothing except temporary gains" could be won through trade union struggles and that, when workers revolted, as they had in Winnipeg, "they laid themselves liable to the fangs and claws of the state; the mounted police and the other thugs and ruffians of the rulers were put into motion." The only solution available to the working class was "political action ... to strip the ruling class of power."[169] Demonstrating further rapprochement on the left as the postwar crisis deepened, Kingsley spoke at an SPC meeting in Vancouver in August 1919 – the first evidence of his public association with the party's platform since the falling out at the beginning of the war.[170]

His renewed political activism in the late stages of the First World War and early phase of the Canadian labour revolt set Kingsley on his own collision path with the Canadian state – harking back to earlier battles with authorities as an SLP organizer in California in the 1890s and during the Vancouver Free Speech fights prior to the war. This was familiar ground for the Old Man of the BC left. But these renewed legal clashes during and after the First World War were intensified by the depth of class conflict both in Canada and globally. Responding to rising working-class opposition

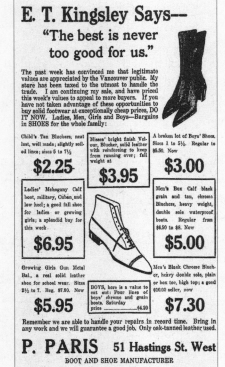

FIGURE 24 Demonstrating Kingsley's notoriety, this shoe store invoked a quotation from Kingsley to sell its product in this 1919 advertisement. | *British Columbia Federationist.*

to militarism and capitalism in Canada, as well as the international context of revolutions in Russia and other European states, the Canadian capitalist class took action to formalize elements of the national security state that had been emerging in preceding decades – with Kingsley among the primary targets of this emboldened security apparatus.

Structuring the Security State during the First World War

As Gregory Kealey has noted, at the outbreak of the First World War, the Canadian state had virtually no security and intelligence capacity.[171] The existing Dominion Police were a small and poorly funded force. Consequently, many policing functions were delegated to other regional police forces, such as the Royal North West Mounted Police, and even contracted out to private detective agencies for undercover services because of funding limitations. We would argue that these problems would be magnified in a sparsely populated province such as British Columbia, which had fewer than 400,000 residents in the 1911 census.[172] At the outset of the First World War, in August 1914, the government enacted the *War Measures Act,* which massively enhanced the federal cabinet's ability to direct the economy to the needs of the war, censor political views deemed to be undermining the war effort, and regulate the lives of enemy aliens and citizens. It simply required an order-in-council by the cabinet to make pivotal and time-sensitive decisions that previously would have been impossible. For this reason, scholars such as Kealey, invoking the work of noted historian Arthur Lower, have succinctly described this as a shift from parliamentary to order-in-council government.[173] It appears that both government and opposition MPs were persuaded by the idea, based on the British experience with the *Defence of the Realm Act,* that the rapidly changing conditions of the war would require them to adopt a long series of legislative amendments because of unforeseen omissions unless a broad piece of emergency legislation was adopted at the outset.[174]

In October 1914, an order-in-council was issued requiring all enemy aliens to report to special registrars for examination and registration. Those who were deemed to be dangerous or failed to register were interned as prisoners of war.[175] As of the summer of 1915, registration offices to process enemy aliens had been established in Sydney, Nova Scotia; Ottawa; Toronto; Brandon; Regina; Calgary; and Victoria.[176] By the end of the First World War, some 80,000 foreign-born Canadians had been subjected to the examination and registration procedures, and nearly 9,000 men, women, and children had been interned.[177] Given that the United States was neutral for most of the war and contained large numbers of immigrants from countries with which Canada was now at war, border security was also a high priority.[178] The regime imposed in Canada on enemy aliens was actually broader than that imposed on British enemy aliens.[179] Section 6 of the *War Measures Act* authorized the governor in council (i.e., the federal cabinet) to suppress publications, writings, maps, plans, photographs, and means of communication. A reverse onus clause required accused persons to demonstrate their innocence, and conviction resulted in a fine of $5,000, five years of imprisonment, or both.[180] In June 1915, in the aftermath of embarrassing press leaks, PC 1330 officially established the Office of the Chief Press Censor, run by Ernest Chambers (1862–1925). Reporting to the secretary of state, Chambers was authorized to suppress sources that were criticizing military policy, causing disaffection, and assisting or encouraging the enemy or preventing the successful prosecution of the war.[181] For the next several years, Chambers would interact with and disrupt Kingsley's political life.

The authority of Chambers was originally limited but gradually increased during the war. British born, he had immigrated to Canada as a young child, developing early ties to the militia in Montreal, and later worked as a field reporter for the Montreal *Daily Star* covering Major-General Middleton's suppression of the Métis uprising in 1885 before enlisting as a volunteer in the Battles of Fish Creek and Batoche.[182] Chambers worked for a time as managing editor of the *Calgary Herald* in the late 1880s and, returning to Montreal, served as proprietor and editor of the *Canadian Military Gazette,* a journal that strongly endorsed Canada's participation in the Boer War. In 1904, Chambers moved to Ottawa when he was appointed the Gentleman Usher of the Black Rod in the Senate, and he continued to publish regimental histories and edit the *Canadian Parliamentary Guide.* With the outbreak of the First World War, he was seconded to do work at military headquarters monitoring international cable and wireless transmissions.[183] His background and contacts in the militia, journalism, and surveillance made Chambers a natural fit when the Office of Chief Press Censor was created in 1915.[184] On assuming this role, he issued detailed instructions on permissible commentary on the war to nearly 1,500 publishers.[185] His authority extended to photographs, movies, theatrical productions, gramophone recordings, and sheet music, and he had the authority to listen to telephone calls, monitor telegraph messages, and open suspicious letters and parcels in a world where postal mail was essential for communication.[186]

Although the Office of Chief Press Censor, located in a tiny space on Elgin Street in downtown Ottawa, was consistently understaffed, Chambers clearly took his role seriously, and the office kept extremely long hours. He received no additional pay, living on his salary as gentleman usher and regarding his press censor work as his contribution to the war effort. Although much of his focus was on censoring the foreign-language press, Chambers attempted to suppress the anti-war newspaper *Le Devoir* on no fewer than five occasions between April 1916 and February 1918.[187]

At times, Canadian censorship exceeded British censorship, apparently on the ground that grisly battle images from the front would be more damaging in Canada in the years before conscription was introduced.[188]

Conscription, introduced by the government of Robert Borden through the *Military Service Act* in August 1917 in the face of severe shortages on the battlefield and the utter failure of volunteer recruitment efforts, was deeply controversial in the Canadian labour movement, especially as wartime conditions in the trenches became more widely known as the war progressed.[189] It also led to the Conscription Crisis in which English-French relations were inflamed. The *Military Service Act* required all men aged twenty to twenty-four who were single or widowers without children to enlist for overseas service. Although Prime Minister Borden had hesitated to introduce conscription because of its immense unpopularity in Quebec and its implications for divisive English-French relations in Canada, he became convinced of its need while visiting with military personnel and political leaders in England.[190] Some farmers and employers, however, joined militant trade unionists in opposing conscription because the denial of manpower threatened their economic viability and the government lacked the requisite statistical capacity to determine manpower needs for each industry in the face of conscription.[191]

One controversial measure that the Borden government took as it considered the thorny and highly divisive issue of conscription was to manipulate the voting rolls to increase its chance of re-election in 1917 through the *War-Time Elections Act*.[192] This statute disenfranchised Canadian citizens of enemy countries naturalized after 1902 and enfranchised the wives, widows, mothers, and sisters of soldiers serving overseas. An exception was made for relatives of recently naturalized citizens serving overseas.[193] Although obviously not consistent with the *Charter* values of the twenty-first century, even in its day this measure was controversial since it retroactively removed a fundamental right granted to citizens. Sir Wilfrid Laurier justifiably regarded the associated bigotry as a blot on Canadian principles of "justice, honesty and fair play."[194] Another piece of legislation, the *Military Voters Act*, granted all British subjects in the military the right to vote, including minors, women, and Indigenous Canadians. Soldiers who did not specify a riding were allowed simply to cast a vote by party, allowing the party to allocate the vote in the riding that would best serve its interests. At this time, women had not yet achieved the franchise, so this was seen as an advance by some feminists that might lead to the franchise for all women.[195]

Press censorship appeared to increase during the war but was not always consistent. Interestingly, abstract socialist propaganda in itself was not necessarily sufficient to warrant prohibition. The law mandated that the staff of Colonel Chambers during the early years were to focus only on communications that undermined the war effort. As the war progressed, the definition was broadened by subsequent orders to include opposition to conscription when it was introduced in 1917. It was broadened yet again in 1918 to include anything that might spread discontent or weaken the people's unanimity behind the war effort.[196] Yet abstract socialist propaganda, though clearly content that Chambers personally found subversive, was always ambiguous as a matter of law. Consequently, a memorandum assessing an issue of the *Western Clarion* in August 1918 noted that there was very little objectionable content but identified a specific paragraph that might have undermined conscription and an article on war bonds that raised alarm among the press censor staff because it suggested that the price of bonds might fall to half of their value at the conclusion of the war.[197] The *Western Clarion* likely did not help its own case given the dramatic writing style typically used by SPC militants and their international comrades. The controversial article on the issue of bonds, written by an American comrade, is worth quoting at length:

By what gentle and benignant methods are these liberty bonds for democracy disposed of?? In all ages, though in this more than any other, freaks, numbskulls, and ordinary slaves with home guard intelligence have been easily found who were willing to crucify, burn at the stake, lynch, or tar and feather those members of their class who had the intelligence and temerity to question what is or to speculate on what is to be. So it is today. Those who do not purchase bonds through the regular agents are interviewed at the shop or their lodging place, and if they fail to respond to a little pressure, more is applied, such as threat of discharge from the job, either open or implied, all the way to tar and feathers, dipping in oil, or lynching.[198]

However, archival documents show that an editorial on the war by Kingsley that appeared in a new Vancouver publication called the *Critic* in August 1917 drew the attention of the censors. The *Critic* was edited by a colourful American Canadian, Louis Taylor, a former long-serving mayor of Vancouver, past managing editor of the *Vancouver World,* and previously circulation editor at the *Vancouver Daily Province*. Chambers received a recommendation that his staff monitor the *Critic,* and the memorandum specifically mentioned Kingsley as an associate editor of the *BC Federationist*.[199]

In the editorial, "Win the War," as the title suggests, Kingsley does not in fact call for the defeat of the Allied forces.[200] His position is emphatically not Lenin's stance of revolutionary defeatism or the defeat of one's own country's troops.[201] Rather, Kingsley merely, if somewhat polemically as was his characteristic writing style, denounces the notion of conscription in the context of the 1917 election campaign that pit Conservatives and those Liberals who joined them in a Unionist coalition against the rump of the Liberal Party led by Sir Wilfrid Laurier. At times, Kingsley bends over backward to emphasize that he is objecting only to conscription and not the war effort and strikes an almost patriotic tone. Whether this was a tactical move undertaken purely to avoid the wrath of Chambers or reflected the fact that Kingsley was not writing for the socialist press in this instance is difficult to determine after the fact. Yet he writes in this editorial that

> I think I know my Canada fairly well, from sea to sea. And what this country is capable of, in men and in resources, if they are properly mobilized, and honestly led, and seriously administered. I think I know something of the fine audacity of Canadians; and what any great prime minister could have done with them, at the very outbreak of this war, in every province, without exception.
>
> And I am convinced that there lingers still in the breast of every son of this free soil of ours, of every province, and of both races and tongues, some sparks of that fire which burned in the hearts of the heroes who fought for our freedom and [illegible] us their fame.[202]

Despite the placid prose in the *Critic,* by this point Kingsley clearly had acquired a notorious reputation in the intelligence world.

State Repression and Censorship at the End of the War

Influenced by a report advocating greater repression and censorship drafted by Conservative politician and lawyer C.H. Cahan, PC 2381 was enacted by an order-in-council on 25 September 1918, authorizing the prohibition of printing, publishing, and possessing any publication in an enemy language, including Russian, Finnish, Ukrainian, and Yiddish.[203] The fact that many speakers of these languages were ardent foes of the kaiser's regime was not thought to be relevant. Subsequent amendments to the order-in-council targeted specific materials. The draconian penalty for violation of the order-in-council was a fine of $5,000 and/or five years in prison.[204]

The promulgation of PC 2384 had even more drastic implications. It prohibited a large number of radical foreign-language publications as well as publications produced outside Canada. Even ads for banned publications in otherwise unobjectionable materials could render the content prohibited.[205] Colonel Chambers would have preferred to go much further and shut down foreign-language publications entirely. PC 2384 also enhanced the law of sedition by prohibiting organizations from advocating economic or political change by force and allowing the Crown to seize the property of such organizations. It remained in effect until April 1919.[206]

Although many organizations were banned, including the Social Democratic Party of Canada, the Socialist Party of Canada was not on the list, perhaps because it had fewer ethnic members or simply because of bureaucratic incompetence.[207] In that year, the *Criminal Code of Canada* was amended to provide for a statutory alternative to PC 2384. Section 97B had a similar effect. The major difference was that it did not permit the government to declare particular organizations illegal. Rather, illegality would have to be established at trial via the prosecution of particular individuals.[208] Although lasting only a few months, a Public Safety Branch was also created by an order-in-council in October 1918 to preserve public safety and order and enforce the war measures enacted toward that end. Cahan served as its only director.[209]

In reality, there were significant limitations to intelligence gathering on the ground. First, language barriers meant that in fact both rank-and-file intelligence officials and the underfunded and understaffed Office of the Chief Press Censor were dependent on speakers fluent in Russian,

Ukrainian, Finnish, or Yiddish. This allowed new immigrants to take advantage of the language barrier either to undermine the law or to pursue their own agendas completely unconnected to national security concerns. In some cases, the office had to rely for translation on speakers fluent in such languages who were themselves political radicals.[210] Second, the geographic size of Canada in a world where commercial air travel did not yet exist meant that staffing issues often resulted in uneven intelligence gathering given the sheer distances that had to be travelled.[211]

The *Western Clarion* was banned by an order-in-council in October 1918.[212] In fact, Chambers had lobbied for the prohibition of the anti-conscription paper for almost a year but had been overruled by his superiors because of concerns that such a controversial measure ought not to be undertaken during the sensitive 1917 election campaign.[213] In September 1918, Chambers made a trip to the *Western Clarion*'s Pender Street offices in Vancouver in the hope of using persuasion to restrain its anti-conscription stance, but he was met by men who simply denied any knowledge of the paper and refused to answer his questions.[214] Although Kingsley himself appears to have been an alien who simply landed at the Port of Victoria and established himself as a socialist in British Columbia in 1902, as a white alien from a non-enemy country, his naturalization status received only cursory attention from the authorities even after amendments to the *Immigration Act* in 1919 authorized the revocation of naturalization of anyone who fomented revolutionary ideas.[215] The Socialist Party of Canada challenged these extensive repressive measures, including house raids on private libraries, which many socialists found particularly egregious and invasive. J.S. Woodsworth buried his collection of radical publications in the back garden.[216] On 22 December 1918, the SPC Local 74 in the town of Alhambra, Alberta, called for an end to press censorship and the release of all political prisoners, adopting a resolution promoted among socialist locals and labour organizations across the country.[217] The Socialist Party of Canada also launched a new publication, the *Red Flag*, in January 1919 to replace the banned *Western Clarion*, and this publication, which apparently attained a circulation of 18,000 across Canada, also came under government scrutiny.[218] In January 1919, the *Red Flag* condemned censorship of the mail and observed that, "This action of the postal officials seems specially designed to seriously impede and cripple this party, both as an organization and in its business of supplying its customers throughout the country with literature on economics, history, sociology and on others of the special sciences."[219] In March 1919, the *Red Flag* reported that the Provincial Executive Committee of the Alberta wing of the Socialist Party of Canada was experiencing financial hardship because of its support for comrades facing steep fines after being charged with sedition or possession of banned literature.[220]

Interestingly, despite personal misgivings, Colonel Chambers acknowledged in a letter to the deputy postmaster general that, under the government's stated policy, it was not deemed to be desirable to prohibit publications such as the *Red Flag*.[221] Chambers took the same position when asked about a number of controversial publications, including Kingsley's iconic pamphlet *The Genesis and Evolution of Slavery*, by the assistant director of the Naval Service.[222] As late as April 1919, Chambers acknowledged that the *Labor Star*, edited by Kingsley, though in his view containing a considerable amount of "poisonous" and "objectionable" matter, was not prohibited since the Consolidated Orders Respecting Censorship were confined to foreign-language publications and publications printed outside Canada.[223] Chambers appears to have been unaware that the *Labor Star* had ceased publication two weeks earlier.

This correspondence is revealing because it demonstrates how government censorship policy was by no means monolithic. Different actors expressed their unique interests and views. Clearly, Colonel Chambers articulated a relatively conservative perspective that erred on the side of repression and censorship in the name of patriotism and encouraging the war effort. He was deeply suspicious of the foreign-language press and focused on an expansive interpretation of his power wherever possible.[224] Yet his power was ultimately constrained by his respect for the rule of law.

A more complicated case is that of C.H. Cahan, a Conservative lawyer and politician in Montreal. He filed an interim report with the minister of justice in July 1918 that identified Bolshevism as a central threat and endorsed the expansion of the Dominion Police and greater cooperation with other security agencies to counter it effectively.[225] In a paper on socialist propaganda delivered to the St. James Literary Society in Montreal in December 1918, Cahan expressed alarm at the radicalization of Finnish immigrants in the most polemical terms.[226] He stated that the revolutionary socialists would burn down the structures that civilization has reared, with all its slowly acquired values, for the purpose of obliterating its obvious defects; but the people of Canada, if they are wise in their day and generation, will devote the energies of Statesmen and of citizens alike ... to maintain on the old foundations the fabric our fathers have built, with new improvements as the health, the moral welfare, the material prosperity and the political and social advancement of our Nation obviously demand. Radical, revolutionary socialism, which is raising its hydra-head and threatening the obliteration of all that civilization has thus far accomplished, can only be stayed by such eternal vigilance as will enable us to discern and eradicate social evils as they appear, without destroying al [*sic*] that is valuable in the Social System which we have so far developed, amid so much of toil and strife and suffering.[227]

Described by the British high commissioner as the mouthpiece of big business interests in Montreal, at the time the largest city in Canada, Cahan was an ambitious man with political experience in the Nova Scotia legislature and legal experience as counsel to the Royal Securities Corporation and a member of corporate boards such as the Canadian Car and Foundry Company.[228] It was in fact his alarmist report, which also called for the establishment of a revamped Dominion Police with regional divisions across the country ready to quell domestic disorder (with his son proposed for an executive appointment), that led to the orders-in-council prohibiting radical publications in the fall of 1918.[229]

However, Newton Rowell, president of the Privy Council and a former leader of the Ontario Liberal Party who joined Prime Minister Borden's Unionist government in 1917 to support the introduction of conscription, typically expressed a more conciliatory approach. As president of the Privy Council, Rowell was the minister in charge of the RNWMP. He argued that PC 2384 risked alienating the labour movement by wrongly banning groups such as the SDPC that sought political reforms but were not a threat to the existing system.[230] Despite efforts by Cahan to bypass the chain of command and appeal directly to the authority of Borden, Rowell's liberal view prevailed, at least partly because Cahan was regarded as having inappropriately failed to follow proper procedure in making his case, and his muted suggestion that cabinet ministers were caving in to red propaganda irritated them rather than enticed them. Cahan's vision for reorganizing the police in a more autonomous direction akin to the American Federal Bureau of Investigation was also rejected.[231]

State monitoring and repression, however, continued and intensified after the Armistice of November 1918 as the government and elites grew increasingly alarmed at the growing radicalization of the Canadian working class. This period of the postwar labour revolt is remembered most for the legendary Winnipeg General Strike, which created an unprecedented political crisis in 1919.[232] After a determined freedom-of-information campaign, Kealey was able to obtain some declassified and redacted reports of intelligence gathering in Vancouver for the month of March 1919. They indicate intense monitoring of radical political activity against both anti-imperialist advocates in the Chinese National League and trade unionists and socialists.[233] The Chinese National League sought to keep Chinese communities overseas in touch with China and celebrate the Canton Uprising. At one point, it operated three daily newspapers in Canada.[234] Colonel Chambers worked to suppress the Chinese National League and tended to make assumptions that Chinese nationalists were uniformly aligned with German imperial interests because of German promises to establish a republic in Beijing if the Germans won the war. Indeed, it has been alleged that his robust attitude toward monitoring Chinese immigrants smacked of racism.[235] As late as 1922, the Defence Committee of Canada Sub-Committee on Intelligence was closely monitoring two Chinese aviation schools in Victoria and Saskatoon for potential affiliation with the Chinese National League.[236]

The Federated Labor Party was also the subject of close scrutiny by intelligence officers. A report notes that Kingsley and Woodsworth were among the prominent speakers delivering talks on Sundays and condemning the capitalist class. Remarkably, the report acknowledges that there was a good deal of truth in many of their arguments for socialism, an unexpectedly frank admission given the source and its intended audience.[237] The police report expresses particular concern about the possibility that socialist propaganda could win over angry soldiers, just returned from military service overseas and disappointed at their economic prospects, to the FLP or SPC cause. Interestingly, though Kingsley was obviously a specific target of this investigation, the report suggests that he was harmless compared with well-known socialists such as Winch, Kavanagh, Lestor, and others.[238] An intelligence report from April 1919 documents how Kingsley, Pritchard, Kavanagh, and Midgley were actively supporting the creation of a soldiers and sailors club. The report specifically identifies the dangers that the radicalization of returned soldiers would pose for the government and how this was clearly a priority for the Vancouver socialists.[239] This concern among the intelligence community is hardly surprising since the *Western Clarion* directly, and in the most polemical terms, raised the issue of the exploitation and marginalization of physically disabled veterans, particularly after unemployment began to rise as the anomalous character of full employment during wartime ended.[240]

In a confidential but blunt document written by Colonel Chambers for his superiors in April 1919 concerning the surveillance of various radical publications, including Kingsley's newly launched but short-lived *Labor Star,* he describes Kingsley in the most polemically imaginable terms. Chambers first observes how Kingsley was forced to resign from the editorship of the *BC Federationist* when press censorship came into effect.[241] He then describes Kingsley as

> an out-and-out red Bolshevik Socialist of pronounced literary capacity and unquestionably one of the most dangerous men in Canada, having education and capacity and knowing how to win the sympathies and acclaim of the more ignorant classes of the community. He would go to any length to secure support for his publication [and] would unquestionably do anything he possibly could to undermine the constituted authority.[242]

Interestingly, Chambers draws a sharp comparison between Kingsley and his long-time collaborator, Richard Parmater Pettipiece. Whereas Kingsley is regarded as irremediably and intractably ideological, Pettipiece is viewed far more favourably and thought to be a patriotic man with a sense of national duty. In fact, Chambers implies that Pettipiece's motivations for public speaking were financial rather than ideological and observes that past arrangements had been made for Pettipiece to be offered a government position. He expresses the wish that perhaps Pettipiece again could be offered a similar arrangement.[243]

Kingsley's impairments seem in no way to have allayed the fears of government authorities about his abilities to engage in subversive action. A month later, in the midst of the Winnipeg General Strike, Chambers would advise a military official in Ottawa that Kingsley's *The Genesis and Evolution of Slavery* had "not previously been drawn to my attention."[244] Although citing the current policy of the federal government "to not interfere with the circulation of literature printed in the English and French languages" under the wartime press censorship powers, Chambers advised the official that he was "endeavouring to keep as complete a record as possible of all questionable literature circulating in Canada for future reference."[245]

It was not only federal officials who objected to Kingsley's radicalism in the immediate postwar period. In a fiery speech at Victoria's Columbia Theatre on 25 January 1919, the weekly Sunday-evening mass meeting of the local FLP branch, Kingsley expressed sympathy for the Russian Bolshevik government and condemned the military intervention of Canada and other Allied countries in Russia's internal affairs – one month after a mutiny erupted in British Columbia's capital city when French Canadian conscripts in the 259th Battalion embarked for Vladivostok.[246] "I don't care what the Bolsheviks are doing to the land barons to win out, so long as they are against the capitalistic gang and bourgeoise and shoot every land baron and general," Kingsley was reported as saying. "We don't want any rough stuff in Canada," he added, "though we have some now in the shape of censorship, which exists though the war is over, in this land of democracy that went abroad to fight the military 'shebang' of Germany ... We demand that restrictions on expression of opinion be removed."[247]

Local authorities and the Board of Trade responded with outrage to Kingsley's speech in Victoria, with Mayor Robert Porter pressuring the manager of the Columbia Theatre, Eugene Clarke, to curb use of the venue for expression of radical political views.[248] Although the leaders of the Victoria FLP branch assured Clarke that "the general tenor of the speeches to be given there by the party's speakers in the future would be modified," the theatre's owners cancelled the next FLP weekly meeting on 1 February, preventing ex-soldier Thomas Barnard from the Great War

Veterans' Association from speaking, citing fears of violence amid agitation by patriotic ex-soldiers.[249] The Victoria mayor's heavy-handed approach reflected pressure from local businessmen, patriotic organizations, and Victoria City Council. Two days after Kingsley's address, the Victoria Board of Trade discussed the content of his speech, with several members favouring restrictions on "the gospel of incendiarism," while the *Victoria Daily Times* called on the government to teach Kingsley and other "frenzied advocates of anarchy that free speech has its limits," and the local branch of the British Campaigners' Association urged the deportation of "all foreign sedition mongers."[250]

The following day Alderman Joseph Patrick proposed a resolution, unanimously adopted by Victoria City Council on 3 February, stating that "it is the duty of the public authorities to prevent the holding of such meetings or the making of such statements" and "to prosecute the persons responsible therefor." The resolution described Kingsley's "treasonable statements" as evidence "that organized efforts are being made in British Columbia and elsewhere in Canada ... to undermine or overthrow Constitutional Government and to encourage sedition and discontent."[251] The resolution also called on the government of Canada to "take immediate steps to deport all enemy aliens and Bolshevik propagandists from Canada" and "henceforth prohibit their entry, inasmuch as their presence constitutes a menace to the peace, order and good government of this Country."[252] Patrick's resolution was adopted following a "stormy half hour of interruptions," with Victoria City Hall packed with a hundred trade unionists, ex-soldiers, and socialists, including one returned soldier in uniform, using crutches, who repeatedly attempted to address the council during Patrick's speech condemning Kingsley. The disabled veteran defiantly declared that "we demand our rights and the time is coming when we will get them."[253] Several months earlier Victoria City Council had exercised its authority (on dubious legal grounds) to prohibit meetings of a local chapter of the Bible Student movement (forerunner to the Jehovah's Witnesses), and Patrick favoured taking a similar strong-arm approach to "suppress Bolsheviki meetings and speeches of the 'fire-brand' type."[254] Again Kingsley's impairments in no way smothered the flames arising from the controversy. His tenacity and organizational ability were clearly perceived as a threat by the authorities.

The controversy over Kingsley's speech in Victoria, combined with clashes between ex-soldiers and leftists in Calgary and Winnipeg, appears to have triggered threats against SPC and FLP meetings in Vancouver. A senior army officer advocated restrictions on "seditious teachings" at a meeting of the Vancouver Rotary Club, and Mayor of Vancouver Robert Gale convened a "peace conference" of returned soldiers' organizations, labour unions, and socialist groups to ensure "no official interference with 'free speech'" as long as "no seditious utterances" were permitted at socialist meetings.[255] Even so, the Vancouver FLP local scrambled to find a new venue for its Sunday mass meetings after the management of the Rex Theatre cancelled the party's standing booking.[256] In a blistering editorial in the *Red Flag,* the Socialist Party of Canada took aim at the *Vancouver Daily Sun* and other "malignant interests in Vancouver that are working might and main to foment trouble and to create sectional antagonisms amongst the working class."[257] Kingsley, meanwhile, published Lenin's "A Letter to American Workingmen" in the *Labor Star* in the immediate wake of the controversy.[258]

The hostility of establishment forces and intelligence agencies was certainly reciprocated by Kingsley and other socialists in publications such as the *Labor Star.* A front-page story, laden with Kingsley's sarcastic wit, blared out the evils of labour-management cooperation, denouncing with venom a speech given by the president of the Trades and Labor Congress of Canada at a Canadian Manufacturers' Association dinner at the Ritz-Carlton in Montreal.[259] Another story headlined not so subtly "The Class War Is Now On!" begins with the statement that "civilization is synonymous with human slavery."[260] One piece, reprinted from the American radical publication the *Nation* on the specific question of civil liberties, eloquently denounces the curtailment of civil liberties in light of the war. It condemns what it describes as the collaboration of capital and labour to allow the abolition of freedom of speech, freedom of the press, freedom of assembly, freedom of petition, and freedom of movement. The final straw, however, in the mind of the anonymous editorial writer was the growing movement to prohibit alcohol.[261] The *Labor Star* also featured advertisements for controversial radical American publications, including the *Liberator,* a magazine edited by noted writer, poet, and radical Max Eastman and his sister, Crystal Eastman, as well as legendary contributing editors such as Helen Keller and Eugene Debs. Kingsley's feminist sister, Clara Kingsley Fuller, owned shares in the *Liberator*, suggesting that its advertising strategy might not have been entirely coincidental. Copies of the *Liberator* had been seized periodically by Canadian customs even though it had not been specifically prohibited.[262]

In the wake of the Victoria Columbia Theatre controversy, federal officials in Regina and Ottawa appear to have considered seriously the prospect of deporting Kingsley from Canada. On 10 April, the commissioner of the RNWMP, A.B. Perry, requested information on whether Kingsley "has been naturalized as a British subject." Inquiries were made to the Department of the Secretary of State and to the head of the Privy Council, Newton Rowell.[263] However, no further move toward deportation appears to have been taken (perhaps on account of Kingsley's naturalization during his provincial candidacy in 1907). Although Kingsley avoided deportation, both he and his socialist cohort remained under close surveillance throughout the spring and into the summer of 1919 as Canada's emerging security apparatus responded to the formation of the One Big Union and the general strike wave that shook Winnipeg, Vancouver, Victoria, and other cities by intensifying its efforts to contain working-class radicalism.

In December 1918, the government of Canada had extended the jurisdiction of the RNWMP into British Columbia and opened detachments at Esquimalt and Vancouver.[264] The following March A.A. McLean, the RNWMP comptroller, advised the federal cabinet that his force was obtaining "accurate and complete information on the whole subject of Western Canada which will prove of the utmost value should vigorous prosecution be considered necessary."[265] In the *Labor Star*, edited by Kingsley, Pettipiece asked readers whether "the establishment of the Royal Northwest Mounted Police force in Canada is the first instalment of the democracy we were fighting for? Or is it just a plain everyday transfer of Hun kultur and kaiserism?"[266] In March and April 1919, RNWMP agents reported on activities within the FLP Vancouver branch, over which Kingsley presided, noting that attendees discussed the One Big Union and the proposed general strike on 1 June as the beginning of the revolution amid talk of "arming the revolutionists"; other police reports highlighted fears about the theft of grenades, arms, and explosives in Vancouver and radicalism within immigrant communities.[267] In May 1919, the Vancouver headquarters of Kingsley's old Socialist Party of Canada were raided by "military and civic police," the opening volley in raids on the homes and offices of socialists and labour leaders from Victoria to Saint John, as the Canadian state responded to working-class militancy in Winnipeg and other cities by initiating a national dragnet around radical organizations and leaders.[268] The arrest of Pritchard and other working-class leaders (and their subsequent conviction and incarceration on trumped-up charges of participating in a seditious conspiracy in connection with the One Big Union and Winnipeg General Strike) highlighted the tangible threat that the socialists were perceived to pose to Canadian capitalism and its state. In July, Vancouver police smashed through the front door of the *Federationist* offices and seized a quantity of paperwork as part of a raid on the Vancouver Labor Temple, the SPC headquarters, and the homes of socialists, including Pritchard, Midgley, Winch, Kavanagh, and Wells. From the home of Wells, police seized the entire records of the BCFL since its inception in 1910, with the *Federationist* accusing the dominion government of conspiring, through the RNWMP, "to establish a reign of terror so far as organized labor is concerned."[269]

In February 1920, the Dominion Police and the RNWMP merged into the newly created Royal Canadian Mounted Police amid bureaucratic infighting and different occupational cultures.[270] The Criminal Investigation Branch was divided into three sections: Criminal and Secret Service, Fingerprints, and Tickets of Leave. There was also a Central Registry that contained hundreds of files on individuals, organizations, and publications regarded as subversive. Finally, by 1922, the position of liaison intelligence officer was established.[271] The first person to fill the position was Charles Frederick Hamilton. A highly paid official, he worked closely with his colleagues at Scotland Yard and in Washington and produced a weekly bulletin on subversive radicals for the federal cabinet and prime minister.[272] Although a full history of the formative years of the RCMP is beyond the scope of our book, what becomes abundantly clear is that, despite the postwar labour revolt centred on the Winnipeg General Strike, the RCMP faced chronic underfunding in the 1920s, limiting its ability to address security concerns in a vast country and to provide training for controlling riots and halting unlawful assemblies.[273] Despite these constraints, the RCMP continued its unrelenting accumulation of security files through the 1920s. It opened nearly 6,800 subject files on radicalism and nearly 4,900 files on suspected agitators during the decade, even as the left declined sharply from its apex of postwar strength.[274]

Personal file number 15 in the RCMP security files was Eugene T. Kingsley, approaching sixty-five years of age as the turbulent decade of world war and class war gave way to the era of "capitalist consolidation" in the 1920s. However, the double amputee and former printshop owner shunned retirement, remaining on the front lines of the "battle of ideas" as president and chief propagandist of the Federated Labor Party. Kingsley was not yet willing to step back from his decades-long role spearheading the movement to conquer state power through constitutional methods – at the same time that the national security state congealed in an attempt to inoculate the Canadian elite against the threat posed by Kingsley and the radicalized working class. It is to this final phase of his political career during his twilight years that we now turn, providing a view of the politics of the left in British Columbia and Canada during the 1920s.

7

The Twilight Years
Kingsley and the 1920s Canadian Left

In an obituary in Vancouver's *Labor Statesman* shortly after the death of E.T. Kingsley in 1929, his former SPC comrade John Sidaway wrote that "the complexities of party strife and the re-alignment of factions left him during the latter part of the World War inactive, so that for some years before his death he had been in retirement."[1] To be sure, Kingsley played a less prominent role in the BC left in the 1920s compared with the intense level of activity that he had sustained since his first involvement with the Socialist Labor Party in California in the wake of his disablement in the early 1890s.[2] He also would never again play an active role in the left-wing publishing world following the demise of the *Labor Star* in the spring of 1919, which had been the central focus of his life for much of the 1900s and 1910s. However, Kingsley continued to exert influence – as a leader, an organizer, and a speaker with the Federated Labor Party, in his final run for elected office as an independent labour candidate in the federal election of 1926, and in his memorialization in the extraordinary fictional portrayal by noted BC author A.M. Stephen in his novel *The Gleaming Archway* (1929).

Regarding Kingsley's personal life, details remain sparse, unfortunately, symptomatic of the general archival record, which sheds much light on his public contributions and statements but little on his personal experiences, struggles, and thoughts. A fragment of information contained in the records of the federal Department of Immigration suggests that Kingsley might have had a brief rapprochement with his family later in life. In 1913, his son Percy Kingsley, then thirty-two years old, entered

Canada by land at the border crossing at Blaine, Washington, south of Vancouver, with his wife Clara and children Donald, age six, and Lucille, age four. The immigration record identifies the family as arriving from Duluth, Minnesota.[3] The nature of Kingsley's relationship with his son and grandchildren (as well as with his younger son, Robert, who had married and apparently settled in Ohio) following his divorce from Myra is not clear.[4] But the fact that Percy made the journey with his family to British Columbia suggests at least some ongoing communication during his father's long years away in California, Washington State, and British Columbia. It is also not clear how long Percy remained in British Columbia, though by 1920 he was living with his family in Nebraska and working, perhaps not entirely coincidentally, as a linotype operator (the 1910 census for Duluth had listed his occupation as printer).[5] Although we do not know for certain that Percy entered Canada in 1913 to visit his father, this seems to be the most probable explanation. His mother, meanwhile, appears to have remained in Minnesota continuously from the time of her divorce from Eugene shortly after his disablement: the 1920 US Census lists Myra Kingsley as living alone in an apartment in Minneapolis, with her marital status listed as divorced. She was fifty-nine at the time and employed as a junior high school teacher.[6]

Socialism through the Federated Labor Party

The final phase of Kingsley's active political involvement (other than a short spurt of activity in the 1926 federal election) was his sustained propaganda and organizational work on behalf of the Federated Labor Party. Kingsley had helped to found the party in 1918 and was at the centre of its leadership in its early years, serving for a time as president of both the provincial party and its Vancouver branch. He gave dozens of lectures from the moment that the party formed to the BC election in 1920, including a speaking tour in the BC Interior and Alberta in the midst of the Winnipeg General Strike. Although Kingsley did not stand for election as an FLP candidate in the 1920 provincial election, he would address numerous meetings and campaign events that year on behalf of FLP candidates (three of whom were elected to the BC legislature).

At an FLP "propaganda meeting" in Vancouver's Royal Theatre in February 1920, Kingsley discussed the topic of "The Ruling Class Debacle." In remarks that bore a strong resemblance to his line of thinking in preceding decades, a *longue durée* approach that traced class struggle across the millennia, Kingsley noted that capitalism would not disappear overnight. The Roman Empire, he said, had taken 1,500 years to grow and 1,300 years to die; similarly, the capitalist system was about 200 years old and had reached its climax and begun to collapse, beginning a process of decline: "It will perish off the face of the earth eventually, without us lifting a finger against it. It may take a hundred years, or two hundred; it may take as long as it has taken to attain its growth."[7] A month later Kingsley appeared again at the Royal Theatre to address the crowd at an FLP event commemorating the forty-ninth anniversary of the Paris Commune of 1871, another familiar topic. At that meeting, chaired by street railway worker Angus MacInnis, Kingsley characterized the massacre of 30,000 Parisien working-class women and men by German and French aristocratic forces as the most stupendous slaughter of slaves since Spartacus, and he predicted that "hundreds of thousands more will be slaughtered before this job is finished and the ruling class dismissed for ever."[8]

At both of these meetings in early 1920, Kingsley took aim at technological changes pursued aggressively in capitalist industries, demonstrating an evolution in his line of thinking and perhaps a glimmer of what would later be described as "postmaterial" considerations. Kingsley posited that mechanization and automation would not reduce the burden on workers and that city life itself was an unfortunate consequence of the capitalist mode of production that would have to be dispensed with in the new age. He suggested that the period of human freedom was marked not by great organized industries but by the utilization of primitive and simple means of production.[9] At a third FLP meeting in the Royal Theatre, convened in late April 1920 on the topic "The End of an Epoch," Kingsley continued to develop this argument, adopting a more ominous tone with the prediction that the machine of capitalist production "will wipe us off the face of the earth if it is allowed to go its course. I believe it will go its course, and this civilization will be wiped out."[10] This prompted the *One Big Union Bulletin*, published in Winnipeg, to comment sardonically that "our old friend E.T. Kingsley ... has become some pessimist, apparently."[11] The chair of that April FLP meeting, a woman named G.H. Taylor, had provided opening remarks to the effect that rising prices and curtailment of production of

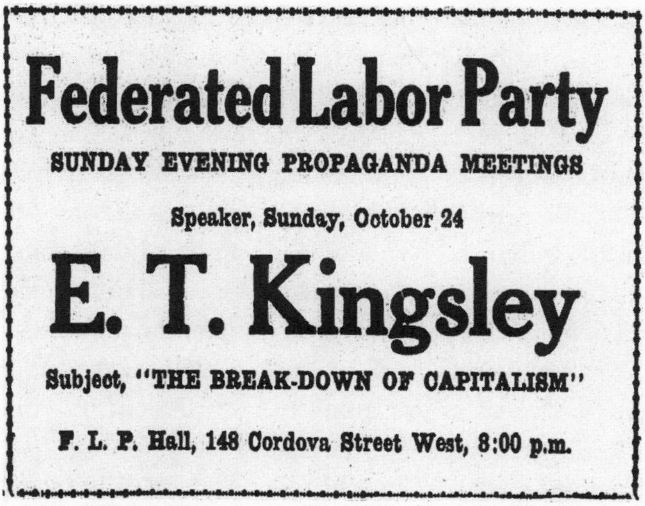

Federated Labor Party

SUNDAY EVENING PROPAGANDA MEETINGS

Speaker, Sunday, October 24

E. T. Kingsley

Subject, "THE BREAK-DOWN OF CAPITALISM"

F. L. P. Hall, 148 Cordova Street West, 8:00 p.m.

FIGURE 25   Advertisement for Kingsley's lecture on "The Break-Down of Capitalism," October 1920. | *British Columbia Federationist.*

essential goods risked exposing a majority of the globe's inhabitants to starvation unless something was done.[12] In October 1920, Kingsley continued to pursue this theme, discussing "The Break-Down of Capitalism" in a meeting at the new FLP hall on Cordova Street in Vancouver.[13]

The BC election of 1920 was hotly contested and the most diverse from a partisan standpoint in the province's political history, with an array of labour, socialist, farmer, and soldier candidates and parties cutting into Liberal and Conservative support. This mirrored patterns in other Canadian provinces, notably Alberta, Manitoba, and Ontario, where the war crisis loosened allegiances to the "old line" parties, creating an opening for the election of a farmer-labour government in Ontario in 1919 and a farmer government in Alberta a year later. However, in British Columbia, this moment of postwar political instability did not result in a break from the old line parties, with the Liberal Party led by John Oliver, a farmer, securing a narrow majority with twenty-five of forty-five legislative seats and 38 percent of the vote.[14] The Federated Labor Party was the strongest third party in the 1920 BC election, with its fourteen candidates capturing 9 percent of the popular vote. Three FLP candidates were elected – miner Tom Uphill in Fernie (who would go on to serve as a Labor MLA for the next forty years, simultaneously serving for most of that period as the town's mayor), typographer Harry Neelands in South Vancouver, and miner Samuel Guthrie in Newcastle (who had been jailed for his role during the 1912–14 Vancouver Island coal strike). Guthrie defeated socialist stalwart James Hawthornthwaite, who contested the election as an independent socialist candidate. His defeat following many years of electoral success revealed a rift within the island socialist movement, particularly in the wake of inflammatory remarks that he made at a public FLP meeting two years earlier against the young Bolshevik government in Russia (describing Lenin and Trotsky as "snakes of the working-class movement"), remarks not looked on favourably by a broad section of the BC working class at the time.[15]

The imprint of Kingsley and the Marxist strain of BC socialism was apparent in the electoral messaging of the Federated Labor Party: "The henchman of the exploiters of Labor will be placed on the defensive," the *Federationist* noted during the campaign. "The bulwarks and institutions of capitalism will be the point of attack."[16] Alongside that party, the Socialist Party of Canada fielded seven candidates of its own in the 1920 election, and collectively they received 3.5 percent of the popular vote, while a loose amalgamation of eleven soldier-farmer and soldier-labour candidates took 3 percent of the vote. Three independent MLAs and one "People's Party" MLA were also elected to the BC legislature, resulting in the most eclectic legislature in the province's history.[17]

Kingsley becomes difficult to track following the BC provincial election in December 1920. In our extensive research, we found only a smattering of sources related to his activities in the years that followed: a speech at an FLP meeting in Vancouver in May 1921; an article during the Canadian parliamentary election in 1921 (lambasting the moral and intellectual bankruptcy of the old line parties), and three speeches in 1925, two of them on the topic of "Civilization versus Nature" (in Nanaimo in March) and the third at an FLP-sponsored educational retreat in the Okanagan Valley on "The Case of the Farmer" (at the Summerland School of Social Science in August).[18] Beyond these fragments of political activity, there is silence in the labour and left-wing press. The usual steady record of speeches, writings, and organizational work that became a mainstay of the socialist, labour, and bourgeois press wherever Kingsley went – providing a continuous marker of his political life from his first involvement in California in the early 1890s to his work in British Columbia in the early 1920s – virtually disappears. This silence presumably signals the beginning of a sustained period of retreat from the rigorous level of activity that Kingsley had maintained more or less continuously for more than twenty-five years. We are left to speculate about the reasons for this retreat in the absence of his own writings or other corroborating material. What is clear is that by the early 1920s Kingsley found himself increasingly separated and isolated from the radical movement that he had helped to nurture as the movement itself entered into a period of decline.

His speech on the forty-ninth anniversary of the Paris Commune offers perhaps the most potent clues about the trajectory of his political thought and isolation in the early 1920s. Likening the slaughter of the Communards in 1871 to the eradication of the slave followers of Spartacus, Kingsley noted that even the most well-versed socialists in radical history did not overcome the German armies. Their failure, he said, was the failure of coming to being a century and a half too soon. The failure of the Winnipeg General Strike, in contrast, was that the revolt, by ignoring the necessity of political action, had made the workers "liable to the fangs and claws of the state."[19] Kingsley went on to speculate that the entire slave civilization was on the verge of collapse and that it would die by its own hand, in a process that was as natural as it was unavoidable. This had been a theme prominent in his early writings and speeches, but a key component was missing: the presence of a revolutionary, constitutionally elected party to usher in the new age.[20]

For Kingsley, this was his final exclusion from radical politics. Beyond the politics of the individual leaders, the entire political field of the BC radical movement quickly changed shape. The Federated Labor Party – his last great political effort, which he had helped to usher onto the political scene – plateaued in the early 1920s, achieving no great electoral coup at any level of government. Rising from the ashes, wrote one editorial of the day, was the One Big Union, the representative of a direct action and general strike sentiment that, though new to BC labour, would have reminded Kingsley of the conflicts that wracked the Socialist Labor Party of America at the turn of the century. He was truly the Old Man now – and his nickname was more apt than ever. No longer could he pull stakes and strike out to virgin soil where no presence of radical politics was felt. What was common ground between British Columbia and San Francisco – the seemingly endless possibility and equal playing field that impossibilism fed on – would need to be pursued elsewhere for the gospel to be brought out further. And Kingsley was far too old to start over again.

Although the politics of the Winnipeg General Strike and wider syndicalist wave embodied in the OBU ideal had isolated Kingsley, his ostracization was complete after the eclipse of the One Big Union as a unifying political force and following the rancorous debate within his old Socialist Party of Canada over affiliation with the Third International. This shift engendered a new dichotomy between revolutionary Bolshevists and non-revolutionary socialists, first by the state, which prosecuted it under those terms, and then by the labour movement, which internalized that division. This would force on BC socialists a decision that completely excluded the old guard of constitutional Marxists from its terms of reference. To be a revolutionary non-Bolshevist was swiftly becoming non-sensical, and, to quote a contemporary appeal in the labour press, "a neutral position was impossible."[21]

Revolutionary Turn: The Birth of the Workers' Party

The early 1920s signalled another period of realignment on the BC and Canadian left as the Socialist Party of Canada was split by a protracted and deeply divisive debate about whether or not to affiliate with the Third International of workers' and socialist parties, the Communist International (Comintern). We do not know Kingsley's position on this debate, but we can surmise based on his uncompromising attitude in earlier debates within the Socialist Labor Party and Socialist Party of Canada that Kingsley likely would have sided with the non-communist camp, which included his friend Wallis Lefeaux as well as party luminaries Bill Pritchard, Ernest Winch, Victor Midgley, and others, who decided to stay out of the Moscow-led Third International and continue to chart an independent, Canadian path to socialism.

The debate was initiated in earnest on 1 January 1921 when the *Western Clarion* published on its front page the conditions issued by Lenin and the Soviet government for joining the Third International, which succeeded the prewar Second International of workers' and socialist parties.[22]

To be sure, debates about the Russian road to socialism and the relationship between the Russian Communist Party and socialists in Canada and other states had comprised a central focus of the Socialist Party of Canada and BC leftists since the Russian Revolution of 1917 (and indeed a focus of SPC propaganda work extending back to the Bloody Sunday massacre in St. Petersburg that served as a catalyst for the Russian Revolution of 1905 and that Kingsley discussed on many occasions in the years that followed).[23] High-profile breaches in the BC socialist movement on the Russian question, such as FLP MLA Hawthornthwaite's public condemnation of the Bolsheviks in January 1919, following discussions with Russian émigré and former Socialist-Revolutionary Party leader Yekaterina Breshkovskaya ("the Grandmother of the Russian Revolution"), highlighted concerns among a section of BC leftists about the authoritarian methods deployed by Lenin and his comrades in their bid to dismantle feudal and capitalist property relations and transform Russia into a socialist republic.[24] Revealing his distance from Kingsley, who had been a close ally, Hawthornthwaite sarcastically remarked at the time that he and Kingsley could follow the example of Lenin and Trotsky, who "abolished the state and established an oligarchy, an oligarchy of four or five men ... My friend Kingsley and I would be great if we established ourselves that way."[25] The fact that this public condemnation of the Lenin government aligned with the ideological and economic imperatives of the Canadian capitalist class (as well as military imperatives at a time when Canadian troops were deployed on four fronts in Russia) was not lost on some leftists, who strongly believed that Hawthornthwaite had entered into a treasonous collaboration with the enemy.[26]

Statements from Lenin and the Bolsheviks, such as a widely circulated "Letter to American Workingmen," which Kingsley published in full in the *Labor Star* in early 1919, established fault lines in a global class struggle that resonated with many SPC members:

> The workers of the whole world, in whatever country they may live, rejoice with us and sympathize with us, applaud us for having burst the iron ring of imperialistic agreements and treaties, for having dreaded no sacrifice, however great, to free ourselves, for having established ourselves as a Socialist republic ... What wonder that we are hated by the capitalist

class the world over. But this hatred of imperialism and the sympathy of the class-conscious workers of all countries give us assurance of the righteousness of our cause.[27]

The undeniable hatred of the Canadian bourgeoisie and state actors for the Lenin government, as exemplified by the sustained attack of business-aligned newspapers and Canada's emerging security state apparatus since 1917, had the effect of driving many Canadian workers and socialists into open sympathy with the Russian Bolsheviks. Their own experience of class inequality and class struggle in Canada provided a framework through which they interpreted events in Russia; in turn, the revolutionary process in Russia increasingly provided a framework through which they came to interpret their own class position and options for social transformation in Canada.

Finally, there were direct connections established between the BC left and the Bolshevik government of Russia (which had rebranded itself the Russian Communist Party in 1918, following the establishment of the Russian Socialist Federative Soviet Republic, the world's first constitutionally socialist state, which itself would merge with other former czarist territories into the Union of Soviet Socialist Republics in 1922). Hawthornthwaite claimed to have met Lenin during his travels in Europe prior to the revolution, when the Soviet leader was in exile.[28] A Victoria longshore worker, who defended the Bolsheviks in a letter to the *Semi-Weekly Tribune* during the controversy over Kingsley's Columbia Theatre speech in January 1919, said that he knew Trotsky personally before the war as Mickey Brennan of Detroit.[29] Other BC leftists travelled to Soviet Russia after the revolution to observe first-hand the social transformation occurring in that country. In the autumn of 1920, on the eve of the publication of Lenin's "21 Points," SPC stalwart Wallis Lefeaux, a Vancouver lawyer and close Kingsley confidant (who would be identified as his "friend" on Kingsley's death certificate), toured Soviet Russia. He travelled via Sweden, with Lenin's trade envoy Lev Kamenev, and spent more than a month in Moscow, mixing with Soviet officials and foreign visitors and closely observing conditions in Soviet Russia. On his return to North America on the Red Star liner *Lapland* in late 1920, Lefeaux was interviewed by the *New York Times*. He said that he was not a communist or in favour of its doctrines, but he predicted that a modified form of communist government would ultimately prevail in Soviet Russia: "The more moderate members of the party will win out in the end, but the people will never return to any of the older forms of government. The Communist Party controls everything and is really well disciplined, with a definite object, and that is the establishment of communism first in Russia and afterward throughout the world." Lefeaux noted the growth of membership in the Russian Communist Party, from 40,000 members at the time of the Bolshevik Revolution to 800,000 members during his visit, and it was "gaining more recruits every day."[30]

As BC socialists debated whether or not to affiliate formally with the Russian communists, the Canadian state closely monitored developments. Publication of Lenin's "21 Points"[31] on the front page of the *Western Clarion* prompted an urgent inquiry from the assistant commissioner of the RCMP, Cortlandt Starnes, to Deputy Minister of Justice E.L. Newcombe. Starnes inquired about whether that particular issue of the newspaper contravened the *Criminal Code of Canada,* particularly Section 97B, which prohibited "any association ... whose professed purpose ... is to bring about any governmental, industrial or economic change within Canada by use of force, violence or physical injury to person or property" (a measure hastily adopted in the midst of the Winnipeg General Strike and sympathy strikes in 1919).[32] The RCMP officer highlighted "a number of passages ... which appear to be revolutionary in character."[33] In his reply to the inquiry from Starnes, the Department of Justice official provided the opinion that the publication fell "within the inhibition of Section 97B of the *Criminal Code.*"[34]

In the midst of the debate about affiliation within the Socialist Party of Canada, the *Federationist* and its editor, Albert Wells of Victoria, would be charged with attempting to force a "government change" by serializing Lenin's *"Left-Wing" Communism: An Infantile Disorder* (1920). The work took aim at "left communists" in Germany, Britain, and elsewhere whom the Russian Bolshevik leader criticized for refusing to work within unions, suggesting that the slogan "no compromises" was an example of using theory as dogma rather than a "guide to action."[35] In March 1921, the *Western Clarion* published Lenin's *"Left-Wing" Communism* on its front page, but no equivalent criminal sanction appears to have been taken against the SPC newspaper.[36]

The debate about Canadian affiliation with the Third International was shaped by the response of Canadian leftists to the class struggle in Canada and to the revolution in Russia and hinged on the degree of authority that they were prepared to vest in the Russian leadership over their activities in Canada, as scholars including Campbell, Kawecki, Isitt, and others have noted.[37] Elements of Lenin's "21 Points," including the first one, were unpalatable to some leftists but resonated with others: "The daily propaganda must bear a truly Communist character ... On the pages of newspapers, at popular meetings, in the labor unions, in the co-operatives, in every place to which the partisans of the Third International have access, they must denounce not only the bourgeoisie, but its assistants, the reformists of all shade and color."[38] Other points insisted on the formation of a parallel illegal apparatus in every country, the adoption of the name Communist Party, and the removal of "all reformists and partisans of the 'centre' ... from all responsible posts in the Labor movement."[39] Although SPC members such as Fred Kaplan of Winnipeg urged comrades "to strive for an affirmative vote in the name of the Revolution," others – including Jack Harrington of Vancouver – argued against the proposal, foreseeing "a series of bitter struggles that would hamper and in the end nullify our educational work," warning that the debate was being shaped by "spite, policy, friendship, [and] jealousy" and not by "class needs."[40] Another party stalwart, former *Western Clarion* editor Chris Stephenson, was in favour of autonomy for Canadian socialists rather than deferral to the leadership of the Russian Bolsheviks:

> I get an impression of the Executive Committee as a General Staff marshalling revolutionary forces in the field of action. However that may be, I count it folly and to the disadvantage of the movement for an E.C., while sitting so far away from the scenes of political activity in all parts of the world, to lay down set regulations to cover widely varying social situations.[41]

In the midst of the debate, the Socialist Party of Canada sent a donation of $152 to the Soviet Russian Medical Relief Committee, raised by Russian immigrants in Vancouver.[42]

As the referendum was under way, events unfolded in eastern Canada that established a new trajectory for a section of the Canadian left. In a barn outside Guelph, Ontario, in late May and early June 1921, twenty-two delegates from Manitoba, Ontario, and Montreal (including one RCMP agent) decided to form the Workers' Party of Canada as a Canadian affiliate to the Third International (it would be renamed the Communist Party of Canada when Parliament allowed the *War Measures Act, 1914* to lapse in 1924).[43] The meeting was held in secret, reflecting the climate of state repression in the immediate postwar years in Canada, as well as the tradition of underground work within the pre-1917 Russian Bolshevik party, which had an influence on organizing practices among its adherents in Canada. Although this founding meeting took place in secret, its existence quickly became common knowledge on the Canadian left: "Enter – the Workers' Party," an editorial in the *Western Clarion* proclaimed.[44]

The results of the SPC referendum on affiliation with the Comintern would never appear in the pages of the *Western Clarion*. But the *Federationist* reported in January 1922 that "the vote went decidedly in favour of affiliation."[45] Several locals had voted unanimously in favour, and though the results cited by the newspaper were incomplete it did list 79 for affiliation compared with 69 opposed to it. In Victoria, members voted 11–6 for affiliation. Vancouver, meanwhile, registered the strongest vote against it: 37 opposed compared with 24 in favour.[46] According to historian Peter Campbell, Pritchard and Kavanagh – shoulder to shoulder for the One Big Union at Calgary in 1919 – nearly came to blows at a meeting in Vancouver in late 1921 as their Socialist Party disintegrated on the divisive question of Russian Communism.[47] Pritchard, who had recently returned to Vancouver after serving his sentence for sedition in connection with the Winnipeg General Strike and would remain in the Socialist Party of Canada rather than join the Communist Party, attributed the decline of the former party squarely to the split associated with the "21 Points" of the Comintern:

> I imagine it was the split that came over Lenin's "21 Points." We wouldn't take it. And we didn't ask for it to be sent to us ... That's the split that took place. It has been an incubus on what I consider to be the socialist

movement ever since ... Their policy is whatever ... happens to be the latest edict from Moscow ... Whether it's Moscow or Jerusalem, if it's the word, reject it. It's got to be subjected to criticism.[48]

Kavanagh, for his part, issued an open letter signed on behalf of twenty former members of SPC Vancouver Local No. 1 dismissing the party as "an academic institution, not a political party of the working class." Although it had once been "one of the clearest Marxist groups on the continent," the organization had deteriorated into a mere debating society, divorced from workers' domestic and global struggles. "To us the road is clear. We will go forward with the revolutionary workers of the Third International."[49]

The split over affiliation with the Third International precipitated a terminal decline for the Socialist Party of Canada. Whereas the earlier split that gave rise to the SDPC in 1907 and the emergence of the Federated Labor Party in 1918 had sapped members, energy, resources, votes, and influence from the Socialist Party of Canada, particularly among workers who had grown impatient waiting for the revolution, and who sought practical improvements to conditions in the here and now, the Workers' Party of Canada posed a more existential threat to the Socialist Party of Canada. This was because it had the same uncompromisingly anti-capitalist and overtly Marxist political orientation of the Socialist Party of Canada but, unlike it, offered an alternative pole of attraction to Canadian workers that was tied to immediate struggles in the workplace as well as to the first example of "actually existing socialism" in the world (however distorted, as socialists would debate for the remainder of the twentieth century). The raison d'être of the Socialist Party of Canada largely disappeared following the debate about affiliation and with the emergence of the Workers' Party of Canada, squeezed between FLP reformism and communist revolutionary politics.

In 1925, the *Western Clarion* suspended publication for the final time, signalling the demise of the Socialist Party of Canada as a vital force on the BC and Canadian left.[50] The death of the newspaper fuelled a brief flurry of introspection among former SPC militants. In a rambling, impressionistic piece in the *Labor Statesman*, Kingsley's friend Wallis Lefeaux reflected on the ideological milieu within which the party had operated: "IWW, OBU, AF of L, Syndicalists, Socialists, Anarchists, Communists and Christians ... each hold forth on their special road and solution of man's ills. The Federation of the World – The Parliament of Man – not yet." The war and the Bolshevik Revolution had "jarred the preconceived notions somewhat," and "the recovery is not yet."[51] Canadian Labor Party Vice-President John Sidaway commented on the Socialist Party of Canada and the demise of the *Western Clarion:*

> Its philosophy was suitable and successful in an era of prosperity when the IWW and the AF of L were flourishing locally. But with the loss of the miners' union on Vancouver Island and industrial stagnation the power of these organizations waned and with it the SP of C and its mouthpiece. The *Clarion* represented an era in the socialist movement which culminated with the Russian Revolution ... Its circle of friends narrowed with the years until of late only a few of the faithful were on hand to prepare its funeral.[52]

The bleakest prognosis appeared in the *Western Clarion* itself and was reprinted in the *Labor Statesman.* Jack Harrington, one of the few SPC faithful in 1925, summed up the waning fortunes of the organization: "From the prophetic preaching of capital's collapse and exhorting to the revolution, we have passed through and beyond back to a period, void and empty to any revolutionary outlook."[53] The *One Big Union Bulletin*, for its part, spared little energy eulogizing the Socialist Party of Canada and its mouthpiece: "The passing of the *Clarion* seems to forecast the burial of the party. There is little regret at the passing of either."[54]

Although a remnant of the party would carry on, revolutionary Marxists had gravitated to the Communist Party, whereas electorally oriented socialists migrated in new directions. In February 1926, the remaining FLP Vancouver branches merged with the Labor Parties of South Vancouver and New Westminster into a new Independent Labor Party (ILP).[55] "The FLP is to be congratulated on sinking its identity for the general good," the *Labor Statesman* commented, hinting that even the Socialist Party of Canada was considering joining the new formation (which does not appear to have occurred).[56] The founding ILP constitution stipulated that all locals must also maintain affiliation with the Canadian Labor Party (CLP), a short-lived coalition of communist, socialist, and labourist forces formed in 1924 as part of a national effort toward independent labour political action. It contested several elections in British Columbia (including the 1924 provincial election, in which CLP candidates maintained three legislative seats with 11 percent of the vote, and the 1925 federal election, in which none of the five BC CLP candidates was elected).[57] There is no evidence that Kingsley either sought a CLP nomination or played a role in supporting the election of CLP candidates in either election. But he would have one more campaign under his belt.

The Final Run

In 1926, Kingsley made his final run for elected office, standing as an independent labour candidate for Parliament in the riding of Vancouver Centre. The motivation behind his candidacy, occurring fifteen years after his last campaign in the 1911 federal election, and without the apparent backing of any party or organization, remains unclear. A news report the day of the election, 14 September, noted that Kingsley had announced he was running "on a Labor ticket," though he had not been endorsed by the Canadian Labor Party.[58] Although the Canadian Labor Party mounted strong campaigns in several ridings, nominating five candidates, including Pritchard in Burnaby and Lefeaux in North Vancouver, it declined to endorse Kingsley, reflecting the Old Man's diminished support on the left.[59] Eleven days before the election, the party made it clear through the *Labor Statesman* that Kingsley (whom it did not name) was running without CLP backing or that of any other working-class organization:

> In order that there may be no misunderstanding regarding the candidature of labour candidates in Vancouver Centre, as announced in Wednesday's *Province*, we desire to make it known that the Canadian Labor Party is not running a labor candidate in Vancouver Centre, neither has it endorsed any candidate and as far as we know, no labor organization, political or industrial, has anything to do with the candidature of any one in that constituency.[60]

On the day of the election, an unnamed "labour leader," quoted by the *Vancouver Sun*, predicted that most workers were voting for Kingsley's Liberal opponent, lawyer and former MP Dugald Donaghy, but "with no candidate of their own ... Labor men will be free to uphold the party of their choice."[61]

At issue was the close federal contest between the Conservatives led by Arthur Meighen and the Liberals led by William Lyon Mackenzie King and the intrigue surrounding the "King-Byng affair" that had seen Canada's governor general decline King's request for an election and briefly install Meighen as prime minister (he subsequently lost a confidence vote and was granted an election). Prior to this transfer of power, King's Liberals were in a tenuous de facto coalition with the two Labor Party MPs (Woodsworth and Heaps of Winnipeg) and some members of the Progressive Party, reflected in an Old Age Pensions Bill that the Liberals introduced in Parliament. A correspondent writing in the *Vancouver Daily Sun* discussed Kingsley's candidacy in this broader context:

> The nomination of E.T. Kingsley as a Labor Independent candidate in Vancouver Centre smacks of the mysterious. He is not supported by the official Labor Party, is not affiliated with any party at all, so far as one can find out. I have heard it suggested he is being financed by a party which is fearing defeat ...
>
> I think the three-cornered contest will go far to defeat any desire Mr. Kingsley may have to further the policy of labor.
>
> Mr. Kingsley, and those who may think of supporting him, should remember that Labor members of the House at Ottawa supported the Old Age Pensions Bill brought in by the Liberals. Any vote next week against Mr. Donaghy would appear to me to be a vote against the chance of pensions for the aged ... I may safely venture to give a warning to voters to beware of the "third party," namely Mr. Kingsley.[62]

Notwithstanding this apparent lack of support from the Vancouver left and the broader public, Kingsley was included among a list of twenty-two "working people and farmers' candidates" recommended by the Finnish newspaper *Vapaus* ("Freedom"), published in Sudbury. This Communist Party–aligned publication (banned during the First World War and threatened with suppression throughout the 1920s) declared confidently (in an article in Finnish) that, once elected to Parliament, these candidates would "expose the shortcomings of the capitalist form of society" and "express

FIGURE 26   Campaign advertisement during Kingsley's final run for public office, as an independent labour candidate for Member of Parliament for Vancouver during the 1926 Canadian federal election. | *Vancouver Daily Province.*

the demands of the Canadian Labor Party and Communist Party's minimum program and act, to the best of their ability, for them to be put into effect."[63] The *Vancouver Daily Province,* meanwhile, described Kingsley as "a veteran Socialist-Labor campaigner," observing that "in earlier days in the city he was a colorful figure in local politics."[64] During the campaign, he hosted at least two meetings, on 9 September in the Hamilton Hall and on 12 September in the Royal Theatre.[65]

On polling day, 14 September 1926, Kingsley was roundly defeated, finishing far back in the three-way race, with a meagre 527 votes compared with nearly 8,500 for the Liberal candidate, Donaghy, and 10,300 for the successful Conservative incumbent (and cabinet minister), H.H. Stevens.[66] No labour or socialist candidate was elected from British Columbia in that election, though Bill Pritchard increased the labour vote in New Westminster from 3,305 to 4,268, and A.W. Neill, an independent candidate in Comox-Alberni who had been endorsed by the Port Alberni

Independent Labor Party, was re-elected to Parliament.[67] Nationally, Labor candidates J.S. Woodsworth and A.A. Heaps were re-elected in Winnipeg, along with Labor candidate H.B. Adshead in East Calgary, Agnes MacPhail representing the farmers of Ontario, Henri Bourassa of Quebec, and eleven members of the United Farmers of Alberta. Despite the election of a Liberal majority government, Labor's representation in Parliament increased slightly to three members, while the "Ginger Group" of farmer and labour MPs expanded to seventeen, strengthening the basis for a socialist-oriented third party in Canada.[68]

At 2.7 percent of the popular vote, Kingsley's federal candidacy in Vancouver in 1926 resulted in the lowest level of support of any of his campaigns for public office (with the exception of his first municipal run in California), revealing his growing political isolation in the years leading up to his death. In comparison, Kingsley had received between 3 and 4 percent in his 1896 and 1898 US congressional runs, about 10 percent in his previous Canadian parliamentary runs for Vancouver MP in 1908 and 1911, and 18 percent in the two-way race against Bowser for Vancouver MLA in the 1907 by-election (see Appendix 2).[69] Among candidates in the 1926 election, the contrast between Kingsley's result in Vancouver City and support received by Pritchard in neighbouring New Westminster and by Woodsworth and others in urban areas elsewhere in the country suggests that there was no general nadir of socialist electoral support in the mid-1920s, at least not in those areas where the working class was sufficiently organized politically. Kingsley's low level of support in 1926 more likely reflected his diminished profile within the Vancouver electorate as well as his political isolation from the working-class parties of the day. During his previous candidacies in the United States and Canada, Kingsley was the leading figure in the Socialist Labor Party and Socialist Party of Canada; by 1926, no working-class party would identify with him. It is puzzling that he chose to stand for office in this context, but this is yet another mystery in his atypical political life.

After the 1926 election, we can find no record of Kingsley's political life. Kingsley appears to have begun retirement in the years immediately leading up to his death, with the 1928 Vancouver city directory identifying him as retired. This period coincided with yet another process of transition for the left in Vancouver, British Columbia, and Canada – one that would produce a more durable organizational form. In 1928, the volatile Canadian Labor Party in British Columbia imploded ostensibly because of the issue of "Oriental" enfranchisement but in fact reflecting deep-seated antipathies between socialists and communists, ending "years of disagreements on an alleged United Front."[70] The Independent Labor Party would carry on, through several organizational permutations, to become, as a reinvigorated Socialist Party of Canada, the BC section of the Co-operative Commonwealth Federation in 1932.[71] This marked the end of the formative phase of BC socialism and the beginning of a more institutionalized phase (to invoke sociologist Leo Zakuta's analytical lens), which continues to the present with the CCF transition into the New Democratic Party in 1961.[72] In four subsequent provincial elections (1972, 1991, 2017, and 2020), the resulting labour-aligned party born from these transitions succeeded in "conquering the public powers," though the extent to which this resulted in the implementation of labour's economic program remains a matter of debate. Kingsley's professed goal – seizing state power to legislate an end to capitalist exploitation – remains an item of unfinished business on the agenda of the BC and Canadian left.

Commemoration in Fiction: *The Gleaming Archway*

A.M. Stephen's novel *The Gleaming Archway,* published the same year as Kingsley's death, is an extraordinary fictional portrayal of the Old Man. Alexander Maitland Stephen (1882–1942), poet, political radical, fiction author, and First World War veteran, penned this novel that so accurately depicts political conflict in British Columbia in the years before the First World War. Born in Ontario, Stephen was raised in Victoria and briefly articled at his uncle's law firm at the age of sixteen. Finding the world of law too stifling for his growing radicalism, he abandoned his career in law to go prospecting for gold in the Klondike.[73] In his early years, Stephen held a wide array of jobs, including life insurance salesman in Victoria, cow puncher in Alberta, and logger in Oregon, until he began studying architecture at the University of Chicago. Ending those studies in 1913, he moved to England before the First World War and enlisted in the military. After injuring his wrist in France, he returned to Vancouver to start his own structural engineering firm.[74]

Stephen was an active member of the SPC for two decades, withdrawing in the 1930s over concerns that the party was veering too much toward social democracy. He was identified by the legendary poet, Earle Birney, as a potential recruit for the nascent Canadian Trotskyist movement following his break from the SPC.[75] Stephen played a pioneering role in the dissemination of birth control information around this time, paving the way for the growth of the Birth Control League of Canada. In the 1920s, he worked for the left-wing weekly the *Western Tribune.* His first book of poetry, *The Rosary of Pan,* appeared in 1923. His first novel, *Kingdom of the Sun,* appeared in 1927. It concerns an adventurer named Richard Anson who sails aboard Sir Francis Drake's galleon, the *Golden Hind,* but ends up with the Haida and meets a golden-haired princess, Auria.[76] Stephen would go on to found the BC branch of the League against War and Fascism and run as a CCF candidate in the riding of Alberni-Nanaimo. He was later expelled from the Co-operative Commonwealth Federation for advocating a popular front with the Communist Party and for his passion for fighting fascism in the Spanish Civil War.[77]

The Gleaming Archway is a historical novel about romantic love and politics set in British Columbia around 1905.[78] It contains not one but two fictional portraits of real-life characters. The protagonist, a journalist named Craig Maitland, is a thinly veiled self-portrait of the author himself. Maitland spends a vacation in the Squamish Valley, where he encounters a cast of colourful characters, including a beautiful Englishwoman, a Russian radical emigré, Kolazoff, a British Tory, and a socialist newspaper editor, Tacey. He falls in love with a married woman, Jocelyn Paget, while struggling to figure out whether the solution to society's problems is through class struggle or more spiritual (theosophical) ideas. The novel ends with Maitland reunited with a newly widowed Paget.[79] Although the self-portrait of Stephen is apparent to the reader, what is not well known is that the novel also features a character (Tacey) clearly based on Kingsley. The evidence is overwhelming since Tacey is referred to affectionately as "the Old Man" and depicted as a socialist amputee who edits a newspaper, the *Beacon,* clearly representing the *Clarion.*[80] Stephen goes so far as to mirror in his character the circumstances of Kingsley's radicalization: Tacey is a former "railroad man" who "lost his arm ... in a wreck": "Best thing ever happen him. He took to readin' books and pretty soon went in for Socialist work altogether."[81]

Stephen's description of Tacey is so detailed that it sheds further light on contemporary understandings of Kingsley:

> Despite the tricks of the politician and a catering to the careless vernacular of the working-man, Tacey's address was logical, convincing, and suggestive of a powerful intellectual grasp of the subject of economics. There could be no doubt of the man's sincerity. The gospel according to Marx was his Bible and the idealistic social State was his religion. He would as willingly die for his dream as any martyr for his interpretation of a Scriptural comma. Body and soul, his idea possessed him. Yet, mellowing his orthodoxy, was a glowing humanitarianism – a great kindliness that drew these rough men to him and held them while he chastised them for their own good. "Slaves," "timber-beasts," "working mules," were among the epithets with which he lovingly belabored them. When he had delivered his last word, they thought that they knew the meaning of "capital," of "class-consciousness," of "bourgeoisie," and of "proletariat." They felt convinced that "the interests of the worker and the employing class were diametrically opposed," and that, to serve their own interests, they must support Labor at the coming election.[82]

This description vividly conveys how Kingsley's orthodox beliefs were respected by his peers even if they did not always agree with his political prescriptions. Stephen also provides potent insight into Tacey's (and by extension Kingsley's) personal characteristics, describing Tacey as being as

> rugged as a bit of granite, stern and uncompromising in his devotion to humanity, [yet] his driving will was tempered by a great kindliness and was rendered strong by loneliness which sought refuge in incessant action. The Old Man, he remembered, had slept homeless and penniless, under the hall wherein he had first discovered his power as an orator. The "masses" had pennies for beer, but very little to spare for those who sacrificed comfort to bring them a message of hope and freedom. It was indeed a long hard road which this man had chosen for himself.[83]

Kingsley's Passing

E.T. Kingsley died in the night of 8 December 1929. His death certificate recorded the cause of death as "syncope and asphyxia from an apparently accidental inhalation of illuminating gas."[84] He died alone in a rooming house at 309 West Pender Street in downtown Vancouver, where he had resided for two months prior to his death. Wallis Lefeaux, a fellow socialist stalwart from the SPC days identified on the death certificate as Kingsley's "friend," provided the particulars.[85] Kingsley's cause of death unfortunately was all too common at the time, with a scholarly study identifying 826 accidental deaths from carbon monoxide poisoning from gas appliances in New York City in 1926 alone (a number that would decline by almost 75 percent in the next quarter-century because of the replacement of gas lighting fixtures, improved design, and more rigid standards of product inspection and testing).[86] The study also notes, however, that "carbon monoxide poisoning by inhalation of raw illuminating gas has also been the most common cause of suicidal death."[87] Although we cannot rule out the possibility that Kingsley took his own life, there is no archival material to support that conclusion. A report in the *Vancouver Daily Sun* noted that his body was found on the morning of 9 December at "about 9:30 a.m." and that "death, which is believed to have been due to heart trouble, came suddenly. There was an odor of gas from a leaking gas plate in the room, but not enough to be dangerous."[88]

Kingsley was cremated at the Mountain View Crematorium, operated by the City of Vancouver, and there is no record of how his ashes were disposed.[89] There is also no indication of a public funeral or any other public expression of grief or remembrance from his socialist comrades or his family – from whom he had been estranged for a number of years. But it appears that Kingsley's former wife, Myra, and sons Percy and Robert were aware of his passing. Myra, then age seventy and still working as a public school teacher in Minneapolis, described herself as a widow to a US Census enumerator less than a month after Eugene's death.[90]

In an obituary in the *Labor Statesman,* which we reproduce in full in Appendix 4, former Socialist MLA Parker Williams asserted that, "on the Labor thought of the province, E.T. Kingsley has left a deeper mark than any other man." Williams provided rare insight into the personal life of

Kingsley, including how he grappled with his life experience as a double amputee:

> While up to recent years the name and face [were] familiar to most of the adult population of the province, still few, if any, really knew the man. He was ever ready to listen and sympathize with the troubles of others; his own troubles were shared with no one. As a young man he lost both his lower limbs in railroading, but he acquired a wonderful mastery over two artificial substitutes. We know that they were a pain and an inconvenience, but even this trouble he held to himself and scorned the sympathy that, to some of us, seems to lighten a burden.[91]

Another SPC comrade, John Sidaway, also reflected on the disability of Kingsley in the wake of his death, suggesting that

> few who saw him carefully thread his way, with the aid of a cane and a pair of artificial limbs, through Vancouver traffic, realized the extent of his physical disabilities. But his grim and resolute determination as a fighter in the class conflict did not fail him in bearing his infirmities without complaint. He would respectfully and sympathetically hear the woes of others, but never mentioned his own.[92]

Reflecting on his legendary oratory and polemical style, Sidaway described Kingsley as "a forceful speaker, an able writer, and a clear thinker, [and] he could, with one terse comment or a casual query, make an adversary and his arguments look foolish."[93] On his contribution to the labour and socialist movements, Sidaway suggested that "his influence as a leader of the Marxian group in Western Canada was to infect most Labor organizations to a greater or lesser degree with the class viewpoint. His favorite theme was the struggle of the slaves through the ages. The Paris Commune of 1871 was a subject which saw him at his best."[94]

Conclusion
Reflections on E.T. Kingsley's Political Life

In the many decades after his death, Eugene T. Kingsley was largely forgotten beyond a small coterie of old socialist comrades and some specialists in the historiography of the BC left. The founder and leader of "the British Columbia School" of socialism (as historian Ross McCormack described it) might have left an imprint on the ideology of the BC and Canadian working class, but there was no trace of a personal legacy or public form of commemoration.[1] To be sure, Kingsley would be mentioned occasionally in the years after his passing, particularly in the left-wing press in Canada and other lands, including in a letter from "A Kingsleyite" in the *One Big Union Bulletin* in the 1930s and a smattering of references in Australian labour newspapers until the 1940s.[2] Generally, however, his contribution to the left and his personal and political struggles were largely forgotten. We hope, therefore, that this work, which applies a critical disability lens to the intellectual and political development of North American labour and society, will help to spur a belated honouring of Kingsley's contribution – all the more remarkable in light of his lived experience as a disabled person.

The Mysterious Absence of E.T. Kingsley
As Bryan Palmer has so poignantly noted, "capitalism disables."[3] A materialist understanding of disablement that analyzes the implications of the rise of capitalism for disabled people has been sorely lacking in the literature.[4] In this book, we implicitly analyze the significance of early socialist theory as articulated by one disabled man. Social theory ultimately plays

out on the level of individual narratives.[5] The biography of one disabled man gives us a view of a lost world and allows us to rethink our understanding of social transformation on the California and BC left in the 1890s through to the 1920s. Disablement manifests itself on every page of Kingsley's story like a hazy mist; it is not quite there at each and every moment, but one can always palpably sense it lurking in the background. Kingsley's provocative and sustained silence about his tangible impairments only enhances the mystery, leaving tantalizing clues for the careful reader to discern.[6]

Yet the political lessons that we learn through his life story are applicable to social justice communities more broadly. From twenty-first-century campaigns for workers' rights to youth-led mobilizations demanding leadership in response to the ecological crisis of capitalism, there are abundant lessons to be learned from Kingsley's lifetime of militant advocacy. As corporate-led globalization continues to lead to downsizing and economic dislocation for billions of inhabitants of this fragile planet, the uncompromising vision of Kingsley, and its hallmark cry of "no compromise, no political trading," are more salient than ever.

One significant reason that Kingsley has been ignored by most scholars is the fact that the rigid brand of impossibilism to which he was deeply wedded during his political life was largely destroyed in the post-1917 political conjuncture. With the rise of the Communist Party and eventually the creation of the social democratic Co-operative Commonwealth Federation in the 1930s, the genuinely creative legacy of socialists such as Kingsley was forgotten. This work, like Peter Campbell's before ours, is an act of rekindling a lost political tradition that continues to have significant insights for us today.[7] In the twenty-first century, it is difficult to grasp the world view that shaped Kingsley and his comrades in the 1890s in California and early in the twentieth century in British Columbia. As Ian McKay has stressed, it entailed a strong belief in the role of popular education that could enlighten the working class. It involved the creation of a rival socialist discourse, including its own holidays, symbols, and myths. This discourse included cartoons, songs, and poems that promoted the socialist cause. Members of the working class themselves were frequently dismissed as foolish and naive for submitting to capitalism.[8] Slogans in the *Western Clarion* even proclaimed "Don't Be a Socialist" unless one had the requisite education on the socialist tradition, up to the point of having formal examinations to test a potential member's knowledge of socialism.[9] One can easily see the emphasis on popular education in the pages of the *Western Clarion,* which Kingsley so lovingly edited.

The socialist world view of the very early twentieth century was also deeply influenced by the theories of evolution from Darwin, Spencer, and others. Spencer's theory of the organic adaptation of society to the external environment through functional and structural differentiation and integration influenced many early socialists. There was a strong feeling that, as a matter of science, socialism would inevitably replace capitalism.[10] With the rise of the Soviet Union, the political yardstick of evaluating social change irrevocably altered. The emphasis on popular education was largely eliminated over time, and the divisions between adherents to social democracy or the Communist Party became sharper. Since Kingsley and other early socialists could not be pigeonholed easily as either incipient CCFers or early Communists, their unique form of socialism was largely marginalized.

Kingsley's relative absence in scholarship on the North American left is striking given the multiple intersections between his life and key moments in the development of the working-class movement in Canada and the United States in the era before the *Wagner Act* and the Rand Formula. Kingsley was a railway worker just before the Pullman Strike, and, like Eugene Debs (the leader of that strike), his experience in the railway industry propelled him down the road of revolutionary socialism. Kingsley was a leading figure in the Socialist Labor Party at the time of the split between De Leon and Debs in 1899 that would give rise to the Socialist Party of America. As a founder and leader of the Socialist Party of Canada and, later, the Federated Labor Party, Kingsley lived through the Russian Revolutions of 1905 and 1917, the Winnipeg General Strike and Canadian labour revolt of 1919, and the birth (and death) of early-twentieth-century millenarian socialism.

Kingsley was disabled on the job and faced a world filled with barriers both environmental and attitudinal, only to find himself deeply at odds with the socialist labour movement that had become his life.[11] The cycle was repeated as he moved further into obscurity in British Columbia, chasing after a party that would match his own radicalism. But, as in the

United States, the labour movements that he shaped intellectually – which would eventually form the crucible for mainstream socialist politics in Canada – cast him aside after the First World War. In reading the *Labor Star*, which Kingsley edited, in 1919, we do not encounter the writing of a beaten man; if anything, it only becomes angrier. There was very little "practical" about the man, who preferred soaring oration to gradualist pencil-pushing. As a rabble-rouser, he was much like Mikhail Bakunin in that, to paraphrase a Parisian police prefect, you would want him by your side on the first day of the revolution and then have him shot on the second.

Disability History

Only relatively recently has disability as a political category come to be regarded as salient in understanding the social and political world. As we have noted, prior to the 1970s, the medical model of disablement predominated, focusing on ameliorating impairment rather than removing structural barriers in the community and exclusionary employment policies at work. To the extent that disability was considered at all, it arose in medical sociology or the history of technology. The dramatic paradigm shift to regarding disabled citizens as part of the community came only when they mobilized to fight against ableist barriers.[12] The field of disability history is even younger, perhaps finding its identity after a seminal article by American historian Catherine Kudlick.[13] Although very little of Kingsley's personal correspondence survives, and it rarely touches on his personal life in any way, there can be no doubt that Kingsley had to adapt repeatedly to a world not constructed with the needs of disabled people in mind. That is not to suggest that he himself had a contemporary understanding of disablement and disability politics. Yet it seems that his life choices were shaped at least partly by how his impairment and environment interacted.

When one considers Kingsley's life, it seems to be clear that it was his 1890 accident at Spring Gulch that led to his political radicalization. We have no evidence of any political activity before his injury. It might also have led indirectly to the radicalization of his suffragist sister, Clara Kingsley Fuller. Yet even beyond that simple fact, the position of newspaper editor and orator was uniquely suited to his needs as a disabled man. The state of technology in 1890 meant that Kingsley simply could

FIGURE 27 Ravi Malhotra at Spring Gulch, Mineral County, Montana – the site of Kingsley's disablement on 15 October 1890. | Courtesy of Ravi Malhotra.

not continue his career as a brakeman after his injury. And as we have seen, the political positions that he took in critiquing unions as irredeemably reformist might have partly reflected his experiences as a disabled man in a trade union hostile or at best indifferent to workers who suffered impairments. Even the underlying rigidity of the *Western Clarion* in focusing on political questions might partly reflect his austere unwillingness to focus on personal matters.[14]

To be sure, Kingsley – as a white man with physical impairments that still allowed him to travel – was relatively privileged when one considers the long history of institutionalization of disabled people in the nineteenth century. Unlike people with mental illnesses or intellectual disabilities,

Kingsley was never institutionalized or confined to a sheltered workshop.[15] In this respect, his story of left-wing activism in the face of disablement has parallels to that of Salem Bland, the Methodist preacher who nurtured a generation of radical clergy in the social gospel tradition at Winnipeg's Wesley College and who became a single amputee at the age of thirty when the lower portion of his right leg was amputated (he had lacked the use of it since an injury as a child).[16] Yet Kingsley undoubtedly had a somewhat visible impairment and was working class, without any advanced education. Other socialists of the era such as Helen Keller certainly had major disabilities. Born a generation later than Kingsley in 1880 in an upper-class family in Alabama, Keller joined the the Socialist Party of America in 1909, radicalizing at roughly the same age as Kingsley.[17]

Perhaps one significant difference between Keller and Kingsley was that it was literally impossible for a casual observer to forget Keller's impairments, which required continuous accommodations in order to achieve communication. The infantilization of disabled people, particularly disabled women, is also a real phenomenon. Kingsley might have been regarded as a dangerous and dogmatic socialist, but he was usually accorded respect and treated as a working-class man even by his political opponents, inside and outside the working-class movement. Despite his American heritage, authorities made no effort to deport him during his first decade of intense political activity in the Socialist Party of Canada (it was only during the postwar crisis that federal police would inquire into his citizenship status, and the matter appears to have been quickly dropped).[18] In contrast, during a 1913 meeting, philanthropist Andrew Carnegie threatened to take Keller across his knees and give her a spanking when he learned that she had become a socialist. Keller was well over thirty at the time, but clearly Carnegie regarded her as a young girl who ought to be disciplined physically when she disobeyed his wishes.[19] Of course, another significant difference between the autodidact Kingsley and Keller is that she was less active politically after the early 1920s. Because she lived into the 1960s and won numerous accolades, including the Presidential Medal of Freedom in 1964, her radical politics is often forgotten or simply unknown. Kingsley, in contrast, remained a socialist to his death.[20]

Although press reports in both the United States and Canada occasionally referred to his amputations, we suspect that the artificial limbs

Kingsley acquired often allowed the casual observer to forget about his impairments. Although we can only speculate, it might well be that, like the case of polio survivor President Franklin D. Roosevelt, who worked hard to keep his impairments completely hidden from the public, large numbers of people who heard Kingsley speak (let alone those who simply read his journalism in the *Western Clarion* and other publications) were simply unaware of his impairments.[21] Nonetheless, the impact of his disablement on his daily life was undeniable. As former Socialist Party legislator Parker Williams noted in his obituary of Kingsley, his artificial limbs were "a pain and an inconvenience."[22] It is therefore all the more remarkable that, as Ross Johnson noted, "in spite of his handicap he managed to travel thousands of miles on speaking and organizing tours, sometimes under the most adverse conditions."[23]

We have endeavoured throughout this book to ground our narrative and analysis in the empirical record given the sharpness of views, currents, and controversies that surrounded Kingsley's life and work. However, our particular locations might have motivated a more discerning examination of his story than was present in earlier works. Like previous scholars of this period, we have political commitments to the left, but we also have specific connections to disability: Malhotra, who has lived with a lifelong impairment to mobility, and Isitt, who has a close friend who became an amputee during this research. In completing this work, we hope that we have shone a fresh light on the dynamics of disablement, class conflict, and political radicalism on the North American industrial frontier at this key moment in the history of the continent. We have also highlighted the extraordinary capacity of people who live with impairments of all sorts to participate actively in shaping their communities and societies – demonstrating a tenacious ability to lead.

Timeline of the Life and Politics of E.T. Kingsley

1856		Eugene Thornton Kingsley is born in the town of Pomfret, Chautauqua County, New York, southwest of Buffalo.
1878		Marries Almyra "Myra" Doan at River Falls, Wisconsin.
1880		US Census records show Eugene and Myra living in Olive, Ohio.
1881		First son, Percy, is born.
1884		Second son, Robert, is born.
1885		The Minnesota Census shows Eugene and family living in St. Paul, Minnesota, where he works as a fireman on the Chicago, St. Paul, Minneapolis and Omaha Railway.
1889		Leaves his family for Montana to work on the Northern Pacific Railroad, stopping at Little Falls, Minnesota, to visit his sister Clara.
1890	14 October	Injured aboard a Northern Pacific Railroad train in the vicinity of Spring Gulch in northwestern Montana and rushed to the railway's hospital in Missoula, where his legs are amputated near the knee. While convalescing, he reads Marx and radicalizes.

1891	April	Discharged from the Missoula hospital. Travels back to River Falls to visit his wife and sons, stopping en route at Little Falls to visit his sister Clara.
	September	Sues the Northern Pacific Railroad Company for $85,000 for the loss of his legs. Unfortunately, the outcome of the litigation is unknown.
1892		Works for a time in St. Paul with the law firm McDonald & Barnard, which had represented him in his tort litigation against Northern Pacific while living in River Falls.
1893		Moves to San Francisco for unknown reasons. Within a year, Myra files for divorce in the US district court in Minneapolis, citing cruel and inhuman treatment.
1894	November	Runs for the San Francisco Board of Supervisors as a candidate in the Tenth Ward, receiving 668 votes (1.2 percent of the vote).
1895		Identified as secretary of the Socialist Labor Party in San Francisco and secretary of the Socialist Hall in the Metropolitan Temple, 115 Turk Street, San Francisco.
	April	Among the signatories in a call to action for labour and reform organizations to host a May Day demonstration in San Francisco.
	April	Delivers a public lecture at the Socialist Hall as part of a Sunday-evening speakers series sponsored by the Socialist Labor Party – the first documented public lecture among hundreds that he would deliver to working-class audiences in Canada and the United States over the next quarter-century.
	October	Arrested for "obstructing a sidewalk" at Seventh Street and Market Street in downtown San Francisco during an SLP street corner meeting. He requests a jury trial.
	October	Addresses a mass meeting on Market Street at which he declares the importance of free speech.
	November	San Francisco Central Labor Council adopts a resolution condemning the arrest of Kingsley and other SLP members.

1896	May	Addresses a May Day meeting in San Francisco.
	May	Elected California state organizer of the Socialist Labor Party.
	August	Arrested midway through a speech during a street corner meeting at Seventh Street and Market Street in San Francisco.
	September	Addresses street corner meetings on Market Street as part of his candidacy for the US Congress.
	November	Runs as the SLP candidate for the US House of Representatives in California's 4th District, receiving 968 votes (3.1 percent of the vote).
1897	May	Addresses a May Day meeting in San Francisco and discusses arrests made by the police.
1898	November	Runs for the US House of Representatives as the SLP candidate for the 5th District, receiving 1,532 votes (3.9 percent of the vote).
		Supports Daniel De Leon in the Kangaroo Revolt within the Socialist Labor Party (a faction that would ultimately become the Socialist Party of America under the leadership of Eugene Debs).
1900	March	Expelled by the San Francisco section of the Socialist Labor Party for allegedly manipulating the party to his own advantage, an action nullified by the party's National Executive Committee since Kingsley was a member of the Santa Clara County section and therefore could not be expelled by the San Francisco section.
	May	Runs for San Jose City Council on a Socialist ticket as a candidate for councilman in the Second Ward, receiving 178 votes (4.7 percent of the vote).
	June	Kingsley is expected to attend the SLP Tenth National Convention in New York City as one of two California delegates but does not attend it because of a shortage of funds.
	c. October	Moves from California to Seattle following a speaking tour in the Pacific Northwest.

	December	Authors a blistering letter in the Seattle *Post-Intelligencer* attacking a proposal to adopt the Minnesota primary law in Washington State as an unjust attempt to "restrict the franchise."
1901	April	Drafts the manifesto of the Revolutionary Socialist League in Seattle, a breakaway group consisting of sixty former SLP members, signalling Kingsley's final break from the Socialist Labor Party.
1902	February	Invited by the Nanaimo Socialist Club to undertake a two-month lecture tour on Vancouver Island.
	March	Arrives in Victoria and immediately delivers public lectures on "The Labor Question from a Socialist Standpoint," with members of the Legislative Assembly, Victoria City Council, and clergy invited to attend.
	March	Arrives in Nanaimo, where he gets along well with members of the Nanaimo Socialist Club, who decide to extend his stay indefinitely. Kingsley would reside in British Columbia for the rest of his life.
	April	Opposes women's suffrage at the Kamloops convention of labour and socialist parties on the grounds that the plank was "irrelevant" and that the class struggle was the real issue.
	May	Spearheads the transformation of the Nanaimo Socialist Club into the Revolutionary Socialist Party of Canada.
	May	Returns to Victoria to deliver six public lectures on topics ranging from "The Earth and Man" to "The Class Struggle." In the years ahead, Kingsley would deliver hundreds of talks to working-class audiences in British Columbia and Canada on behalf of the Socialist Party of British Columbia, the Socialist Party of Canada, and the Federated Labor Party of British Columbia.
	June	Travels to the Kootenay region to organize socialist locals.
	October	Brokers the merger of the Revolutionary Socialist Party of Canada and the Socialist Party of British Columbia with a platform calling for the abolition of private property and production for profit.

1903		Identified as the proprietor of the Nanaimo Fish Market in the city directory, turning to private enterprise to sustain himself as a socialist organizer.
	September	Described as "the legless wonder of social economics" by the *Victoria Daily Colonist* prior to a public meeting in the capital city during the BC provincial election campaign.
	Fall	Moves from Nanaimo to Vancouver, where he would live for the rest of his life.
	November	Appointed as editor of the *Western Clarion,* a position that he would hold until 1908 and then again briefly in 1912.
	December	SPBC Revelstoke local passes a strong resolution condemning Kingsley for his anti-union views.
1904	December	Participates in the convention decision to transform the SPBC into the Socialist Party of Canada and is appointed to continue serving as editor of the *Western Clarion.* Also appointed as dominion organizer of the party, a role that he would hold until 1908. Also elected to the Dominion Executive Committee of the party, a role that he would hold until 1911.
1905		Purchases the *Western Clarion* printshop from Richard Parmater "Parm" Pettipiece, which he operates as E.T. Kingsley Printing Ltd. until 1914, devoting a portion of the surplus estimated at $100 per month to subsidize publication of the paper.
1906	March	Delivers a lecture in Vancouver's Sullivan Hall on the anniversary of the establishment of the Paris Commune.
		Resists attempts to form a BC section of the Canadian Labor Party, welcoming a resolution of labour delegates endorsing the Socialist Party of Canada.
1907	February	Runs for the BC Legislative Assembly as an SPC candidate in the multiple-member Vancouver City riding, receiving 617 votes (2.0 percent of the vote).

	2 August	Speaks at an open-air mass meeting in Vancouver's Recreation Park with Keir Hardie, leader of the British Labour Party, declaring that "socialism, in its fundamental conceptions, is the same in the new world as in the old."
	August	Runs again for the BC Legislative Assembly as the SPC candidate in a by-election in the Vancouver City riding, prompted by the appointment of William Bowser to the cabinet, receiving 521 votes (18 percent of the vote in the two-way race).
1908	May	Embarks on a speaking tour to eastern Canada, delivering talks in Calgary, Winnipeg, Port Arthur, Toronto, Hamilton, Guelph, Berlin, Cobalt, Montreal, and other points.
	October	Runs for the House of Commons as the SPC candidate for Vancouver City, receiving 1,194 votes (10.9 percent of the vote). Appears in a series of editorial cartoons by James Fitzmaurice in the *Vancouver Daily Province*.
		Stops working as *Western Clarion* editor and as SPC dominion organizer while continuing to write editorials for the newspaper, financially subsidize its operations through his printing business, and serve on the party's Dominion Executive Committee.
1909	May	Predicts the outbreak of the First World War in an editorial in the *Western Clarion*.
	May	Addresses a Free Speech meeting at Vancouver City Hall during the controversy over the arrest of socialist speakers during the Free Speech fight that year.
	November	Runs for the BC Legislative Assembly as an SPC candidate in the multiple-member Vancouver City riding, receiving 1,883 votes (3.7 percent of the vote).
1910		Declares Christianity and socialism to be identical during a speech in Victoria.
1911	September	Runs for the House of Commons as the SPC candidate for Vancouver City, receiving 1,056 votes (8.98 percent of the vote).

1912	January	Temporarily appointed as *Western Clarion* editor and SPC dominion secretary on the resignation of R.I. Matthews, assuming responsibility for the publication of the newspaper, a task that Kingsley admits "is not to my liking."
	February	Speaks at a protest meeting attended by 2,500 people at Vancouver's Horse Show Building, condemning the "Bloody Sunday" police attacks on left-wing speakers and citizens during the Vancouver Free Speech fight.
	November	Suspends publication of the *Western Clarion,* citing losses of "considerably over one hundred dollars per month" from his personal funds since 1904.
1913		Presumably visits with his son Percy, then age thirty-two, his daughter-in-law Clara, and his grandchildren Donald, age six, and Lucille, age four, after the family enters Canada at the US border crossing at Blaine, Washington. This is the only evidence of any association with his family since he left for California in the early 1890s.
		Speaks against the military occupation of the Vancouver Island coalfield and the arrest and imprisonment of miners during the "Vancouver Island War" (the Vancouver Island Miners' Strike, 1912–14) at meetings organized by the Miners' Liberation League, later embarking on a propaganda tour in the strike zone.
1914		Condemns racist attacks against Sikh, Hindu, and Muslim passengers aboard the *Komagata Maru* as well as local Sikh residents in a speech in Vancouver on the topic of "The Battle of Coal Harbour."
		Writes a controversial editorial for the *Western Clarion* criticizing German workers for patriotic aggression and is permanently removed from the editorial work of the newspaper. Signals the end of Kingsley's active role in the Socialist Party of Canada.
1915		Begins writing for the BCFL's *Federationist* newspaper, later serving as associate editor and editor.

1916		Publishes a booklet entitled *The Genesis and Evolution of Slavery* with Parm Pettipiece, the only official published version of his political thought.

1916   Publishes a booklet entitled *The Genesis and Evolution of Slavery* with Parm Pettipiece, the only official published version of his political thought.

1917   Shares a platform opposing the *Military Service Act, 1917,* with former Socialist Party comrades Bill Pritchard and others in a series of anti-conscription meetings in Vancouver organized by the BCFL, the VTLC, and the Socialist Party of Canada.

Writes an article for the inaugural issue of L.D. Taylor's newspaper the *Critic,* attracting the attention of Canada's immigration inspector for British Columbia as well as the chief press censor.

1918   Resigns as editor of the *Federationist* following the imposition of press censorship, according to Canada's chief press censor, Colonel Ernest J. Chambers.

February   Helps to found the Federated Labor Party, speaking at the founding convention, at which Kingsley is elected vice-president, later assuming the role of president.

1919 January   Founds the *Labor Star* newspaper with Pettipiece, which publishes for two months until March 1919.

Delivers a speech at the founding FLP meeting in Victoria saying that, according to the daily press, he does not care what the Bolsheviks do in Russia as long as they "shoot every land baron and general," prompting the cancellation of FLP meetings in the Columbia Theatre and a Victoria City Council resolution proposing the suppression of seditious meetings and the deportation of foreign-born radicals such as Kingsley.

June   Embarks on a speaking and organizing tour for the Federated Labor Party in the Okanagan, Kootenays, Crow's Nest Pass, and Alberta.

1920 March   Speaks at a Vancouver meeting commemorating the anniversary of the Paris Commune.

November   Speaks in support of FLP candidates during the 1920 provincial election campaign.

1921	9 May	Delivers his final documented lecture for the Federated Labor Party at the party's hall on Cordova Street West in Vancouver.
	December	Writes an editorial for *British Columbia Labor News* exposing the moral and intellectual bankruptcy of the Canadian ruling class during the 1921 parliamentary election campaign.
1923	3 July	Comments on immigration and internationalism.
1925	August	Delivers a lecture on "The Case of the Farmer" at the Summerland School of Social Science, a two-week educational retreat that the Federated Labor Party sponsored in the Okanagan Valley in the 1920s, bringing together leftists from across the country.
1926	September	Runs for the House of Commons as an independent labour candidate for Vancouver Centre, receiving 527 votes (2.7 percent of the vote).
1929	9 December	Dies in his apartment in Vancouver, the cause of death identified as asphyxiation from an apparently accidental inhalation of illuminating gas. Kingsley is cremated at the Mountain View Crematorium, with no record of the final resting place of his remains. His friend and comrade Wallis Lefeaux provides the particulars on the death certificate.
	13 December	Kingsley is eulogized in the VTLC *Labor Statesman* as having "left a deeper mark than any other man" on labour thought in the province and infecting "most Labor organizations to a greater or lesser degree with the class viewpoint."
1930	January	His ex-wife, Myra, identifies herself as a "widow" to a US Census enumerator in Minneapolis.

E.T. Kingsley's Election Results

1894 San Francisco Municipal Election

Candidate for Supervisor for the Tenth Ward for the City of San Francisco's Board of Supervisors, 6 November 1894

Candidate	Votes	
	%	N
Dray, Homer C.	0.71	391
Hinton, William M.	39.4	21,564
Kingsley, E.T.	1.2	668
McBride, M.J.	2.5	1,368
Spreckels, Adolph B.	49.6	27,115
Vetter, Fred J.	6.6	3,604

1896 United States Congressional Election

Candidate for Member of the House of Representatives for California's 4th Congressional District, 3 November 1896

Candidate	Votes	
	%	N
Kingsley, E.T. (Socialist Labor)	3.09	968
MacGuire, James G. (Democratic, incumbent)	61.0	19,074
O'Brien, Thomas B. (Republican)	35.0	10,940
Rowell, Joseph (Prohibition)	0.96	299

Tinted background denotes elected candidate(s)

1898 United States Congressional Election

Candidate for Member of the House of Representatives for California's 5th Congressional District, 8 November 1898

Candidate	Votes	
	%	N
Craig, William (Democratic)	44.3	17,352
Kingsley, E.T. (Socialist Labor)	3.9	1,532
Lourd, Eugene F. (Republican, incumbent)	51.8	20,254

1900 San Jose Municipal Election

Candidate for Councilman for the Second Ward for the Common Council of the City of San Jose, California, 21 May 1900

Candidate	Votes	
	%	N
Cherrie, J.J.	61.0	2,304
Kingsley, E.T. (Socialist)	4.7	178
Millard, Byron	34.3	1,298

1907 British Columbia Provincial Election

Candidate for Member of the Legislative Assembly for Vancouver City (multiple-member district), 2 February 1907

Candidate	Votes	
	%	N
Bowser, William John (Conservative, incumbent)	10.5	3,152
Dubberley, John Edward (Socialist)	2.0	599
Farris, John Wallace deBeque (Liberal)	7.0	2,096
Garden, James Ford (Conservative, incumbent)	10.2	3,080
Henderson, Alexander (Liberal)	7.5	2,248
Kingsley, Eugene Thornton (Socialist)	2.0	617
MacGowan, Alexander Henry Boswell (Conservative, incumbent)	10.4	3,141
McGuire, George Albert (Conservative)	9.9	2,994
McInnes, William Wallace Burns (Liberal)	7.4	2,233
McLennan, Robert Purvis (Liberal)	7.7	2,316
McVety, James Hackett (Socialist)	2.0	616
Neelands, Thomas Fletcher (Liberal)	6.8	2,063
Perry, Albert George (Canadian Labor Party)	0.9	281
Pettipiece, Richard Parmater (Socialist)	2.0	602
Stebbings, Albion Richard (Socialist)	2.0	598
Tatlow, Robert Garnet (Conservative, incumbent)	10.4	3,136
Williams, Francis (Canadian Labor Party)	1.3	401

1907 British Columbia Provincial By-Election

Candidate for Member of the Legislative Assembly for Vancouver
City, 3 August 1907

Candidate	Votes	
	%	*N*
Bowser, William John (Conservative, incumbent)	81.9	2,364
Kingsley, Eugene Thornton (Socialist)	18.1	521

1908 Canadian Federal Election

Candidate for Member of Parliament for Vancouver City,
26 October 1908

Candidate	Votes	
	%	*N*
Cowan, George Henry (Conservative)	42.1	4,621
Kingsley, Eugene T. (Independent)	10.9	1,194
Martin, Joseph (Independent)	19.3	2,120
McInnes, William Wallace Burns (Liberal)	27.7	3,039

1909 British Columbia Provincial Election

Candidate for Member of the Legislative Assembly for Vancouver
City (multiple-member district), 25 November 1909

Candidate	Votes	
	%	*N*
Bowser, William John (Conservative, incumbent)	10.6	5,441
Campbell, John Bell (Liberal)	6.3	3,227
Garvie, Peter (Socialist)	2.4	1,227
Kingsley, Eugene Thornton (Socialist)	3.7	1,883
MacDonald, George Ernest (Liberal)	7.8	3,984
MacGowan, Alexander Henry Boswell (Conservative, incumbent)	10.1	5,190
McGregor, Moses (Socialist)	2.4	1,218
McGuire, George Albert (Conservative, incumbent)	9.4	4,286
MacKenzie, William Murray (Socialist)	2.4	1,231
Pettipiece, Richard Parmater (Socialist)	2.8	1,428
Senkler, John Harold (Liberal)	8.0	4,110
Stables, James (Liberal)	6.5	3,356
Tisdall, Charles Edward (Conservative)	9.8	5,051
Wade, Frederick Coate (Liberal)	7.7	3,942
Watson, Henry Holgate (Conservative)	10.1	5,202

1911 Canadian Federal Election

Candidate for Member of Parliament for Vancouver City,
21 September 1911

Candidate	Votes %	Votes N
Kingsley, Eugene T. (Socialist)	8.98	1,056
Senkler, John Harold (Liberal)	32.3	3,796
Stevens, Henry Herbert (Conservative)	58.7	6,902

1926 Canadian Federal Election

Candidate for Member of Parliament for Vancouver Centre,
9 September 1926

Candidate	Votes %	Votes N
Donaghy, Dugald (Liberal)	43.8	8,471
Kingsley, Eugene Thornton (Labor)	2.7	527
Stevens, Henry Herbert (Conservative, incumbent)	53.4	10,326

Sources: "Registrar of Voters' Report," in San Francisco Board of Supervisors, *San Francisco Municipal Reports, for the Fiscal Year 1894–1895, Ending June 30, 1895* (San Francisco: Hinton Printing Company, 1895), 59; Michael J. Dubin, *United States Congressional Elections, 1788–1997: The Official Results of the Elections of the 1st through 105th Congresses* (Jefferson, NC: McFarland, 1998), 313, 322; "Official Returns of the Election," *San Francisco Call,* 14 December 1898, 5; "Results of the Municipal Election Held May 21st, 1900," in Minutes of the Common Council of the City of San Jose, 23 May 1900, City Council Records, San Jose Public Library; Elections British Columbia, *An Electoral History of British Columbia, 1871–1986* (Victoria: Elections British Columbia, 1988), 103, 106, 113; "Socialist Could Not Have Retired," *Vancouver Daily Province,* 5 August 1907, 1; Parliament of Canada, "Elections and Ridings," https://lop.parl.ca/sites/ParlInfo/default/en_CA/ElectionsRidings.

Partial Record of E.T. Kingsley's
Public Speeches and Lectures

This is not an exhaustive list; it is confined to Kingsley's speeches reported in articles that we consulted in the socialist and non-socialist press. In particular, speeches from outside the Lower Mainland of British Columbia – for example, his SPBC, SPC, and FLP organizing tours in 1902–04, 1905–14, and 1918–20, respectively, have not been comprehensively documented because of our selected review of the small-town press in British Columbia and Alberta. Kingsley's speeches on behalf of the Socialist Labor Party in California in the 1890s and the Revolutionary Socialist League in Seattle in 1901 are also not comprehensively documented here because of a paucity of archival material.

1895

San Francisco, 1153 Mission Street, 18 March, meeting of unions re
    San Francisco City Charter
San Francisco, Metropolitan Labor Temple, 28 April, SLP lecture course
San Francisco, Metropolitan Labor Temple, 1 May, re International
    Labor Day
San Francisco, corner of Market and Seventh, 1 October, open-air meeting
    resulting in Kingsley's arrest
San Francisco, corner of Market and Seventh, 12 October, SLP American
    Branch open-air meeting with Mrs. A.F. Smith and others re Free Speech
San Francisco, Pythian Hall, 27 October, SLP meeting re "The Aims of
    Socialism"

1896

San Francisco, Pythian Hall, 16 February, SLP meeting re "How and to
    What Extent Do We Now Co-Operate?" with T.E. Zant

San Francisco, Metropolitan Labor Temple, 18 March, SLP meeting re
anniversary of the inauguration of the Paris Commune

San Francisco, Metropolitan Labor Temple, 1 May, SLP May Day
demonstration

San Francisco, SLP Jewish Branch Headquarters, 970 Folsom Street,
30 June, organizing meeting for Thirteenth Assembly District Branch

San Francisco, Metropolitan Labor Temple, 8 July, SLP Liberty Branch
meeting re "Economic Errors"

San Francisco, SLP Jewish Branch Headquarters, 970 Folsom Street, 9 July,
SLP Jewish Branch meeting re labour unions and party politics

San Francisco, corner of Market and Seventh, 8 August, open-air meeting
with William Costley and George Speed

San Francisco, corner of Market and Seventh, 15 August, open-air meeting
resulting in Kingsley's arrest along with seven other socialists

San Francisco, Metropolitan Labor Temple, 19 August, SLP meeting
protesting the arrest of Kingsley and others

San Francisco, corner of Pine and Kearney, 31 August, open-air meeting to
protest the arrest of SLP leaders and police incursions on free speech

San Francisco, Pythian Hall, 6 September, SLP meeting re confusion

San Francisco, corner of Pine and Kearney, 14 September, open-air meeting
with Charles Sunflower and Barnaby

San Francisco, Fifth Street, 26 September, open-air meeting with William
Costley and George Aspen

1897

San Francisco, 18 March, SLP meeting re anniversary of Paris Commune,
with G. Aspden, G. Benham, P. Grottkau, and M.W. Wilkins

San Francisco, 4 April, SLP propaganda meeting, with William Costley,
George Speed, S. Seller, and W.M. Wilkinson

San Francisco, Metropolitan Labor Temple, 1 May, SLP May Day celebration, address on the topic of "The Modern Labor Movement"

1898

San Francisco, 31 July, SLP meeting re "Surplus Value"

San Francisco, Washington Hall, Eddy Street, 13 November, SLP meeting
re 1898 election campaign

1899

San Francisco, Metropolitan Labor Temple, 30 May, SLP meeting
protesting US imperialism in Cuba and the Philippines

Salinas (CA), Good Templars' Hall, 14 July, SLP meeting re practical means
to improve the condition of the masses

1902

Victoria, 16 March, to Victoria CSL branch

Victoria, Labour Hall, 19 March, CSL meeting re "The Labor Problem from
a Socialist Standpoint"

Victoria, Labour Hall, 20 March, CSL meeting re "The Capitalist and
Labourer"

Nanaimo, 22 March, Nanaimo Socialist Club open-air meeting

Nanaimo, Free Press Hall, 23 March, Nanaimo Socialist Club propaganda
meeting

Kamloops, Raven's Hall, 15–16 April, Convention on Labour Political
Action

Nanaimo, 4 May, Nanaimo Socialist Club meeting re International Labor
Day

Victoria, 12 May, CSL meeting re "The Earth and Man"

Victoria, 13 May, CSL meeting re "Man as Savage and Barbarian"

Victoria, 14 May, CSL meeting re "The History of Civilization"

Victoria, 15 May, CSL meeting re "The Capitalist System"

Victoria, 16 May, CSL meeting re "The Class Struggle"

Victoria, 17 May, CSL meeting re "The Politics of Labour"

Vancouver, City Hall, 23 June, chaired meeting with American socialist
leader Eugene Debs

Nanaimo, Socialist Hall, July, RSPC inaugural meeting, on "Lessons for the
Workers in the Great Coal Strike and Its Relation to the Class Struggle"

Nanaimo, Opera House, 1 September, Labour Day demonstration

Ladysmith, Gould's Hall, 6 December, re provincial by-election, with James
Hawthornthwaite and Parker Williams

1903

Victoria, Labour Hall, 1 February, SPBC meeting re the labour problem

Nanaimo, Opera House, 19 February, re railway expansion

Nanaimo, Opera House, 17 March, SPBC meeting re socialism

Vancouver, Labour Hall, 1 May, re International Labor Day

Cumberland, June, SPBC propaganda meeting re "Evolution of Man"

Cumberland, June, SPBC propaganda meeting re "Economics"

Cumberland, June, SPBC propaganda meeting re "Working Class Politics"

Courtenay, June, SPBC propaganda meeting re "The Condition of the Small
Farmer"

Cedar (Vancouver Island), Wheatsheaf Hotel, 20 June, SPBC propaganda
    meeting, with James Hawthornthwaite
Ladysmith, 5 July, SPBC campaign meeting re "The Coming Campaign"
Vancouver, open-air meeting, 25 July, SPBC propaganda meeting
Vancouver, Socialist Hall, 44 Hastings Street West, 26 July, SPBC propaganda
    meeting
Texada Island, August, SPBC propaganda meeting
Fernie, August, SPBC campaign meeting, with Parm Pettipiece
Greenwood, 19 August, SPBC campaign meeting in support of Ernest
    Burns
Phoenix, Miners' Union Hall, 13 September, SPBC meeting re socialism
Phoenix, open-air meeting, 16 September, Labour Day demonstration
Victoria, corner of Yates and Broad, 22 September, SPBC open-air
    meeting
Victoria, Spring Ridge Odd Fellows' Hall, 23 September, SPBC campaign
    meeting for J.C. Watters
Victoria, corner of Yates and Broad, 26 September, SPBC open-air meeting
    re "The Labour Problem"
Victoria, Spring Ridge Odd Fellows' Hall, 27 September, SPBC campaign
    meeting for J.C. Watters
Nanaimo, Opera House, 30 September, SPBC propaganda meeting
Vancouver, 18 October, SPBC propaganda meeting
Victoria, Labour Hall, 8 November, SPBC meeting re "Karl Marx's Definition
    of Capital"
Saanich, 9 November, organizational meeting to establish a Gordon Head
    SPBC branch

1904

Vancouver, Crystal Theatre, 20 March, SPBC meeting re anniversary of
    inauguration of Paris Commune
Vancouver, Sullivan Hall, 14 August, SPBC educational meeting
Ladysmith, Pavilion Green, 22 August, SPBC lecture re socialism
Victoria, Crystal Theatre, 4 September, SPBC lecture re "The Labour Problem"
Victoria, City Hall, 5 September, Victoria Trades and Labor Council–
    sponsored Labour Day mass meeting
Ladysmith, Opera House, 12 October, SPBC campaign meeting for federal
    candidate William Fenton, with James Hawthornthwaite
Victoria, Ancient Order of United Workmen Hall, 27 October, SPBC
    campaign meeting for J.C. Watters and other federal candidates

Vancouver, City Hall, 31 October, SPBC campaign meeting for J.T. Mortimer and other federal candidates

1905

New Westminster, Eagle Hall, 26 March, SPC propaganda meeting

Vancouver, City Hall, 29 July, SPC debate re "The Single Tax vs. Socialism," with John White

Nanaimo, Opera House, 31 July, SPC debate re "The Single Tax vs. Socialism," with John White

Victoria, 4 August, SPC debate re "The Single Tax vs. Socialism," with John White

Vancouver, Sullivan Hall, 3 September, SPC propaganda meeting

Seattle, Socialist Hall, 406 Pine Street, 23 September (afternoon), Socialist Party Seattle Local meeting

Seattle, Socialist Hall, 406 Pine Street, 23 September (evening), Socialist Party Seattle Local meeting

Vancouver, City Hall, 5 November, SPC meeting re Russian Revolution

Seattle, Temple, 17 December, Socialist Party of Washington State propaganda meeting

Vancouver, City Hall, 18 December, SPC meeting re "The Mission of the Working Class"

1906

Vancouver, City Hall, 21 January, SPC meeting re anniversary of Bloody Sunday massacre, St. Petersburg, Russia

Vancouver, Sullivan Hall, 18 March, SPC meeting re thirty-fifth anniversary of the Paris Commune

Vancouver, 29 April, SPC meeting re "The Politics of Labour"

Crow's Nest Pass, c. April, SPC propaganda tour

Boundary district, c. April, SPC propaganda tour

Vancouver, Grand Theatre, 26 August, SPC propaganda meeting

Vancouver, City Hall, 2 September, SPC propaganda meeting

Vancouver, Grand Theatre, 23 September, SPC propaganda meeting with James Simpson, Toronto

Nelson, Miners' Union Hall, 6–8 October, SPC fourth provincial convention

Nelson, Fraternity Hall, 7 October, SPC meeting re socialism

Revelstoke, Selkirk Hall, 11 October, SPC meeting re socialism

Vancouver, Grand Theatre, 2 December, SPC propaganda meeting re "The Carnival of Crime"

1907

Nanaimo, Opera House, 19 January, re SPC provincial campaign, with J.H. Hawthornthwaite

Vancouver, Sullivan Hall, 3 March, SPC meeting re evolution of human society

Vancouver, Grand Theatre, 17 March, SPC meeting re anniversary of inauguration of the Paris Commune

Vancouver, Recreation Park, 2 August, SPC open-air mass meeting with Keir Hardie, leader of the British Labour Party

1908

Vancouver, City Hall, 9 February, SPC propaganda meeting

Vancouver, City Hall, 1 May, SPC May Day celebration

Fernie, Miners' Hall, 23 May, SPC interprovincial convention

Calgary, 27 May, SPC propaganda meeting

Winnipeg, Hay Market, 28 May, SPC open-air meeting, joined by Polish and Ruthenian speakers

Winnipeg, Trades Hall (James Street), 29 May, SPC public lecture on "Socialism"

Port Arthur, c. June, SPC propaganda meeting

Montreal, June, SPC propaganda meeting

Toronto, June, SPC propaganda meeting

Toronto, June, SPC propaganda meeting

Peterborough, c. June, SPC propaganda meeting

Hamilton, c. June, SPC propaganda meeting

Sarnia, c. June, SPC propaganda meeting

Port Huron, c. June, SPC propaganda meeting

Lindsay (ON), c. June, SPC propaganda meeting

Guelph, c. June, SPC propaganda meeting

Berlin (ON), c. June, SPC propaganda meeting

Allendale (ON), c. June, SPC propaganda meeting

Cobalt, c. July, SPC propaganda meeting

Winnipeg, Ruthenian Hall, 18 July, SPC propaganda meeting

Winnipeg, Trades Hall, 28 July, SPC propaganda meeting

Calgary, Trades and Labour Hall, 2 August, SPC meeting re socialism

Edmonton, Club Hall, 12 August, SPC propaganda meeting

Lethbridge, Oliver's Hall, 24 August, SPC meeting re "Labour and Its Economies"

Denoro (near Greenwood, BC), 18 September, People's Dinner Hour address re socialism

Kaslo, c. 19 September, SPC propaganda meeting

Revelstoke, Opera House, 20 September, SPC meeting re "The Cause of Strikes"

Vancouver, City Hall, 30 September, SPC candidates' meeting during federal election campaign

Vancouver, City Hall, 7 October, SPC campaign meeting during federal election

Vancouver, Opera House, 19 October, VTLC meeting during federal election campaign

Vancouver, City Hall, 21 October, SPC campaign meeting during federal election

Vancouver, Opera House, 23 October, SPC campaign meeting during federal election

Revelstoke, Opera House, 11 November, Liberal rally meeting re socialism

Vancouver, Rose Theatre, 13 December, SPC meeting

1909

Victoria, Grand Theatre, 24 January, SPC meeting

Victoria, Grand Theatre, 28 February, SPC meeting re "Signs upon the Horizon"

Vancouver, City Hall, 18 March, SPC meeting commemorating the thirty-eighth anniversary of inauguration of the Paris Commune

Vancouver, City Hall, 10 April, VTLC mass meeting re eight-hour day

Vancouver, Cambie Street Grounds, 1 May, May Day celebration hosted by the Socialist Party of Canada

Vancouver, Cameraphone Theatre, 2 May, May Day celebration hosted by the Socialist Party of Canada, with W. Dreaver and L.T. English

Vancouver, City Hall, 17 May, SPC protest meeting against arrest of street corner orators during Vancouver Free Speech fight, with T.M. Beamish, James McVety, and Leo T. English

Revelstoke, 6 September, Revelstoke Trades and Labour Council–sponsored Labour Day celebration re "The Labour Question"

Vancouver, National Theatre, 12 September, SPC propaganda meeting

Vancouver, National Theatre, 17 October, SPC propaganda meeting

Vancouver, City Hall, 17 November, provincial candidates' meeting for Vancouver City, hosted by the Socialist Party of Canada

1910

Victoria, Romano Theatre, 23 January, SPC propaganda meeting

Vancouver, 10 April, SPC propaganda meeting re control of the state

Vancouver, Cambie Street Grounds, 1 May, SPC May Day demonstration, with James Hawthornthwaite, Parker Williams, and Parm Pettipiece

Nelson, Crystal Theatre, 11 September, SPC meeting re "The Class War"

Vancouver, Empress Theatre, 25 September, SPC meeting re "The Class War"

Vancouver, Empress Theatre, 30 October, SPC propaganda meeting

Victoria, Grand Theatre, 27 November, SPC meeting

Vancouver, Empress Theatre, 4 December, SPC propaganda meeting

1911

Vancouver, Empress Theatre, 8 January, SPC propaganda meeting

Vancouver, Empress Theatre, 5 February, SPC propaganda meeting

Vancouver, Empress Theatre, 19 March, SPC propaganda meeting

Vancouver, Empress Theatre, 9 April, SPC propaganda meeting

Vancouver, Crystal Theatre, 4 June, SPC Local 15 meeting

Vancouver, Pender Hall, 6 September, SPC campaign meeting re "Enslavement of Workers"

Eburne (South Vancouver), Odd Fellows' Hall, 8 September, SPC campaign meeting re socialism

Vancouver, Horse Show Building, 19 September, federal campaign meeting with J.H. Senkler and H.H. Stevens

1912

Vancouver, Dominion Hall, 1 February, SPC- and IWW-sponsored protest meeting against the "Bloody Sunday" attacks and incursions on freedom of speech

Vancouver, Horse Show Building, 3 February, SPC-, IWW-, and VTLC-sponsored protest meeting attended by 2,500 people against the "Bloody Sunday" attacks and incursions on freedom of speech

Vancouver, Grand Theatre, 18 February, SPC propaganda meeting

Vancouver, Electric Theatre, 17 March, SPC propaganda meeting

Vancouver, Electric Theatre, 24 March, SPC propaganda meeting

Vancouver, Electric Theatre, 21 April, SPC propaganda meeting

Nanaimo, 1 May, SPC May Day celebration

New Westminster, City Theatre, 6 October, SPC propaganda meeting

Nanaimo, 20 October, SPC propaganda meeting

1913

Vancouver, Labor Temple, 26 January, SPC propaganda meeting re socialism

Vancouver, Empress Theatre, 2 March, SPC propaganda meeting

Vancouver, Empress Theatre, 16 March, SPC propaganda meeting

Vancouver, Dominion Hall, 10 November, Miners' Liberation League meeting re Vancouver Island Miners' Strike

Vancouver, Horse Show Building, 8 December, Miners' Liberation League
  meeting re Vancouver Island Miners' Strike
Nanaimo, Athletic Club, 14 December, SPC meeting re socialism

1914

Vancouver, Empress Theatre, 22 March, SPC meeting re anniversary of the
  Paris Commune
Vancouver, Empress Theatre, 3 May, SPC propaganda meeting
Cumberland, 21 May, SPC propaganda meeting
Nanaimo, 24 May, SPC propaganda meeting
Vancouver, Empress Theatre, 28 June, SPC propaganda meeting
Vancouver, Empress Theatre, 26 July, SPC meeting re the *Komagata Maru*
  incident and "The Battle of Coal Harbour"
Vancouver, 17 August, SPC meeting re "The World Situation and the
  Revolutionary Movement"

1916

Vancouver, Labor Temple, 11 September, with Robert Gosden re corruption
  in provincial politics

1917

Vancouver, Orpheum Theatre, 3 June, against conscription
Vancouver, Empress Theatre, 13 June, against conscription, with W.A.
  Pritchard, J.H. McVety, R.P. Pettipiece, and Wallis Lefeaux
Vancouver, Avenue Theatre, 26 July, against conscription, with Helena
  Gutteridge and Jack Kavanagh
Victoria, Knights of Pythias Hall, 10 November, in support of federal labour
  candidates, with Albert Wells and Joseph Taylor
Saanich, St. Mark's Hall, 23 November, in support of federal labour candi-
  dates Joseph Taylor and Albert Wells
Victoria, Princess Theatre, 24 November, in support of federal labour candi-
  dates Joseph Taylor and Albert Wells
Chase River, 25 November (afternoon), in support of federal labour candi-
  dates Joseph Taylor and Albert Wells
Nanaimo, Dominion Hall, 25 November (evening), in support of federal
  labour candidates Joseph Taylor and Albert Wells
South Vancouver, McBride School, 28 November, in support of federal
  labour candidate J.H. McVety
North Vancouver, Knights of Pythias Hall, 12 December, in support of federal labour candidate Victor Midgley

1918

Vancouver, Labor Temple, 1 February, FLP founding meeting

Vancouver, Labor Temple, 23 February, first FLP public propaganda
 meeting

New Westminster, St. George's Hall, 9 March, FLP propaganda meeting

Vancouver, University of British Columbia Assembly Hall, 14 March,
 Vancouver Institute meeting re "Capital, Labour, and the State"

Vancouver, Colonial Theatre, 17 March, FLP meeting re "Paris Commune
 and the Bolsheviki"

Vancouver, Colonial Theatre, 31 March, FLP meeting re "Civilization: Its
 Cause and Cure"

Vancouver, Rex Theatre, 14 April, FLP meeting re "The Collapse of
 Capitalism"

Vancouver, Rex Theatre, 12 May, FLP meeting re "The Civic Employees
 Strike and Bigger Things"

Vancouver, Rex Theatre, 28 July, FLP meeting re "Road to Freedom"

Vancouver, Rex Theatre, 13 October, FLP meeting re "Reconstruction of
 Society"

Vancouver, Rex Theatre, 24 November, FLP meeting re "Now! What?"
 following the Armistice in Europe

Vancouver, Empress Theatre, 1 December, FLP propaganda meeting

Vancouver, Empress Theatre, 29 December, VTLC meeting re censorship
 regulations and Allied intervention in Russia

1919

Vancouver, Rex Theatre, 5 January, FLP propaganda meeting

Victoria, Columbia Theatre, 26 January, FLP Victoria Local meeting re
 "The Bolsheviki"

Vancouver, Dominion Theatre, 2 February, FLP propaganda meeting

Vancouver, Broadway Theatre, 2 February, FLP propaganda meeting

New Westminster, Columbia Theatre, 16 February, FLP meeting re "Problems
 of the Hour"

North Vancouver, Knights of Pythias Hall, 23 February, FLP propaganda
 meeting

Nanaimo, Dominion Hall, 2 March, FLP meeting re the Russian and industrial situation

Vancouver, Royal Theatre, 30 March, FLP meeting re "One Big Union"

Vancouver, Royal Theatre, 20 April, FLP meeting re "The Class Struggle"

Revelstoke, 27 April, FLP meeting re "The World Unrest and Its Causes"

Silverton, late April, FLP propaganda meeting

Nelson, late April, FLP propaganda meeting

Fernie, Grand Theatre, 1 May, Gladstone Local May Day celebration

Victoria, Crystal Theatre, 4 May, FLP meeting re "The Machine"

Vancouver, Columbia Theatre, 1 June, FLP meeting re "Capitalism"

Salmon Arm, 3 June, FLP propaganda meeting

Summerland, Campbell Hall, 4 June, FLP propaganda meeting

Nelson, 6 June, FLP propaganda meeting

Fernie, 8 June, FLP propaganda meeting

Lethbridge, 15 June, FLP propaganda meeting

Calgary, 22 June, FLP propaganda meeting

Vancouver, Columbia Theatre, 13 July, FLP meeting re "Labour and Political
Action"

Vancouver, Columbia Theatre, 31 August, FLP meeting re "The Machinery
of Slavery"

Vancouver, National Theatre, 22 November, FLP meeting re "Civilization"

1920

Vancouver, Royal Theatre, 2 February, FLP meeting re "The Ruling Class
Debacle"

Vancouver, Royal Theatre, 21 March, re anniversary of the Paris Commune

Vancouver, Royal Theatre, 25 April, re "The End of an Epoch"

Vancouver, FLP Hall (Cordova Street West), 24 October, re "The Break-
Down of Capitalism"

Vancouver, Columbia Theatre, 26 December, re "Bankruptcy of Capitalism"

1921

Vancouver, FLP Hall (Cordova Street West), 29 May, FLP propaganda
meeting

1925

Nanaimo, McGarrigle Hall, 29 March, re "Civilization versus Nature"

Nanaimo, Foresters Hall, 29 March, re "Civilization versus Nature"

Summerland, Log Cabin, 26 August, Summerland School of Social Science
lecture re "The Case of the Farmer"

1926

Vancouver, Hamilton Hall, 9 September, re federal election campaign

Vancouver, Royal Theatre, 12 September, re federal election campaign

Obituary for E.T. Kingsley

"E.T. Kingsley"

By Parker Williams,
Socialist Member of the Legislative Assembly for Newcastle, 1903–1917

During the night of December 9th E.T. Kingsley "passed on." Kingsley first came to British Columbia 27 years ago at the invitation of the Vancouver Island miners. From the first day he took a leading part in the class fight. As a speaker he was ready for any emergency or any opponent, and many a hesitating Labor candidate gathered courage from the moment "the old warhorse" put a foot in his district. For some years Kingsley edited and published the "Western Clarion." This went down during the opening years of the war. He was then, for some considerable time, engaged on "The B.C. Federationist." Kingsley was, at different times, nominated both for the Provincial and the Dominion Parliaments. On Labor matters he had very definite opinions, and the courage to hold them even if standing alone. A rigid Marxian student, he found in this theory the answers to the riddle of economic tendencies, as well as human antics. On the Labor thought of the province, E.T. Kingsley has left a deeper mark than any other man.

While up to recent years the name and face [were] familiar to most of the adult population of the province, still few, if any, really knew the man. He was ever ready to listen and sympathize with the troubles of others; his own troubles were shared with no one. As a young man he lost both his lower limbs in railroading, but he acquired a wonderful mastery over two artificial substitutes. We know that they were a pain and an inconvenience, but even this trouble he held to himself and scorned the sympathy that, to some of us, seems to lighten a burden.

During the years that Kingsley lived in our province, his life work was to make the world a better place to live in. At the end of the journey, when values become real, we know of nothing that he could regret.

"The old warhorse" passed out in the night, and alone, and, from what we know of the man, we believe that he would wish it in this way.

Source: Parker Williams, "E.T. Kingsley," *Labor Statesman,* 13 December 1929, 4.

Notes

Epigraph: W.A. Pritchard, interview with David Millar, 17 September 1969, Los Angeles, Accession No. 1970–0010, David Millar Fonds, Library and Archives Canada (hereafter LAC). Ironically, Pritchard had not yet immigrated to Canada at the time of this candidates' meeting during the 1908 federal election campaign (he would arrive in Vancouver in 1911). Although Pritchard did not mention this in his 1969 interview with Millar, telling the story as if he had been a first-hand observer, Pritchard presumably was recounting a story that had become a legend within the Socialist Party of Canada, emblematic of Kingsley's rhetorical style. He might also have heard the story from his father, James Pritchard, a Welsh-born coal miner closely involved in bringing Kingsley to Canada in the first place and who might have attended the 1908 campaign meeting, with the younger Pritchard later adopting the story as his own.

Chapter 1: Kingsley in Context

1 E.T. Kingsley, *The Genesis and Evolution of Slavery: Showing How the Chattel Slaves of Pagan Times Have Been Transformed into the Capitalist Property of To-Day* (Vancouver: Federationist Publishing, 1916); see also "Political Notes of Interest," *Victoria Daily Colonist*, 24 September 1903, 6; Colonel Ernest J. Chambers (Chief Press Censor) to A.A. MacLean (Comptroller Royal North West Mounted Police [RNWMP]), 2 April 1919, file 279–1, "The Red Flag/The Soviet," vol. 602, Office of the Chief Press Censor Files, Record Group (hereafter RG) 6, Department of the Secretary of State Fonds, LAC; and "Socialism," *Voice* [Winnipeg, hereafter not noted], 22 May 1908, 3.

2 W.A. Pritchard, interview with A. Ross McCormack, 16 August 1971, Vancouver, Tape "No. 1, Track No. 1," Accession No. T0225, British Columbia Archives (hereafter BCA).

3 For a discussion on the struggle of achieving statehood, see Dave Walter, "'The Right Kind of Nail': Reactions to J.K. Toole's Montana Statehood Speech," *Montana: The Magazine of Western History* 37, no. 4 (1987): 46–57. Regarding terminology, we use

the name Northern Pacific Railroad Company throughout this book, which was Kingsley's employer at the time of his disablement and subsequent litigation. In 1896, the Northern Pacific Railroad Company sold its assets to a new company, the Northern Pacific Railway Company. The sale attracted controversy from creditors, and was considered in the US Supreme Court in the 1913 decision in *Northern Pacific Railroad Company and Northern Pacific Railway Company, Appts, v Joseph H. Boyd*, 228 US 482.

4 William L. Lang, "Corporate Point Men and the Creation of the Montana Central Railroad, 1882–87," *Great Plains Quarterly* 10 (1990): 152. Pockets of Montana would eventually embrace the reform socialism advocated by the Socialist Party. See Jerry Calvert, "The Rise and Fall of Socialism in a Company Town, 1902–1905," *Montana: The Magazine of Western History* 36, no. 4 (1986): 2–13, describing the growth of the Socialist Party in Anaconda, Montana, after 1902.

5 "Heavy Damages Demanded for Serious Injury," *St. Paul Daily Globe*, 9 September 1891, 8; "Eugene T. Kingsley," *Manitoba Daily Free Press* [Winnipeg], 11 September 1891, 6.

6 "Eugene T. Kingsley," *Manitoba Daily Free Press* [Winnipeg], 11 September 1891, 6; "Eugene Kingsley," *Little Falls Transcript*, 10 April 1891, 3. Malhotra erroneously stated in an earlier article on Kingsley that his hospitalization was in Oakland, California. See Ravi Malhotra, "Electioneering and Activism at the Turn of the Century and the Politics of Disablement: The Legacy of E.T. Kingsley (1856–1929)," *Review of Disability Studies* 7, nos. 3–4 (2011): 34.

7 For a biography of De Leon, see L. Glen Seretan, *Daniel De Leon: The Odyssey of an American Marxist* (Cambridge, MA: Harvard University Press, 1979).

8 Peter Campbell, *Canadian Marxists and the Search for a Third Way* (Montreal and Kingston: McGill-Queen's University Press, 1999), 3.

9 Ian McKay, *Reasoning Otherwise: Leftists and the People's Enlightenment in Canada, 1890–1920* (Toronto: Between the Lines, 2008), 518; Ross McCormack, *Reformers, Rebels, and Revolutionaries: The Western Canadian Radical Movement 1899–1919* (Toronto: University of Toronto Press, 1977), 60.

10 McCormack, *Reformers, Rebels, and Revolutionaries*, 26–34, 60–61, 70. See also Gordon Hak, *The Left in British Columbia: A History of Struggle* (Vancouver: Ronsdale Press, 2013), 40. Like others, Hak repeats the erroneous claim that Kingsley's disability arose from "an industrial accident in California." Hak provides the useful suggestion that Kingsley was "recruited by Nanaimo miners to serve as their propagandist."

11 Paul Fox, "Early Socialism in Canada," in *The Political Process in Canada: Essays in Honour of R. MacGregor Dawson*, ed. J.H. Aitchison (Toronto: University of Toronto Press, 1963), 91–92. See also David Akers, "Rebel or Revolutionary? Jack Kavanagh and the Early Years of the Communist Movement in Vancouver, 1920–1925," *Labour/ Le Travail* 30 (1992): 15.

12 McKay, *Reasoning Otherwise*. See also Ian McKay, *Rebels, Reds, Radicals: Rethinking Canada's Left History* (Toronto: Between the Lines, 2005).

13 William S. McClure, "Trend of Social Evolution," *Western Clarion*, 25 November 1905, 3.

14   Please note that we use the term "disabled people" rather than "people with disabilities" throughout this book as a reflection of our commitment to disability rights. This is increasingly common practice. For a brief discussion, see Art Blaser, "Taking Disability Rights Seriously," *New Political Science* 25, no. 4 (2003): 593.

15   Edward Slavishak, "Artificial Limbs and Industrial Workers' Bodies in Turn-of-the-Century Pittsburgh," *Journal of Social History* 36 (Winter 2003): 368.

16   Ibid., 370.

17   Ibid.

18   Ibid., 372.

19   Ibid., 371.

20   Ibid., 379.

21   Ibid., 371.

22   Although Kingsley did not discuss his impairments in his extensive body of published work, there are tantalizing references to injured workers. See, for example, E.T. Kingsley, "Killed and Maimed in Peace as in War," *British Columbia Federationist* (hereafter cited as *Federationist*) (Vancouver), 9 June 1916, 1.

23   Dianne Pothier and Richard Devlin, *Critical Disability Theory: Essays in Philosophy, Politics, Policy and Law* (Vancouver: UBC Press, 2006). See also Helen Meekosha, Russell Shuttleworth, and Karen Soldatic, "Disability and Critical Sociology: Expanding the Boundaries of Critical Social Inquiry," *Critical Sociology* 39, no. 3 (2013): 319–23.

24   Jennifer Esmail and Christopher Keep, "Victorian Disability: Introduction," *Victorian Review* 35, no. 2 (2009): 46; Michel Foucault, *The History of Sexuality, Volume 1: An Introduction,* trans. Robert Hurley (1976; repr., London: Allen Lane, 1979), and subsequent volumes; Richard Wolin, *The Terms of Cultural Criticism: The Frankfurt School, Existentialism, Postmodernism* (New York: Columbia University Press, 1992).

25   John Witt, *The Accidental Republic: Crippled Workingmen, Destitute Widows, and the Remaking of American Law* (Cambridge, MA: Harvard University Press, 2004).

26   William W. Fisher III, "Texts and Contexts: The Application to American Legal History of the Methodologies of Intellectual History," *Stanford Law Review* 49, no. 5 (May 1997): 1068. See also Assaf Likhovski, "Czernowitz, Lincoln, Jerusalem and the Comparative History of American Legal Thought," *Theoretical Inquiries in Law* 4, no. 2 (January 2003): 621–57.

27   Reva B. Siegel, "Home as Work: The First Woman's Rights Claims Concerning Wives' Household Labor, 1850–1880," *Yale Law Journal* 103, no. 5 (March 1994): 1073–217. For another pioneering example, see J.G.A. Pocock, *The Machiavellian Moment: Florentine Political Thought and the Atlantic Republican Tradition* (Princeton, NJ: Princeton University Press, 1975).

28   McKay, *Reasoning Otherwise.*

29   John Williams-Searle, "Cold Charity: Manhood, Brotherhood, and the Transformation of Disability, 1870–1900," in *The New Disability History: American Perspectives,* ed. Paul K. Longmore and Lauri Umansky (New York: New York University Press, 2001),

157–86. See also Witt, *The Accidental Republic,* 37; and Barbara Young Welke, *Recasting American Liberty: Gender, Race, Law, and the Railroad Revolution, 1865– 1920* (New York: Cambridge University Press, 2001).

30 Alan Sears, "Immigration Controls as Social Policy: The Case of Canadian Medical Inspection, 1900–1920," *Studies in Political Economy* 33, no. 1 (1990): 91–112; Valentina Capurri, "Canadian Public Discourse around Issues of Inadmissibility for Potential Immigrants with Disabilities and/or Disability, 1902–2002" (PhD diss., York University, 2010).

31 Gregory S. Kealey, "Spymasters, Spies, and their Subjects: The RCMP and Canadian State Repression, 1914–1939," in *Whose National Security? Canadian State Surveillance and the Creation of Enemies,* ed. Gary Kinsman, Dieter K. Buse, and Mercedes Steedman (Toronto: Between the Lines, 2000), 18–33.

Chapter 2: Incident at Spring Gulch

1 "Northern Pacific," *Railroad Gazette* [New York], 2 January 1891, 18. The journal refers to the opening of the Spring Gulch line.

2 "Heavy Damages Demanded for Serious Injury," *St. Paul Daily Globe,* 9 September 1891, 8.

3 "Crushed by the Cars: Frightful Accident to a Northern Pacific Brakeman," *Standard* [Anaconda, MT], 17 October 1890, 8. This is hardly surprising since the mortality rate for amputations was extremely high. Erin O'Connor suggests that it was as high as 75 percent for amputations performed at the hip in the nineteenth century. Erin O'Connor, "'Fractions of Men': Engendering Amputation in Victorian Culture," *Comparative Studies in Society and History* 39, no. 4 (1997): 746.

4 The age of Kingsley is determined from the 1860 US Census records, which identify him as being four years old. He identified his place of birth as Pomfret on his 1878 marriage record, though another source identifies his place of birth as Marcellus, New York, near Syracuse, where his father was born. See United States, Eighth Census of the United States, 12 June 1860, Town of Spring, Boone County, Illinois, 408, roll M653–157, Family History Library film 803157, from the *1860 United States Federal Census Online Database,* www.ancestry.com; and marriage record, 16 October 1878, Hudson, Wisconsin, vol. 1, 203, from the *Wisconsin, Marriage Index, 1820–1907 Online Database,* www.ancestry.com.

5 See United States, Census Records, 1860–1900, from the *United States Federal Census Online Databases,* www.ancestry.com; *St. Paul City Directory, 1884,* 476; California State Voters' List, "Register 2nd Precinct, 30th Assembly District, San Francisco County, 1896," California State Library, California History Section, Great Registers 1866–1898, collection 4–2A, roll 93, Family History Library roll 977613, from the *California, Voter Registers, 1866–1898 Online Database,* www.ancestry.com.

6 For a discussion of Frederick Jackson Turner's famous "frontier thesis" on the relationship of the frontier to American democracy, see Martin Ridge, "The Life of an Idea: The Significance of Frederick Jackson Turner's Frontier Thesis," *Montana: The Magazine of Western History* 41, no. 1 (1991): 2–13.

7   United States, Ninth Census of the United States, 11 June 1870, Morristown, Rice County, Minnesota, 5, sheet 436, from the *1870 United States Federal Census Online Database*, www.ancestry.com.

8   See Clara K. Fuller, *History of Morristown and Todd Counties, Minnesota: Their People, Industries, and Institutions* (Indianapolis: B.F. Bowen, 1915). Although many details of Eugene Kingsley's life remain vague, we have access to detailed accounts of Clara Kingsley Fuller's health status, teaching career, social life, and quotidian comings and goings, all documented in great detail in the *Little Falls Transcript* from 1885 onward as a result of her husband's position as a newspaper proprietor. In 1893, the newspaper reported that Clara had been visiting her parents in the town of Parker (presumably in Ohio) and had returned to her home in Minneapolis. See "Randall Notes," *Little Falls Transcript*, 31 March 1893, 3.

9   Marriage record, 16 October 1878, Hudson, Wisconsin, vol. 1, 203, from the *Wisconsin, Marriage Index, 1820–1907 Online Database*, www.ancestry.com.

10 See United States, Tenth Census of the United States, 7 June 1880, Caldwell, Noble County, Ohio, 163A, roll 1055, Family History Library film 1255055, from the *1880 United States Federal Census Online Database*, www.ancestry.com.

11 Minnesota, Minnesota State Census, 15 May 1885, City of St. Paul, Ramsey County, Minnesota, 4th Ward, 342, microfilm reels 1–47 and 107–64, from the *Minnesota, Territorial and State Censuses, 1849–1905 Online Database*, www.ancestry.com.

12 See *St. Paul City Directory, 1884–85*, 476; *St. Paul City Directory, 1885*, 496; *St. Paul City Directory, 1886*, 567; *St. Paul City Directory, 1887*, 696; and *St. Paul City Directory, 1888*, 670. The family lived at 455 Goodhue Street in St. Paul.

13 "Personal," *Little Falls Transcript*, 22 March 1889, 3. This issue of the newspaper, published by Kingsley's future brother-in-law, notes that "Mr. E.T. Kingsley of St. Paul ... was in Little Falls yesterday visiting his sister, Miss Clara Kingsley. He was on his way to Montana."

14 For an account of the global depression that spread after 1873, see Eric Hobsbawm, *The Age of Empire 1875–1914* (New York: Random House, 1987), 34–36. See also Howard H. Quint, *The Forging of American Socialism: Origins of the Modern Movement* (Indianapolis: Bobbs-Merrill, 1953).

15 "Schedule for Trainmen," 1894, folder 15 "Northern Pacific Railway," box 161, collection 5149, Brotherhood of Railway Trainmen Records, Kheel Center for Labor-Management Documentation and Archives, Cornell University Library (hereafter cited as BRT Records, Cornell). See also James H. Ducker, *Men of the Steel Rails: Workers on the Atchison, Topeka and Santa Fe Railroad, 1869–1900* (Lincoln: University of Nebraska Press), 106–7.

16 Sherman to Sheridan, 7 October 1872, cited in David D. Smits, "The Frontier Army and the Destruction of the Buffalo: 1865–1883," *Western Historical Quarterly* 25, no. 3 (1994): 335.

17 Ibid., 317; see also Robert Wooster, *The Military and United States Indian Policy, 1865–1903* (New Haven, CT: Yale University Press, 1988), 171–72.

18 For the importance of railway infrastructure in the settlement of Montana, see Dale Martin, *Ties, Rails, and Telegraph Wires: Railroads and Communities in Montana and the West* (Helena: Montana Historical Society Press, 2018).

19 Gordon Morris Bakken and Alexandra Kindell, eds., *Encyclopedia of Immigration and Migration in the American West* (Thousand Oaks, CA: Sage, 2006), 383; Melvyn Dubofsky, "The Origins of Western Working Class Radicalism, 1890–1905," *Labor History* 7, no. 2 (1966): 134.

20 Thomas A. Clinch, "The Northern Pacific Railroad and Montana's Mineral Lands," *Pacific Historical Review* 34, no. 3 (1965): 326–32. See *Barden v Northern Pacific Railroad Co*, (1894) 154 US 288.

21 Montana, *Reports of the Inspector of Mines and Deputy Inspector of Mines for the Year Ending November 30th, 1890* (Helena: Journal Publishing, 1890); *Railroad Gazette* [New York] 23 (1891): 18, 71; "Missoula County," *Independent-Record* [Helena], 22 November 1890, 5; "Splendid Prospects," *Semi-Weekly Spokesman-Review* [Spokane], 30 July 1891, 2. See also Carlos Schwantes, "How Railroads Took the 'Wild' Out of the West," *Wild West* 20, no. 6 (2008): 42–49.

22 Dubofsky, "The Origins of Western Working Class Radicalism," 138; Joan London, *Jack London and His Times: An Unconventional Biography* (1939; repr., Seattle: University of Washington Press, 1968), 124.

23 "Heavy Damages Demanded for Serious Injury," *St. Paul Daily Globe,* 9 September 1891, 8.

24 "Crushed by the Cars: Frightful Accident to a Northern Pacific Brakeman," *Standard* [Anaconda, MT], 17 October 1890, 8. Thanks to Professor Mark Aldrich of Smith College for his technical insight on drawbars. Mark Aldrich email to Ravi Malhotra, 24 May 2013.

25 "Eugene T. Kingsley," *Manitoba Daily Free Press* [Winnipeg], 11 September 1891, 6.

26 Katherine Ott, "The Sum of Its Parts: An Introduction to Modern Histories of Prosthetics," in *Artificial Parts, Practical Lives: Modern Histories of Prosthetics,* ed. Katherine Ott, David Serlin, and Stephen Mihm (New York: New York University Press, 2002), 15. See also Tal Golan, "The Emergence of the Silent Witness: The Legal and Medical Reception of X-Rays in the USA," *Social Studies of Science* 34, no. 4 (2004): 469–72.

27 Ironically, given his later political career in Canada, some of the most detailed coverage of his litigation appeared in the *Manitoba Daily Free Press*. See "Eugene T. Kingsley," *Manitoba Daily Free Press* [Winnipeg], 11 September 1891, 6. Given the importance of the railways to the economy in Winnipeg, litigation by injured railway workers was likely of great interest to the business community there.

28 W.A. Pritchard, interview with David Millar, 17 September 1969, Los Angeles, Accession No. 1970–0010, David Millar Fonds, LAC. Kingsley's use of artificial limbs is confirmed in several other sources, including a report on his 1896 arrest during an open-air meeting in San Francisco, an account of his 1908 organizing tour across Canada, and an obituary in the *Labor Statesman*. See "Socialists Explain Their Principles," *San Francisco Examiner,* 17 August 1896, 4; George Weston Wrigley,

"How Working-Class Leaders Travel," *Western Clarion*, 12 September 1908, 1; Parker Williams, "E.T. Kingsley," *Labor Statesman* [Vancouver], 13 December 1929, 4. Clearly, some reports of Kingsley's political activities did occasionally reference his impairments. It might also simply be that nineteenth-century newspaper reporting practices did not include references to disabilities. We thank David Serlin for discussion on this point.

29 "Annual Report Ending 1893," box 143.L.10.6 (F), Northern Pacific Railway Company Records, Minnesota Historical Society. (In 1896, the Northern Pacific Railroad Company sold its assets to a new company, the Northern Pacific Railway Company. The sale attracted controversy from creditors, and was considered in the US Supreme Court in the 1913 decision in *Northern Pacific Railroad Company and Northern Pacific Railway Company, Appts, v Joseph H. Boyd*, 228 US 482.) Kingsley left the Missoula hospital for his family home in River Falls, Wisconsin, by way of the home of his sister Clara in Little Falls, Minnesota, by April 1891. See "Eugene Kingsley," *Little Falls Transcript*, 10 April 1891, 3. The other Northern Pacific Railroad hospitals were located in Brainerd, Minnesota; Glendive, Montana; and Tacoma, Washington. See "Railway Hospital Post Cards," n.d., Railway Surgery, http://railwaysurgery.org/Hospitals.htm.

30 "How Kingsley Became a Socialist," *Voice*, 29 May 1908, 4. See also Ross McCormack, *Reformers, Rebels, and Revolutionaries: The Western Canadian Radical Movement 1899–1919* (Toronto: University of Toronto Press, 1977), 26.

31 Dubofsky, "The Origins of Western Working Class Radicalism," 132–33. For a discussion of changing legal doctrines in late-nineteenth-century America tied to the rise of corporations and legal recognition of corporate personhood, see Morton Horwitz, *The Transformation of American Law, 1870–1960: The Crisis of Legal Orthodoxy* (Oxford: Oxford University Press, 1992), 65–107.

32 See "N.P. Directors," *Missoula Weekly Gazette*, 22 October 1891, 9; "Northern Pacific Directors Elected," *Missoula Weekly Gazette*, 22 October 1891, 8; "Through a Trestle," *Missoula Weekly Gazette*, 22 October 1891, 1; "A Brave Engineer," *Missoula Weekly Gazette*, 22 October 1891, 3; "Killed in the Cage," *Missoula Weekly Gazette*, 22 October 1891, 6; untitled article, *Missoula Weekly Gazette*, 22 October 1891, 12, regarding the death of Sir Thomas Gorsett at Mission, British Columbia. The *Missoula Weekly Gazette* appears never to have mentioned Kingsley or his disablement or litigation during its three-year print run, in contrast to coverage in the St. Paul and Winnipeg press. A report regarding the death of a railway worker on the Northern Pacific line near Helena and a resolution expressing sympathy (but not outrage) from his union, Division 262 of the Brotherhood of Locomotive Engineers, appeared in the *Missoula Weekly Gazette* the same day as the incident at Spring Gulch involving Kingsley. See "Resolutions of Sympathy," *Missoula Weekly Gazette*, 15 October 1890, 5.

33 J.A. Phillips III, "Genealogy and the Northern Pacific," *Mainstreeter* [Kirkland, WA], 28, no. 1 (2009): 14, 18.

34 "Eugene Kingsley," *Little Falls Transcript*, 10 April 1891, 3.

35 "Covering Up the Tracks," *Western Clarion*, 4 September 1909, 1. See also "Three Times Widowed by Horrors of Mine," *Western Clarion*, 27 January 1912, 1.

36 *St. Paul City Directory, 1892–93,* 787.

37 See *Langley's San Francisco Directory for the Year 1893,* 822; *Davidson's Minneapolis Directory, 1894–95,* 536; and "School Teachers of Minneapolis," *Minneapolis Tribune,* 1 June 1899, 4.

38 See "Briefs in the Courts," *Minneapolis Star Tribune,* 17 June 1894, 5; "District Court Calendar," *Minneapolis Star Tribune,* 17 June 1894, 22. In the 1920 US Census, Myra Kingsley is identified as divorced, confirming the outcome of these legal proceedings. However, intriguingly, she would identify herself as "widowed" a month after Kingsley's death according to the record produced by a US Census enumerator in January 1930. See United States, "Fourteenth Census of the United States: 1920 – Population," Minneapolis, Minnesota, Curtis Court Hotel and Apts, 3 January 1920, in *1920 US Census Online Database,* www.ancestry.com; and United States, "Fifteenth Census of the United States: 1930 – Population," Minneapolis, Minnesota, 3 January 1930, in *1930 US Census Online Database,* www.ancestry.com.

39 Robert Kingsley, "Cruelty as a Ground for Divorce in Minnesota," *Minnesota Law Review* 16, no. 3 (February 1932): 260.

40 Garrity would die of typhoid fever in 1906. John Garrity, telephone interview with Ravi Malhotra, 9 April 2020. See also "Thomas A. Garrity Dead," *Irish Standard* [Minneapolis, MN], 20 January 1906, 5.

41 Horwitz, *The Transformation of American Law,* 80. For a more detailed discussion of some of the activities of the Minneapolis branch of the Socialist Labor Party, see Joseph Dorfman, *The Economic Mind in American Civilization, Vol. 3, 1865–1918* (New York: Viking Press, 1949), 137–39.

42 See BRT Records, Cornell. The Brotherhood of Railway Trainmen would later merge into the United Transportation Union. See also Paul Michel Taillon, *Good, Reliable, White Men: Railroad Brotherhoods, 1877–1917* (Champaign: University of Illinois Press, 2009); Joel Isaac Seidman, *The Brotherhood of Railroad Trainmen: The Internal Political Life of a National Union* (New York: Wiley, 1962); and Walter F. McCaleb, *Brotherhood of Railway Trainmen, with Special Reference to the Life of Alexander F. Whitney* (New York: Albert and Charles Boni, 1936).

43 "Honorary Register of the Disabled," 1879–1904, box 1, collection 5611, Brotherhood of Locomotive Firemen and Enginemen Honorary Register of Disabled, Kheel Center for Labor-Management Documentation and Archives, Cornell University Library (hereafter cited as BLF Records, Cornell).

44 "Constitution and By-Laws of the Brotherhood of Railroad Brakemen, 1884," folder 1, box 1, BRT Records, Cornell.

45 See, for example, "Assessment for March 1888, Assessment No. 17," 1 March 1888, folder 1, box 146, collection 5141, BLF Records, Cornell.

46 "A Cold-Blooded Document," *Railroad Trainmen's Journal* 7 (1890): 68.

47 Ibid., 68–70.

48 See John Williams-Searle, "Cold Charity: Manhood, Brotherhood, and the Transformation of Disability, 1870–1900," in *The New Disability History: American Perspectives,* ed. Paul K. Longmore and Lauri Umansky (New York: New York University Press, 2001), 157–86.

49 See "Program for the Sixtieth Anniversary of the Brotherhood of Railroad Train-men," box 22, collection 5149, BRT Records, Cornell; also see McCaleb, *Brotherhood of Railway Trainmen,* 33.

50 Mark Aldrich, *Death Rode the Rails: American Railway Accidents and Safety, 1828–1965* (Baltimore: Johns Hopkins University Press, 2006), 2.

51 John Witt, *The Accidental Republic: Crippled Workingmen, Destitute Widows, and the Remaking of American Law* (Cambridge, MA: Harvard University Press, 2004), 27.

52 Mark Aldrich, *Safety First: Technology, Labor, and Business in the Building of American Work Safety 1870–1939* (Baltimore: Johns Hopkins University Press, 1997), 17, noting that British railways had a fatality rate for railworkers 50 percent higher than American railways despite four times the traffic density.

53 Mark Aldrich, "Train Wrecks to Typhoid Fever: The Development of Railway Medicine Organizations, 1850 to World War I," *Bulletin of the History of Medicine* 75, no. 2 (2001): 264. For a discussion of the impact of railway accidents on passengers, see Barbara Young Welke, *Recasting American Liberty: Gender, Race, Law and the Railroad Revolution, 1865–1920* (New York: Cambridge University Press, 2001).

54 Sarah Rose, "'Crippled' Hands: Disability in Labour and Working-Class History," *Labor: Studies in Working-Class History in the Americas* 2, no. 1 (2005): 34. Rose notes (48) how employers became more restrictive in their hiring of disabled employees after the 1880s.

55 Ibid., 37. See also Charles H. Clark, "The Railway Safety Movement in the United States: Origins and Development, 1869–1893" (PhD diss., University of Illinois at Urbana, 1966), 10, commenting on how "the constant injection of new brakemen into train crews prevented any one combination of men from gaining the experience necessary for efficient operation of trains."

56 Aldrich, *Death Rode the Rails,* 16. See also Williams-Searle, "Cold Charity"; and John Williams-Searle, "Broken Brothers and Soldiers of Capital: Disability, Manliness and Safety on the Rails, 1863–1908" (PhD diss., University of Iowa, 2004).

57 Witt, *The Accidental Republic,* 34.

58 Ibid. See also John Witt, "The Transformation of Work and the Law of Workplace Accidents, 1842–1910," *Yale Law Journal* 107, no. 5 (1998): 1470–73.

59 John Williams-Searle, "Risk, Disability, and Citizenship: U.S. Railroaders and the Federal Employers' Liability Act," *Disability Studies Quarterly* 28, no. 3 (2008): n. pag., http://dsq-sds.org/article/view/113/113.

60 Edward Slavishak, *Bodies of Work: Civic Display and Labor in Industrial Pittsburgh* (Durham: Duke University Press, 2008), 2–4.

61 Williams-Searle, "Broken Brothers and Soldiers of Capital," 7; Ducker, *Men of the Steel Rails,* 9, 112.

62 Ducker, *Men of the Steel Rails,* 10–11.

63 Ibid., 11–12.

64 Aldrich, *Death Rode the Rails,* 6.

65 See Fred A. Benham, "Misplaced Confidence," *Railroad Trainmen's Journal* 7 (1890): 480. This article describes hosting for three months a trainman falsely making a total disability claim.

66 Williams-Searle, "Broken Brothers and Soldiers of Capital," 302.

67 Witt, "The Transformation of Work," 1477.

68 Kim Nielsen observes that, during the Progressive Era, institutional settings gradually became less devoted to educational improvement of disabled people, as had been the case in earlier years, and more purely carceral sites that warehoused disabled people. See Kim E. Nielsen, *A Disability History of the United States* (Boston: Beacon Press, 2012), 118–19.

69 Rose, "'Crippled' Hands," 51; Sarah F. Rose, *No Right to Be Idle: The Invention of Disability, 1840s–1930s* (Chapel Hill: University of North Carolina Press, 2017), 1416. See also Witt, *The Accidental Republic*, 36.

70 See Liat Ben-Moshe, Chris Chapman, and Allison C. Carey, eds., *Disability Incarcerated: Imprisonment and Disability in the United States and Canada* (London: Palgrave Macmillan, 2014). For a good overview of British policy during industrialization, see Colin Barnes, *Disabled People in Britain and Discrimination: A Case for Anti-Discrimination Legislation* (London: C. Hurst, 1991), Chapter 2. See also David L. Braddock and Susan L. Parish, "An Institutional History of Disability," in *Handbook of Disability Studies*, ed. Gary L. Albrecht, Katherine D. Seelman, and Michael Bury (Thousand Oaks, CA: Sage Publishing, 2001), 11–68; and Marta Russell and Ravi Malhotra, "Capitalism and Disability," in *Socialist Register 2002: A World of Contradictions*, ed. Leo Panitch and Colin Leys (Halifax: Fernwood Publishing, 2001), 211–28. A more theoretical treatment is Michel Foucault's classic work on madness, *Madness and Civilization: A History of Insanity in the Age of Reason*, trans. Richard Howard (New York: Vintage Books, 1964).

71 Rose, *No Right to Be Idle*, 116.

72 Rose, "'Crippled' Hands," 48–49.

73 Williams-Searle, "Broken Brothers and Soldiers of Capital," 299–301.

74 For the origins of workers' compensation schemes in the United States, see Price V. Fishback and Shawn Everett Kantor, "The Adoption of Workers' Compensation in the United States, 1900–1930," *Journal of Law and Economics* 41, no. 2 (1998): 305–41; and Price V. Fishback and Shawn Everett Kantor, *A Prelude to the Welfare State: The Origins of Workers' Compensation* (Chicago: University of Chicago Press, 2000). For an influential report on the development of workers' compensation laws in Canada, see William Ralph Meredith, *Final Report on Laws Relating to the Liability of Employers* (Toronto: L.K. Cameron, 1913).

75 Williams-Searle, "Broken Brothers and Soldiers of Capital," 300–1.

76 Ibid., 302.

77 Ibid., 303.

78 Ibid., 303–4.

79 Ibid., 304, noting that only 40 percent of BLE members were part of the insurance plan in the late 1860s and early 1870s.

80 Ibid., 308.

81 Ibid., 308–9.

82 Ducker, *Men of the Steel Rails*, 44–45; Rose, *No Right to Be Idle*, 117–18.

83 Rose, *No Right to Be Idle*, 117.

84   Williams-Searle, "Cold Charity," 169–76.

85   For a discussion of adaptation to social roles after the acquisition of an impairment, see David M. Engel and Frank W. Munger, *Rights of Inclusion: Life Stories of Americans with Disabilities* (Chicago: University of Chicago Press, 2003).

86   See Dorfman, *The Economic Mind in American Civilization*, 222–25; and Albert C. Stevens, "Analysis of the Phenomena of the Panic in the United States in 1893," *Quarterly Journal of Economics* 8, no. 1 (1894): 121–48.

87   "Married," *Little Falls Transcript*, 2 February 1894, 3.

88   Court of Appeals of the District of Columbia, *Transcript of Record, No. 3122, Jamison et al. v District of Columbia* (Washington, DC: Law Reporter Printing Company, 1917); New York, Senate of the State of New York, Joint Legislative Committee Investigating Seditious Activities, *Revolutionary Radicalism: Its History, Purpose and Tactics with an Exposition and Discussion of the Steps Being Taken and Required to Curb It, Part I: Revolutionary and Subversive Movements at Home and Abroad, Volume II* (Albany: J.B. Lyon, 1920), 1253.

89   "Program for the Sixtieth Anniversary of the Brotherhood of Railroad Trainmen," 1943, box 22, collection 5149, BRT Records, Cornell.

90   Ibid. This seems to be an allusion to an address given by President Benjamin Harrison to Congress the same year. See Nielsen, *A Disability History of the United States*, 124–25. Nielsen appears to state the wrong year.

91   Aldrich, *Death Rode the Rails*, 4–5.

92   Ibid., 5.

93   Aldrich, *Safety First*, 26–39. For a further discussion of injuries to railway passengers, see Welke, *Recasting American Liberty*.

94   Lorenzo S. Coffin, "Safety Appliances on the Railroads," *Annals of Iowa* 5, no. 8 (1903): 562.

95   Clark, "The Railway Safety Movement in the United States," 121.

96   Ibid., 111.

97   Williams-Searle, "Broken Brothers and Soldiers of Capital," 164.

98   Clark, "The Railway Safety Movement in the United States," 125.

99   Ibid., 128.

100 *Safety Appliance Act, 1893*, 27 Stat 531; Aldrich, *Safety First*, 9, 36–40. See also William Hayes, "Letter," *Locomotive Engineers' Monthly Journal* [Cleveland], April 1893, 326–27, discussing the importance of railworkers working with state railway boards.

101 Lawrence M. Friedman and Jack Ladinsky, "Social Change and the Law of Industrial Accidents," *Columbia Law Review* 67, no. 1 (1967): 64.

102 David W. Louisell and Kenneth M. Anderson, "The Safety Appliance Act and the FELA: A Plea for Clarification," *Law and Contemporary Problems* 18, no. 3 (1953): 281. See also Williams-Searle, "Cold Charity," 166–67.

103 Benjamin Harrison, "State of the Union Address, 1889," 3 December 1889, American History, http://www.let.rug.nl/usa/presidents/benjamin-harrison/state-of-the-union-1889.php.

104 Ibid. Advocates of labour often compared injured workers to veterans.

105 Witt, *The Accidental Republic*, 25.

106 Aldrich, *Safety First,* 33–36. See also "The Safety Coupler Law," *Railroad Trainmen's Journal* 7 (1900): 81–82.

107 "Safety Appliances," *Railroad Firemen's Magazine* [Terre Haute, IN], 26 January 1899, 93.

108 Williams-Searle, "Cold Charity," 167. Later in 1902, the US circuit court for the northern district in Iowa handed down its decision in the case of *Voelker v Chicago, Milwaukee and St. Paul Railway Company,* denying an appeal by the company and sustaining a finding of legal liability for failure to install an automatic coupler, upholding an award of damages for $9,000 for the death of a twenty-nine-year-old brakeman. See *Voelker v Chicago, Milwaukee and St. Paul Railway* (16 June 1902), reprinted from the *Federal Reporter,* vol. 116, 867, in "Defective Safety Appliances: Decision of the United States Circuit Court," n.d. [c. 1902], and associated correspondence, folder 11, box 19, BRT Records, Cornell.

109 Louisell and Anderson, "The Safety Appliance Act and the FELA," 282. The *FELA* abolished the employer defences of contributory negligence and assumption of risk. See also George W. Alger, "The Present Situation of Employers' Liability," *Railroad Trainmen's Journal* 24 (1907): 244–45.

110 Ducker, *Men of the Steel Rails,* 45.

111 Aldrich, "Train Wrecks to Typhoid Fever," 265.

112 Ibid., 266–67.

113 See, for example, Clark Bell, "The True Field of Duty of the Railway Surgeon," *Medico-Legal Studies* 12 (1894): 374–86, arguing that railway surgeons had to put the interests of their patients first.

114 Aldrich, "Train Wrecks to Typhoid Fever," 265.

115 Ibid.

116 Ibid., 267. Epistemic communities can be defined as "professional networks with authoritative and policy-relevant expertise." See Mai'a K. Davis Cross, "Rethinking Epistemic Communities Twenty Years Later," *Review of International Studies* 39, no. 1 (2013): 137. Although epistemic communities are frequently global, we would argue that the concept can be applied appropriately here.

117 "Railway Hospital Post Cards," n.d., Railway Surgery, http://railwaysurgery.org/Hospitals.htm; W.H. Allport, "American Railway Relief Funds I," *Journal of Political Economy* 20, no. 1 (1912): 49–78.

118 Ducker, *Men of the Steel Rails,* 45–46.

119 Ibid., 46.

120 Ibid., 46–47.

121 Vanessa Warne, "'To Invest a Cripple with Peculiar Interest': Artificial Legs and Upper-Class Amputees at Mid-Century," *Victorian Review* 35, no. 2 (2009): 83.

122 Slavishak, "Artificial Limbs and Industrial Workers' Bodies in Turn-of-the-Century Pittsburgh," 382. As late as 1910, funding from employers to assist workers in purchasing artificial limbs varied from $800 to as little as $50.

123 "Socialists Explain Their Principles," *San Francisco Examiner,* 17 August 1896, 4.

124 Slavishak, *Bodies of Work,* 248.

125 Ryan Sweet, "'Get the Best Article in the Market': Prostheses for Women in Nineteenth-Century Literature and Commerce," in *Rethinking Modern Prostheses in*

Anglo-American Commodity Cultures, 1820–1939, ed. Claire L. Jones (Manchester: Manchester University Press, 2017), 114. See also the discussion of surgeon-artists in Caroline Lieffers, "Itinerant Manipulators and Public Benefactors: Artificial Limb Patents, Medical Professionalism, and the Moral Economy in Antebellum America," in *Rethinking Modern Prostheses in Anglo-American Commodity Cultures, 1820–1939,* ed. Claire L. Jones (Manchester: Manchester University Press, 2017), 141.

126　Stephen Mihm, "'A Limb Which Shall Be Presentable in Polite Society': Prosthetic Technologies in the Nineteenth Century," in *Artificial Parts, Practical Lives: Modern Histories of Prosthetics,* ed. Katherine Ott, David Serlin, and Stephen Mihm (New York: New York University Press, 2002), 283. For a more recent discussion of patents in the context of prosthetics, see Lieffers, "Itinerant Manipulators."

127　Mihm, "'A Limb Which Shall Be Presentable in Polite Society,'" 282–83; Slavishak, "Artificial Limbs and Industrial Workers' Bodies," 370. Slavishak dates the rise of industrial accidents to the turn of the century, but the evidence, including President Harrison's address to Congress, clearly indicates widespread concerns about the increase of accidents as far back as the 1880s.

128　Lisa Herschbach, "Prosthetic Reconstructions: Making the Industry, Re-Making the Body, Modelling the Nation," *History Workshop Journal* 44 (1997): 27–28. Interestingly, Confederate veterans with disabilities received far worse pensions than their Northern counterparts.

129　Lieffers, "Itinerant Manipulators," 137.

130　Ibid.

131　Ibid., 139.

132　Katherine Ott, "Disability Things: Material Culture and American Disability History, 1700–2010," in *Disability Histories,* ed. Susan Burch and Michael Rembis (Champaign: University of Illinois Press, 2014), 127. Many amputees and paraplegics have long complained that popular fashion trends prioritize designs that are impossible or difficult for amputees and wheelchair users to wear.

133　Warne, "'To Invest a Cripple with Peculiar Interest,'" 83–86.

134　See Deborah Harris-Moore, *Media and the Rhetoric of Body Perfection: Cosmetic Surgery, Weight Loss and Beauty in Popular Culture* (Burlington, VT: Ashgate, 2014).

135　Slavishak, "Artificial Limbs and Industrial Workers' Bodies," 370; Ott, "The Sum of Its Parts," 10.

136　See Susan Schweik, *The Ugly Laws: Disability in Public* (New York: New York University Press, 2009).

137　Herschbach, "Prosthetic Reconstructions," 35.

138　Slavishak, "Artificial Limbs and Industrial Workers' Bodies," 376.

139　Ibid., 372.

140　Daniel T. Rodgers, *The Work Ethic in Industrial America, 1850–1920* (Chicago: University of Chicago Press, 1978), xi, cited in Rose, *No Right to Be Idle,* 30.

141　See, for example, Michael Oliver, *The Politics of Disablement* (London: Macmillan, 1990); Marta Russell, *Beyond Ramps: Disability at the End of the Social Contract* (Monroe, ME: Common Courage, 1998); and Rose, *No Right to Be Idle,* 1–3. For a discussion in the context of American veteran pensions in the First World War, see

Paul R.D. Lawrie, "'Salvaging the Negro': Race, Rehabilitation, and the Body Politic in World War America, 1917–1924," in *Disability Histories,* ed. Susan Burch and Michael Rembis (Champaign: University of Illinois Press, 2014), 331.

142 Lawrie, "'Salvaging the Negro,'" 331.

143 Rose, *No Right to Be Idle,* 2. The third point has less salience in the case of Kingsley since there was very little income support legislation for injured workers at the time of his accident in 1890.

144 Witt, *The Accidental Republic,* 23. For further discussion, see John M. Kinder, "'Lest We Forget': Disabled Veterans and the Politics of War Remembrance in the United States," in *Disability Histories,* ed. Susan Burch and Michael Rembis (Champaign: University of Illinois Press, 2014), 169.

145 Sweet, "'Get the Best Article in the Market,'" 117–22.

146 O'Connor, "'Fractions of Men,'" 744. See also Erin O'Connor, *Raw Material: Producing Pathology in Victorian Culture* (Durham, NC: Duke University Press, 2000), 104; and Cassandra S. Crawford, *Phantom Limb: Amputation, Embodiment and Prosthetic Technology* (New York: New York University Press, 2014), 9, discussing the phantom-prosthetic issue.

147 O'Connor, "'Fractions of Men,'" 754.

148 "Heavy Damages Demanded for Serious Injury," *St. Paul Daily Globe,* 9 September 1891, 8; "Suit against the Northern Pacific," *Star Tribune* [Minneapolis], 9 September 1891, 3; "Pioneer Press," *Little Falls Transcript,* 11 September 1891, 3; "Eugene T. Kingsley," *Manitoba Daily Free Press* [Winnipeg], 11 September 1891, 6. Given that a federal court would have had jurisdiction if Kingsley were living in another state, the fact that his case was heard in a state court indicates that he returned to Minnesota, where his sister Clara taught in Little Falls, after his rehabilitation.

149 But see Aldrich, *Death Rode the Rails,* xv (suggesting that the availability of new products over time makes it problematic to evaluate awards for damages in the distant past simply by adjusting for inflation).

150 "Heavy Damages Demanded for Serious Injury," *St. Paul Daily Globe,* 9 September 1891, 8.

151 "Suit against the Northern Pacific," *Star Tribune* [Minneapolis], 9 September 1891, 3. Attorneys William H. McDonald and Lynas D. Barnard operated a firm at 303 and 305 Grand Avenue in St. Paul. See *St. Paul City Directory, 1891–92,* 891; and *St. Paul City Directory, 1891–92,* 787.

152 Peter Karsten, "Enabling the Poor to Have Their Day in Court: The Sanctioning of Contingency Fee Contracts, a History to 1940," *DePaul Law Review* 47, no. 2 (1998): 258.

153 "In Special Term: Legal Problems Passed Upon by District Judges," *St. Paul Daily Globe,* 24 January 1892, 8.

154 "Judicial Portraits: William Dalton Cornish," 2012, *Ramsey County Law Library Blog,* http://ramseylawlibrary.org/?p=426; "W.D. Cornish Found Dead in Chicago," *New York Times,* 8 November 1908, 11.

155 *Saint Paul: History and Progress* (St. Paul: Pioneer Press, 1897), 64–65, http://www.minnesotalegalhistoryproject.org/assets/St.%20P%20B&B%20(1897).pdf.

156 "Five Thousand for Kingsley," *St. Paul Daily Globe*, 28 July 1892, 2.

157 Alger, "The Present Situation of Employers' Liability," 244–45.

158 "The Price of a Leg," *St. Paul Daily Globe*, 25 March 1892, 2.

159 Peter Karsten, *Heart versus Head: Judge-Made Law in Nineteenth Century America* (Chapel Hill: University of North Carolina Press, 1997), 258–63.

160 G.E. White, *Tort Law in America: An Intellectual History* (Oxford: Oxford University Press, 2003), 16.

161 Ibid., Chapter 3. A systematic treatment of legal realism and its impact on tort law is beyond the scope of this work.

162 Witt, *The Accidental Republic*, 43–44, referring to Holmes's *The Common Law*.

163 White, *Tort Law in America*, 18. See also Witt, *The Accidental Republic*, 34, for a discussion of how scholars such as Holmes regarded themselves as "expounders, systematizers and historians, clarifying the law and making possible its orderly development."

164 *Farwell v Boston and Worcester Rail Road*, 45 Mass (4 Met) 49 (1842).

165 Witt, "The Transformation of Work," 1469. In *Farwell*, an engineer sought compensation for injuries stemming from a train accident resulting from the negligence of a switchman.

166 Witt, "The Transformation of Work," 1477n53; Randolph E. Bergstrom, *Courting Danger: Injury and Law in New York City, 1870–1910* (Ithaca, NY: Cornell University Press, 1992), 65. See also White, *Tort Law in America*, 51. In the specific context of Minnesota, see *Charles N Ling v St Paul, Minneapolis & Manitoba Railway Co*, 50 Minn 160; 52 NW 378; 1892 Minn LEXIS 270 [*Ling*].

167 *Chicago & Milwaukee R R v Ross*, 112 US 377 (1884).

168 Ibid., 390–91.

169 *Winterbottom v Wright*, 152 Eng Rep 402, 403 (Ex 1842).

170 John C.P. Goldberg and Benjamin C. Zipursky, "The Moral of Macpherson," *University of Pennsylvania Law Review* 146, no. 6 (August 1998): 1750.

171 Ibid.

172 Ibid.

173 Ibid.

174 Karsten, *Heart versus Head*, 278.

175 Witt, *The Accidental Republic*, 50.

176 Witt, "The Transformation of Work," 1476. In the specific context of Minnesota, see *John Birmingham v Duluth, Missabe and Northern Railway Company*, 70 Minn 474; 73 NW 409; 1897 Minn LEXIS 91.

177 Horwitz, *The Transformation of American Law*, 225. For a dissenting view, arguing that nineteenth-century innovations in tort doctrine were primarily designed to assist victims of torts to obtain justice, see Karsten, *Heart versus Head*, 294.

178 R. Blake Brown, "Cecil A. Wright and the Foundations of Canadian Tort Law Scholarship," *Saskatchewan Law Review* 64 (2001): 204.

179 Witt, *The Accidental Republic*, 50–51. See also White, *Tort Law in America*, 41, discussing Holmes's endorsement of the assumption of risk principle.

180 Witt, *The Accidental Republic*, 57–58.

181 Ibid., 67–68.

182 Ibid., 62.

183 "The Human Cost of Industry," *Railroad Trainmen's Journal* 25 (1908): 421.

184 See Walter M. Licht, "Nineteenth Century American Railwaymen: A Study in the Nature and Organization of Work" (PhD diss., Princeton University, 1977); and Walter Licht, *Working for the Railroad: The Organization of Work in the Nineteenth Century* (Princeton, NJ: Princeton University Press, 1983).

185 "A Cold-Blooded Document," *Railroad Trainmen's Journal* 7 (1890): 68–70.

186 "The Human Cost of Industry," *Railroad Trainmen's Journal* 25 (1908): 419–20.

187 Ibid., 418.

188 Alger, "The Present Situation of Employers' Liability," 244–45.

189 Witt, *The Accidental Republic,* 55.

190 Ibid.

191 Bergstrom, *Courting Danger,* 17–20.

192 Witt, *The Accidental Republic,* 59.

193 Ibid., 61.

Chapter 3: California Radical

1 See Dustin Galer, "A Friend in Need or a Business Indeed? Disabled Bodies and Fraternalism in Victorian Ontario," *Labour/Le Travail* 66 (2010): 9–36, for a discussion of stigma in the Victorian era.

2 Howard H. Quint, *The Forging of American Socialism: Origins of the Modern Movement* (Indianapolis: Bobbs-Merrill, 1953), 173; Frank Girard and Ben Perry, *The Socialist Labor Party 1876–1991: A Short History* (Philadelphia: Livra Books, 1991); J. Anthony Lukas, *Big Trouble: A Murder in a Small Western Town Sets Off a Struggle for the Soul of America* (New York: Simon and Schuster, 1997), 208. As Lukas writes, "then, in 1893, work dried up. That spring, a financial panic, starting with ruinous collapse on Wall Street, had sent a tidal wave of repercussions crashing through the land. In the worst economic crisis the country had yet experienced, mines, factories, railroads, and retail establishments went belly-up, disgorging thousands of unemployed men and women into skid row and 'hobo jungles.'" But see also Carlos A. Schwantes, "Left-Wing Unionism in the Pacific Northwest: A Comparative History of Organized Labor and Socialist Politics in Washington and British Columbia, 1885–1917" (PhD diss., University of Michigan, 1976), 161, noting that the SLP sections in the Pacific Northwest were eliminated after the Panic of 1893. It should be remembered that the impact of macro-economic crises was not cushioned by state policy as it would be in the twentieth century. For an account of political protests arising from the Panic of 1893, see Benjamin F. Alexander, *Coxey's Army: Popular Protest in the Gilded Age* (Baltimore: Johns Hopkins University Press, 2015).

3 Paul Fox, "Early Socialism in Canada," in *The Political Process in Canada: Essays in Honour of R. MacGregor Dawson,* ed. J.H. Aitchison (Toronto: University of Toronto Press, 1963), 89.

4 Melvyn Dubofsky, "The Origins of Western Working Class Radicalism, 1890–1905," *Labor History* 7, no. 2 (1966): 138–41.

5   Ibid., 143.

6   Charles M. White, "The Socialist Labor Party, 1890–1903" (PhD diss., University of Southern California, 1959), 1. Although White cites more recent SLP statements, they have remained constant since the 1890s.

7   These concepts are further developed in the Canadian context in Peter Campbell, *Canadian Marxists and the Search for a Third Way* (Montreal and Kingston: McGill-Queen's University Press, 1999).

8   Ralph Shaffer, "Radicalism in California, 1869–1929" (PhD diss., University of California, Berkeley, 1962), 331–33; Hecht to Kuhn, 16 January 1898, reel 16, collection US Mss 3A, Socialist Labor Party of America Records, Wisconsin Historical Society (hereafter cited as SLP Records, WHS).

9   Quint, *The Forging of American Socialism*, 15–18; Gerald Sorkin, *A Time for Building: The Third Migration 1880–1920* (Baltimore: Johns Hopkins University Press, 1992), 117.

10 Quint, *The Forging of American Socialism*, 18.

11 Joan London, *Jack London and His Times: An Unconventional Biography* (1939; repr., Seattle: University of Washington Press, 1968), 106.

12 For an account of the questionable trial in the Haymarket Affair, see Harvey O'Connor, "Henry Demarest Lloyd: The Prophetic Tradition," in *American Radicals: Some Problems and Personalities,* ed. Harvey Goldberg (New York: Monthly Review Press, 1957), 82–83; and Quint, *The Forging of American Socialism,* 32–35. But Timothy Messer-Kruse, *The Haymarket Conspiracy: Transatlantic Anarchist Networks* (Champaign: University of Illinois Press, 2012), argues that there was a violent conspiracy.

13 David Herreshoff, "Daniel De Leon: The Rise of Marxist Politics," in *American Radicals: Some Problems and Personalities,* ed. Harvey Goldberg (New York: Monthly Review Press, 1957), 200. De Leon was among the earliest of a number of West Indian radicals to immigrate to the United States. Others included Hubert Harrison and C.L.R. James. See Jeffrey B. Perry, *Hubert Harrison: The Voice of Harlem Radicalism, 1883–1918* (New York: Columbia University Press, 2010); and Paul Buhle, *C.L.R. James: The Artist as Revolutionary* (London: Verso, 1988). For an account of De Leon's teaching days at Columbia University, see L. Glen Seretan, *Daniel De Leon: The Odyssey of an American Marxist* (Cambridge, MA: Harvard University Press, 1979), 13–16.

14 Joseph Dorfman, *The Economic Mind in American Civilization, Vol. 3, 1865–1918* (New York: Viking Press, 1949), 142–46.

15 Ibid., 145–48. Nonetheless, Marx respected George's attempt to critique mainstream economic thinking.

16 Quint, *The Forging of American Socialism,* 143; Edward Bellamy, *Looking Backward: From 1887 to 2000* (Boston: Ticknor, 1888). George was known as a supporter of a single tax.

17 Dorfman, *The Economic Mind in American Civilization,* 149–51.

18 Quint, *The Forging of American Socialism,* 73–79.

19 Ibid., 81–82.

20 Ibid., 144–45. De Leon became editor of the *People* in 1891.

21 James D. Young, *Socialism since 1889: A Biographical History* (London: Pinter, 1988), 51–54. See also Seretan, *Daniel De Leon,* 63.

22 Seretan, *Daniel De Leon,* 84–97.

23 Quint, *The Forging of American Socialism,* 146.

24 The *People,* 8 December 1895, cited in White, "The Socialist Labor Party," 77.

25 Quint, *The Forging of American Socialism,* 146.

26 For an account of the 1896 California SLP State Convention, including Kingsley's endorsing a resolution in favour of the creation of the Trade and Labor Alliance, see "Socialists in State Convention," *San Francisco Chronicle,* 24 February 1896, 9; and "Socialists Organizing," *San Francisco Call,* 24 February 1896, 7.

27 See Joseph G. Rayback, *A History of American Labor* (New York: Free Press, 1959), 227–31.

28 James A. Stevenson, "Daniel De Leon: The Relationship of Socialist Labor Party and European Marxism, 1890–1914" (PhD diss., University of Wisconsin, Madison, 1977), 137.

29 Seretan, *Daniel De Leon,* 116–21; Dorfman, *The Economic Mind in American Civilization,* 219. See also Mike Davis, *Old Gods, New Enigmas: Marx's Lost Theory* (London: Verso, 2018), 50–51, noting the employer's use of the blacklist to punish Pullman strikers led by Debs.

30 Michael Kazin, "The Great Expectation Revisited: Organized Labor and Politics in San Francisco and Los Angeles, 1870–1940," *Pacific Historical Review* 55, no. 3 (1986): 379.

31 Ibid., 379–81; Michael Rogin, "California Populism and the 'System of 1896,'" *Western Political Quarterly* 22, no. 1 (1969): 182; also see Michael Kazin, *Barons of Labor: The San Francisco Building Trades and Union Power in the Progressive Era* (Champaign: University of Illinois Press, 1989).

32 Kazin, "The Great Expectation Revisited," 384.

33 Richard Walker, "Industry Builds the City: The Suburbanization of Manufacturing in the San Francisco Bay Area, 1850–1940," *Journal of Historical Geography* 27, no. 1 (2001): 38.

34 Seretan, *Daniel De Leon,* 108; David B. Griffiths, "Anti-Monopoly Movement in California: 1873–1898," *Southern California Quarterly* 52, no. 2 (1970): 105–6. See also Dorfman, *The Economic Mind in American Civilization,* 22; and James F. Hudson, *The Railways and the Republic,* 3rd ed. (New York: Harper and Brothers, 1889).

35 Dorfman, *The Economic Mind in American Civilization,* 224–25. During the 1890s, a "free silver" policy would gain traction among sections of the American working class.

36 Shaffer, "Radicalism in California," 128–30. For an account of the impact of the Pullman Strike in California, see William W. Ray, "Crusade or Civil War? The Pullman Strike in California," *California History* 58, no. 1 (1979): 29. It seems to have had a much greater impact in Sacramento than San Francisco.

37 Shaffer, "Radicalism in California," 117; Kazin, *Barons of Labor,* 38; Alexander Saxton, "San Francisco Labor and the Populist and Progressive Insurgencies," *Pacific Historical Review* 34, no. 4 (1965): 436–37. For a discussion of the Populist-led alliance to elect

Mayor Sutro, see John D. Hicks, *Populist Revolt: A History of the Farmers' Alliance and the People's Party* (Minneapolis: University of Minnesota Press, 1931), 339.

38 Shaffer, "Radicalism in California," 117–19.

39 Kazin, "The Great Exception Revisited," 386.

40 Shaffer, "Radicalism in California," 115.

41 Seretan, *Daniel De Leon,* 108. Mayor Sutro's popular campaign slogan was "down with corporations." He won by a landslide, partly because of his opposition to Southern Pacific's monopoly of the city's streetcar system. See John A. Lawrence, "Behind the Palaces: The Working Class and the Labor Movement in San Francisco, 1877–1901" (PhD diss., University of California, Berkeley, 1979), 370; and Steven P. Erie, "The Development of Class and Ethnic Politics in San Francisco 1870–1910: A Critique of the Pluralist Interpretation" (PhD diss., University of California, Los Angeles, 1975), 249.

42 London, *Jack London and His Times,* 123.

43 Shaffer, "Radicalism in California," 114–15.

44 Michael J. Dubin, *United States Congressional Elections, 1789–1997: The Official Results of the Elections of the 1st through 105th Congresses* (Jefferson, NC: McFarland, 1998), 313, 322.

45 Stephen Coleman, *Daniel De Leon* (Manchester: Manchester University Press, 1990), 61.

46 Edel Hecht to Daniel De Leon, 12 February 1898, De Leon Collection, as cited in Ira Kipnis, *The American Socialist Movement, 1897–1912* (New York: Columbia University Press, 1952), 23.

47 Lawrence, "Behind the Palaces," 324.

48 Ibid., 325–26. Unfortunately, the poor state of the economy until the outbreak of the Spanish-American War meant that affiliated unions had fallen to fifteen by 1897. See ibid., 328–29.

49 Ibid., 327–28.

50 Ibid., 330.

51 Ibid., 331–33; Hecht to Kuhn, 16 January 1898, reel 16, SLP Records, WHS; Benham to Kuhn, 20 March 1897, reel 13, SLP Records, WHS.

52 Shaffer, "Radicalism in California," 129; Jonah Raskin, "Introduction," in *The Radical Jack London: Writings on War and Revolution,* ed. Jonah Raskin (Berkeley: University of California Press, 2008), 19.

53 Jack London, "Letter to Editor," *Oakland Times,* 29 July 1896, in *The Letters of Jack London, Vol. 1: 1896–1905,* ed. Earle Labor, Robert C. Leitz III, and I. Milo Shepard (Stanford, CA: Stanford University Press, 1988), 3–5.

54 Joseph Noel, *Footloose in Arcadia: A Personal Record of Jack London, George Sterling, Ambrose Bierce* (New York: Carrick and Evans, 1940), 34. See also Philip S. Foner, "Jack London: American Rebel," in Philip S. Foner, ed., *Jack London: American Rebel* (New York: Citadel Press, 1964; orig. pub. 1947), 27.

55 For a discussion of London's Social Darwinism and its impact on his novels, see Clarice Stasz, "Social Darwinism, Gender and Humor in 'Adventure,'" in *Rereading Jack London,* ed. Leonard Cassuto and Jeanne C. Reesman (Stanford, CA: Stanford

University Press, 1996), 130–40. On Social Darwinism as a theme of De Leon's thought and the influence of Darwin and Spencer on De Leon, see Mark Pittenger, *American Socialists and Evolutionary Thought, 1870–1920* (Madison: University of Wisconsin Press, 1993), 101–3. For a discussion of Darwinism in the *Western Clarion,* journal of the Socialist Party of Canada and edited by Kingsley, see Ian McKay, *Reasoning Otherwise: Leftists and the People's Enlightenment in Canada, 1890–1920* (Toronto: Between the Lines, 2008), 70–77.

56 Ronald Grantham, "Some Aspects of the Socialist Movement in British Columbia, 1898–1933" (MA thesis, University of British Columbia, 1942), Appendix 4, 2. The *Western Clarion* also serialized the *Iron Heel* in 1913–14. See, for example, "The Iron Heel," *Western Clarion,* 3 January 1914, 4; "The Iron Heel," *Western Clarion,* 18 July 1914, 4; and David Buchanan, "'Yours for the Revolution': Communication and Identity in the *Western Clarion,*" *English Studies in Canada* 41, nos. 2–3 (2015): 153.

57 Shaffer, "Radicalism in California," 20.

58 Ibid., 21–22. Haskell clearly came from a different class background than Kingsley and London.

59 Ibid., 22–23.

60 Ibid., 25.

61 *Yick Wo v Hopkins,* 118 US 356 (1886). For a discussion of *Yick Wo,* see Thomas W. Joo, "*Yick Wo* Re-Revisited: Nonblack Nonwhites and Fourteenth Amendment History," *University of Illinois Law Review* 5 (2008): 1427–40. For a comprehensive discussion of anti-Chinese racism in California, see Alexander Saxton, *The Indispensable Enemy: Labor and the Anti-Chinese Movement in California* (Berkeley: University of California Press, 1971).

62 Shaffer, "Radicalism in California," 81.

63 Griffiths, "Anti-Monopoly Movement in California," 95.

64 Walton Bean, "Idea of Reform in California," *California Historical Quarterly* 51, no. 3 (1972): 217; Shaffer, "Radicalism in California," 30–32, 49, 94. Shaffer concludes that it seems to have had no direct connection with the organization led by Mikhail Bakunin in Europe. He also notes that there is no evidence that the International Workmen's Association actually used dynamite. Ibid., 34–35.

65 Lawrence, "Behind the Palaces," 194.

66 Shaffer, "Radicalism in California," 24.

67 Ibid., 45. A rather shrill document articulating Haskell's philosophy of anarchist revolution is reproduced in Chester M. Destler, *American Radicalism: 1865–1901* (1946; repr., Chicago: Quadrangle Books, 1966), 82–100.

68 Shaffer, "Radicalism in California," 90; Bean, "Idea of Reform in California," 216–17; Dorfman, *The Economic Mind in American Civilization,* 153. George Speed, along with many other radicals, broke with Haskell over his mismanagement of the Kaweah colony. See Shaffer, "Radicalism in California," 83. For an example of Nationalist ideology in the San Francisco Bay Area, see A.A. Denison, *Some Aspects of Modern Socialism: A Paper Read before the Oakland Nationalist Club* (Oakland: Enquirer Publishing House, 1891), and the announcement of the meeting at which Denison presented his paper is "The Nationalists," *Tribune* [Oakland], 3 April 1891, 1.

69 Whether this club actually had working-class members is not clear. See Charles Postel, *The Populist Vision* (New York: Oxford University Press, 2007), 226.

70 Shaffer, "Radicalism in California," 116. Other Nationalists, such as Job Harriman, entered the Socialist Labor Party and ran for vice-president on the SLP ticket in 1898. See Griffiths, "Anti-Monopoly Movement in California," 96. Harriman was eventually the running mate of Debs in his 1900 campaign for president.

71 The election for supervisor took place on 6 November 1894, and Kingsley received 668 votes (1.2 percent) compared with 27,115 votes (49.6 percent) for the victorious candidate, businessman and sugar baron Adolph Spreckels. See "The Municipal Ticket," *San Francisco Examiner,* 25 October 1894, 9; "Vote of the City," *San Francisco Chronicle,* 7 November 1894, 9; "Municipal Ticket," *San Francisco Examiner,* 8 November 1894, 2; "The Local Ticket," *San Francisco Chronicle,* 9 November 1894, 12; "Winners and Losers," *San Francisco Chronicle,* 25 December 1894, 14; and Appendix 2 and "Registrar of Voters' Report," in San Francisco Board of Supervisors, *San Francisco Municipal Reports, for the Fiscal Year 1894–1895, Ending June 30, 1895* (San Francisco: Hinton Printing, 1895), 59.

72 "Will Carry a Red Flag," *San Francisco Call,* 26 April 1896, 21. The figure of several thousand SLP members in San Francisco might well be an exaggeration, and the internal correspondence of the SLP leadership suggests a lower figure. See Benham to Kuhn, 20 March 1897, reel 13, SLP Records, WHS. In 1901, the Metropolitan Labor Temple was identified as the "Trades Union Headquarters" and the location of the Temple Bar. See advertisement for the "Temple Bar," *Advance* [San Francisco], 27 April 1901, 7.

73 Edgar Painter, *Langley's San Francisco Directory for the Year 1895* (San Francisco: J.B. Painter, n.d. [c. 1894]), 862, 1443.

74 "A Challenge to Debate," *San Francisco Examiner,* 28 October 1894, 8.

75 "Discussed the Charter," *San Francisco Call,* 19 March 1895, 4. See also "Socialists Want Representation," *San Francisco Call,* 19 November 1896, 9, for Kingsley's participation on an SLP committee to lobby the mayor of San Francisco, James Phelan, for equitable representation for the socialists on a committee of 100 entrusted to draft a new charter for the city.

76 "To Celebrate Labor Day," *San Francisco Call,* 9 April 1895, 11.

77 "Socialist Labor Party," *San Francisco Call,* 19 April 1896, 32; "Will Carry a Red Flag," *San Francisco Call,* 26 April 1896, 21; "Socialists Are Active," *San Francisco Call,* 3 May 1896, 9; Hecht to Kuhn, 15 May 1896, reel 7, SLP Records, WHS. It appears that Ross McCormack is mistaken in suggesting that Kingsley was awarded the post of state organizer for his loyalty during the split of the "Kangaroos" who went on to support the Socialist Party of Eugene Debs. These events did not occur until 1898–99. See Ross McCormack, *Reformers, Rebels, and Revolutionaries: The Western Canadian Radical Movement 1899–1919* (Toronto: University of Toronto Press, 1977), 26.

78 "Socialists Celebrate," *San Francisco Call,* 2 May 1896, 5. See also "Will Carry a Red Flag," *San Francisco Call,* 26 April 1896, 21; "Socialists Will March," *San Francisco Examiner,* 28 April 1896, 5. Kingsley would repeat this simile in a controversial column shortly after his appointment as managing editor of the *Western Clarion* in December 1903. See "The Annual Farce," *Western Clarion,* 5 December 1903, 1.

79 Jerome A. Hart, *In Our Second Century: From an Editor's Note-Book* (San Francisco: Pioneer Press, 1931), http://www.sfmuseum.net/hist2/kalloch.html.

80 "Socialists Keep Labor Day Holy," *San Francisco Call,* 2 May 1897, 9.

81 "The Socialists," *San Francisco Call,* 19 March 1896, 9.

82 "In Socialist Ranks," *San Francisco Call,* 19 July 1897, 10; "Klondyke a Great Curse," *San Francisco Call,* 2 August 1897, 5.

83 "Prof. Jordan to Lecture," *San Francisco Call,* 31 May 1897, 10.

84 "Socialists' Meetings," *San Francisco Call,* 15 November 1897, 10.

85 "Meetings," *Twentieth Century* [New York] 14, no. 16 (1895): 16. For more on Pentecost, see Benjamin Tucker, "Mr. Pentecost's Belief in the Ballot," *Liberty* (Boston, MA), 19 January 1889, http://fair-use.org/benjamin-tucker/instead-of-a-book/mr-pentecosts-belief-in-the-ballot.

86 "Aims of Socialism," *San Francisco Call,* 28 October 1895, 10. The Knights of Pythias fraternal order had some 7,000 members in the Bay Area in this time period. See "Oakland Will Greet Knights of Pythias," *San Francisco Call,* 14 August 1902, 11. For a meeting on the topic of "How and to What Extent Do We Now Co-Operate?" featuring speeches by T.E. Zant and Kingsley, see "Socialist Meeting," *San Francisco Call,* 17 February 1896, 7. For other speeches by Kingsley in San Francisco, see "Socialism and the Economy," *San Francisco Call,* 9 July 1896, 9; "The Socialists," *San Francisco Examiner,* 10 July 1896, 10; "The Socialists' Idea," *San Francisco Call,* 11 July 1896, 11; "Labor Day at the Big Temple," *San Francisco Call,* 7 September 1896, 12; "The Socialists," *San Francisco Call,* 5 April 1897, 5; and "Socialist Labor Party Is Working," *San Francisco Examiner,* 1 August 1898, 5.

87 "Frank Hadsell's Red Wagon House," *San Francisco Call,* 2 July 1896, 13; "Socialist Labor Party Is Working," *San Francisco Examiner,* 1 August 1898, 5. For a discussion of a lecture that Kingsley delivered in Salinas, California, see "The Socialist Labor Party," *Californian* [Salinas], 14 July 1899, 3.

88 Kingsley to Kuhn, 4 June 1898, reel 17, SLP Records, WHS.

89 "Report of the National Executive Committee, SLP, to the 9th National Convention, July 4th, 1896," 15, reel 35, SLP Records, WHS. See also "Socialists in State Convention," *San Francisco Chronicle,* 24 February 1896, 9; "Socialists Organizing," *San Francisco Call,* 24 February 1896, 7; "Advocates of Socialism," *San Francisco Call,* 17 June 1896, 20; "Convention of City Socialists," *San Francisco Call,* 29 June 1896, 8; "Socialists Organizing," *San Francisco Call,* 1 July 1896, 8; "State Socialists against Silver," *San Francisco Examiner,* 20 July 1896, 8; "Socialism in the Country," *San Francisco Call,* 14 August 1896, 10; "Socialists in the Country," *San Francisco Call,* 8 March 1897, 12; and E. Hecht, letter to the editor, *Appeal to Reason* [Girard, KS], 20 June 1896, 4.

90 Hecht to Kuhn, 25 September 1896, reel 9, SLP Records, WHS.

91 "Socialism and Economy," *San Francisco Call,* 9 July 1896, 9.

92 Ibid.

93 For the Free Speech fights in the early twentieth century, see Terry R. Willis, "The Black Hole of Seattle: The Socialist Free Speech Movement, 1906–1907," *Pacific North West Quarterly* 91, no. 3 (2000): 124; Jeffrey A. Johnson, *"They Are All Red*

Out Here": Socialist Politics in the Pacific Northwest, 1895–1925 (Norman: University of Oklahoma Press, 2008), 76–77; Emma Goldman, Candace Falk, Barry Pateman, and Jessica M. Moran, *Emma Goldman: A Documentary History of the American Years – Making Speech Free, 1902–1909* (Berkeley: University of California Press, 2003), 413, 531; Gerald Meyer, *The Lost World of Italian American Radicalism: Politics, Labor, and Culture* (Westport, CT: Greenwood Publishing Group, 2003), 195; Paul B. Bushue, "Dr. Hermon F. Titus and Socialism in Washington State, 1900–1909" (MA thesis, University of Washington, 1967); and various issues of the Seattle *Socialist,* October–December 1907. One rare treatment briefly discussing the SLP protests in 1896 in San Francisco, but without explaining the context of SLP politics, is Richard S. Street, *Beasts of the Field: A Narrative History of California Farmworkers, 1769–1913* (Stanford: Stanford University Press, 2004), 596.

94   "Arrested Socialists," *San Francisco Call,* 8 October 1895, 9.

95   Ibid.; "A Constitutional Right," *San Francisco Call,* 13 August 1895, 6; "Arrest of T.F. Burns," *San Francisco Call,* 15 August 1895, 12; "Right of Free Speech," *San Francisco Call,* 21 August 1895, 11. In the earlier case involving the cigar makers' union official, Judge Conlan had dismissed the charges against Burns, stating that "the streets constitute the people's forum, and so long as no riot is threatened the police should not attempt to interfere."

96   "Labor Council," *San Francisco Call,* 16 November 1895, 16.

97   See "Socialists and Free Speech," *San Francisco Call,* 13 October 1895, 7.

98   Ford to Kuhn, 25 August 1896, reel 8, SLP Records, WHS.

99   "Socialists Explain Their Principles," *San Francisco Examiner,* 17 August 1896, 4.

100   "Eight Socialists Arrested," *San Francisco Chronicle,* 16 August 1896, 28; "The Right of Free Speech," *San Francisco Call,* 16 August 1896, 16; "City News in Brief," *San Francisco Call,* 16 August 1896, 7; "Socialists Explain Their Principles," *San Francisco Examiner,* 17 August 1896, 4; "Poor May Speak under the Sky," *San Francisco Call,* 17 August 1896, 12; "Jury Trials Will Be Asked For," *San Francisco Call,* 21 August 1896, 7; Shaffer, "Radicalism in California," 240; Ford to Kuhn, 25 August 1896, reel 8, SLP Records, WHS. The 1896 Free Speech controversy in San Francisco began in early July with Costley's arrest and was followed by several challenges to police authority, including an open-air meeting on 8 August 1896 at Seventh and Market, where Kingsley spoke. See "A Socialist under Arrest," *San Francisco Call,* 3 July 1896, 11; "Fear Free Speech Is in Jeopardy," *San Francisco Call,* 6 July 1896, 7; "Stood for Free Speech," *San Francisco Call,* 1 August 1896, 5; "City News in Brief," *San Francisco Call,* 1 August 1896, 7; "Socialist Open-Air Meeting," *San Francisco Chronicle,* 9 August 1896, 32; "William Edlin Will Be Fined," *San Francisco Call,* 15 August 1896, 11. The implications of an African American socialist who challenged the police are discussed neither in the news reports of the day nor in the SLP internal correspondence. However, Costley was not in fact the first African American in a leadership position within the Socialist Labor Party. Peter Clark had run as a socialist candidate for Congress decades earlier. See Nikki M. Taylor, *America's First Black Socialist: The Radical Life of Peter H. Clark* (Lexington: University Press of Kentucky, 2013). Costley would go on to play a role in the Socialist Party led by Debs.

101 "Jury Trials Will Be Asked For," *San Francisco Call,* 21 August 1896, 7; "Socialists in Court," *San Francisco Call,* 18 August 1896, 7; "Granted a Continuance," *San Francisco Examiner,* 18 August 1896, 10; "Right of Free Speech," *San Francisco Call,* 23 August 1896, 32.

102 "The Right of Free Speech," *San Francisco Call,* 16 August 1896, 16.

103 Ibid.; "Socialists in Public Protest," *San Francisco Call,* 20 August 1896, 8; "The Socialists Make Protest," *San Francisco Examiner,* 20 August 1896, 8. The San Jose Branch of the Socialist Labor Party and the State Executive Committee, and the San Francisco Cigar-Makers' Union and Pacific Coast Fresco Painters Union, also adopted resolutions protesting the arrests in San Francisco. See "Socialist Labor Protest," *San Francisco Call,* 18 August 1896, 4; "Socialist Labor Party," *San Francisco Call,* 19 August 1896, 10; "The Labor Unions," *San Francisco Call,* 19 August 1896, 11; "Will Aid the Socialists," *San Francisco Call,* 22 August 1896, 7; "Socialists Are Angry," *San Francisco Call,* 4 September 1896, 11.

104 "More Socialists under Arrest," *San Francisco Call,* 30 August 1896, 16; "Silent Socialism Is Not Golden," *San Francisco Chronicle,* 30 August 1896, 27; "Will Speak in Black Letters," *San Francisco Call,* 28 August 1896, 9; "Police Attacked by Socialists," *San Francisco Call,* 31 August 1896, 12; "Sunflower's Invitation," *San Francisco Call,* 1 September 1896, 10; Shaffer, "Radicalism in California," 240.

105 "Socialists Convicted," *San Francisco Examiner,* 26 August 1896, 16; "Socialists Were Held Guilty," *San Francisco Call,* 26 August 1896, 9; "Right of Free Speech," *San Francisco Call,* 27 August 1896, 11; "Jurors Will Not Convict Them," *San Francisco Call,* 4 September 1896, 8; "The Jury Disagreed," *San Francisco Call,* 12 September 1896, 7; "Socialists Are Free," *San Francisco Call,* 15 September 1896, 14. According to the *San Francisco Examiner,* Kingsley and the other accused, who had "decided to allow their cases to be governed by that of Costley, were also judged guilty of the same crime [obstructing the street], and all of them were instructed to appear in court this morning for sentence."

106 Hecht to Kuhn, 15 September 1896, reel 9, SLP Records, WHS.

107 "Sunflower's Invitation," *San Francisco Call,* 1 September 1896, 10; "They Were Not Disturbed," *San Francisco Examiner,* 15 September 1896, 8; "Mum's the Word," *San Francisco Call,* 17 September 1896, 8; "Socialist Labor Party," *San Francisco Call,* 27 September 1896, 4.

108 "Socialists Keep Labor Day Holy," *San Francisco Call,* 2 May 1897, 9. See also "Socialists in the Country," *San Francisco Call,* 8 March 1897, 12; and "International Labor Day," *San Francisco Call,* 16 April 1897, 9.

109 See Noel, *Footloose in Arcadia,* 34. Controversy surrounding open-air meetings in San Francisco would continue in the years ahead. See, for example, "Gives Views on Ordinance," *San Francisco Call,* 17 March 1904, 4.

110 "Socialists Name Their Candidates," *San Francisco Call,* 3 August 1896, 5; "Political Action," *Los Angeles Herald,* 3 August 1896, 1; "Socialist Convention," *Los Angeles Times,* 3 August 1896, 2; "Socialists in Session," *San Francisco Examiner,* 3 August 1896, 5; "A Capitalistic Quarrel," Seattle *Post-Intelligencer,* 3 August 1896, 1; untitled, *Evening Sentinel* [Santa Cruz, CA], 29 September 1896, 2; "Socialist Labor Party's

Ticket," *San Francisco Call,* 30 September 1896, 8; "Socialist Ticket," *Los Angeles Herald,* 1 October 1896, 1; "Socialist Labor Party," *San Francisco Chronicle,* 1 October 1896, 4; "Socialist Labor Party Ticket," *San Francisco Call,* 1 October 1896, 5; "These Are the Candidates," *San Francisco Chronicle,* 17 October 1896, 9; "Official State Ballot," *Sacramento Record-Union,* 24 October 1896, 5; "Socialists Nominate a Ticket," *San Francisco Call,* 22 August 1898, 2; Dubin, *United States Congressional Elections,* 313, 322. Kingsley had moved to San Jose by 1898.

111 "Socialist Labor Party," *San Francisco Call,* 19 April 1896, 32; *New Charter* (Santa Cruz), 10 February 1897, 4.

112 G.B. Benham, "California," *People* [New York], 4 April 1897, 1.

113 Hecht to Kuhn, 15 May 1896, reel 7, SLP Records, WHS. Hecht was also a member of the State Executive Committee. See "Will Carry a Red Flag," *San Francisco Call,* 26 April 1896, 21.

114 Hecht to Kuhn, 15 May 1896, reel 7, SLP Records, WHS; Lawrence, "Behind the Palaces," 333; "Socialists Celebrate," *San Francisco Call,* 2 May 1896, 5.

115 Lawrence, "Behind the Palaces," 333. The leadership of the San Francisco branch was enthusiastic about the relocation of the *New Charter* under the leadership of M.W. Wilkins from Fresno to Santa Clara. See Hecht to Kuhn, 13 January 1897, reel 12, SLP Records, WHS; Benham to Kuhn, 20 March 1897, reel 13, SLP Records, WHS; and Shaffer, "Radicalism in California," 120.

116 Hecht to Kuhn, 15 May 1896, reel 7, SLP Records, WHS; Lawrence, "Behind the Palaces," 333–34; "Socialists Celebrate," *San Francisco Call,* 2 May 1896, 5. McIvor actually spoke before Kingsley in the program but anticipated many of his arguments.

117 Lawrence, "Behind the Palaces," 333–34.

118 Benham to Kuhn, 20 March 1897, reel 13, SLP Records, WHS. For a list of publications by Benham, see "Book Catalog of the Socialistic Co-Operative Publishing Association," 1901, Early American Marxism: A Repository of Source Material, 1864–1946, http://www.marxisthistory.org/subject/usa/eam/spapubs-scpa.html. Benham would go on to support the Debsian Socialist Party. See Kipnis, *The American Socialist Movement,* 85.

119 Benham to Kuhn, 20 March 1897, reel 13, SLP Records, WHS.

120 "More Socialists Organize," *San Francisco Call,* 17 May 1897, 4.

121 Remarkably, long after Kingsley had left the Socialist Party of Canada, an article by George Aspden would be published in the dying days of the *Western Clarion* in 1923. See George Aspden, "A Short History of the Chameleon," *Western Clarion,* 16 May 1923, 6.

122 Benham to Kuhn, 20 March 1897, reel 13, SLP Records, WHS.

123 Ibid.

124 Job Harriman was the SLP vice-presidential candidate in 1898. Maguire was likely James Maguire, the Democratic member of the House of Representatives for the Fourth District of California between 1893 and 1899.

125 Benham to Kuhn, 20 March 1897, reel 13, SLP Records, WHS.

126 Ibid.

127 Ibid.
128 Hecht to Kuhn, 2 May 1897, reel 13, SLP Records, WHS. This is presumably the Metropolitan Temple that served as a venue for many SLP events.
129 Ibid.
130 Ibid.
131 Mark Sherry, "A Sociology of Impairment," *Disability and Society* 31, no. 6 (2016): 734, 738. For a classic phenomenological account of limb loss, see Maurice Merleau-Ponty, *The Phenomenology of Perception*, trans. Donald A Landes (New York: Routledge, 2014 [1945]), 73–89. Merleau-Ponty comments on phantom limbs thoughtfully at 81: "This phenomenon, distorted equally by physiological and psychological explanations, is, however, understood in the perspective of being-in-the-world. What it is in us which refuses mutilation and disablement is an *I* committed to a certain physical and inter-human world, who continues to tend toward his world despite handicaps and amputations and who, to this extent, does not recognize them *de jure*." Clearly, Merleau-Ponty was influenced by Husserl and Heidegger. For interesting treatments of Merleau-Ponty, see Richard Wolin, *The Terms of Cultural Criticism: The Frankfurt School, Existentialism, Postmodernism* (New York: Columbia University Press, 1992); and Dermot Moran, *Introduction to Phenomenology* (New York: Routledge, 2000), 391–434.
132 Judith Butler, *Gender Trouble: Feminism and the Subversion of Identity* (New York: Routledge, 1990), 140–41.
133 Erin O'Connor, "'Fractions of Men': Engendering Amputation in Victorian Culture," *Comparative Studies in Society and History* 39, no. 4 (1997): 744. See also Erin O'Connor, *Raw Material: Producing Pathology in Victorian Culture* (Durham, NC: Duke University Press, 2000), 104; and Cassandra S. Crawford, *Phantom Limb: Amputation, Embodiment and Prosthetic Technology* (New York: New York University Press, 2014), 9.
134 Walker, "Industry Builds the City," 40.
135 Peter E. Newell, *The Impossibilists: A Brief Profile of the Socialist Party of Canada* (London: Athena Press, 2008), 157.
136 Kingsley is first identified in the San Francisco city directory in 1893 living at 34 Ellis Street, three blocks from the Metropolitan Temple at 115 Turk Street. In 1894, the directory shows him living at 863 ½ Market Street, about eight blocks away; we speculate that the number might be an error since this location is substantially farther away from his workplace than any of his other recorded residences after his disablement until his death. In 1895 and 1896, Kingsley is listed in the directory as residing in a room at the Metropolitan Temple. The state voters' list for 1896 identifies him as living in a room at 474 Jessie Street, suggesting that he moved midway through the year. The 1897 directory shows him living at the same location at 474 Jessie Street. Kingsley is not listed in any San Francisco directory after 1897, following his move to San Jose, where he would reside until 1900. See *Langley's San Francisco Directory for the Year 1893*, 822; *Langley's San Francisco Directory for the Year 1894*, 819; *Langley's San Francisco Directory for the Year 1895*, 862; *Langley's San Francisco Directory for the Year 1896*, 902; *Langley's San Francisco Directory for the Year 1897*,

984; "Register 2nd Precinct, 30th Assembly District, San Francisco County, 1896," California State Library, California History Section, Great Registers 1866–1898, collection 4–2A, roll 93, Family History Library roll 977613, from the *California, Voter Registers, 1866–1898 Online Database,* www.ancestry.com.

137   Sherry, "A Sociology of Impairment," 738.

138   Ryan Sweet, "'Get the Best Article in the Market': Prostheses for Women in Nineteenth-Century Literature and Commerce," in *Rethinking Modern Prostheses in Anglo-American Commodity Cultures, 1820–1939,* ed. Claire L. Jones (Manchester: Manchester University Press, 2017), 116. See also Erving Goffman, *Stigma: Notes on the Management of Spoiled Identity* (Englewood Cliffs, NJ: Prentice-Hall, 1963).

139   Dubin, *United States Congressional Elections,* 322; "Socialists Nominate a Ticket," *San Francisco Call,* 22 August 1898, 2; "Positions Assigned to District Candidates," *San Francisco Call,* 12 October 1898, 2; "California State Ticket," *Sacramento Record-Union,* 12 October 1898, 5; "Republican Banner Now Belongs to San Francisco," *San Francisco Chronicle,* 9 November 1898, 9; "Gage Has Swept the City," *San Francisco Call,* 9 November 1898, 5; "How the City Cast Its Vote," *San Francisco Call,* 10 November 1898, 3; "Semi-Official Count Settles All Doubts," *San Francisco Call,* 11 November 1898, 3; "California's Vote," *Los Angeles Times,* 14 December 1898, 3; "Official Returns of the Election," *San Francisco Call,* 14 December 1898, 5; "The Official Vote," *Santa Cruz Daily Sentinel,* 15 December 1898, 1; "The Official Figures," *Napa Journal,* 15 December 1898, 2. An article in the *Sacramento Record-Union* in October 1898 identified Kingsley as being based in San Jose. See "California State Ticket," *Sacramento Record-Union,* 12 October 1898, 5.

140   "Socialists' Meeting," *San Francisco Call,* 14 November 1898, 5.

141   The 1899 San Jose city directory places Kingsley at 240 South 1st Street, and the 1900 directory and June 1900 US Census show him living in a room at 22 North 1st Street – the SLP headquarters – in the centre of San Jose. See *San Jose City Directory Including Santa Clara County, 1899–1900* (San Jose: F.M. Husted, 1899), 259, 382; *San Jose City Directory Including Santa Clara County, 1900–1901* (San Jose: F.M. Husted, 1900), 277; and United States, "Twelfth Census of the United States, Schedule No. 1 – Population," San Jose Ward 2, Santa Clara County, California, 1 June 1900, 1, enumeration district 66, FHL microfilm 1240111, in *1900 United States Federal Census Online Database,* www.ancestry.com.

142   "Closing Day of the Campaign at San Jose," *San Francisco Call,* 20 May 1900, 16; "Results of the Municipal Election Held May 21st, 1900," in Minutes of the Common Council of the City of San Jose, 23 May 1900, City Council Records, San Jose Public Library.

143   McCormack, *Reformers, Rebels, and Revolutionaries,* 26. See also Morris Hillquit, *History of Socialism in the United States,* rev. ed. (New York: Russell and Russell, 1909), 296 (discussing how dissident SLP members originally rejected the leadership's conception of trade unions); Frank Girard and Ben Perry, *The Socialist Labor Party 1876–1991: A Short History* (Philadelphia: Livra Books, 1991); and Charles M. White, "The Socialist Labor Party, 1890–1903" (PhD diss., University of Southern California, 1959).

144 "Imperialism Denounced by the Socialists," *San Francisco Call,* 31 May 1899, 7. In March 1898, it appears that Kingsley travelled from San Jose to San Francisco, with an "E.S. Kingsley" of San Jose identified in the guest list at the New Western Hotel. See "Hotel Arrivals," *San Francisco Call,* 1 March 1898, 14.

145 "Imperialism Denounced by the Socialists," *San Francisco Call,* 31 May 1899, 7.

146 Howard H. Quint, "American Socialists and the Spanish-American War," *American Quarterly* 10, no. 2 (Summer 1958), 133–34.

147 Ibid., 136. For an overview of later third camp politics and debates, see Sean Matgamna, *The Fate of the Russian Revolution: Lost Texts of Critical Marxism* (London: Phoenix Press, 1998).

148 Lambert to National Board of Appeals, 30 March 1900, reel 34, SLP Records, WHS.

149 E.B. Mercadier, "A Few Corrections," the *People,* 19 November 1899, 3. Harriman obtained 5,600 votes for governor of California on the SLP ticket.

150 United States, "Twelfth Census of the United States, Schedule No. 1 – Population," San Jose Ward 2, Santa Clara County, California, 1 June 1900, 1, enumeration district 66, FHL microfilm 1240111, in *1900 United States Federal Census Online Database,* · www.ancestry.com.

151 Lambert to National Board of Appeals, 30 March 1900, reel 34, SLP Records, WHS.

152 Ibid.

153 King to Slobodin, 4 April 1900, folder 12 "California," box 1, microfilm R-7124, reel 4, Socialist Labor Party Records (hereafter SLP Records), Tamiment Library and Robert F. Wagner Labor Archives, New York University. See also Bersford to Slobodin, 20 June 1900, reel 4, SLP Records, New York University.

154 "Report of the National Executive Committee," in Socialist Labor Party, *Proceedings of the Tenth National Convention of the Socialist Labor Party* (New York: New York Labor News, 1900), 39.

155 Decision of the SLP National Board of Appeals, 13 May 1900, folder "National Board of Appeal Minutes, 1900," reel 34, SLP Records, WHS. See also Boal to National Board of Appeals, 13 March 1900, reel 34, SLP Records, WHS; and "Report of the National Board of Appeals," in Socialist Labor Party, *Proceedings of the Tenth National Convention of the Socialist Labor Party* (New York: New York Labor News, 1900), 71–73.

156 "Report of the National Executive Committee," in Socialist Labor Party, *Proceedings of the Tenth National Convention,* 54–55; see also "Appeal of County Committee, Section Los Angeles, to National Board of Appeals," April 1900, reel 34, SLP Records, WHS.

157 Socialist Labor Party, *Proceedings of the Tenth National Convention,* 5.

158 Ibid., 134.

159 "Report of the National Executive Committee," in Socialist Labor Party, *Proceedings of the Tenth National Convention,* 37–38. See also United States, "Twelfth Census of the United States, Schedule No. 1 – Population," San Jose Ward 2, Santa Clara County, California, 1 June 1900, 1, enumeration district 66, FHL microfilm1240111, in *1900 United States Federal Census Online Database,* www.ancestry.com.

160   Carlos A. Schwantes, *Radical Heritage: Labor, Socialism and Reform in Washington and British Columbia, 1885–1917* (Seattle: University of Washington Press), 110–11; "A New Local Organization of Socialists," Seattle *Socialist,* 24 March 1901, 2.

161   *Polk's Seattle City Directory* (Seattle: Polk's Seattle Directory, 1901), 689. According to the city directory, another resident of the home at 502 21st Avenue (and potentially the owner who provided lodging to Kingsley) was Annie Fisher. See Ibid., 465.

162   "He Wants to Be President," *Spokane Chronicle,* 25 September 1900, 6.

163   Untitled article, *Advance* [San Francisco], 4 May 1901, 2.

164   E.T. Kingsley, "Republican Tyranny: The Primary Election Law Criticized from the Standpoint of the Weaker Parties," Seattle *Socialist,* 16 December 1900, 1. In fact, Washington State adopted election law reform only in 1907. See Kevin Pirche, "Political Parties in the Evergreen State," in *Governing the Evergreen State: Political Life in Washington,* ed. Cornell W. Clayton et al. (Pullman: Washington State University Press, 2018), 45–52; also see Hugh D. Spitzer, "Be Careful What You Wish For: Private Political Parties, Public Primaries, and State Constitutional Restrictions," *Washington Law Review* 94, no. 2 (2019): 823–50; and Claudius O. Johnson, "The Adoption of the Initiative and Referendum in Washington," *Pacific Northwest Quarterly* 35, no. 4 (1944): 291–303.

165   E.T. Kingsley, "Against the Primary," Seattle *Post-Intelligencer,* 12 December 1900, 4.

166   Kingsley, "Republican Tyranny."

167   "That Boasted Primary Law," Seattle *Socialist,* 9 December 1900, 2.

168   Kingsley, "Republican Tyranny."

169   "Rich Man's Primary Law," Seattle *Socialist,* 23 December 1900, 2; "The New Primary Law," Seattle *Socialist,* 27 January 1901, 1; "That Infamous Primary Law," Seattle *Socialist,* 3 February 1901, 1; "A Frank Fair Statement," Seattle *Socialist,* 17 February 1901, 1.

170   For further discussion of the socialist critique of the proposed primary law, see Bushue, "Dr. Hermon F. Titus and Socialism in Washington State," 41–43.

171   "A New Local Organization of Socialists," Seattle *Socialist,* 24 March 1901, 2.

172   E.T. Kingsley, "Statement by the Revolutionary Socialist League of Seattle," Seattle *Socialist,* 28 April 1901, 3. For more on Titus, see Bushue, "Dr. Hermon F. Titus and Socialism in Washington State."

173   Kingsley, "Statement by the Revolutionary Socialist League of Seattle," Seattle *Socialist,* 28 April 1901, 3. The Seattle *Socialist* would continue to engage in polemics with Kingsley even after his arrival in British Columbia.

174   Ibid.

175   Ibid.

176   "Report of the National Executive Committee," in Socialist Labor Party, *Proceedings of the Tenth National Convention,* 56. During debate at the SLP national convention in 1900 on the process for electing officers to the National Executive Committee, Washington State delegate W.S. Dalton spoke in favour of the "old method" as the "most practical and sensible one." Whether this issue contributed in any way to the split in the Washington Socialist Labor Party is unclear. Another reference to

Dalton in the 1900 convention proceedings is an invitation from De Leon to convention delegates to attend a special event marking the opening of a new printing press for the party organ, the *Daily People*. Dalton, who served at the time as secretary of the party's press committee, was scheduled to read "a salutory poem," which would be printed in the presence of delegates as the first publication on the new press. See Socialist Labor Party, *Proceedings of the Tenth National Convention*, 77, 124, 185.

177　Daniel De Leon, "Unity of Insight," *Daily People* [New York], 30 March 1901, http://www.slp.org/pdf/de_leon/eds1901/mar30_1901.pdf. See also "Unity of Insight," *Weekly People*, 6 April 1901, 4.

178　De Leon, "Unity of Insight."

179　Ibid.

180　Ibid.

181　E.T. Kingsley, "Organizer Kingsley's Letter," Seattle *Socialist*, 15 November 1903, 2. See also "Cannot Fool Daniel," *Western Clarion*, 27 April 1907, 1.

182　McCormack, *Reformers, Rebels, and Revolutionaries*, 26, also 178n51, citing McCormack's interviews with Pritchard, 16–18 August 1971, and a personal letter from Pritchard to McCormack, 26 September 1971.

183　G. Weston Wrigley, "BC Socialist Party Convention Reflections," *Western Socialist*, 11 October 1902, 11. Animosity between De Leon and Kingsley was apparent when the former visited British Columbia in 1907, with De Leon lambasting "vagabond journalists" such as Kingsley. See Schwantes, *Radical Heritage*, 180.

184　William Griffiths to Editor, *Weekly People*, 10 September 1904, 5.

185　Press Committee to Editor, *Weekly People*, 27 February 1904, 5.

186　"De Leon in Vancouver," *Weekly People*, 4 May 1907, 6.

187　Eugene V. Debs, "The Social Democratic Convention Has Emphasized Startling Truths," *Appeal to Reason* [Girard, KS], 24 March 1900, 3.

188　"Socialist Unity Secured," Seattle *Socialist*, 11 August 1901, 1, 4. See also "Unity Convention," Seattle *Socialist*, 23 June 1901, 3.

189　See George R. Taft, "Socialism in North America: The Case of British Columbia and Washington State, 1900–1960" (PhD diss., Simon Fraser University, 1983), 401; Bushue, "Dr. Hermon F. Titus and Socialism in Washington State," 31–33.

Chapter 4: Crossing the Line

1　"A Small Flutter," *Western Clarion*, 26 December 1903, 2.

2　G. Weston Wrigley, "BC Socialist Party Convention Reflections," *Western Socialist*, 11 October 1902, 11. Wrigley invokes the common trope of overcoming a handicap rather than a recognition of the societal barriers that restrict disabled people.

3　Ena Chadha, "'Mentally Defectives' Not Welcome: Mental Disability in Canadian Immigration Law, 1859–1927," *Disability Studies Quarterly* 28, no. 1 (2008): n. pag., http://www.dsq-sds.org/article/view/67/67. See also Judith Mosoff, "Excessive Demand on the Canadian Conscience: Disability, Family, and Immigration," *Manitoba Law Journal* 26 (1999): 149–77; and Rose Voyvodic, "Into the Wasteland: Applying Equality Principles to Medical Inaccessibility in Canadian Immigration Law," *Canadian Journal of Law and Social Policy* 16 (2001): 131. The discriminatory exclusion of disabled people as an excessive burden is a policy issue that still plagues Canadian immigration law.

4 *An Act Respecting Emigrants and Quarantine,* Consolidated Statutes of Canada 1859, c 40, ss 10(2) and 11(2).

5 *An Act Respecting Emigrants and Quarantine,* Consolidated Statutes of Canada 1866, c 40, s 8(1).

6 *An Act Respecting Emigrants and Quarantine,* Consolidated Statutes of Canada 1859, c 40, s 11(1); *An Act Respecting Emigrants and Quarantine,* Consolidated Statutes of Canada 1866, c 40, s 11(1).

7 Chadha, "'Mentally Defectives' Not Welcome," n. pag.; Barbara Roberts, *Whence They Came: Deportation from Canada 1900–1935* (Ottawa: University of Ottawa Press, 1988), 53–54.

8 Comprehensive medical inspections were not required by law until 1902, shortly after Kingsley's arrival, and likely implemented only in phases. For further discussion, see Alan Sears, "Immigration Controls as Social Policy: The Case of Canadian Medical Inspection, 1900–1920," *Studies in Political Economy* 33, no. 1 (1990): 96–98.

9 *An Act Respecting Immigration and Immigrants,* SC 1869, c 10; Chadha, "'Mentally Defectives' Not Welcome," n. pag.; Isaac Shin Imai, "Canadian Immigration Law and Policy: 1867–1935" (LL.M. thesis, York University, 1983), 17–19.

10 *An Act Respecting Immigration and Immigrants,* SC 1869, c 10, s 9.

11 Chadha, "'Mentally Defectives' Not Welcome," n. pag. See also Sears, "Immigration Controls as Social Policy," 103, noting the use of medical inspections to exclude African Americans. A full treatment of the racist history of Canadian immigration law, including the Chinese exclusion statute, is beyond the scope of our research.

12 Jay Dolmage and Jen Rinaldi, "'Of Dark Type and Poor Physique': Law, Immigration Restriction, and Disability in Canada, 1900–30," in *Disabling Barriers: Social Movements, Disability History, and the Law,* ed. Ravi Malhotra and Benjamin Isitt (Vancouver: UBC Press, 2017), 98–99. See also David Mitchell and Sharon Snyder, "The Eugenic Atlantic: Race, Disability, and the Making of an International Eugenic Science, 1800–1945," *Disability and Society* 18, no. 7 (2003): 843–64.

13 See Erica Dyck, *Facing Eugenics: Reproduction, Sterilization, and the Politics of Choice* (Toronto: University of Toronto Press, 2013), 3. For a compelling discussion of the operations of the Alberta Eugenics Board, see Jana Grekul, Harvey Krahn, and Dave Odynak, "Sterilizing the 'Feeble-Minded': Eugenics in Alberta, Canada, 1929–1972," *Journal of Historical Sociology* 17, no. 4 (2004): 358–84.

14 *An Act Respecting Immigration and Immigrants,* RSC 1886, c 65.

15 Ibid., s 17(2); Chadha, "'Mentally Defectives' Not Welcome," n. pag.

16 Fiona Alice Miller, "Making Citizens, Banishing Immigrants: The Discipline of Deportation Investigations, 1908–1913," *Left History* 7, no. 1 (2000): 64–67.

17 Cited in ibid., 67.

18 Sears, "Immigration Controls as Social Policy," 95.

19 Constance Backhouse, *Colour Coded: A Legal History of Racism in Canada, 1900–1950* (Toronto: University of Toronto Press, 1999).

20 *An Act to Amend the Immigration Act,* SC 1902, c 14, s 24A.

21 Barbara Roberts, "Doctors and Deports: The Role of the Medical Profession in Canadian Deportation, 1900–1920," *Canadian Ethnic Studies* 18, no. 3 (1986): 18.

22 *An Act to Amend the Immigration Act,* SC 1902, c 14, s 24A; Roberts, "Doctors and Deports," 18; Roberts, *Whence They Came,* 54.

23 Miller, "Making Citizens," 64.

24 On the conflicts between physicians who worked as medical inspectors at ports of entry and the lay bureaucracy, see Roberts, "Doctors and Deports," 17–19.

25 Dolmage and Rinaldi, "'Of Dark Type and Poor Physique,'" 107.

26 Parker Williams, "E.T. Kingsley," *Labor Statesman* [Vancouver], 13 December 1929, 4. See also John Sidaway, "Kingsley Led Vanguard in Fight for Workers," *Labor Statesman* [Vancouver], 27 December 1929, 5.

27 "Nanaimo All Right," Seattle *Socialist,* 19 January 1901, 4.

28 "British Columbia," Seattle *Socialist,* 7 July 1901, 2. See also "British Columbia," Seattle *Socialist,* 23 June 1901, 2; and "From British Columbia," Seattle *Socialist,* 30 June 1901, 2. Titus also commented on the rift between labourists and Marxists in the province, stating that "the Independent Labor Party of British Columbia is a tool of the capitalists to side track the real labor party represented by the Socialists." When the SPBC considered removing a reference to its composition as a "working-class movement" later in 1901 (retreating from an earlier endorsement of the class-conscious SPA program), the Seattle *Socialist* railed against the move. See "Opportunism in British Columbia," Seattle *Socialist,* 29 December 1901, 1. See also Minutes of the Executive Meeting, 4 February 1902, in "The Socialist Movement in British Columbia," *Lardeau Eagle* [Ferguson, BC], 13 February 1902, 3. For the statement of principles adopted by the SPBC at its convention in Vancouver on 3 October 1901, see "The Socialist Movement in British Columbia," *Lardeau Eagle* [Ferguson, BC], 20 February 1902, 3.

29 The *Lardeau Eagle,* British Columbia's first socialist newspaper (published in the mining town of Ferguson by Richard Parmater "Parm" Pettipiece), carried an SPBC report dated the day that Kingsley arrived in Canada (15 March 1902) and published in the next issue of the newspaper to the effect that "the Nanaimo Comrades have engaged Comrade Kingsley of Oakland, Cal., to spend a month in Nanaimo and vicinity in propaganda work. They have kindly offered his services to Victoria for one or more meetings, which we hope will do much good." The *Victoria Daily Colonist* reported the day after Kingsley arrived that his services had been secured "for two months." We have opted to cite the latter time period. See "Sidelights from the Capital," *Lardeau Eagle* [Ferguson, BC], 20 March 1902, 3; and "The World of Labor," *Victoria Daily Colonist,* 16 March 1902, 10. Ross Johnson, relying on the *Lardeau Eagle* report, states that Kingsley's initial contract was for one month. Ross McCormack says that Kingsley was engaged for "a brief propaganda tour." See Ross Alfred Johnson, "No Compromise – No Political Trading: The Marxian Socialist Tradition in British Columbia" (PhD diss., University of British Columbia, 1975), 128–29; and Ross McCormack, *Reformers, Rebels, Revolutionaries: The Western Canadian Radical Movement 1899–1919* (Toronto: University of Toronto Press, 1977), 26. According to Johnson, Kingsley was brought to Nanaimo to "assist in organization"

of the club, seeking to exploit a rift between Marxists and labourists within the Nanaimo (Independent) Labor Party to expand its membership and influence. Historian Gordon Hak suggests that Kingsley was "recruited by Nanaimo miners to serve as their propagandist." See Johnson, "No Compromise," 128–29; and Gordon Hak, *The Left in British Columbia: A History of Struggle* (Vancouver: Ronsdale, 2013), 40; also see Ian McKay, *Reasoning Otherwise: Leftists and the People's Enlightenment in Canada, 1890–1920* (Toronto: Between the Lines, 2008), 149.

30 "Pioneers Pass On," *Western Socialist,* May–June 1952, n. pag., http://www.socialist history.ca/Docs/SocialistParty/Morgan-Pritchard.htm.

31 "The World of Labor," *Victoria Daily Colonist,* 16 March 1902, 10.

32 John Douglas Belshaw, *Colonization and Community: The Vancouver Island Coal-field and the Making of the British Columbian Working Class* (Montreal and Kingston: McGill-Queen's University Press, 2002), 3.

33 Ibid., photo caption, n. pag.

34 See Desmond Morton, "Aid to the Civil Power: The Canadian Militia in Support of Social Order, 1867–1914," *Canadian Historical Review* 51, no. 4 (1970): 410; also see Jeremy Mouat, "The Politics of Coal: A Study of the Wellington Miners' Strike of 1890–91," *BC Studies* 77 (1988): 8.

35 W.A. Taylor, *Crown Land Grants: A History of the Esquimalt and Nanaimo Railway Land Grants* (Victoria: BC Ministry of Environment, Lands and Parks, 1975); Will Horter, "Vancouver Island's Great E & N Railway Land Grab," *Watershed Sentinel,* December 2008, n. pag., https://watershedsentinel.ca/articles/vancouver-island -land-grab.

36 McCormack, *Reformers, Rebels, and Revolutionaries,* 8–9.

37 Jack Kavanagh, *The Vancouver Island Strike* (Vancouver: BC Miners' Liberation League, c. 1913), 1.

38 Mouat, "The Politics of Coal," 5.

39 Ibid., 3–29; Thomas R. Loosmore, "The British Columbia Labor Movement and Political Action, 1879–1906" (MA thesis, University of British Columbia, 1954), 88–149; John Tupper Saywell, "Labour and Socialism in British Columbia: A Survey of Historical Development before 1903," *British Columbia Historical Quarterly* 15, nos. 3–4 (1951): 129–50.

40 Cited in Johnson, "No Compromise," 127–28; Loosmore, "The British Columbia Labor Movement and Political Action," 172–79; Paul Fox, "Early Socialism in Canada," in *The Political Process in Canada: Essays in Honour of R. MacGregor Dawson,* ed. J.H. Aitchison (Toronto: University of Toronto Press, 1963), 86–87; John R. Hinde, *When Coal Was King: Ladysmith and the Coal-Mining Industry of Vancouver Island* (Vancouver: UBC Press, 2003), 139. See also Elections British Columbia, *An Electoral History of British Columbia, 1871–1986* (Victoria: Elections British Columbia, 1988), 55, 56, 72, 73, 81, 83, 87.

41 J.A. Hobson, *Canada Today* (London: Unwin, 1906), 33.

42 "From the Island Coal Camp," *Western Clarion,* 14 April 1906, 1; Canada, *Fourth Census of Canada* (Ottawa: King's Printer, 1921), 244. See also Nelson Wiseman and

Benjamin Isitt, "Early Socialism in Canada: International and Regional Impulses," *American Review of Canadian Studies* 43, no. 4 (2013): 521.

43 Mouat, "The Politics of Coal," 8–9, citing "The Late Calamity," *Nanaimo Free Press,* 11 May 1887, 3.

44 Belshaw, *Colonization and Community;* also Hinde, *When Coal Was King.* In contrast to the heavily British character of the settler population in Nanaimo, the pattern of migration and settlement in nearby Wellington was more ethnoculturally diverse, with the 1893 *British Columbia Directory* observing that the population of that community was "most cosmopolitan, having representatives from every quarter of the globe." See *The Williams Official British Columbia Directory 1893* (Victoria: Williams' BC Directory, 1893), 248, as cited in Mouat, "The Politics of Coal," 9.

45 For the historical antipathy of white settlers in British Columbia toward workers from Asia, which gave rise to the demand for "Asiatic Exclusion," see David Goutor, *Guarding the Gates: The Canadian Labour Movement and Immigration, 1872–1934* (Vancouver: UBC Press, 2008); Gillian Creese, "Class, Ethnicity, and Conflict: The Case of Chinese and Japanese Immigrants, 1880–1923," in *Workers, Capital, and the State in British Columbia* (Vancouver: University of British Columbia Press, 1988), 55–85; Gillian Creese, "Exclusion or Solidarity? Vancouver Workers Confront the 'Oriental Problem,'" *BC Studies* 80 (1988–89): 24–51; Patricia E. Roy, *A White Man's Province: British Columbia Politicians and Chinese and Japanese Immigrants, 1885–1914* (Vancouver: UBC Press, 1989); Patricia Roy, *The Oriental Question: Consolidating a White Man's Province, 1914–41* (Vancouver: UBC Press, 2003); and Peter Ward, *White Canada Forever: Popular Attitudes and Public Policy toward Orientals in British Columbia,* 3rd ed. (Montreal and Kingston: McGill-Queen's University Press, 2002). For a contemporary view of labour's attitude toward Asian workers, see "The Asiatic Question," *BC Trades Unionist* [Vancouver], April 1908, 4.

46 "Socialist Lectures," *Victoria Daily Colonist,* 19 March 1902, 2; untitled article, *Victoria Daily Times,* 20 March 1902, 5; "The Socialist Movement in British Columbia," *Lardeau Eagle* [Ferguson, BC], 27 March 1902, 3.

47 "The World of Labor," *Victoria Daily Colonist,* 16 March 1902, 10.

48 "A Convincing Speaker," *Nanaimo Daily News,* 24 March 1902, 4.

49 Johnson, "No Compromise," 129.

50 Ibid.

51 "A New Method," Seattle *Socialist,* 16 November 1902, 3.

52 Johnson, "No Compromise," 129.

53 Wrigley, "BC Socialist Party Convention Reflections."

54 *Henderson's British Columbia Gazetteer and Directory, 1903* (Victoria: Henderson Publishing, 1903), 364, 1133; *Henderson's British Columbia Gazetteer and Directory, 1904* (Victoria: Henderson Publishing, 1904), 379, 1207; "Political Notes of Interest," *Victoria Daily Colonist,* 24 September 1903, 6. See also Johnson, "No Compromise," 129.

55 "Third Annual Convention," *Western Clarion,* 11 September 1903, 3.

56 "Organizer's Fund" and "In the Provincial Field," *Western Socialist,* 17 January 1903, 4.

57   For a sample of Kingsley's speeches, see "Kamloops Convention," *Nanaimo Daily News*, 19 April 1902, 4; "Socialistic Meeting," *Nanaimo Daily News*, 3 May 1902, 4; "Socialist Meeting," *Nanaimo Daily News*, 10 May 1902, 4; "Socialists in New Hall," *Nanaimo Daily News*, 11 July 1902, 4; "Labor Day Celebration," *Nanaimo Daily News*, 2 September 1902, 4; "Socialists," *Nanaimo Daily News*, 6 September 1902, 4; untitled article, *Victoria Daily Times*, 31 January 1903, 5; "The Labor Problem," *Victoria Daily Times*, 2 February 1903, 3; and "International Labor Day," *Vancouver Daily Province*, 2 May 1903, 8. For Kingsley's movements to and from Nanaimo and Vancouver, see "From Vancouver," *Nanaimo Daily News*, 6 October 1902, 3; "Personal Mention," *Nanaimo Daily News*, 22 November 1902, 4; "From Vancouver," *Nanaimo Daily News*, 30 November 1903, 4; "From Vancouver," *Nanaimo Daily News*, 30 September 1904, 2; and "Hotel Arrivals," *Nanaimo Daily News*, 28 November 1904, 4.

58   "Local News," *Victoria Daily Colonist*, 11 May 1902, 5; untitled article, *Victoria Daily Times*, 10 May 1902, 5; "City News in Brief," *Victoria Daily Times*, 13 May 1902, 5.

59   E.T. Kingsley, *The Genesis and Evolution of Slavery: Showing How the Chattel Slaves of Pagan Times Have Been Transformed into the Capitalist Property of To-Day* (Vancouver: Federationist Publishing, 1916); we discuss this work in Chapter 6.

60   "Eugene V. Debs," *Independent* [Vancouver, hereafter not noted], 28 June 1902, 1. Two days after the speech by Debs, delegates at a convention of the Socialist Party of Washington State "proclaimed their allegiance" to the Socialist Party of America. See "Working-Class Platform," Seattle *Socialist*, 6 July 1902, 1. The *Vancouver Daily Province* noted the arrival of Debs in Vancouver on 24 June 1902: "Mr. Eugene V. Debs, the labor orator, arrived this morning by the steamer North Pacific from Seattle. He will deliver a lecture this evening in the City Hall on Why I Am a Socialist. A large party of influential local labor people met Mr. Debs at the steamer." The newspaper also reported on Kingsley's presence in the city: "Mr. E.T. Kingsley of Nanaimo is spending several days in the city." A few days earlier, on 19 June, it had noted that "Mr. E.T. Kingsley of Nanaimo is spending several days in the city in visiting friends here." See "Men and Women," *Vancouver Daily Province*, 24 June 1902, 3; and "Men and Women," *Vancouver Daily Province*, 19 June 1902, 3.

61   "Labor Day in Nanaimo," *Independent*, 6 September 1902, 1, 3.

62   "Executive Committee Vote," *Western Socialist*, 17 January 1903, 4.

63   Imai, "Canadian Immigration Law and Policy," 27–28; *An Act Respecting Naturalization and Aliens*, SC 1881, c 13, ss 10–12. For the evolution of Canadian immigration and citizenship law and policy, see Ninette Kelley and Michael Trebilcock, *Making of the Mosaic: A History of Canadian Immigration Policy* (Toronto: University of Toronto Press, 1998).

64   *An Act Respecting Naturalization and Aliens*, SC 1881, c 13, s 1.

65   Imai, "Canadian Immigration Law and Policy," 29.

66   Ibid., 5.

67   Ibid., 22–23. Imai notes how Canada's population remained steady despite a massive push to attract more desirable immigrants as many new immigrants departed, presumably for the United States.

68 *Chinese Immigration Act, 1885,* SC 1885, c 71; Imai, "Canadian Immigration Law and Policy," 26–27. A full discussion of the exclusion of Chinese immigration is beyond the scope of our book.

69 *Alien Labour Act, 1897,* SC 1897, c 11; Imai, "Canadian Immigration Law and Policy," 44–45.

70 Imai, "Canadian Immigration Law and Policy," 67.

71 Ibid.

72 *Reference re Alien Labour Act, s 6 (Can),* [1906] JCJ No 2 at para 7 (Lexis Nexis).

73 Saywell, "Labour and Socialism in British Columbia," 143–44; Loosmore, "The British Columbia Labor Movement and Political Action," 109; Fox, "Early Socialism in Canada," 89–90.

74 Untitled article, Seattle *Socialist,* 20 October 1901, 2; McCormark, *Reformers, Rebels, and Revolutionaries,* 25; Fox, "Early Socialism in Canada," 88. See also "Wants Labor Party to Join Socialists," *Lardeau Eagle* [Ferguson, BC], 2 January 1902, 1; and "The City," *Nelson Daily Miner,* 28 December 1901, 4. These articles report on J.M. Cameron's organizing efforts in the Kootenays, establishing branches of the SPBC at Rossland, Grand Forks, Greenwood, Phoenix, Ymir, and Trail. See also "Socialist Movement in British Columbia," *Lardeau Eagle* [Ferguson, BC], 20 March 1902, 3.

75 See "Announcement," *Western Socialist,* 20 September 1902, 2; "Brief Historical Review," *Western Clarion,* 12 January 1907, 2; "A Brief History of the Labor Press," *Federationist,* 7 January 1916, 3; and "The Rise of the Labor Press," *Federationist,* 9 November 1917, 9. The *Western Socialist* was published from September 1902 to May 1903. Kingsley was mentioned in nearly every issue of the paper given his leading role in the SPBC. For a letter summarizing the ideology of the newspaper's editor, George Dale, in response to an inquiry from a comrade in Ladysmith, see "Inquiry and Reply," *Western Socialist,* 24 April 1903, 1. For the earlier history of the labour press in British Columbia and Canada, see Ron Verzuh, *Radical Rag: The Pioneer Labour Press in Canada* (Ottawa: Steel Rail Publishing, 1988). For a study of Pettipiece and the *Lardeau Eagle,* see David Thompson, "The 'Indignity of Speaking for Others': The Early Brainwork of R. Parm Pettipiece and the *Lardeau Eagle,*" unpublished paper, University of Victoria, cited in McKay, *Reasoning Otherwise,* 556.

76 Fox, "Early Socialism in Canada," 88–90. See also Hak, *The Left in British Columbia,* 37–39.

77 Margaret Ormsby, *British Columbia: A History* (Vancouver: Macmillan, 1958), 316.

78 Carlos A. Schwantes, *Radical Heritage: Labor, Socialism, and Reform in Washington and British Columbia, 1885–1917* (Seattle: University of Washington Press, 1979), 130, citing the *Social Democratic Herald* [Chicago], 4 November 1899, 1; 11 November 1899, 1.

79 Melvyn Dubofsky, "The Origins of Western Working Class Radicalism, 1890–1905," *Labor History* 7, no. 2 (1966): 150–52; Fox, "Early Socialism in Canada," 90–91.

80 "Provincial Progressive Party," *Independent,* 19 April 1902, 1; "Labor Convention Opened at Kamloops," *Vancouver Daily Province,* 15 April 1902, 1; "A Big Convention," *Lardeau Eagle* [Ferguson, BC], 27 March 1902, 1. See also "Labor Politics in British Columbia," Seattle *Socialist,* 13 April 1902, 4; and Johnson, "No Compromise," 136–44.

The decision of delegates early in the convention (recorded in the verbatim transcript of proceedings in the *Independent*) that "no candidate for permanent office be eligible unless he be a British subject and a voter" would have prevented Kingsley from standing for election to the executive of the new party; however, there is no evidence that he sought a position as an officer of the party at that convention.

81 "Provincial Progressive Party," *Independent*, 19 April 1902, 3; Loosmore, "The British Columbia Labor Movement and Political Action," 157.

82 "Provincial Progressive Party," *Independent*, 19 April 1902, 3. Foley would later fall out with sections of the BC socialist movement as it gravitated toward Marxism under Kingsley's influence. See, for example, "The Defeat of Foley," *Voice*, 6 February 1903, 6; and William Small, "Local Option in Vermont," *Voice*, 6 February 1903, 1. For a discussion of Foley, elected Provincial Progressive Party president at the 1902 Kamloops convention, see Loosmore, "The British Columbia Labor Movement and Political Action," 164–72; and "Socialism," *Voice*, 6 February 1903, 3.

83 "Provincial Progressive Party," *Independent*, 19 April 1902, 1, 3; "Provincial Progressive Party," *Independent*, 3 May 1902, 1; "Progressive Party," *Independent*, 28 June 1902, 1; Loosmore, "The British Columbia Labor Movement and Political Action," 151–62; Saywell, "Labour and Socialism in British Columbia," 146–48; Fox, "Early Socialism in Canada," 90.

84 "Kamloops Convention," *Nanaimo Daily News*, 19 April 1902, 4.

85 "A New Socialist Party" and "Platform of the Revolutionary Socialist Party of Canada," Seattle *Socialist*, 18 May 1902, 4. The paper had reported earlier on political conditions in British Columbia in "From British Columbia," Seattle *Socialist*, 30 June 1901, 2.

86 "Socialists in New Hall," *Nanaimo Daily News*, 11 July 1902, 4; "Brief Historical Review," *Western Clarion*, 12 January 1907, 2.

87 Hinde, *When Coal Was King*, 138–39.

88 Loosmore, "The British Columbia Labor Movement and Political Action," 164.

89 "Call to Convention," *Western Socialist*, 20 September 1902, 1; "Second Annual Convention of the BC Socialist Party," *Western Socialist*, 11 October 1902, 1; "Socialist Platform," *Phoenix Pioneer*, 25 October 1902, 2. Also see "BC Socialist Party Platform," *Western Socialist*, 17 January 1903, 4; "Platform of the Socialist Party of BC," *Western Clarion*, 11 September 1903, 3; and Fox, "Early Socialism in Canada," 91. McCormack has challenged the view that the SPBC convention in 1902 marked "the beginning of the ascendancy of Island impossibilism over all lesser doctrines," citing delegates' affirmation of their commitment to trade unions and language from the Washington State party platform. See McCormack, *Reformers, Rebels, and Revolutionaries*, 30.

90 "Party News," Seattle *Socialist*, 16 November 1902, 3.

91 "Burnt His Bridges," *Victoria Daily Colonist*, 16 October 1902, 5. See also Loosmore, "The British Columbia Labor Movement and Political Action," 172–79.

92 "Provincial Progressive Party," *Independent*, 19 April 1902, 3.

93 "Burnt His Bridges," *Victoria Daily Colonist*, 16 October 1902, 5.

94 Johnson, "No Compromise," 134, 188, 221; "BC Socialist Party," *Independent*, 1 March 1902, 1; "Socialist Party," *Independent*, 12 April 1902, 5; "BC Socialist Party,"

Independent, 15 March 1902, 1; "Socialist Meetings," *Independent,* 31 May 1902, 1; "Important Socialist Meetings," *Western Socialist,* 20 September 1902, 4; "In the Provincial Field," *Western Socialist,* 17 January 1903, 4.

95 "Revolutionary Jargon," Seattle *Socialist,* 12 January 1902, 4.

96 "Letter to the Editor," *Western Clarion,* 25 June 1904, 4.

97 Linda Kealey, *Enlisting Women for the Cause: Women, Labour, and the Left in Canada, 1890–1920* (Toronto: University of Toronto Press, 1998), 100–1; see also Linda Kealey, "Canadian Socialism and the Woman Question, 1900–14," *Labour/Le Travail* 13 (1984): 77–100; "Socialist Party of BC," *Western Socialist,* 22 November 1902, 4; "Socialist Party of BC," *Western Socialist,* 3 January 1903, 4.

98 Kealey, *Enlisting Women for the Cause,* 101.

99 "City News in Brief" and "Socialist Campaigning," *Victoria Daily Times,* 29 September 1903, 5; "City News in Brief," *Victoria Daily Times,* 23 September 1903, 5; "Political Notes of Interest," *Victoria Daily Colonist,* 24 September 1903, 6; "Straws in the Life Stream," *Western Clarion,* 11 September 1903, 4; "Straws in the Life Stream," *Western Clarion,* 17 September 1903, 4.

100 See "Organizer Kingsley's Address," *Western Socialist,* 7 February 1903, 1; "In the World of Labor," *Victoria Daily Colonist,* 8 February 1902, 12; "Workingmen's Parliament," *Victoria Daily Colonist,* 22 January 1903, 2; and McCormack, *Reformers, Rebels, and Revolutionaries,* 31. Kingsley's contentious speech on unions took place in Victoria's Labour Hall on 1 February 1903. According to the *Victoria Daily Colonist,* Kingsley "bitterly condemned trades unions in a ranting fashion" and rejected established labour orthodoxy. He also took aim at the provincial legislature, which he described as "a tin-horn affair." Applause for his remarks at the meeting indicated (according to the correspondent) that "there are in Victoria people who think like Mr. Kingsley."

101 "In the World of Labor," *Victoria Daily Colonist,* 8 February 1902, 12; G. Weston Wrigley, "Unionism with Socialism," *Western Socialist,* 28 February 1903, 1; "Socialist Party of BC," *Western Socialist,* 27 March 1903, 4; "Socialist Party of BC," *Western Socialist,* 24 April 1903, 4; Alex Lang, "Local Victoria Attention," *Western Clarion,* 10 July 1903, 4; Johnson, "No Compromise," 173; McCormack, *Reformers, Rebels, and Revolutionaries,* 31, 33. McCormack suggests that Wrigley Sr. would later come around to supporting Kingsley. The Victoria local, in requesting that he be relieved as organizer, suggested that local party member James C. "Jimmy" Watters should be appointed in his place. (Watters would stand as the SPBC and SPC candidate in provincial and federal elections and serve as president of the Trades and Labor Congress of Canada from 1911 to 1918.) See Lang, "Local Victoria Attention." For Wrigley's praise of Kingsley, describing his articles in the *Western Clarion* as "magnificent," see G. Weston Wrigley, "Among the Workers," *Western Clarion,* 9 December 1905, 4.

102 Fox, "Early Socialism in Canada," 94.

103 "The Annual Farce," *Western Clarion,* 5 December 1903, 1. Kingsley also suggested that the inevitable outcome of trade union action was a "stupid rebellion against the inevitable downward trend of wages."

104 "A Small Flutter," *Western Clarion,* 26 December 1903, 2; Johnson, "No Compromise," 171.

105 "A Small Flutter," *Western Clarion*, 26 December 1903, 2; Fox, "Early Socialism in Canada," 94; McCormack, *Reformers, Rebels, and Revolutionaries*, 56; Mark Leier, *Red Flags and Red Tape: The Making of a Labour Bureaucracy* (Toronto: University of Toronto Press, 1995), 150.

106 See, for example, "The New Politics," *Nanaimo Daily News*, 18 March 1903, 1, 2; David M. Halliday, "Organizer Kingsley in Cumberland," *Western Clarion*, 26 June 1903, 1; G. Weston Wrigley, "News from the Seat of War," *Western Clarion*, 26 June 1903, 1, 3; "Straws in the Life Stream," *Western Clarion*, 24 July 1903, 4; "E.T. Kingsley's Rousing Meetings," *Western Clarion*, 31 July 1903, 4; "Political Notes," *Nanaimo Daily News*, 29 September 1903, 4; "'Small and Early' Given by Socialists," *Nanaimo Daily News*, 1 October 1903, 2, 3; "Straws in the Life Stream," *Western Clarion*, 22 October 1903, 4; untitled article, *Western Clarion*, 13 August 1904, 4; "News of the Day at Ladysmith," *Victoria Daily Colonist*, 23 August 1904, 3; and "Local News," *Victoria Daily Colonist*, 4 September 1904, 5.

107 "Labor Day," *Victoria Daily Colonist*, 27 August 1904, 5; untitled article, *Victoria Daily Times*, 27 August 1904, 5; "Big Celebration on Monday Next," *Victoria Daily Times*, 3 September 1904, 3; "Victoria Pays Tribute to Labor," *Victoria Daily Colonist*, 5 September 1904, 2; "Incidents of the Labor Day Celebration at the Provincial Capital," *Western Clarion*, 10 September 1904, 5. McNiven had attended the PPP founding convention in 1902 in Kamloops as a delegate from the Victoria Trades and Labor Council, and he was elected as the founding secretary-treasurer of the short-lived party. He would later serve as British Columbia's deputy minister of labour. See "Provincial Progressive Party," *Independent*, 19 April 1902, 1, 3.

108 Parker Williams, "E.T. Kingsley," *Labor Statesman* [Vancouver], 13 December 1929, 4.

109 Fox, "Early Socialism in Canada," 87.

110 Elections British Columbia, *An Electoral History of British Columbia*, 82–83; Fox, "Early Socialism in Canada," 88.

111 "Enthusiastic for McInnes," *Victoria Daily Colonist*, 14 December 1902, 2. See also "Rumor," *Vancouver World*, 8 December 1902, 1; and "Views of Two Men," *Nanaimo Daily News*, 13 December 1902, 2.

112 See Elections British Columbia, *An Electoral History of British Columbia*, 89, 93–94; and Loosmore, "The British Columbia Labor Movement and Political Action," 180–81.

113 "Enthusiastic for McInnes," *Victoria Daily Colonist*, 14 December 1902, 2. McInnes was the son of a former lieutenant-governor, Thomas Robert McInnes, and the younger brother of Thomas Robert Edward "Tom" MacInnes (note the slightly different spelling), a poet and an outspoken white supremacist in British Columbia in the 1920s. See Tom MacInnes, *The Oriental Occupation of British Columbia* (Vancouver: Vancouver Sun Publishing, 1927); and Martin Robin, *Shades of Right: Nativist and Fascist Politics in Canada, 1920–1940* (Toronto: University of Toronto Press, 1992), 1–24.

114 "Mildly Riotous – Public Meeting Captured by Socialists," *Nanaimo Free Press*, 20 February 1903, 1, 4. See also "Theory and Practice," *Nanaimo Free Press*, 4 March 1903, 2.

115 "Saint Hawthornthwaite," *Nanaimo Free Press,* 10 March 1903, 4.

116 "A New Civic Staff," *Nanaimo Daily News,* 6 April 1903, 4.

117 The coal miners' strike was settled in early July 1903 when a majority of miners reluctantly voted in favour of a return to work, accepting a two-year agreement with Dunsmuir that provided no apparent material gain for the miners, who had lost half a million dollars in wages during the strike. See "Extension Miners Accept Agreement," *Victoria Daily Colonist,* 3 July 1903, 1.

118 "Party News," Seattle *Socialist,* 16 November 1902, 3.

119 W.A. Pritchard, interview with David Millar, 17 September 1969, Los Angeles, Accession No. 1970–0010, David Millar Fonds, LAC; Paul A. Phillips, *No Power Greater: A Century of Labour in British Columbia* (Vancouver: Boag Foundation, 1967), 38–41.

120 "Third Annual Convention," *Western Clarion,* 11 September 1903, 3; Halliday, "Organizer Kingsley"; Wrigley, "News"; "Telegraphic Items – Nanaimo," *Cumberland News,* 19 May 1903, 1. According to correspondent David Halliday from Cumberland, Kingsley was "the first socialist who lectured to an audience in Cumberland."

121 Wrigley, "News."

122 "Socialist Party Candidates," *Western Clarion,* 11 September 1903, 1.

123 See "Telegraphic Items – Nanaimo," *Cumberland News,* 19 May 1903, 1; "Straws in the Life Stream," *Western Clarion,* 10 July 1903, 4; and "Third Annual Convention," *Western Clarion,* 11 September 1903, 3.

124 E.T. Kingsley, "Time for Action," *Western Clarion,* 19 June 1903, 2.

125 "Extension Miners Accept Agreement," *Victoria Daily Colonist,* 3 July 1903, 1.

126 "Robillard-Caulfield," *Boundary Creek Times* [Greenwood, BC, hereafter not noted], 21 August 1903, 1; "Socialist Meetings," *Fernie Free Press,* 29 August 1903, 1; "The Dignity of Labor," *Boundary Creek Times,* 28 August 1903, 1; "Third Annual Convention," *Western Clarion,* 11 September 1903, 3; "Political Meeting," *Fernie Free Press,* 19 September 1903, 1; "Brief News Notes," *Phoenix Pioneer,* 19 September 1903, 7; "It Is Now Brown MPP," *Boundary Creek Times,* 9 October 1903, 1.

127 "City News in Brief," *Victoria Daily Times,* 28 September 1903, 5; "Socialist Campaigning," *Victoria Daily Times,* 29 September 1903, 5; "City News in Brief," *Victoria Daily Times,* 23 September 1903, 5.

128 E.T. Kingsley, "Organizer Kingsley's Letter," Seattle *Socialist,* 15 November 1903, 2; see also Alec Lang, "BC Secretary Explains," Seattle *Socialist,* 25 October 1903, 3.

129 "Editorial Croppings," *Slocan Drill,* 14 August 1903, 4.

130 See Wiseman and Isitt, "Early Socialism in Canada," 521.

131 Elections British Columbia, *An Electoral History of British Columbia,* 91–96.

132 "Campaign in the Boundary," *Western Clarion,* 4 August 1906, 1; Elections British Columbia, *An Electoral History of British Columbia,* 93–96; "Victory in British Columbia," Seattle *Socialist,* 11 October 1903, 1; "Brief Historical Review," *Western Clarion,* 12 January 1907, 2; Loosmore, "The British Columbia Labor Movement," 183–94.

133 "The Real Issue before Workers," *Western Clarion,* 17 September 1903, 4; "Socialist News," Seattle *Socialist,* 20 September 1903, 2. The same issue of the *Western Clarion*

highlighted Hawthornthwaite's advocacy for reforms in the legislature, including a proposed amendment to the *Trade Unions Act* in May 1903 (defeated on a vote of 4–29) that would have recognized the right of an employee "to join any trade union or similar labor association" and prohibited any discrimination or disciplinary measures by an employer against an employee for exercising this right, imposing a penalty of up to $1,000. See "Hawthornthwaite's Bill and Its Friends," *Western Clarion,* 17 September 1903, 4.

134 "Third Annual Convention," *Western Clarion,* 11 September 1903, 1, 3; "Political Notes of Interest," *Victoria Daily Colonist,* 24 September 1903, 6.

135 "Third Annual Convention," *Western Clarion,* 11 September 1903, 3; "Socialist News," Seattle *Socialist,* 20 September 1903, 2.

136 Untitled article, *Victoria Daily Times,* 9 November 1903, 5; "Local News," *Victoria Daily Colonist,* 10 November 1918, 5.

137 Tadeusz Adam Kawecki identifies the *Western Clarion* of 11 September 1903 as a source of information on Kingsley replacing Pettipiece as editor of the newspaper; we consulted that issue but did not find the reference. The most reliable reference that we have found appears on the front page of a special issue of the *Western Clarion* on 28 November 1903. See "The *Clarion's* Mission," *Western Clarion,* 28 November 1903, 1; and Tadeusz Adam Kawecki, "Canadian Socialism and the Origin of the Communist Party of Canada, 1900–1922" (MA thesis, McMaster University, 1980), 41.

138 "Enthusiastic for McInnes," *Victoria Daily Colonist,* 14 December 1902, 2; "Political Notes of Interest," *Victoria Daily Colonist,* 24 September 1903, 6.

Chapter 5: No Compromise

1 Jack Harrington, interview with Paul Fox, quoted in Ross McCormack, *Reformers, Rebels, and Revolutionaries: The Western Canadian Radical Movement 1899–1919* (Toronto: University of Toronto Press, 1977), 60.

2 Ross Alfred Johnson, "No Compromise – No Political Trading: The Marxian Socialist Tradition in British Columbia" (PhD diss., University of British Columbia, 1975), 159.

3 "The Wail of the Wallopped MPP," *Victoria Daily Times,* 23 May 1911, 9.

4 See "Factious Opposition," *Week,* 3 August 1907, 16.

5 "Socialism," *Voice,* 22 May 1908, 3; McCormack, *Reformers, Rebels, and Revolutionaries,* 70.

6 Most of the dozens of references to Kingsley's work in the Australian labour press consist of excerpts and quotations from *The Genesis and Evolution of Slavery* (1916) and articles from the *Labor Star* in 1919. However, complete articles by Kingsley were also published in Australian labour newspapers, for example "How Capitalism Gets Rich Quick," *Australian Worker,* 26 December 1918, 17; "The Pleasing Hallucinations of Wealth," *Australian Worker,* 30 January 1919, 15; "Gold – The Sacred Ikon of Payment," *Australian Worker,* 13 February 1919, 15; "An International Madhouse," *Australian Worker,* 22 May 1919, 15; "Capitalist Civilization," *Australian Worker,* 24 July 1919, 21; and "The Financial Problem," *Australian Worker,* 24 April

1919, 5. There were also reports reproduced from Kingsley's speeches as originally published in the *Federationist*, for example his talk of 21 March 1920 in Vancouver on the Paris Commune. See "Paris Commune," *Worker* [Brisbane], 22 July 1920, 22, originally published in "Kingsley on the Commune," *Federationist*, 26 March 1920, 4.

7   See Dorothy G. Steeves, *The Compassionate Rebel: Ernest Winch and the Growth of Socialism in Western Canada* (Vancouver: Boag Foundation, 1977), 14; McCormack, *Reformers, Rebels, and Revolutionaries*, 26–34, 60–61, 70; A. Ross McCormack, "The Emergence of the Socialist Movement in British Columbia," *BC Studies* 21 (1974): 15–27; and Sunit Sarvraj Singh, "Echoes of Freedom: Radical Indian Thought and International Socialism, 1905–1920" (PhD diss., University of Chicago, 2018), 172, 175–76. For the more typical scholarly treatment of Kingsley, see Carlos A. Schwantes, *Radical Heritage: Labor, Socialism and Reform in Washington and British Columbia, 1885–1917* (Seattle: University of Washington Press, 1979), 110–11, 180.

8   Paul Fox, "Early Socialism in Canada," in *The Political Process in Canada: Essays in Honour of R. MacGregor Dawson*, ed. J.H. Aitchison (Toronto: University of Toronto Press, 1963), 95. For a familiarly fleeting and dismissive treatment of "doctrinaire socialists," see also George R. Taft, "Socialism in North America: The Case of British Columbia and Washington State, 1900–1960" (PhD diss., Simon Fraser University, 1983), 315–17, 331–32, 397, 402, and references to Kingsley at 373 and 375; and notes of interviews with John Harrington and Wallis Lefeaux, c. 1961, by Paul Fox, in "Herrington [sic] Vancouver – 1 Notes," folder 37, and "Lefeaux Notes – 1," folder 43, box 10A "Transcripts of Taped Interviews for CBC Broadcast: Socialism in Canada, 1961," Woodsworth Memorial Collection, Thomas Fisher Rare Book Library, University of Toronto.

9   Fox, "Early Socialism in Canada," 96. See also Ian McKay, *Reasoning Otherwise: Leftists and the People's Enlightenment in Canada, 1890–1920* (Toronto: Between the Lines, 2008), 161–64.

10   *Western Clarion*, 20 February 1909, as cited in McCormack, *Reformers, Rebels, and Revolutionaries*, 70.

11   "Something Missing," *Western Clarion*, 8 October 1910, 2.

12   "Socialists Meet," *Daily Canadian* [Nelson], 8 October 1906, 1.

13   Ibid.

14   Steeves, *The Compassionate Rebel*, 14.

15   C.M. O'Brien, "Ukrainian Convention," *Western Clarion*, 3 September 1910, 3.

16   "Socialists Meet in Fernie," *Fernie District Ledger*, 2 May 1908, 6.

17   "E.T. Kingsley's Rousing Meetings," *Western Clarion*, 31 July 1903, 4.

18   Grace MacInnis, interview (presumably with Richard Stuart), 9 January 1968, as cited in Richard G. Stuart, "The Early Political Career of Angus MacInnis" (MA thesis, University of British Columbia, 1967), 233, also 14.

19   Oblique references to Kingsley's influence were peppered throughout the mainstream and labour press in this era. See, for example, a reference to an "embryonic Kingsley friend" in "A Word on School Affairs by Proletarian," *Ladysmith Daily Ledger*, 4 January 1905, 1.

20 E.T. Kingsley, "Notes by the Way," *Western Clarion*, 15 August 1908, 1, cited in McKay, *Reasoning Otherwise*, 162.

21 McKay, *Reasoning Otherwise*, 164.

22 See "Platform of the Revolutionary Socialist Party of Canada" and "A New Socialist Party," Seattle *Socialist*, 18 May 1902, 4; "Second Annual Convention of the BC Socialist Party," *Western Socialist*, 11 October 1902, 1; "Socialist Platform," *Phoenix Pioneer*, 25 October 1902, 2; "BC Socialist Party Platform," *Western Socialist*, 17 January 1903, 4; "Platform of the Socialist Party of BC," *Western Clarion*, 11 September 1903, 3; "Report of the Proceedings," *Western Clarion*, 28 January 1905, 2–4; "Socialism Spreading," *Victoria Daily Colonist*, 5 January 1905, 5; and "Platform – Socialist Party of Canada," *Western Clarion*, 20 February 1909, 4.

23 "Kingsley Makes Good Points," *Federationist*, 18 July 1919, 2.

24 United States, "Twelfth Census of the United States, Schedule No. 1 – Population," San Jose Ward 2, Santa Clara County, California, 1 June 1900, 1, enumeration district 66, FHL microfilm 1240111, in *1900 United States Federal Census Online Database*, www.ancestry.com.

25 McKay, *Reasoning Otherwise*, 157; Mark Leier, "Workers and Intellectuals: The Theory of the New Class and Early Canadian Socialism," in *Making Western Canada: Essays on European Colonization and Settlement*, ed. Catherine Cavanaugh and Jeremy Mouat (Toronto: Garamond, 1996), 144.

26 Sarah Rose, "'Crippled' Hands: Disability in Labour and Working-Class History," *Labor: Studies in Working-Class History in the Americas* 2, no. 1 (2005): 51. See also Dustin Galer, "Disabled Capitalists: Exploring the Intersections of Disability and Identity Formation in the World of Work," *Disability Studies Quarterly* 32, no. 3 (2012): n. pag., http://dsq-sds.org/article/view/3277/3122.

27 Galer, "Disabled Capitalists."

28 Leier, "Workers and Intellectuals," 141, 143. See also James Mark Leier, "Through the Lense [*sic*] of Syndicalism: Fragmentation on the Vancouver and British Columbia Left before the Great War" (MA thesis, Simon Fraser University, 1987), 84. For Kingsley's printshop's status as a union shop (one of eighteen in Vancouver in 1908), see "Demand the Label on Your Printing," *Trades Unionist* [Vancouver], 1 June 1908, 13. For Kingsley's advertisement indicating his use of paper bearing the papermakers' watermark, see "E.T. Kingsley" [advertisement], *Western Clarion*, 3 January 1914, 4.

29 Leier, "Workers and Intellectuals," 141. For a discussion of paying Stan Lefeaux fifteen dollars per month "for services as accountant to the [SPC] committees and the *Western Clarion*," see "Dominion Executive Committee," *Western Clarion*, 2 March 1912, 3.

30 W.A. Pritchard, interview with Ross McCormack, 17 August 1971, Tape 3, Accession No. T0225, BCA; McKay, *Reasoning Otherwise*, 157.

31 Pritchard interview with McCormack, 17 August 1971, tape 3, t-225, BCA.

32 *Henderson's British Columbia Gazetteer and Directory, 1903* (Victoria: Henderson Publishing, 1903), 364; Johnson, "No Compromise," 129; "Political Notes of Interest," *Victoria Daily Colonist*, 24 September 1903, 6.

33 BC Statistics, "Census Population of BC and Canada, 1871 to 2011," http://www. bcstats.gov.bc.ca/StatisticsBySubject/Census/2011Census/PopulationHousing/ BCCanada.asp.

34 See *Henderson's British Columbia Gazetteer and Directory, 1903*, 1187; and *Henderson's Greater Vancouver City Directory Part 2, 1914* (Vancouver: Henderson Publishing Company, 1914), 1851–52.

35 "A New Deal," *Western Clarion*, 9 November 1912, 2; Johnson, "No Compromise," 177n37. Johnson claims that Kingsley "bought" the printing business from Pettipiece. The two men appear to have had a complicated political and business relationship difficult to discern properly. They collaborated closely several times in the 1900s and 1910s: in 1904–05, when Pettipiece managed and Kingsley edited the *Western Clarion*; around 1912–14, when Pettipiece served as managing editor and Kingsley as printer of the *British Columbia Federationist*; in 1916, when Pettipiece published Kingsley's work *The Genesis and Evolution of Slavery*; around 1917–18, when Pettipiece served as managing editor and Kingsley as associate editor of the *British Columbia Federationist*; and in 1919, when Pettipiece managed and Kingsley edited the short-lived *Labor Star* newspaper. However, several sources point to tensions and intrigue between them, calling into question the extent to which they were friends rather than business associates brought together by occupations and interests in the left-wing publishing world of Vancouver. For example, in 1904, Kingsley wrote to Hawthornthwaite describing his attempts to "force the ... Pettipiece outfit off the premises." By 1905, Kingsley was in control of the *Western Clarion*, and Pettipiece's association with the SPC newspaper appears to have been conclusively over. In 1914, during debate at the BC Federation of Labor's annual convention, Pettipiece described in detail a campaign of organized intrigue against the *Federationist* that he claimed was orchestrated by Kingsley: "The big noise is ... Kingsley. These conspiracies were hatched in the 'bear-pit' of the Vancouver Labor Temple." See Kingsley to Hawthornthwaite, 7 November 1904, folder 4, box 1, James H. Hawthornthwaite Fonds, McC 47, Simon Fraser University Special Collections (hereafter Hawthornthwaite Fonds, SFUSC); "Fourth Annual Convention of BC Federation of Labor," *Federationist*, 6 February 1914, 8; and "Official Proceedings 4th Annual Convention," *Federationist*, 6 February 1914, 8.

36 See Bessie Lamb, "Origin and Development of Newspapers in Vancouver" (MA thesis, University of British Columbia, 1942), 110.

37 For the incorporation of E.T. Kingsley, Ltd., see "New Companies," *Victoria Daily Times*, 8 December 1911, 5; and "New Incorporations," *Pulp and Paper Magazine of Canada* [Toronto], February 1912, 15. For Kingsley's partnership with English, see invoices from Kingsley and English in 1905, including "Socialist Party of Canada," *Western Clarion*, 20 May 1905, 4; "Socialist Party of Canada," *Western Clarion*, 17 June 1905, 4; and "Socialist Party of Canada," *Western Clarion*, 15 July 1905, 6. For evidence that Kingsley's business extended at times beyond printing, see a notice from Kingsley & Stow regarding the sale of three sixty-five-dollar sewing machines from the National Sewing Machine Company: "To Clarion Readers," *Western Clarion*,

16 March 1907, 3. *Henderson's City Directory* for Vancouver for 1906 identified Kingsley as being associated with the firm Kingsley, Arnason & Stow in the basement of the Flack Block (where his printshop was located); personal listings for Annie Arnason and John Stow can be found in that directory, both living at 160 16th Avenue East. The directory for 1907 listed Kingsley himself with the business Kingsley & Stow at the same location in the Flack Block. By 1908, Kingsley was identified as a sole proprietor – as a "printer and publisher" – still at the Flack Block basement. His business was not listed in the Vancouver city directory for 1912, which appears to have been an oversight. By 1913, he was listed in his new location, where he moved the printing shop and business at the end of 1911, in the Labor Temple at 411 Dunsmuir Street. For Stow and Arnason's move from Victoria to Vancouver in 1905, see Harold Burnett, "Victoria Local No. 2," *Western Clarion*, 4 November 1905, 4. Also see *Henderson's City of Vancouver Directory, 1906–1914* (Vancouver: Henderson Publishing, 1906–14).

38 "E.T. Kingsley – Printer, Publisher" [advertisement], *Western Clarion*, 23 December 1911, 4; untitled notice, *Western Clarion*, 6 January 1912, 1; "E.T. Kingsley – Printer, Publisher" [advertisement], *Western Clarion*, 13 January 1912, 4; "The New Labor Temple," *Western Clarion*, 18 May 1912, 1; "The Rise of the Labor Press," *Federationist*, 9 November 1917, 9.

39 In May 1914, an advertisement appeared in the *Western Clarion* for "Lefeaux Bros., Successors to E.T. Kingsley," operating out of the same location in the Vancouver Labor Temple. In September 1914, the *Federationist* described a sale of the printing plant: "During the week Messrs. Cowan & Brookhouse purchased the printing plant of Lefeaux Bros. (E.T. Kingsley) and have moved from the Dunsmuir lane corner of the Labor Temple to the basement occupied by the latter, and *The Federationist* is issued from the 'merger' premises this week." See "Printing – Lefeaux Bros, Successors to E.T. Kingsley" [advertisement], *Western Clarion*, 23 May 1914, 4; and "Print Shop Conditions," *Federationist*, 18 September 1914, 1. See also *Henderson's Greater Vancouver City Directory, 1915* (Vancouver: Henderson Publishing, 1915), 1219; and *Henderson's Vancouver Directory, 1920* (Vancouver: Henderson Publishing, 1920), 1154.

40 E.T. Kingsley, "Organizer Kingsley's Letter," Seattle *Socialist*, 15 November 1903, 2.

41 "The *Western Clarion*," *Western Clarion*, 9 September 1905, 3.

42 "Brief Historical Review," *Western Clarion*, 12 January 1907, 2.

43 For Pettipiece's role as an organizer in the International Typographical Union, see "Pettipiece in the West Again," *Western Clarion*, 21 December 1907, 1. For English's membership in the union, see Leier, "Through the Lense [*sic*] of Syndicalism," 54.

44 E.T. Kingsley advertisement, *Western Wage-Earner* [Vancouver], February 1909, 24. See also "Vancouver Trades and Labor Council," *Federationist*, 6 May 1912, 2. An advertisement in 1912 described Kingsley's printshop as "the shop where progressive thought is merged with the artistics." See "Printing – E.T. Kingsley," *Federationist*, 20 January 1912, 4. For an example of Kingsley's business with organized labour, see a bill payable by the Vancouver Trades and Labor Council from 1909 in the amount of $16.25 for "bill heads, rate cards, subscription books." Minutes of the Regular

Meeting of the Vancouver Trades and Labor Council, 6 May 1909, book 3 "Minutes," box 16, Vancouver and District Labour Council Fonds, University of British Columbia Rare Books and Special Collections (hereafter VDLC Fonds, UBCSC). Demonstrating Kingsley's fame in British Columbia, a Vancouver shoe company invoked a quotation from Kingsley to promote its product in "Pierre Paris Shoes – Advertisement," *Federationist,* 27 October 1919, 8.

45 "A New Deal," *Western Clarion,* 9 November 1912, 2.

46 For Kingsley's editorship of the *Federationist,* see "Rousing Meeting Held at Coal City," *Federationist,* 23 November 1917, 5; also see Chambers to MacLean, 2 April 1919, file 279–1, vol. 602, RG 6, Secretary of State Fonds, LAC. According to Chambers, Kingsley resigned as *Federationist* editor when "the Directors were compelled to agree to observe the requirements of the Press Censorship." For Kingsley's role as editor of the *Labor Star,* see "Banned Book Is Published Here," *Vancouver World,* 21 January 1919, 3, copied in Office of the Chief Press Censor Files, file 279–1, vol. 602, RG 6, Secretary of State Fonds, LAC; also see various issues of the *Labor Star* [Vancouver], January–March 1919; and Pritchard interview with McCormack, 16 August 1971, tape 1, t-225, BCA.

47 Kingsley to Hawthornthwaite, 4 January 1904, folder 4, box 1, Hawthornthwaite Fonds, SFUSC. For Bird's legal work, see Janet Mary Nicol, "'Not to Be Bought, Not for Sale': The Trials of Joseph Edward Bird," *Labour/Le Travail* 78 (2016): 219–36. In 1904, the SPBC provincial executive considered the question of patronage appointments, with Kingsley introducing a resolution (duly carried) expressing the opinion that elected members should refuse requests from private citizens for assistance in securing patronage appointments from the government, on the grounds that "such members have no influence nor do they wish to acquire any influence, except such as may be obtained upon the floor of the legislature." See Minutes of Provincial Executive Meeting, 5 June 1904, in "Socialist Party of B.C.," *Western Clarion,* 9 July 1904, 4.

48 Kingsley to Hawthornthwaite, 5 May 1905, folder 4, box 1, Hawthornthwaite Fonds, SFUSC.

49 Ibid. For further discussion of this proposed business venture between Kingsley and Hawthornthwaite, see Allen Seager, "Hawthornthwaite, James Hurst," in *Dictionary of Canadian Biography* (2005), http://www.biographi.ca/en/bio.php?BioId=42322.

50 Kingsley to Hawthornthwaite, 5 May 1907, folder 4, box 1, Hawthornthwaite Fonds, SFUSC.

51 Ibid.

52 Bird to Hawthornthwaite, 20 December 1907, folder 7, box 1, Hawthornthwaite Fonds, SFUSC.

53 Ibid.

54 Ibid.

55 Kingsley to Hawthornthwaite, 17 February 1908, folder 8, box 1, Hawthornthwaite Fonds, SFUSC.

56 "Petition No. 23 – John McLarty," 16 February 1909, and "Attorney General's Statement in Reply," in British Columbia, *Sessional Papers, Third Session, Eleventh Parliament* (Victoria: King's Printer, 1909), 197–200.

57 Kingsley to Hawthornthwaite, 19 May 1909, folder 9, box 1, Hawthornthwaite Fonds, SFUSC.

58 "New Million and Half Dollar Company Opens for Business" [advertisement], *Vancouver World*, 28 March 1911, 11; "A Gilt Edged Investment" [advertisement], *Vancouver World*, 11 May 1911, 5; "The Coal Supply of Prince Rupert and the New North Country" [advertisement], *Victoria Daily Times*, 16 May 1911, 9. The company ran dozens of ads seeking to attract investors between March and September 1911 in newspapers in Victoria, Vancouver, Nanaimo, and Calgary before disappearing, apparently without initiating mining operations on the Graham Island coal deposit.

59 "Aroused by Speeches Defending Red Guard," *Victoria Daily Colonist*, 29 January 1919, 11.

60 From 1906 to 1913, according to Vancouver city directories, Kingsley was living in a room at #10, 309 West Cordova Street. He appeared in the 1903 and 1904 directories for Nanaimo as the proprietor of the Nanaimo Fish Market, with his residence as a boarder at "Dunsmuir" (presumably the information for the 1904 Nanaimo directory was gathered in 1903 prior to his move to Vancouver that autumn). Kingsley is not listed in the 1904 or 1905 Vancouver city directory. The listings for him for 1906 to 1911 provide the West Cordova residence as well as his place of work in the Flack Block, 163 West Hastings Street. He is missing from the 1912 directory, but the 1913 directory lists him as continuing to live at 309 West Cordova, and the location of his printing business moves to 311 [*sic*, 411] Dunsmuir Street, the Labor Temple. The 1914 directory lists only his workplace in the Labor Temple. In 1915, Kingsley is recorded as living in a room at 307 West Pender Street, and his business listing no longer appears, replaced by Cowan & Brookhouse in the Labor Temple (they purchased the business from Kingsley to merge with their own operation). There is no record of a business address after that date. Kingsley is not listed in the 1916 and 1917 directories. In 1918, he is identified as "editor B C Federationist" and living in a room at 748 Richards Street, with the *Federationist* offices in the Labor Temple at 405 Dunsmuir. Henderson's 1919 directory shows Kingsley living in a room at 647 Seymour Avenue – the farthest location from the socialist and labour offices of all the residences that we are aware of during his time in Vancouver – three and a half blocks away from the Labor Temple. Kingsley is not listed in the 1920 and 1921 city directories published by either Henderson's or Wrigley's (which would merge in 1924). In 1922, he is listed as a resident at 537 Richards. From 1923 to shortly before his death in 1929, he lived in a room at 110 Water Street before moving for a final time to 309 West Pender, where he died in December. Beginning in 1928, Kingsley is identified as "retired." See *Henderson's British Columbia Gazetteer and Directory, 1903–1904* (Victoria: Henderson Publishing, 1903, 1904); *Henderson's City of Vancouver Directory, 1906–1923* (Victoria: Henderson Publishing, 1906–1923); and *Wrigley's British Columbia Directory, 1924–1929* (Vancouver: Wrigley Directories, 1924–29).

61 See "Socialists Explain Their Principles," *San Francisco Examiner*, 17 August 1896, 4; and George Weston Wrigley, "How Working-Class Leaders Travel," *Western Clarion*, 12 September 1908, 1.

62 "Certification of Registration of Death – Eugene Thomas [*sic*] Kingsley," 13 December 1929, record 23286, vol. 417, GR-2952, BCA; *Wrigley's British Columbia Directory, 1928* (Vancouver: Wrigley Directories, 1928), 1178.

63 Although Linda Kealey suggests that Kingsley's wife "occasionally took part in organizing activities in the party," we have not found evidence that she lived in British Columbia or maintained contact with Kingsley after the early 1890s. See Linda Kealey, "Canadian Socialism and the Woman Question, 1900–14," *Labour/Le Travail* 13 (1984): 88n22.

64 "Certification of Registration of Death – Eugene Thomas [*sic*] Kingsley," 13 December 1929, record 23286, vol. 417, GR-2952, BCA.

65 "Petition No. 23 – John McLarty," 16 February 1909, and "Attorney General's Statement in Reply," in British Columbia, *Sessional Papers, Third Session, Eleventh Parliament* (Victoria: King's Printer, 1909), 197–200.

66 "If Necessary Let Them Use Clubs," *Vancouver Daily Province*, 1 October 1908, 2.

67 "Political Notes of Interest," *Victoria Daily Colonist*, 24 September 1903, 6.

68 Ronald Grantham, "Some Aspects of the Socialist Movement in British Columbia, 1898–1933" (MA thesis, University of British Columbia, 1942), 16.

69 "Politicians out of the Past," *Western Socialist* [Vancouver] 26, no. 7 (1959): 9–11, http://www.worldsocialism.org/canada/politicians.out.of.the.past.1959.v26n211. htm.

70 "Will Discuss Labor Topics," *Federationist*, 23 November 1917, 5; "Snapshots of the City," *Vancouver World*, 13 March 1918, 9; "Defines Capital – Control of Labor," *Vancouver Daily Sun*, 15 March 1918, 14; "Capital, Labor and State," *Vancouver World*, 15 March 1918, 11.

71 See "Prisoners and Labourers," *Western Clarion*, 4 March 1904, 1; untitled article, *Western Clarion*, 17 November 1906, 2; untitled article, *Western Clarion*, 8 December 1906, 4; untitled article, *Western Clarion*, 11 May 1907, 3; "Labor," *Western Clarion*, 1 June 1907, 4; "The Horrors of Peace," *Western Clarion*, 6 January 1912, 1; and "Capitalism's Toll," *Western Clarion*, 15 June 1912, 1.

72 "Another Mine Explosion," *Western Clarion*, 4 March 1905, 1. See also "Gas, Coal Dust and the Law," *Western Clarion*, 16 July 1904, 1; and untitled article, *Western Clarion*, 13 May 1905, 1.

73 Untitled article, *Western Clarion*, 4 August 1906, 2.

74 "Outcropping of Canada's Slave Market," *Western Clarion*, 13 October 1906, 4. See also "Safety Appliances Cost Much Money," *Western Clarion*, 16 March 1907, 4.

75 Untitled article, *Western Clarion*, 8 December 1906, 4. See also "Covering Up the Tracks," *Western Clarion*, 4 September 1909, 1.

76 Untitled article, *Western Clarion*, 11 May 1907, 3.

77 "One Thing and Another," *Western Clarion*, 20 May 1905, 3. See also a report on a lecture in Vancouver delivered by J.B. Osborne, "the blind orator." "Blind Orator to Give Address on Unionism," *BC Federationist*, 12 June 1914, 1.

78 E.T. Kingsley, "Reconstruction," *Labor Star*, 27 February 1919, 1.

79 See "A New Lease of a Larger Life," *Western Clarion*, 7 May 1903, 1. In January 1902, Pettipiece addressed the Canadian Socialist League branch in Victoria, expressing

his desire to establish a socialist newspaper "somewhere in British Columbia, most likely at Victoria." See letter to the editor of the Seattle *Socialist,* 26 January 1902, 4. Also see "Socialism Spreading," *Victoria Daily Colonist,* 5 January 1905, 5. In early 1903, the Nanaimo Socialist Party obtained control of the *Nanaimo Clarion* from Hawthornthwaite, who had served as editor "for several months," according to a report in the *Victoria Daily Colonist:* "The local socialist party now own the paper and will conduct it by a press committee." See "In the World of Labor," *Victoria Daily Colonist,* 8 February 1903, 12.

80 "Must the *Clarion* Go Down?" *Western Clarion,* 22 October 1903, 1; "To Arms, Comrades," *Western Clarion,* 5 November 1903, 1. Also see "Financial Statement," *Western Clarion,* 17 July 1903, 3. Kingsley had earlier issued an appeal to SPBC members to support the newspaper, noting the debt that Pettipiece was incurring and advising that he had personally purchased stocks in the Western Socialist Publishing Company to ensure its financial viability. Stating his preference for "placing the *Western Clarion* and plant absolutely under the control of the Socialist Party of B.C.," Kingsley made a public request to the company "that when such stock is issued it be turned over to our Provincial Executive, to be voted [on] and controlled by that body in the interest of our Party. This [is] to include all stock taken or subscribed for by me up to the present time." See E.T. Kingsley, "Time for Action," *Western Clarion,* 19 June 1903, 2.

81 Untitled notice, *Western Clarion,* 6 January 1912, 1.

82 Steeves, *The Compassionate Rebel,* 13.

83 A.M. Stephen, *The Gleaming Archway* (London: J.M. Dent and Sons, 1929), 133.

84 "The *Clarion's* Mission," *Western Clarion,* 28 November 1903, 1; see also untitled article, *Voice,* 4 December 1903, 12. For the factors leading to suspension of the publication, see "Must the *Clarion* Go Down?" *Western Clarion,* 22 October 1903, 1.

85 "The *Western Clarion,*" *Western Clarion,* 5 December 1903, 2; "The *Western Clarion,*" *Western Clarion,* 5 June 1904, 2.

86 "Notice to *Western Clarion* Readers," *Western Clarion,* 26 December 1903, 2. See also "To All Concerned," *Western Clarion,* 5 December 1903, 4.

87 Kingsley to Hawthornthwaite, 28 December 1903, folder 3, box 1, Hawthornthwaite Fonds, SFUSC.

88 G. Weston Wrigley, "Thinks," *Western Clarion,* 7 July 1903, 2.

89 "Socialist Party of BC," *Western Clarion,* 18 June 1904, 3.

90 "To All Concerned," *Western Clarion,* 5 December 1903, 4; "A New Deal," *Western Clarion,* 9 November 1912, 2. See also "Dominion Executive Committee Meeting of June," *Western Clarion,* 8 June 1912, 3; and "A Plain Statement of Fact," *Western Clarion,* 22 June 1912, 2.

91 Kingsley to Hawthornthwaite, 7 November 1904, folder 4, box 1, Hawthornthwaite Fonds, SFUSC. While Kingsley was away in the BC Interior, English took on the responsibilities of editing and distributing the newspaper.

92 See "The *Western Clarion,*" *Western Clarion,* 18 June 1904, 2.

93 "A New Deal," *Western Clarion,* 9 November 1912, 2.

94 Kingsley to Hawthornthwaite, 7 November 1904, folder 4, box 1, Hawthornthwaite Fonds, SFUSC. In December 1903, Kingsley was reimbursed for seven dollars for expenses incurred in relation to an organizing trip on behalf of the SPBC to Texada Island. In July 1904, he was reimbursed five dollars for a trip to Victoria the previous April. See "Socialist Party of BC," *Western Clarion*, 5 December 1903, 3; and "Socialist Party of BC," *Western Clarion*, 16 July 1904, 3. For a report in advance of Kingsley's trip to Texada Island in 1903, see "Straws in the Life Stream," *Western Clarion*, 7 August 1903, 4. For a strike of Texada Island miners in 1907, see "Strike at Texada," *Western Clarion*, 4 April 1907, 2.

95 Johnson, "No Compromise," 175–76, 190n57, 341–42.

96 See Fox, "Early Socialism in Canada," 92–93; also see BC Statistics, "Census Population of BC and Canada, 1871 to 2011," http://www.bcstats.gov.bc.ca/StatisticsBySubject/Census/2011Census/PopulationHousing/BCCanada.aspx.

97 "News and Views," *Western Clarion*, 2 December 1905, 4.

98 "A New Deal," *Western Clarion*, 9 November 1912, 2. See also "A Job for November," *Western Clarion*, 7 November 1908, 2; "To Canadian Socialists," *Western Clarion*, 20 November 1909, 4; "Among Canada's Wage-Earners," *Lethbridge Herald*, 31 December 1909, 3; and "Announcement," *Western Clarion*, 20 January 1912, 2. In November 1909, the *Western Clarion* claimed that "the Socialist Party of Canada took the paper over about a year and a half ago. Comrade Kingsley paid the deficit for the first six months and since then the S.P. of C. has been sustaining the *Clarion*."

99 "Notice," *Western Clarion*, 20 January 1912, 2.

100 "Dominion Executive Committee," *Western Clarion*, 2 March 1912, 3.

101 See *Western Clarion* from July to October 1911.

102 "Introductory," *Western Wage-Earner*, February 1909, 12. The earlier VTLC-aligned newspaper *BC Trades Unionist*, was published in Vancouver from January 1908 to January 1909. See "Trades Council and the *Trades Unionist*," *BC Trades Unionist*, 1 December 1908, 8.

103 E.T. Kingsley advertisement, *Western Wage-Earner*, February 1909, 24.

104 See *British Columbia Federationist*, 6 January 1912 to 5 June 1925. For the founding of the BCFL, which took place at a convention on 2 May 1910 chaired by James C. "Jimmy" Watters, see Martin Robin, *Radical Politics and Canadian Labour, 1880–1930* (Kingston: Queen's University Industrial Relations Centre, 1968), 104–5.

105 "A New Deal," *Western Clarion*, 9 November 1912, 2. In June 1912, Kingsley warned the SPC Dominion Executive Committee and *Western Clarion* readers that he could no longer subsidize the cost of publishing the newspaper from his personal finances. See "Dominion Executive Committee Meeting of June," *Western Clarion*, 8 June 1912, 3; and "A Plain Statement of Fact," *Western Clarion*, 22 June 1912, 2.

106 "The Passing of the *Clarion*," *Federationist*, 15 November 1902, 4.

107 "A New Deal," *Western Clarion*, 9 November 1912, 2.

108 "Notice to 'Clarion' Subscribers," *Federationist*, 15 November 1902, 4.

109 "Socialist Party Directory," *Western Clarion*, 15 November 1912, 4; "Socialist Party Directory," *Western Clarion*, 22 November 1912, 4.

110 "Dominion Executive Committee," *Federationist,* 17 January 1913, 3; "Dominion Executive Committee," *Federationist,* 24 January 1913, 3; "Resurgam," *Western Clarion,* 1 March 1913, 2; "What Is It to Be?" *Western Clarion,* 10 May 1913, 2. For the revival of the *Western Clarion,* see "Notice," *Western Clarion,* 1 March 1913, 1; "Resurgam," *Western Clarion,* 1 March 1913, 2; and untitled article, *Western Clarion,* 1 March 1913, 3.

111 Pritchard interview with McCormack, 17 August 1971, tape 3, t-225, BCA.

112 Ibid.

113 "Notes by Secretary," *Western Clarion,* 12 March 1905, 4.

114 Pritchard interview with McCormack, 17 August 1971, tape 3, t-225, BCA. All publications from the Kerr Company were banned in a federal government order on 2 October 1918, pursuant to the Consolidated Orders Respecting Censorship of 21 May 1918 under the federal government's extraordinary wartime powers under the *War Measures Act, 1914.* See Censorship Notice, 2 October 1918, *Canada Gazette* 52, no. 14 (1918): 1294; also see Allen Ruff, "Repression of the Press in the World War I Era: The Case of Charles H. Kerr & Company," *Journal of Newspaper and Periodical History* 5, no. 2 (1989): 2–19; Allen Ruff, *"We Called Each Other Comrade": Charles H. Kerr & Company, Radical Publishers* (Oakland, CA: PM Press, 2011); and Malcolm Reid to Colonel Ernest Chambers, 22 January 1919, and Colonel Ernest Chambers to Malcolm Reid, 27 January 1919, file 279-1, vol. 602, RG 6, Secretary of State Fonds, LAC. See also "Theatre Royal Meeting Packed," *Federationist,* 29 November 1918, 8, and "The Censorship of Literature," *Federationist,* 6 December 1918, 8, for speeches by Pritchard and Lefeaux condemning the suppression of literature from the Kerr Company.

115 Grantham, "Some Aspects of the Socialist Movement in British Columbia," Appendix 4, 2.

116 "Report of the Proceedings," *Western Clarion,* 28 January 1905, 2–4. See also Peter E. Newell, *The Impossibilists: A Brief Profile of the Socialist Party of Canada* (London: Athena Press, 2008), 25–27.

117 "Socialism Spreading," *Victoria Daily Colonist,* 5 January 1905, 5.

118 Ibid.; "Report of the Proceedings," *Western Clarion,* 28 January 1905, 2–4; Johnson, "No Compromise," 190–91.

119 "Socialism Spreading," *Victoria Daily Colonist,* 5 January 1905, 5. For a resolution of the SPC Dominion Executive Committee in 1909 declining to consider affiliation with the International Socialist Bureau, because of concerns about "fusion or compromise" that would contravene the SPC constitution, see "International Affiliation," *Western Clarion,* 7 August 1909, 3. The resolution was reprinted shortly after the outbreak of war; see "Resolution of the DEC on Question of Affiliation with ISB," *Western Clarion,* 21 November 1914, 2. See also Newell, *The Impossibilists,* 50–51.

120 See "Platform – Socialist Party of Canada," *Western Clarion,* 20 February 1909, 4. For the earlier iteration of the platform in the SPBC and RSPC, see "Second Annual Convention of the BC Socialist Party," *Western Socialist,* 11 October 1902, 1; and "Platform of the Revolutionary Socialist Party of Canada," Seattle *Socialist,* 18 May 1902, 4.

121 "Socialism Spreading," *Victoria Daily Colonist,* 5 January 1905, 5. The SPC MLAs would try repeatedly to reduce the candidate deposit, with Hawthornthwaite introducing an amendment to the provincial *Elections Act* in 1906 to reduce the deposit from $200 to $50. The amendment was defeated after second reading following a rigorous debate, with Premier Richard McBride indicating his support for the lower deposit but other MLAs, including Finance Minister R.G. Tatlow opposed to it. During the debate, Tatlow informed Hawthornthwaite that "he came to the House with an entirely different mandate from that on which the member for Nanaimo came to the legislature. Mr. Hawthornthwaite was sent to introduce certain reforms. He [Tatlow] was not sent for that purpose and he was not going to be forced into consenting to such a decision." Later that year Hawthornthwaite and Williams succeeded in mustering a majority of votes in the legislature in favour of reducing the deposit from $200 to $100. See "Proceedings of the Legislature," *Victoria Daily Times,* 9 February 1906, 3; "The Red Flag of Socialism," *Victoria Daily Times,* 27 June 1906, 3; *Provincial Elections Act Amendment Act, 1906,* SBC 1906, c 19; Patricia E. Roy, *Boundless Optimism: Richard McBride's British Columbia* (Vancouver: UBC Press, 2012), 96–97; and "Eight-Hour Bill in the Provincial House," *Western Clarion,* 2 April 1905, 1. As the Socialist Party of Canada noted in the wake of the provincial election in 1907, "we have an election deposit of $100 for each candidate to put up, which is forfeited unless the candidate polls at least one half as many votes as the successful nominee. In Vancouver alone it cost our Local $500 in forfeited deposits to record over 600 votes for the abolition of wage-slavery." See John T. Mortimer, "Note and Comment," *Western Clarion,* 2 March 1907, 2.

122 Johnson, "No Compromise," 190–91; "Report of the Proceedings," *Western Clarion,* 28 January 1905, 2–4.

123 Pritchard interview with McCormack, 17 August 1971, tape 3, t-255, BCA; Harry Gutkin and Mildred Gutkin, *Profiles in Dissent: The Shaping of Radical Thought in the Canadian West* (Edmonton: NeWest Publishers, 1997), 99. Pritchard's comments on geography arose in response to a question by interviewer McCormack about whether the SPC Dominion Executive Committee consisted almost exclusively of members from Vancouver. "Yes, it had to be because of geography," Pritchard answered before discussing the organizational constraints imposed by lines of communication in the early twentieth century.

124 Notes of interviews with John Harrington and Wallis Lefeaux, c. 1961, by Paul Fox, in "Herrington [*sic*] Vancouver – Notes," folder 37, and "Lefeaux Notes – 1," folder 43, box 10A "Transcripts of Taped Interviews for CBC Broadcast: Socialism in Canada, 1961," Woodsworth Memorial Collection, Thomas Fisher Rare Book Library, University of Toronto. McCormack, who consulted these interviews, suggested that the Socialist Party of Canada had 3,000 members during its prewar peak. See McCormack, *Reformers, Rebels, and Revolutionaries,* 68.

125 See "Dominion Executive" and "BC Provincial Executive," *Federationist,* 6 December 1912, 4; and "1911 Executive," *Western Clarion,* 24 December 1910, 2. At the same meeting in December 1911 at which Kingsley and others were elected to the SPC Dominion Executive Committee, members of Vancouver Local No. 1 repudiated

any association with the "red dentist," Dr. W.J. Curry, who was described as "no longer a member of the party." See "1911 Executive," *Western Clarion*, 24 December 1910, 2.

126 In March 1905, Kingsley postponed a planned organizing trip with Hawthornthwaite into the BC Interior in order to attend to *Western Clarion* business. The Revelstoke local responded by expressing disappointment. See "B.C. Provincial Executive: Socialist Party of Canada," *Western Clarion*, 11 March 1905, 4; and "B.C. Provincial Executive: Socialist Party of Canada," *Western Clarion*, 25 March 1905, 4.

127 The minutes of DEC meetings, including the lists of attendees, were usually printed in the *Western Clarion*. See, for example, "Dominion Executive Meeting," *Western Clarion*, 25 March 1905, 4.

128 Fox, "Early Socialism in Canada," 93–94. Early members of the SPC Dominion Executive Committee included Kingsley as organizer, J.M. Cameron, A.J. Wilkinson, C. Peters, John E. Dubberly, W.H. Flowers, Alfred Lea, and Pettipiece (who served as secretary). Other prominent SPC members at this time included James Pritchard of Nanaimo and J.G. "Geordie" Morgan of Vancouver. See "Dominion Executive Meeting," *Western Clarion*, 25 March 1905, 4; "Pioneers Pass On," *Western Socialist*, May–June 1952, n. pag., http://www.socialisthistory.ca/Docs/SocialistParty/Morgan-Pritchard.htm; and McCormack, *Reformers, Rebels, and Revolutionaries*, 60. See also "Ukrainian Convention," *Western Clarion*, 3 September 1910, 3.

129 For the *Western Clarion's*, and potentially Kingsley's, views on the impacts of a "low-class of foreign labour" on working conditions, see untitled article, *Western Clarion*, 26 May 1906, 3. For the historical antipathy of white settlers in British Columbia toward workers from Asia, which gave rise to the demand for "Asiatic exclusion," see Chapter 4, note 45. For anti-Asian sentiment among white workers in Washington State in the 1880s, see Carlos A. Schwantes, "Protest in a Promised Land: Unemployment, Disinheritance, and the Origin of Labor Militancy in the Pacific Northwest, 1885–1886," *Western Historical Quarterly* 13, no. 4 (1982): 373–90; and Carlos A. Schwantes, "Perceptions of Violence on the Wageworkers' Frontier: An American-Canadian Comparison," *Pacific Northwest Quarterly* 77, no. 2 (1986): 52–57.

130 "Preparing an Issue," *Western Clarion*, 14 September 1907, 2.

131 Ibid.

132 "The Dominion Elections," *Vancouver World*, 17 September 1908, 6. A correspondent to the *Western Clarion* also invoked Kingsley's statement to the effect that "the conditions of the workers would be ever getting worse" in discussing conditions among Asian workers, but it is not apparent from this letter that Kingsley himself made this association. See "Too Coarse for John," *Western Clarion*, 29 April 1911, 4, stating that "Kingsley often said that the condition of the worker would ever be getting worse. That the standard of living would reduce itself to its lowest level, viz., rice and rats of the Orientals."

133 "Socialist Intentions," *Winnipeg Tribune*, 30 May 1908, 16.

134 "Socialist Mass Meeting," *Vancouver World*, 4 February 1911, 37. See also "Tokio Anarchists Executed Today," *Vancouver World*, 24 January 1911, 1; "Japanese Plotters

Pay Full Penalty," *Saskatoon Star-Phoenix*, 1 February 1911, 6; "Arrived," *Western Clarion*, 28 January 1911, 2; and "Propaganda Meeting," *Western Clarion*, 28 January 1911, 3.

135 Peter Campbell, "East Meets Left: South Asian Militants and the Socialist Party of Canada in British Columbia, 1904–1914," *International Journal of Canadian Studies* 20 (1999): 35–65; Singh, "Echoes of Freedom."

136 "On the 'Battle of Coal Harbor,'" *Federationist*, 31 July 1914, 3. See also "Hindu Invasion from Socialist Viewpoint," *Vancouver Daily Sun*, 28 July 1914, 2.

137 "Organizer Kingsley's Address," *Western Socialist*, 7 February 1903, 1. Kingsley's full statement on the matter was paraphrased in the *Western Socialist* as follows: "The labor problem is not a matter of excluding the Chinese, negroes, etc. nor of getting a ten per cent rise in wages or an hour's less toil per day, it is a problem of securing for labor all the wealth it creates." Exploitation of workers and the working class would continue, Kingsley said, until "the working class capture the powers of government and establish collective ownership of all means of producing and distributing wealth."

138 Linda Kealey, *Enlisting Women for the Cause: Women, Labour, and the Left in Canada, 1890–1920* (Toronto: University of Toronto Press, 1998), 100–1.

139 "Why Women Should Be Socialists," *American Labor Union Journal* [Butte, MT], 6 August 1903, 2, cited in ibid., 105.

140 Joan Sangster, *Dreams of Equality: Women on the Canadian Left, 1920–1950* (Toronto: McClelland and Stewart, 1989), 15.

141 McKay, *Reasoning Otherwise*, 301. See also "Women's Suffrage," *Western Clarion*, 23 July 1910, 1; "An Interesting Discussion of Woman Suffrage," *Western Clarion*, 27 January 1912, 4; and "Shall Women Be Given the Rights of Citizenship?" *Western Clarion*, 10 August 1912, 1.

142 Untitled article, *Western Clarion*, 25 September 1909, 1; "A Woman's Column," *Western Clarion*, 12 September 1908, 2; untitled article, *Western Clarion*, 22 August 1908, 3; Kealey, *Enlisting Women for the Cause*, 123; Kealey, "Canadian Socialism and the Woman Question," 89. See also "Here and Now," *Western Clarion*, 18 August 1909, 3.

143 "Home," *Western Clarion*, 28 May 1910, 2. See also "Women and Wages in New York City," *Western Clarion*, 8 October 1910, 4; "More Blots than One," *Western Clarion*, 15 October 1910, 1; "Must Woman Emancipate Herself?" *Western Clarion*, 17 February 1912, 2; "Socialism and Motherhood," *Western Clarion*, 22 June 1912, 1; "Woman in Society," *Western Clarion*, 3 August 1912, 2; "Shall Women Be Given the Rights of Citizenship?" *Western Clarion*, 10 August 1912, 1; "Women in Industry," *Western Clarion*, 19 July 1913, 1; "Future Woman's Demand," *Western Clarion*, 13 September 1913, 2; "Woman and Socialism," *Western Clarion*, 27 September 1913, 1; "Will Woman Suffrage Solve Economic Problem?" *Western Clarion*, 20 December 1913, 4; and "The Feminine Point of View," *Western Clarion*, 1 July 1920, 8. In 1911, a female SPC member, M.H.T. Alexander, wrote in the *Western Clarion* that she had attended a meeting of the Women's Political Equality League, a leading suffragist organization in British Columbia, and decided that she could not join the

group, which, she said, talked "largely of upholding private property interests." See "A Lady's View," *Western Clarion,* 2 December 1911, 1.

144   John Douglas Belshaw, *Colonization and Community: The Vancouver Island Coalfield and the Making of the British Columbian Working Class* (Montreal and Kingston: McGill-Queen's University Press, 2002), 115.

145   See Andrew Parnaby, *Citizen Docker: Making a New Deal on the Vancouver Waterfront, 1919–1939* (Toronto: University of Toronto Press, 2008), 75–99; Andrew Parnaby, "'The Best Men that Ever Worked the Lumber': Aboriginal Longshoremen on Burrard Inlet, BC, 1863–1939," *Canadian Historical Review* 87, no. 1 (2006): 53–78.

146   "Provincial Parliament," *Western Clarion,* 27 January 1906, 3. Occasional reporting on Indigenous issues could be found in the *Western Clarion.* For example, in 1904 the newspaper reported on a strike of Indigenous fishers on the Skeena River, adhering to a class position that described the canning companies as "playing one bunch of workers against another" after Japanese fishers joined the strike "as a result of the influence brought to bear upon them by the Indians." In 1906, an anonymous letter writer from Nanaimo compared conditions on the Snuneymuxw reserve, where "all land is held in common," with deplorable working conditions in the adjacent Western Fuel Company mine. Commenting on a *Herald* newspaper report on how "the peasants in Russia are killing the landed proprietors," the *Western Clarion* correspondent questioned "how long it will be before the slaves in this country get up courage enough to do likewise." Earlier in 1906, a report discussed accusations against the Cape Mudge Indians of selling children who passed as white to "white purchasers ... in British Columbia for the highest bidder," suggesting that this was an ordinary occurrence "in this age of buying and selling." In July 1909, Vancouver's "red dentist," Dr. W.J. Curry, similarly raised Indigenous issues as a foil against capitalist property relations, commenting on the use of "the land stolen from the Indian" as an example of the capitalist drive for profit. Like the earlier commentary, Curry made no effort to treat in a serious way the Indigenous grievance over land dispossession. In contrast to these generally respectful reports, we find one blatantly dismissive one by former *Western Clarion* publisher Pettipiece encouraging white settlers to join the voters list in advance of the 1909 provincial election: "A man without a vote is classified with the Indians, lunatics and dead men. Be a live one. See that your name appears on the voters' list." See untitled article, *Western Clarion,* 9 July 1904, 1; "From the Slave Pens," *Western Clarion,* 28 July 1906, 3; untitled article, *Western Clarion,* 13 January 1906, 5; untitled article, *Western Clarion,* 3 July 1909, 3; and "Notes from the Trail," *Western Clarion,* 17 July 1909, 2. For a passing reference to "Indian squaws" in Vancouver, see also "A Peep Inside," *Western Clarion,* 10 July 1909, 3.

147   For Capilano's delegation to London, see Parnaby, *Citizen Docker,* 87. For the broader pattern of Indigenous political organization, see Paul Tennant, *Aboriginal People and Politics: The Indian Land Question in British Columbia, 1849–1989* (Vancouver: UBC Press, 1990); and Paul Tennant, "Native Indian Political Organization in British Columbia, 1900–1969: A Response to Internal Colonialism," *BC Studies* 55 (1982): 3–49.

148 "Notes by the Way," *Western Clarion,* 15 August 1908, 1; McKay, *Reasoning Otherwise,* 162, 393.

149 E.T. Kingsley, *The Genesis and Evolution of Slavery: Showing How the Chattel Slaves of Pagan Times Have Been Transformed into the Capitalist Property of To-Day* (Vancouver: Federationist Publishing, 1916). See also Karl Marx and Friedrich Engels, *The Communist Manifesto,* ed. and introd. David McLellan (1848; repr., Oxford: Oxford University Press, 1992), 7; James S. Woodsworth, *Strangers within Our Gates: Or, Coming Canadians* (Toronto: Missionary Society of the Methodist Church, n.d. [c. 1908]), 194; Diane Paul, "'In the Interests of Civilization': Marxist Views of Race and Culture in the Nineteenth Century," *Journal of the History of Ideas* 42, no. 1 (1981): 115–38; Erik van Ree, "Marx and Engels's Theory of History: Making Sense of the Race Factor," *Journal of Political Ideologies* 24, no. 1 (2019): 54–73; and Lawrence Krader, ed., *The Ethnological Notebooks of Karl Marx* (Assen, Netherlands: Van Gorcum, 1974).

150 The Socialist Party of Canada organized weekly meetings on a broad range of topics, as well as special events, such as debates in 1905 in Vancouver, Nanaimo, and Victoria on the question of the single tax or socialism, featuring Kingsley and speaker John White from Chicago. See "A Socialist Debate" [advertisement], *Western Clarion,* 29 July 1905, 4; "Interesting Debate," *Victoria Daily Colonist,* 6 August 1905, 5; and "Sincere Repentance," *Western Clarion,* 12 August 1905, 3.

151 Fox, "Early Socialism in Canada," 95.

152 George Hardy, *Those Stormy Years: Memories of the Fight for Freedom on Five Continents* (London: Lawrence and Wishart, 1956), 28.

153 "Socialists Hold Mass Meeting," *Vancouver Daily Province,* 22 January 1906, 9; "'Bloody Sunday' Commemoration," *Western Clarion,* 27 January 1906, 4; "To Remember Bloody Sunday," *Western Clarion,* 20 January 1906, 1; "Commune Anniversary," *Western Clarion,* 24 March 1906, 4. Intriguingly, the fictionalized account of Kingsley written a quarter of a century later, Stephen's novel *The Gleaming Archway,* describes a socialist meeting in Vancouver on the topic of Bloody Sunday at which a collection is taken to aid Russian revolutionaries. It is a distinct possibility that Stephen attended this meeting, though no mention of his role is included in contemporary media reports. See Stephen, *The Gleaming Archway,* 131–33, 143. For an earlier speech by Kingsley on the topic of the Russian Revolution of 1905, see "Big Meeting in City Hall," *Western Clarion,* 11 November 1905, 3; and "Workers Mass Meeting," advertisement, *Western Clarion,* 4 November 1905, 4. For an "open air" demonstration in 1910 at Vancouver's Cambie Street Grounds, which featured speeches by Kingsley and others, see "Here and Now," *Western Clarion,* 23 April 1910, 2.

154 Pritchard interview with McCormack, 17 August 1971, tape 4, t-225, BCA.

155 Pritchard interview with McCormack, 17 August 1971, tape 3, t-225, BCA.

156 "United Brotherhood of Carpenters, L.U. 617," *Federationist,* 14 February 1913, 1. See also "The Brotherhood of Carpenters Plan Big Program for This Year," *Federationist,* 9 May 1913, 4.

157 In the spring of 1905, Kingsley cancelled a planned propaganda tour in the BC Interior "because of *Clarion* business" but promised that he and Hawthornthwaite would go there once the legislature adjourned. The SPC local in Revelstoke expressed disappointment at the cancellation. In 1906, Kingsley made at least two trips into the Interior, including to Crow's Nest Pass, Nelson, and Revelstoke, where he delivered a lecture on a familiar topic, socialism. In October 1906, he convened with other delegates at the Miners' Union Hall in Nelson for the fourth SPC provincial convention. In 1908, he travelled as far east as Quebec and spoke closer to home at Ladysmith and points in the Kootenays and Boundary country. Prior to a meeting in 1909 in Victoria, the party ran a tongue-in-cheek "wanted" ad for 700 men and women to hear Kingsley speak. See "BC Provincial Executive," *Western Clarion*, 11 March 1905, 4; "Socialists Meet," *Daily Canadian* [Nelson], 8 October 1906, 1; "Proletarian Conference," *Western Clarion*, 20 October 1906, 1; "A Provincial Organization," *Western Clarion*, 27 October 1906, 4; "Socialists' Meeting," *Revelstoke Mail-Herald*, 26 September 1908, 3; and "Wanted" advertisement, *Victoria Daily Colonist*, 22 January 1909, 17.

158 "Liberal Candidates," *Kootenay Mail* [Revelstoke], 19 November 1904, 2. See also "Socialism Explained," *Mail-Herald* [Revelstoke], 13 October 1903, 13. For a lecture in Ladysmith, see "Socialist Leader Attacks Green," *Ladysmith Daily Ledger*, 15 August 1906, 1, 2.

159 "Third Annual Convention," *Western Clarion*, 11 September 1903, 3.

160 "A Trip to Seattle," *Western Clarion*, 30 September 1905, 4.

161 Advertisement, *Western Clarion*, 16 December 1905, 3; "Kingsley Calls Them All Loons," *Vancouver World*, 20 December 1905, 9.

162 "Western Socialists in Convention," *Vancouver Daily Province*, 30 May 1908, 23; "Socialists Meet in Fernie," *Fernie District Ledger*, 2 May 1908, 6; "Socialists Meet in Convention," *Fernie District Ledger*, 30 May 1908, 3; "Port Arthur Election," *Voice*, 29 May 1908, 1. See also "Dominion Executive Committee," *Western Clarion*, 25 January 1908, 3; and J. Castell Hopkins, *Canadian Annual Review of Public Affairs, 1908* (Toronto: Annual Review Publishing, 1909), 100.

163 "Dominion Organization and Fund," *Western Clarion*, 25 January 1908, 3; "Dominion Organization Fund," *Western Clarion*, 2 May 1908, 3.

164 George Weston Wrigley, "How Working-Class Leaders Travel," *Western Clarion*, 12 September 1908, 1. Hawthornthwaite was originally scheduled to join Kingsley on the trip to the east but ended up not going. Kingsley's presence in Cobalt and Hamilton was discussed briefly in a letter by Wilfred Gribble in the *Western Clarion* on 4 July 1908. In 1909, a correspondent identified as "The Rambler" suggested that, when Kingsley reached Port Arthur on his tour in 1908, "some of the kinks" in the SPC local "were straightened out." For Kingsley's tour in 1908, see Wilfred Gribble, "Cobalt and Elsewhere," *Western Clarion*, 4 July 1908, 2; The Rambler, "A Bit of History," *Western Clarion*, 21 August 1909, 3; "Socialist Intentions," *Winnipeg Tribune*, 30 May 1908, 16; "Socialist Meeting," *Calgary Herald*, 1 August 1908, 10; "Socialists Will Surely Come to Power in British Columbia," *Lethbridge Herald*, 25 August 1908,

1; Hopkins, *Canadian Annual Review of Public Affairs, 1908,* 100; and McKay, *Reasoning Otherwise,* 185.

165 Wrigley, "How Working-Class Leaders Travel." For other SPC organizing efforts outside British Columbia, see "Nelson, BC," *Western Clarion,* 11 December 1909, 3; and "Dominion Executive Committee," *Western Clarion,* 29 June 1912, 3.

166 Johnson, "No Compromise," 14n16.

167 Clarence V. Hoar, "Socialism Defended," *Saint John Sun,* 8 June 1909, 4. The letter writer was responding to an attack in the newspaper on renowned socialist John Spargo. Hoar's letter prompted a rebuttal in an editorial in the same issue of the paper. See "Socialism," *Saint John Sun,* 8 June 1909, 4. For an extensive treatment of Spargo, see McKay, *Reasoning Otherwise,* references at 639.

168 Johnson, "No Compromise," 208. For the broader contours of the socialist movement in the Maritimes, see David Frank and Nolan Reilly, "The Emergence of the Socialist Movement in the Maritimes, 1899–1916," *Labour/Le Travail* 4 (1979): 85–113.

169 See, for example, "Mass Meeting on Saturday," *Semi-Weekly World* [Vancouver], 9 April 1909, 10; "Mass Meeting This Evening," *Vancouver World,* 10 April 1909, 1, regarding a mass meeting at Vancouver City Hall at which Kingsley was to speak on the issue of the eight-hour workday. See also "Socialist Meeting," *Victoria Daily Times,* 21 January 1910, 2; "Jottings from Vancouver Meeting," *Western Clarion,* 16 April 1910, 3; and "Here and Now," *Western Clarion,* 23 April 1910, 3.

170 See J. Castell Hopkins, *Canadian Annual Review of Public Affairs, 1910* (Toronto: Annual Review Publishing, 1911), 316, as cited in Richard Allen, "The Social Gospel and the Reform Tradition in Canada, 1890–1928," *Canadian Historical Review* 49, no. 4 (1968): 388–89. Allen suggests that this meeting took place in Montreal, but Hopkins says that the meeting occurred in Victoria, and that is consistent with the following source: "Socialist Speaks on 'Ancient Lowly,'" *Victoria Daily Colonist,* 22 November 1910, 19.

171 "Socialist Speaks on 'Ancient Lowly,'" *Victoria Daily Colonist,* 22 November 1910, 19.

172 "Red Flag Waved by Socialists Last Night," *Vancouver Daily Province,* 12 January 1907, 2–3. See also Hopkins, *Canadian Annual Review of Public Affairs, 1908,* 316.

173 "Will Celebrate May Day in the Diamond City," *Federationist,* 5 April 1912, 1; "Propaganda Meeting," *Western Clarion,* 23 March 1912, 1; "News and Views," *Voice,* 5 April 1912, 7; "New Westminster Propaganda Meeting," *Western Clarion,* 5 October 1912, 1; "A Page for Socialists," *Federationist,* 6 December 1912, 4.

174 "Precious Pedagogues," *Federationist,* 29 August 1913, 2; see also untitled article, *Federationist,* 29 August 1913, 2. For the 1912–14 Vancouver Island coal miners' strike, see Jack Kavanagh, *The Vancouver Island Strike* (Vancouver: BC Miners Liberation League, c. 1913); William Bennett, *Builders of British Columbia* (Vancouver: Broadway Printers, 1937), 65–76; Paul A. Phillips, *No Power Greater: A Century of Labour in British Columbia* (Vancouver: Boag Foundation, 1967), 58–60; and Hardy, *Those Stormy Years,* 48–54.

175   See Kavanagh, *The Vancouver Island Strike,* 13–14; "Minutes," 12 August 1914, box 3.2, Accession No. 80–59, Victoria Labour Council Fonds, University of Victoria Archives and Special Collections; "Around Vancouver," *Vancouver Daily Province,* 13 December 1913, 22. MLA Jack Place, who had succeeded Hawthornthwaite in Nanaimo, was charged with two counts of rioting and one count of being in possession of stolen goods. See "John Place MPP and Thos. Moore Sent Up for Trial," *Nanaimo Daily News,* 27 August 1913, 1; "John Place Charged," *Nanaimo Free Press,* 27 August 1913, 1; and "Decide to Take Speedy Trial," *Victoria Daily Colonist,* 30 August 1913, 1.

176   "The B.C. Miners' Liberation League," *Federationist,* 12 December 1913, 3. See also "United Labor Will Voice Unanimous Protest," *Federationist,* 7 November 1913, 1; "Big Mass Meeting Voices Strong Protest," *Federationist,* 14 November 1913, 1; "McBride, Bowser and City Members Invited," *Federationist,* 5 December 1913, 1; "Around Vancouver," *Vancouver Daily Province,* 13 December 1913, 22; and Mark Leier, *Rebel Life: The Life and Times of Robert Gosden, Revolutionary, Mystic, Labour Spy,* rev. ed. (Vancouver: New Star Books, 2013), 31–32. The British Columbia Federation of Labor was founded at a convention in Vancouver in May 1910, with the first annual convention taking place the following spring, in March 1911, in Victoria. See "Proceedings of First Annual Convention of British Columbia Provincial Federation of Labor," *Vancouver World,* 25 March 1911, 4–5.

177   "Comrade Kingsley for Organizer," *Western Clarion,* 5 May 1914, 1; "Secretarial," *Western Clarion,* 23 May 1914, 3.

178   Hardy, *Those Stormy Years,* 54.

179   Phillips, *No Power Greater,* 61.

180   The estimate of the number of defectors is provided in Kealey, *Enlisting Women for the Cause,* 115–16.

181   "We Women," *Western Socialist,* 31 January 1903, 3, as cited in Kealey, *Enlisting Women for the Cause,* 101; see also Kealey, "Canadian Socialism and the Woman Question," 80.

182   Ira Kipnis, in his history of socialism in the United States, characterized Mills (known as the "little giant" on account of his stature at four feet and six inches) as an oratorical mercenary, enlisted by moderates in factional fights in various states; an earlier talk by Mills in Victoria in December 1906 prompted charges against him in the Socialist Party of Washington State, culminating in the expulsion of the Seattle local. See Ira Kipnis, *The American Socialist Movement, 1897–1912* (New York: Columbia University Press, 1952), 180; untitled article, *Victoria Daily Times,* 27 December 1906, 10; "Shall Seattle Socialists Condone Compromise?" Seattle *Socialist,* 14 April 1907, 2; Erwin B. Ault, "Socialist Party News Notes," Seattle *Socialist,* 27 April 1907, 3; "The Origin of the Charges," Seattle *Socialist,* 4 May 1907, 1; "Trial of Walter Thomas Mills," Seattle *Socialist,* 4 May 1907, 1; Erwin B. Ault, "Local Notes," Seattle *Socialist,* 1 June 1907, 3; and Erwin B. Ault, "Local's Charter Is Revoked," Seattle *Socialist,* 27 July 1907, 4. See also Paul B. Bushue, "Dr. Hermon F. Titus and Socialism in Washington State, 1900–1909" (MA thesis, University of Washington, 1967), 71–74, 97–109. During a lecture in Vancouver on 8 February 1907 on the topic of

"Socialism and Industrial Evolution," which "a large number attended," Mills applied "the doctrine of evolution ... to present day socialism." In comments that diverged sharply from the usual SPC emphasis on the class struggle against capitalism, Mills said that "socialism will never bring about a revolution ... but vice versa. Evolution was taking place every day and the new era was gradually approaching." See "Notice: Socialism and Industrial Evolution," *Vancouver World,* 7 February 1907, 12; and "Socialism of the Scientific Order," *Vancouver World,* 9 February 1907, 5.

183 The Burnses insisted that they hosted the controversial lecture on 8 March 1907 "in a private capacity, instead of as agents of the party." At a raucous special meeting of the SPC Vancouver local a few days prior to the Mills lecture, members defeated on a vote of 26–15 resolutions moved by Mortimer and seconded by Kingsley to expel or suspend Ernest Burns from the party. However, at a subsequent "smaller" meeting, a motion to suspend (which required a simple majority to pass under the party's constitution rather than a two-thirds vote required to expel) was carried on a vote of 15–9. Bertha alleged that the suspension was "engineered by the same persons" (Mortimer and Kingsley), and Ernest protested that he had been denied an opportunity to provide a defence of the charges against him. See Bertha Burns, "Another Socialist Party," *Voice,* 10 May 1907, 1; "Do You Wish to Understand Socialism?" *Vancouver World,* 4 March 1907, 12; "Burns Suspended by Socialists," *Vancouver Daily Province,* 8 March 1907, 12; Leeds, "Correspondence," *Western Clarion,* 9 March 1907, 2; and "Fusion Rejected," *Western Clarion,* 16 March 1907, 2. For the SPC Vancouver local's vote against hosting the Mills meeting of 8 March 1907, which carried on a vote of 20–6 with a resolution stating "that we publicly disavow all connection with Walter Thomas Mills' meeting," see Leeds, "Correspondence," *Western Clarion,* 9 March 1907, 2. For an earlier debate within the SPBC about "fusion" with other parties, including Kingsley's position that independent candidates in the federal election of 1904 were "the worst enemies the workers had," see William Griffiths, "Correspondence," *Vancouver Daily Province,* 30 November 1904, 4.

184 "Seceding Socialists to Form New Party," *Victoria Daily Colonist,* 2 April 1907, 3; Elections British Columbia, *An Electoral History of British Columbia, 1871–1986* (Victoria: Elections British Columbia, 1988), 91, 99; "Get Ready for Next Campaign," *Western Clarion,* 9 February 1907, 1.

185 Bertha M. Burns to Mrs. Ramsay MacDonald, 26 July 1906, J.R. MacDonald Papers, as quoted in Kealey, *Enlisting Women for the Cause,* 116, 281n8.

186 "Seceding Socialists to Form New Party," *Victoria Daily Colonist,* 2 April 1907, 3.

187 Ibid.

188 "Another Socialist Party," *Voice,* 10 May 1907, 1.

189 "Platform of the Social-Democratic Party of Canada," quoted in C.H. Cahan, *Socialistic Propaganda in Canada: Its Purposes, Results and Remedies, Address Delivered to St. James Literary Society, Montreal, 12 December 1918* (Montreal:, n.d. [c. 1918]), 5, cited in Fox, "Early Socialism in Canada," 96.

190 Bertha M. Burns to Mrs. Ramsay MacDonald, 9 April 1907, J.R. MacDonald Papers, as quoted in Kealey, *Enlisting Women for the Cause,* 116, 281n8.

191 "Fusion Rejected," *Western Clarion,* 16 March 1907, 2. See also "Factions in the Socialist Party," *Western Clarion,* 2 March 1907, 1; "Another Family Row," *Western Clarion,* 2 March 1907, 2; "The Death of Socialism in British Columbia," *Western Clarion,* 2 March 1907, 4; "Mills' Apologist Admits Fusion," *Western Clarion,* 9 March 1907, 3; and Johnson, "No Compromise," 280–82.

192 "Gleanings 'Long the Road," *Weekly People,* 4 May 1907, 1. For De Leon's talk in Vancouver attended by Kingsley, see "De Leon in Vancouver," *Weekly People,* 4 May 1907, 6.

193 The geographic scope of the SDPC is discussed in Johnson, "No Compromise," 298n36. As Kealey has noted, women played prominent roles in the SDPC, including serving as secretaries of the Vancouver and Victoria locals. See Kealey, *Enlisting Women for the Cause,* 116, 134.

194 Johnson, "No Compromise," 287–88. Prominent Socialist James C. "Jimmy" Watters, who had contested the 1903 provincial election and the 1904 federal election as the SPBC candidate in Victoria, also joined the SDPC, on the eve of his election as president of the Trades and Labor Congress of Canada, the central body of Canadian unions at the time. See Phillips, *No Power Greater,* 51. For an earlier controversy regarding the election of Watters as president of the Victoria Trades and Labor Council, since he was a known member of the SPBC, see "Tempest in a Tea Pot," *Western Clarion,* 14 August 1903, 3.

195 Hawthornthwaite to McKenzie, Secretary, Provincial Executive Committee of the Socialist Party of Canada, 14 March 1911, in "The Wail of the Wallopped MPP," *Victoria Daily Times,* 23 May 1911, 9; "Hawthornthwaite's Resignation," *Western Clarion,* 6 May 1911, 3; "Hawthornthwaite's Side," *Cranbrook Herald,* 1 June 1911, 6; "The Reason," *Western Clarion,* 16 December 1911, 2; Johnson, "No Compromise," 287–88; Grantham, "Some Aspects of the Socialist Movement," 82. McKenzie would die from blood poisoning at Alberni in 1918. See "The Late D.G. McKenzie," *Federationist,* 25 January 1918, 2.

196 McKay, *Reasoning Otherwise,* 177; McCormack, *Reformers, Rebels, and Revolutionaries,* 74–75; Fox, "Early Socialism in Canada," 96. Building on the Socialist Party of Canada's limited inroads among "language locals," the SDPC developed a more durable and extensive presence within ethnocultural communities that had recently arrived from Southern and Eastern Europe – establishing German, Polish, Jewish, Ukrainian, and Finnish locals (a foundation that communists would expand in the 1920s).

197 McCormack, *Reformers, Rebels, and Revolutionaries,* 75.

198 "Philosophers Only," *Western Clarion,* 9 March 1912, 9.

199 Pritchard interview with McCormack, 17 August 1971, tape 3, t-225, BCA.

200 "Built on Marxianism," *Voice,* 2 November 1906, 6. See also Martin Robin, *Radical Politics and Canadian Labour, 1880–1930* (Kingston: Queen's University Industrial Relations Centre, 1968), 96–97.

201 "Hardie at Vancouver," *Voice,* 16 August 1907, 1; "Keir Hardie's Visit," *Voice,* 9 October 1908, 9. See also "Mr. Martin Withdraws from Vancouver Contest," *Victoria Daily Colonist,* 3 August 1907, 1, and "Keir Hardie Will Speak Next Friday," *Vancouver*

Daily Province, 27 July 1907, 1, for additional information on Hardie's visit to Vancouver, including declining a request from the Canadian Club to speak; "Labor Leader Who Is Visiting Canada," *Victoria Daily Times,* 1 August 1907, 3, for Hardie's speaking tour in Canada in 1907; "Keir Hardie in Winnipeg," *Voice,* 2 August 1907, 1, for a report on Hardie's lecture in Winnipeg; "Keir Hardie before the Canadian Club," *Voice,* 9 August 1907, 1, and "Socialism: By J. Keir Hardie," *Ottawa Citizen,* 23 July 1907, 11, for reports on a lecture by Hardie to the Canadian Club in Toronto on 22 July 1907; "British Labor Leader Will Deliver Address in This City To-Morrow," *Victoria Daily Times,* 3 August 1907, 11, and "Keir Hardie at Victoria," *Manitoba Morning Free Press* [Winnipeg], 6 August 1907, 1, for Hardie's lecture in Victoria's Ancient Order of United Workmen Hall on 4 August 1907.

202 "Keir Hardie's Visit," *Voice,* 9 October 1908, 9. A correspondent to the Winnipeg *Voice* would later comment favourably on Hardie's attack on "aggressive socialists" not in touch with the modern socialist movement at all. See "The Elections," *Voice,* 9 October 1908, 6. See also McCormack, *Reformers, Rebels, and Revolutionaries,* 60.

203 "Question Time," *Western Clarion,* 8 December 1906, 4. See also Mark Leier, *Where the Fraser River Flows: The Industrial Workers of the World in British Columbia* (Vancouver: New Star Books, 1990), 35. A blistering attack on the Industrial Workers of the World can be found in "Proving Its Case," *Western Clarion,* 18 July 1914, 2.

204 "Come It, Comet, Come-Off-It," *Western Clarion,* 19 March 1910, 2. For a rebuttal to this letter by a Kingsley supporter, see "Take 'Em," *Western Clarion,* 16 April 1910, 2. Kingsley would elaborate his theories of economic organization under capitalism in a three-page article, "Economic Organization," *Western Clarion,* July 1911, 18–20.

205 "Something Is Holding Us Back," *Western Clarion,* 2 October 1909, 4. For other criticism of Kingsley, see "Wages and Prices," *Western Clarion,* 22 January 1910, 2.

206 "Kingsley, McKenzie and Co.," *Western Clarion,* 11 June 1910, 2.

Chapter 6: Kingsley and the State

1 Gregory S. Kealey and Reg Whitaker, eds., *RCMP Security Bulletins: The Early Years, 1919–1929* (St. John's: Committee on Canadian Labour History, 1994), 383. See also 472 for a subject file associated with Kingsley, file 538 "OBU E.T. Kingsley – Organizer 175/P15," folder 175 "Classification: Bolsheviki and Agitators," [1919], vol. 2448, RCMP Security Service Files, Record Group 18, Royal Canadian Mounted Police Fonds, Library and Archives Canada (hereafter RG 18, RCMP Fonds, LAC).

2 Chambers to MacLean, 2 April 1919, file 279–1, vol. 602, RG 6, Secretary of State Fonds, LAC.

3 E.T. Kingsley, "Sacrificial Victims," *Federationist,* 30 August 1910, 1.

4 Parliament of Canada, "Elections and Ridings," https://lop.parl.ca/sites/ParlInfo/default/en_CA/ElectionsRidings; Elections British Columbia, *An Electoral History of British Columbia, 1871–1986* (Victoria: Elections British Columbia, 1988), 103, 106, 113; "Socialist Could Not Have Retired," *Vancouver Daily Province,* 5 August 1907, 1.

5 Allen Seager, "Hawthornthwaite, James Hurst," in *Dictionary of Canadian Biography* (2005), http://www.biographi.ca/en/bio.php?BioId=42322.

6   "8-Hour Bill for Coal Miners," *Western Clarion*, 6 April 1905, 1. See also "Capitalists Disturbed by Labor Legislation," *Western Clarion*, 4 March 1905, 1; Patricia E. Roy, *Boundless Optimism: Richard McBride's British Columbia* (Vancouver: UBC Press, 2012), 96–97.

7   "Campaign in the Boundary," *Western Clarion*, 4 August 1906, 1. See also "The Provincial Parliament," *Western Clarion*, 27 January 1906, 1, 3; "Hawthornthwaite Scores," *Western Clarion*, 24 February 1906, 1; "Class War in the Local House," *Western Clarion*, 12 January 1907, 1; "The Provincial House Once More in Session," *Western Clarion*, 16 March 1907, 1; "Week's Doings in the House in Victoria," *Western Clarion*, 19 February 1910, 1; "Much Cry and Little Wool," *Western Clarion*, 26 March 1910, 1; "J.H. Hawthornthwaite's Record in the Legislature," *Federationist*, 2 February 1917, 5.

8   See Peter Campbell, "'Making Socialists': Bill Pritchard, the Socialist Party of Canada, and the Third International," *Labour/Le Travail* 30 (1992): 42–65; Peter Campbell, *Canadian Marxists and the Search for a Third Way* (Montreal and Kingston: McGill-Queen's University Press, 1999); and Paul Fox, "Early Socialism in Canada," in *The Political Process in Canada: Essays in Honour of R. MacGregor Dawson*, ed. J.H. Aitchison (Toronto: University of Toronto Press, 1963), 94.

9   Fox, "Early Socialism in Canada," 94.

10   See ibid., 95; and "Socialist Platform," *Phoenix Pioneer*, 25 October 1902, 3.

11   Thomas R. Loosmore, "The British Columbia Labor Movement and Political Action, 1879–1906" (MA thesis, University of British Columbia, 1954), 196–97.

12   "Socialists Select Their Candidates," *Vancouver Daily Province*, 2 January 1907, 1.

13   We have not been able, unfortunately, to locate the original article cited by McCormack. For the perspective of SPC members on revolutionary violence, see the *Western Clarion*, 16 March 1907; 2 May 1908; 25 June 1908; 5 June 1909; and 2 October 1909, as cited in Ross McCormack, *Reformers, Rebels, and Revolutionaries: The Western Canadian Radical Movement 1899–1919* (Toronto: University of Toronto Press, 1977), 58–59.

14   Martin Robin, *Radical Politics and Canadian Labour, 1880–1930* (Kingston: Queen's University Industrial Relations Centre, 1968), 97; see also Ronald Grantham, "Some Aspects of the Socialist Movement in British Columbia, 1898–1933" (MA thesis, University of British Columbia, 1942), 53; Ross Alfred Johnson, "No Compromise – No Political Trading: The Marxian Socialist Tradition in British Columbia" (PhD diss., University of British Columbia, 1975), 255–56; "Alderman Bird Says City Was Never So Wicked," *Vancouver Daily Province*, 20 May 1907, 2; and Richard G. Stuart, "The Early Political Career of Angus MacInnis" (MA thesis, University of British Columbia, 1967).

15   Kingsley to Hawthornthwaite, 28 December 1903, folder 3, box 1, Hawthornthwaite Fonds, SFUSC. An article in the *Western Socialist* in January 1903 noted that "the local municipal campaign is over, but not a whisper is murmured about the city acquiring the telephone system. The socialists will certainly take a hand in the game next year." See "Notes," *Western Socialist*, 17 January 1903, 2.

16   Kingsley to Hawthornthwaite, 28 December 1903, folder 3, box 1, Hawthornthwaite Fonds, SFUSC.

17 "Labor Will Have Ticket in Next Civic Election," *Vancouver Daily Province*, 27 March 1909, 4. Pettipiece, a delegate of the typographers' union, would later serve as general secretary of the VTLC. See "Central Labor Body Holds Rousing Meeting," *Federationist*, 20 February 1912, 1.

18 "Will Socialists Enter the Municipal Field Next Year?" *Federationist*, 12 October 1912, 1; Johnson, "No Compromise," 255–56.

19 "The Socialists and the Municipal Elections," *Voice*, 18 October 1912, 12. See also "Will Socialists Enter Municipal Field Next Year?" *Federationist*, 12 October 1912, 1.

20 "Municipal Politics," *Western Clarion*, 9 November 1912, 1. See also "Municipal Comment," *Western Clarion*, 21 November 1908, 2.

21 "The Mirage of Municipal Politics," *Western Clarion*, 30 October 1909, 2.

22 The SPC candidates in Kootenay, Victoria, and Yale – James Baker, James C. "Jimmy" Watters, and Ernest Mills – received between 10 and 12 percent of the vote. The candidate in Nanaimo – named Fenton – running against former labour leader Ralph Smith, received 22 percent of the vote compared with 43 percent for Smith. See Parliament of Canada, "Elections and Ridings," https://lop.parl.ca/sites/ParlInfo/default/en_CA/ElectionsRidings; and Loosmore, "The British Columbia Labor Movement and Political Action," 194–95.

23 "The Selections of the Socialists," *Victoria Daily Colonist*, 27 October 1904, 3. For his comments at an SPBC campaign meeting in Ladysmith, where Kingsley equated labour to any other commodity, including fish, see "Socialists Start the Campaign Here," *Ladysmith Daily Ledger*, 13 October 1904, 1, 4. For his appearance at an SPBC campaign meeting in Vancouver, see "Last Big Meeting of Socialists," *Vancouver Daily Province*, 1 November 1904, 2.

24 For the nomination of the five SPC candidates in the multiple-member Vancouver City riding, see "Socialists Select Their Candidates," *Vancouver Daily Province*, 2 January 1907, 1; "Politics in Vancouver," *Western Clarion*, 5 January 1907, 2; "Socialist Party Candidates," *Western Clarion*, 19 January 1907, 3; and "The Nominations," *Boundary Creek Times* [Greenwood, BC], 1 February 1907, 2.

25 "Mortimer Will Run on Socialist Ticket," *Vancouver Daily Province*, 10 January 1907, 1. This story regarding Kingsley's disqualification would be reported again twenty years later in "Twenty Years Ago in Vancouver," *Vancouver Daily Province*, 11 January 1927, 24. For the statutory requirements regarding qualifications to run for the provincial legislature, see *Constitution Act*, RSBC 1897, c 47, s 30; also see *Provincial Elections Act*, SBC 1903–04, c 17.

26 "Seventeen Candidates to Run in Vancouver," *Vancouver World*, 17 January 1907, 1; "Mortimer Will Run on Socialist Ticket," *Vancouver Daily Province*, 10 January 1907, 1. The *Vancouver World* reported that "some doubt was entertained in many quarters as to whether the nomination of Mr. Kingsley would be accepted, but the nomination passed in without question."

27 "Red Flag Waved by Socialists Last Night," *Vancouver Daily Province*, 12 January 1907, 2–3.

28 "McInnes Was Roasted by Socialists Last Night," *Vancouver Daily Province*, 30 January 1907, 7. A controversy arose during the campaign over McInnes's previous

application for membership in the Nanaimo Socialist Party. See "Will Pledge Anything," *Daily Canadian* [Nelson], 15 January 1907, 3.

29 "The Labor Vote Issue," *Vancouver Daily Province,* 9 January 1907, 13. See also "Red Flag Waved by Socialists Last Night," *Vancouver Daily Province,* 12 January 1907, 1–3. For Kingsley's organizing work in other districts during the election campaign in British Columbia in 1907, see "Provincial Executive Committee," *Western Clarion,* 29 December 1906, 3.

30 "Working Men and Socialism," *Vancouver Daily Province,* 19 January 1907, 6.

31 "Socialists Warned to Prepare for the Campaign," *Vancouver Daily Province,* 24 December 1906, 7. For a speech by Kingsley in Nanaimo during the provincial election campaign in 1907, see "A Public Meeting" [advertisement], *Nanaimo Daily News,* 18 January 1907, 4. In the wake of the election that year, Kingsley and fellow socialist D.G. McKenzie would be appointed as commissioners in Vancouver for taking affidavits under the provincial *Elections Act.* See "New Commissioner Named for Osoyoos," *Vancouver Daily Province,* 4 May 1907, 1.

32 "The Triumph of Capitalism," *Western Clarion,* 9 February 1907, 4; also see "Socialist Vote," *Western Clarion,* 9 February 1907, 1; "Get Ready for Next Campaign," *Western Clarion,* 9 February. 1907, 1; "Note and Comment," *Western Clarion,* 2 March 1907, 2; and "Lost Deposits," *Nanaimo Daily News,* 6 February 1907, 4.

33 Elections British Columbia, *An Electoral History of British Columbia,* 99–104; also see Fox, "Early Socialism in Canada," 93.

34 Elections British Columbia, *An Electoral History of British Columbia,* 106; "Three Candidates in By-Election on Saturday," *Vancouver Daily Province,* 1 August 1907, 1; "Bowser Martin Kingsley," *Nanaimo Daily News,* 1 August 1907, 1; "BC Candidates," *Edmonton Journal,* 2 August 1907, 4; "Election Tomorrow," *Nanaimo Daily News,* 2 August 1907, 1; "Socialists in the Fray," *Voice,* 2 August 1907, 1.

35 "Mr. Martin Withdraws from Vancouver Contest," *Victoria Daily Colonist,* 3 August 1907, 1. See also "Martin Is Running, but Not for Election," *Vancouver Daily Province,* 2 August 1907, 1; "Election on in Vancouver," *Nanaimo Daily News,* 3 August 1907, 1; "Martin Has Dropped Out," *Mail-Herald* [Revelstoke], 3 August 1907, 1; "Socialist Could Not Have Retired," *Vancouver Daily Province,* 5 August 1907, 1; "Joe Martin Is Out," *Star-Phoenix* [Saskatoon], 5 August 1907, 6; "Martin Not a Candidate," *Brandon Daily Sun,* 3 August 1907, 8; and "News Briefs," *Moyie Leader,* 10 August 1907, 4. During the by-election campaign, the *Week* newspaper would lambaste Kingsley as "an illogical, irreconcilable, revolutionary demagogue of the worst type." See "Factious Opposition," *Week* [Victoria], 3 August 1907, 16. The circumstances of Martin's withdrawal during the by-election were described in greater detail in a retrospective article five decades later by James Morton, the *Victoria Daily Colonist*'s long-standing legislative reporter: "When W.J. Bowser was appointed attorney-general, [Martin] announced himself in opposition. He held an open-air meeting in Recreation Park, where he vigorously addressed a large audience seated in the grandstand. Not a murmur of applause reached his ears and the next day he announced his withdrawal from the contest, leaving Mr. Bowser with a walkover against

E.T. Kingsley, the lone Socialist candidate." James Morton, "Courtroom Fireball," *Victoria Daily Colonist Islander Magazine,* 7 February 1960, 2.

36 Elections British Columbia, *An Electoral History of British Columbia,* 103, 106; "Kingsley Has Lost His Deposit," *Vancouver Daily Province,* 3 August 1907, 1; "Mr. Bowser Carries By-Election Easily," *Nanaimo Daily News,* 5 August 1907, 1; "Vote Remained Stationary," *Voice,* 9 August 1907, 1.

37 "Vancouver Socialist Candidate," *Victoria Daily Colonist,* 29 July 1908, 11. See also "Socialists Name Kingsley," *Vancouver World,* 28 July 1908, 1; "The Bodies Recovered," *Star-Phoenix* [Saskatoon], 15 July 1908, 1; "Vancouver Socialists," *Gazette* [Montreal], 29 July 1908, 1; "Socialist Candidate Chosen," *Calgary Herald,* 29 July 1908, 7; and "Local Notes," *Keremeos Trumpet,* 7 August 1908, 1.

38 "Socialist Plans for Next Election," *Victoria Daily Colonist,* 24 April 1908, 2.

39 "Kingsley for the Socialists," *Vancouver World,* 17 September 1908, 10. According to this report, City Hall was "fairly well filled by those who follow the cause of the Red Flag, and included quite a number of ladies."

40 "Kingsley for the Socialists," *Vancouver World,* 17 September 1908, 10; "Political Pointers," *Express* [North Vancouver], 18 September 1908, 4. The Socialist Party of Canada had publicly disclaimed any association with the September 1908 nomination meeting. See "Public Notice," *Vancouver Daily Province,* 16 September 1908, 16; and "Public Notice," *Vancouver World,* 16 September 1908, 12.

41 "If Necessary Let Them Use Clubs," *Vancouver Daily Province,* 1 October 1908, 2.

42 "Four Candidates on One Platform," *Victoria Daily Colonist,* 21 October 1908, 14; see also "'Make the Laws to Suit Ourselves,'" *Vancouver Daily Province,* 8 October 1909, 8.

43 "M'Innes and Martin Fought Verbal Duel," *Vancouver Daily Province,* 20 October 1908, 12. See also "Invite Candidates to Joint Meeting," *Vancouver Daily Province,* 9 October 1908, 1; "Joint Meeting in Vancouver," *Voice,* 23 October 1908, 7; "Four Characteristic Addresses," *Western Clarion,* 24 October 1908, 1, 4; and "Socialists Met at Opera House," *Vancouver Daily Province,* 24 October 1908, 3.

44 "All Ready to Start," *Vancouver Daily Province,* 16 October 1908, 1; "Wandering Willie's Sad Behavior," *Vancouver Daily Province,* 20 October 1908, 1; untitled cartoon, *Vancouver Daily Province,* 22 October 1908, 1; "On the Mercy Seat," *Vancouver Daily Province,* 26 October 1908, 1; "Back to the Tall Timber," *Vancouver Daily Province,* 27 October 1908, 1; "Dull Times in the Art Department," *Vancouver Daily Province,* 28 October 1908, 1; Robin Anderson, "The British Columbia View of Cartoonist, J.B. Fitzmaurice, 1908–1909," *Journal of Canadian Studies* 42, no. 1 (2008): 36–37; Peter Desbarats and Terry Mosher, *The Hecklers: A History of Canadian Political Cartooning and a Cartoonists' History of Canada* (Toronto: McClelland and Stewart, 1979), 34, describing Fitzmaurice's work for the *Vancouver Daily Province* as milquetoast.

45 "Bribery in Vancouver," *Victoria Daily Colonist,* 30 October 1908, 1; news briefs, *Victoria Daily Colonist,* 1 November 1908, 4. Kingsley's candidacy is also discussed in "The Dominion Elections," *Semi-Weekly World* [Vancouver] 18 September 1908,

5; and "Your Candidates Will Go to the Polls," *Vancouver Daily Province,* 19 October 1908, 7.

46 Elections British Columbia, *An Electoral History of British Columbia,* 113; "Socialists to Run," *Vancouver Daily Province,* 27 October 1909, 1; "Vancouver Socialists Nominate Candidates," *Edmonton Journal,* 27 October 1909, 1; "Secretarial," *Western Clarion,* 30 October 1909, 3; "Among Canada's Wage-Earners," *Lethbridge Herald,* 6 November 1909, 9; "Analysis of Last Election Results," *Vancouver Daily Province,* 8 November 1909, 19; "Socialist Candidates," *Western Clarion,* 13 November 1909, 1; "Provincial Elections Candidates in the Field," *Victoria Daily Times,* 15 November 1909, 10; "Vancouver City," *Victoria Daily Times,* 26 November 1909, 7; "British Columbia Endorses McBride," *Star-Phoenix* [Saskatoon], 26 November 1909, 1; "The Vancouver Vote," *Western Clarion,* 4 December 1909, 1; "Candidates Who Lost Deposits," *Vancouver Daily Province,* 2 February 1908, 1; "Story of the Last Election," *Victoria Daily Colonist,* 3 April 1910, 24. Kingsley was among five Socialist candidates nominated to stand in the multiple-member Vancouver City district at a joint meeting of the Finnish- and English-speaking SPC locals in Vancouver on 26 October 1909. See "Socialists to Run," *Vancouver Daily Province,* 27 October 1909, 1; and "Vancouver Socialists Nominate Candidates," *Edmonton Journal,* 27 October 1909, 1. In the 1909 provincial election, James McVety served as the official agent for Kingsley and the other Socialist candidates. See "Provincial Elections Act," *Vancouver Daily Province,* 17 November 1909, 25.

47 "Mr. Kingsley May Run," *Vancouver Daily Province,* 4 December 1909, 1. Kingsley did not run for mayor of Vancouver in the 1910 municipal election or at any other time. He appears never to have contested a municipal seat in British Columbia.

48 "Politicians Talked to Socialists and Workers," *Vancouver Daily Province,* 18 November 1909, 4. See also "Vancouver's Joint Meeting," *Western Clarion,* 27 November 1909, 3.

49 Elections British Columbia, *An Electoral History of British Columbia,* 109–15; also see Fox, "Early Socialism in Canada," 93.

50 "Election Prospects," *Week* [Victoria], 2 September 1911, 13; "S.P. of C. Candidates," *Western Clarion,* September 1911, 8; "Three Candidates Formally Nominated," *Vancouver Daily Province,* 14 September 1911, 1; "Nominations," *Victoria Daily Times,* 14 September 1911, 18. Kingsley was acclaimed as the SPC candidate for Vancouver City in the 1911 federal election, receiving the unanimous support of members of the Vancouver local who attended a meeting at party headquarters on Water Street on 8 August 1911. See "Would Nominate Attorney-General," *Vancouver Daily Province,* 8 August 1911, 3; "Liberals Inaugurate Campaign in City," *Vancouver Daily Province,* 9 August 1911, 19; "The Political Pot Is Boiling," *Winnipeg Tribune,* 10 August 1911, 3; "Manitoba Machine Out of Action," *Victoria Daily Times,* 10 August 1911, 1; "Way Clear for D. Ross," *Omineca Herald,* 12 August 1911, 1. Ray Isaac Matthews served as Kingsley's agent during the 1911 federal campaign. See "Electoral Division of Vancouver City," *Vancouver World,* 16 September 1911, 12. The Socialist Party of Canada also fielded a candidate in the Victoria riding in 1911 to challenge legal restrictions on street-corner meetings.

51 "Socialist Party of Canada," *Western Call* [Vancouver], 18 August 1911, 8. During the 1911 election campaign, Kingsley also addressed a crowd at the Odd Fellows' Hall in Eburne (now the Marpole neighbourhood in south Vancouver). See "Eburne Meeting Poorly Attended," *Vancouver World*, 8 September 1911, 10.

52 Pritchard interview with McCormack, 16 August 1971, tape 1, t-225, BCA. See also "Crowded Meeting at Vancouver," *Nanaimo Daily News*, 19 September 1911, 1; "Socialist Meeting Well Attended," *Vancouver Daily Province*, 7 September 1911, 30.

53 Parliament of Canada, "Elections and Ridings," https://lop.parl.ca/sites/ParlInfo/default/en_CA/ElectionsRidings; "Six Opposition in the Province," *Victoria Daily Times*, 22 September 1911, 1; "Vancouver," *Ottawa Citizen*, 22 September 1911, 14; "Analysis of Vote in the Recent Election," *Vancouver Daily Province*, 4 November 1911, 13.

54 "Public Notice," *Western Clarion*, 2 December 1911, 3.

55 Elections British Columbia, *An Electoral History of British Columbia*, 115–19; "To Secretaries of BC Locals," *Western Clarion*, 2 March 1912, 1. For the SPC nomination process in Vancouver prior to the election, see E.T. Kingsley, "Vancouver Convention," *Western Clarion*, 2 March 1912, 2. Jack Place earlier served as secretary of the SPC Nanaimo Local No. 3. Presumably, he left that party and joined the SDPC when members of the local defected as a block. For his work on behalf of the Socialist Party of Canada, including reporting funds in the amount of $136.20 in advance of the 1908 federal campaign, see "Nanaimo Riding Campaign," *Western Clarion*, 22 August 1908, 3.

56 "O'Brien, Socialist, Elected by a Majority of 32," *Coleman Miner*, 26 March 1909, 4.

57 Weston Wrigley, "How Toronto Movement Progresses," *Western Clarion*, 20 May 1905, 1.

58 "C.M. O'Brien, MPP, Arrested," *Coleman Miner*, 20 August 1909, 1; "O'Brien Gets His," *Western Clarion*, 21 August 1909, 2. See also "Alberta Legislature," *Western Clarion*, 31 December 1910, 1.

59 "Eastern Tour," *Western Clarion*, 10 June 1911, 1. See also "O'Brien Reports," *Western Clarion*, 16 December 1911, 3.

60 "An Earnest Suggestion," *Western Clarion*, 18 July 1914, 1.

61 E.T. Kingsley, "The Affirmation of 'German Culture,'" *Western Clarion*, 24 October 1914, 2. In 1909, the SPC Dominion Executive Committee had adopted a resolution declining to pursue affiliation with the International Socialist Bureau because of its class-collaborationist character. The resolution was republished in the *Western Clarion* in November 1914 as the failure of the Second International was brought into sharp focus by the responses of European socialists to the outbreak of war. See "Resolution of the DEC on Question of Affiliation with ISB," *Western Clarion*, 21 November 1914, 2; also see the original resolution in "International Affiliation," *Western Clarion*, 7 August 1909, 3. The resolution cited concerns about "fusion or compromise" that would contravene the SPC constitution.

62 Kingsley, "Affirmation."

63 E.T. Kingsley, "War Is Hell, for Workers," *Western Clarion*, 1 May 1909, 1.

64 Local Vancouver BC No. 1 to Dominion Executive Committee, 28 October 1914, "Vancouver," *Western Clarion*, 7 November 1914, 3. The Vancouver local grounded

its objection to the editorial in the context of the party's position on the war as well as "the fundamentals of the Socialist Philosophy itself." It insisted that the enemy of socialists was capitalism and that all "German 'culture,' Allied 'culture,' or Neutral 'culture'" was bourgeois and violently opposed to "the revolutionary working class." The resolution also noted that Kingsley's suggestion that neutral countries should enter the war was "directly contrary to the class struggle."

65 W.M. Braes, 22 October 1914, "Cumberland, BC," *Western Clarion,* 7 November 1914, 3. The Cumberland local declared that "so far as we understand the workings of the capitalist system we consider this war is a capitalist war, fought in the interest of the capitalist class, therefore we, as a part of the international working class, abhor the horrors of war, instead of aiding and abetting it, as the article seems to do."

66 T. Sanders, "Edmonton," And. Manson, "Nelson, BC," J. Pilkington, "Enderby, BC," Thos. Hanwell, "Brandon, Man," *Western Clarion,* 7 November 1914, 3.

67 Minutes of DEC meeting of 23 October 1914, Vancouver, in "Dominion Executive Committee," *Western Clarion,* 7 November 1914, 3; "Secretarial Note," *Western Clarion,* 7 November 1914, 2. The new editorial board made its stance toward the war clear when the next issue of the *Western Clarion* featured a blaring front-page headline and full-page story highlighting British hypocrisy as a global imperialist power. See "What Is the British Ruling Class After?" *Western Clarion,* 7 November 1914, 1.

68 "Secretarial Note," *Western Clarion,* 7 November 1914, 2.

69 Minutes of DEC meeting of 30 October 1914, Vancouver, in "Dominion Executive Committee," *Western Clarion,* 21 November 1914, 3. See also Dale Michael McCartney, "A Crisis of Commitment: Socialist Internationalism in British Columbia during the Great War" (MA thesis: Simon Fraser University, 2010), 40, 52; Pritchard interview with McCormack, 17 August 1971, tape 3, t-225, BCA; Grantham, "Some Aspects of the Socialist Movement in British Columbia," 89.

70 Pritchard interview with McCormack, 17 August 1971, tape 3, t-225, BCA.

71 "Riff-Raff of the Raging Sea of Politics," *Federationist,* 8 September 1916, 16.

72 "Little Pin-Head Bunch in Vancouver," *Vancouver World,* 31 December 1915, 3. O'Brien left the Socialist Party of Canada after the leaders in Vancouver attempted to impose restrictions to prevent members from accepting speaking engagements hosted by organizations other than the party. According to Kingsley, "on the principle, perhaps, that actions speak louder than words, Charles O'Brien has simply withdrawn from the rule of the little pin-head bunch here and has gone to organize across the line."

73 "Socialists to Run One Man," *Vancouver Daily Province,* 26 July 1916, 4.

74 Reg Whitaker, Gregory S. Kealey, and Andrew Parnaby, *Secret Service: Political Policing in Canada from the Fenians to Fortress America* (Toronto: University of Toronto Press, 2012).

75 Donald Avery, *"Dangerous Foreigners": European Immigrant Workers and Labour Radicalism in Canada, 1896–1932* (Toronto: McClelland and Stewart, 1979).

76 "Arouse Ye Slaves," *Appeal to Reason,* 10 March 1906, 1. See also "*Appeal to Reason* Is Cast Out of Canada," *Labor World* [Duluth], 5 May 1906, 1. For other SPC advocacy in relation to the persecution of American socialist labour leaders Moyer, Haywood,

and others, see "Vancouver Local No. 1" and "A Question of Power," *Western Clarion,* 31 March 1906, 3, 4.

77   Untitled article, *Appeal to Reason,* 12 May 1906, 1.

78   Ibid. See also "Debs Sounds a Warning," *Western Clarion,* 17 March 1906, 2.

79   See "City Hall Meeting," *Western Clarion,* 2 June 1906, 1.

80   "Canada Aflame with Indignation," *Appeal to Reason,* 12 May 1906, 1.

81   See "Mass Meeting Held Last Sunday at the Empress," *Federationist,* 3 January 1919, 7.

82   For the Victoria Free Speech fight, see "Victoria's Turn," *Western Clarion,* August 1911, 41-42; and Mark Leier, *Where the Fraser River Flows: The Industrial Workers of the World in British Columbia* (Vancouver: New Star Books, 1990), 73-74. See also Gregory S. Kealey, *Toronto Workers Respond to Industrial Capitalism, 1867-1892* (1980; repr., Toronto: University of Toronto Press, 1991), 402; "Would Sweep Back the Tide," *Western Clarion,* 5 August 1905, 1; "Big Demonstration in Seattle," *Montana News* [Helena], 3 October 1907, 1; "The Fight for Free Streets," Seattle *Socialist,* 16 November 1907, 1; "On Free Streets," Seattle *Socialist,* 23 November 1907, 4; "Seattle's Free Speech Fight," Seattle *Socialist,* 30 November 1907, 2; "Victory for Free Speech in Spokane," Seattle *Socialist,* 7 December 1907, 2; "Free Speech Report," Seattle *Socialist,* 14 December 1907, 3; "Speak on the Streets," *Vancouver Daily Province,* 9 March 1909, 14; "Judge Mann Dismisses Free Speech Case," *Spokane Press,* 2 November 1909, 1; "Bread and Water or Street Work," *Wenatchee Daily World,* 24 May 1910, 1; "Free Speech," *Los Angeles Herald,* 12 July 1908, 4. Although the socialists at times made common cause with the Salvation Army, which also faced municipal restrictions and police interventions for street-corner gatherings, the Vancouver Trades and Labor Council adopted a strongly worded resolution in March 1909 condemning the immigration methods of the Salvation Army in chartering steamers to bring immigrants from the old country to Canada. See "Salvation Army Is Condemned by Labor," *Vancouver Daily Province,* 19 March 1909, 28.

83   Mark Leier, "Solidarity on Occasion: The Vancouver Free Speech Fights of 1909 and 1912," *Labour/Le Travail* 23 (1989): 42. See also Leier, *Where the Fraser River Flows,* 74-85; Dorothy G. Steeves, *The Compassionate Rebel: Ernest Winch and the Growth of Socialism in Western Canada* (Vancouver: Boag Foundation, 1977), 14-15; and Paul A. Phillips, *No Power Greater: A Century of Labour in British Columbia* (Vancouver: Boag Foundation, 1967), 48. We do not fully endorse Leier's perspective that the IWW comprised the only genuine advocates of working-class democracy and that the SPC and VTLC simply sold out the IWW and the working class in the face of police repression.

84   Leier, "Solidarity on Occasion," 42; "Notes of the Work of the C.I.B. Division for the Week Ending 21st October," in *RCMP Security Bulletins: The Early Years, 1919-1929,* ed. Gregory S. Kealey and Reg Whitaker (St. John's: Committee on Canadian Labour History, 1994), 227.

85   Leier, "Solidarity on Occasion," 42-43. An SPC member even produced a street map as evidence that there was no violation of the law.

86   Ibid., 43.

87   "Socialists Will Dare Police," *Vancouver Daily Province,* 7 April 1909, 1.

88 Leier, "Solidarity on Occasion," 44.

89 Ibid., 45.

90 "Propaganda Zeal of City Officials," *Western Clarion*, 22 May 1909, 1, 4.

91 See "Rousing Labor Union Meeting," *Federationist*, 5 February 1912, 4; "Central Labor Body Meeting Holds Rousing Meeting" and "Free Speech Suppression Called Off," *Federationist*, 20 February 1912, 1; "Pettipiece Trial This Week," *Federationist*, 20 May 1912, 4; "Right of Free Speech Vindicated," *Federationist*, 8 June 1912, 3; and "Trades Council Discuss Police Affairs," *Federationist*, 7 September 1912, 1. For the enforcement of vagrancy laws in pre–First World War Calgary, see David Bright, "Loafers Are Not Going to Subsist on Public Credulence: Vagrancy and the Law in Calgary, 1900–1914," *Labour/Le Travail* 36 (1995): 37.

92 See Johnson, "No Compromise," 14n16.

93 Leier, "Solidarity on Occasion," 48–49.

94 "Union Jack Is Torn Down and Hurled to Floor," *Vancouver Daily Province*, 2 February 1912, 35. See also "Socialists Tore Flags from Walls," *Brandon Weekly Sun*, 8 February 1912, 10.

95 "Mule Story Was His Theme," *Vancouver Daily Province*, 5 February 1912, 3.

96 "Notes on Current Events," *Western Call* [Vancouver], 9 February 1912, 1.

97 "Free Speech Suppression Called Off," *Federationist*, 20 February 1912, 1; Leier, "Solidarity on Occasion," 52–54; Phillips, *No Power Greater*, 55. See also Pritchard interview with McCormack, 16 August 1971, tape 2, t-225, BCA.

98 "The Rise of the Labor Press," *Federationist*, 9 November 1917, 9. For the printing of the *Federationist* at Kingsley's plant and the sale of the plant to a competing firm, Cowan & Brookhouse, which moved its operations into the Labor Temple, see "Print Shop Conditions," *Federationist*, 18 September 1914, 1; and "Printing – Lefeaux Bros, Successors to E.T. Kingsley" [advertisement], *Western Clarion*, 23 May 1914, 4.

99 Gerald Friesen, "Yours in Revolt: Regionalism, Socialism, and the Western Canadian Labour Movement," *Labour/Le Travail* 1 (1976): 142.

100 "The Rise of the Labor Press," *Federationist*, 9 November 1917, 10; "Rousing Meeting Held at Coal City," *Federationist*, 23 November 1917, 5; "Will Celebrate May Day at South Wellington," *Federationist*, 20 April 1917, 4.

101 Colonel Ernest J. Chambers (Chief Press Censor) to A.A. MacLean (Comptroller RNWMP), 2 April 1919, file 279-1, "The Red Flag/The Soviet," vol. 602, Office of the Chief Press Censor Files, RG 6, Secretary of State Fonds, LAC. See also J. Castell Hopkins, *Canadian Annual Review of Public Affairs, 1918* (Toronto: Annual Review Publishing, 1919), 309–11. A *Victoria Daily Times* report on a speech by Kingsley in Victoria in November 1917 referred to him as "E.T. Kingsley, editor of the *BC Federationist*, Vancouver," but the *Federationist* itself referred to him as an "associate editor" and a member of its "editorial staff." See "The Rise of the Labor Press," *Federationist*, 9 November 1917, 10; "Rousing Meeting Held at Coal City," *Federationist*, 23 November 1917, 5; "Will Celebrate May Day at South Wellington," *Federationist*, 20 April 1917, 4.

102 For the removal of Pettipiece as managing editor of the *Federationist*, see "Minutes of the Directors of the *BC Federationist*," 20 May–28 December 1918, 76–94,

Vancouver Trades and Labor Council Fonds, University of British Columbia Special Collections (hereafter VTLC Fonds, UBCSC), as cited in McCartney, "A Crisis of Commitment," 27. Another report in the paper around this time made no mention of the financial scandal but suggested that Pettipiece intended to move with his family the following spring to a farm that he had purchased with his brother-in-law at the mouth of the Campbell River at Mud Bay south of Vancouver. See "Parm's Real 'Potato Patch,'" *Federationist*, 5 July 1918, 8.

103 E.T. Kingsley, *The Genesis and Evolution of Slavery: Showing How the Chattel Slaves of Pagan Times Have Been Transformed into the Capitalist Property of To-Day* (Vancouver: Federationist Publishing, 1916). See also advertisement, *Federationist*, 23 February 1917, 4.

104 See "The Genesis and Evolution of Slavery," *Federationist*, 8 September 1916, 5–15; "Just Off the Press" [advertisement], *Federationist*, 6 October 1916, 4; and "A Crackerjack Pamphlet," *Federationist*, 13 October 1916, 1.

105 Pritchard interview with McCormack, 17 August 1971, tape 3, t-225, BCA.

106 "A Crackerjack Pamphlet," *Voice*, 3 November 1916, 2.

107 "The Work that Counts," *Federationist*, 10 November 1916, 4.

108 "Men 'Who Pay the Printer,'" *Federationist*, 20 October 1916, 4; John L. Martin, "Letters to the Fed.," *Federationist*, 20 October 1916, 4.

109 Kingsley, *The Genesis and Evolution of Slavery*, 5.

110 Ibid., 8.

111 Ibid.

112 Ibid. See also Marx and Engels to Bebel, Liebknecht, Fritzsche, Geiser, Hasenclever, and Bracke, 17–18 September 1879, Marxists Internet Archive, https://www.marxists.org/archive/marx/works/1879/09/17.htm.

113 Kingsley, *The Genesis and Evolution of Slavery*, 43–45.

114 Ibid., 54.

115 Ibid., 55.

116 Ibid.

117 Ibid., 56.

118 Ibid., 59–60.

119 "Gosden Voted 1400 Pluggers, He Declares," *Vancouver Daily Sun*, 12 September 1916, 13.

120 Elections British Columbia, *An Electoral History of British Columbia*, 123–28.

121 In March 1915, Kingsley was nominated to stand as the SPC provincial candidate in Slocan and as a candidate in Vancouver City by the Carpenters Union Local 617. However, the following month, a convention of SPC members in Vancouver declined to nominate him as one of their candidates in the multiple-member Vancouver City riding; when one of the nominated candidates, Jack Harrington, declined to accept the nomination, Kingsley was offered the vacant spot, but he also declined to run after conferring with Hawthornthwaite during a meeting in Victoria. See "Mr. Kingsley Declined," *Federationist*, 23 April 1915, 1; also see "Socialist Ticket," *Vancouver Daily Sun*, 12 March 1915, 1; "For Other Ridings," *Vancouver Daily Sun*, 17 March 1915, 4; "Kaslo and Islands Select Candidates," *Victoria Daily Times*, 17

March 1915, 12; "Other Socialists Named," *Vancouver Daily Province,* 17 March 1915, 7; "City Liberal Convention to Be Held This Evening," *Vancouver Daily Sun,* 19 March 1915, 4; "Political Rumblings," "Trades Council to Nominate Candidates Next Thursday," and "Election Matters Warming Up in Revelstoke," *Federationist,* 19 March 1915, 1; "Socialists Nominating for Coming Elections," *Prince Rupert Journal,* 24 March 1915, 1; "Brotherhood of Carpenters" and "Mr. Kingsley's Position," *Federationist,* 26 March 1915, 1; "Nominations for Provincial Election," *Victoria Daily Times,* 31 March 1915, 12; and "Here Are the Standardbearers," *Saturday Chinook* [Vancouver], 1 January 1916, 4.

122 "Socialists to Run One Man," *Vancouver Daily Province,* 26 July 1916, 4.

123 "Killed and Maimed in Peace as in War," *Federationist,* 9 June 1916, 1.

124 William Bennett, *Builders of British Columbia* (Vancouver: Broadway Printers, 1937), 86; "Will Celebrate May Day at South Wellington," *Federationist,* 20 April 1917, 4; "The Russian Situation," *Federationist,* 18 May 1917, 2.

125 "Empress Theatre Meeting of June 13," *Federationist,* 15 June 1917, 7. See also "Mass-Meeting at Orpheum Theatre Sunday Evening," *Federationist,* 1 June 1917, 1; "Bloated War Barons Scored," *Vancouver World,* 5 June 1917, 16; "Organized Labor Pulls Off Big Meeting," *Federationist,* 8 June 1917, 1, 8; "Conscriptionists Plan Monster Mass Meeting Next Week," *Vancouver Daily Sun,* 14 June 1917, 4; "Anti-Conscription Meeting" [advertisement], *Vancouver World,* 25 July 1917, 14; and "Very Good Meeting Held in Avenue Theatre," *Federationist,* 27 July 1917, 1, 6. An editorial in the *Federationist* in May 1917, potentially authored by Kingsley, discussed the overthrow of the czar in the March revolution in Russia. See "The Russian Situation," *Federationist,* 18 May 1917, 4. Comments by Kingsley at the Orpheum Theatre meeting on 3 June 1917 provoked a sharp reaction from George Murray, editor of the Vancouver *Standard* weekly newspaper, whom Kingsley had accused of hypocritical conduct for being physically fit and avoiding military service while endorsing strong measures by the Canadian state to enforce the conscription law. See "Let George Do It!" *Federationist,* 15 June 1917, 2.

126 McCartney, "A Crisis of Commitment," 97–98.

127 "Fighting Now and Paying Later," *Federationist,* 31 August 1917, 23.

128 See "Albert Goodwin Shot and Killed by Police Officer Near Comox Lake," *Federationist,* 2 August 1918, 1; "Trades and Labor Council Endorse 24-Hr. Protest," *Federationist,* 2 August 1918, 1; "Goodwin Buried at Cumberland," *Federationist,* 9 August 1918, 1; "Labor Temple Scene of Trouble and Rioting" and "A Statement to the Public by the Executive of the Trades and Labor Council," *Federationist,* 9 August 1918, 1; Susan Mayse, *Ginger: The Life and Death of Albert Goodwin* (Madeira Park, BC: Harbour Publishing, 1990); and Roger Stonebanks, *Fighting for Dignity: The Ginger Goodwin Story* (St. John's: Canadian Committee on Labour History, 2004).

129 "Labor's Statement to the Electorate," *Federationist,* 9 November 1917, 1; *War-Time Elections Act,* SC 1917, c 39; Martin Robin, "Registration, Conscription, and Independent Labour Politics, 1916–17," in *Conscription 1917,* ed. A.M. Willms et al. (Toronto: University of Toronto Press, 1969), 60–77; Canada, *The Military Service Act, 1917* (Ottawa: J. de Labroquerie Taché, 1917); H.A.C. Machin, *Report of the*

Director of the Military Service Branch to the Honourable Minister of Justice on the Operation of the Military Service Act, 1917 (Ottawa: J. de Labroquerie Taché, 1919).

130 Kingsley had been put forward when the VTLC considered its endorsement for the by-election in May 1917, securing two votes at a preliminary meeting compared with twelve for McVety and one for Smith, among a smattering of other nominees. However, Kingsley declined to stand, with organized labour ultimately fielding five candidates in BC: Victor Midgley in Burrard, James McVety in Vancouver South, Joseph Taylor in Nanaimo, A.S. Wells in Victoria, and Thomas Biggs in East Kootenay. See "Labor's Political Slogan Is 'Pull Together and Win,'" *Federationist*, 23 March 1917, 1; "Candidates Named for Submission to Referendum," *Federationist*, 20 April 1917, 1; "Labor Party Nominees," *Federationist*, 4 May 1917, 6; and "Labor's Statement to the Electorate," *Federationist*, 9 November 1917, 1.

131 "Politicians Find a Sudden Love for Labor Class," *Federationist*, 7 December 1917, 5. Reflecting a shift in its editorial line, the Victoria *Week*, which had attacked Kingsley as "an illogical, irreconcilable, revolutionary demagogue of the worst type" a decade earlier, would commend him during the federal election campaign in 1917 for making a "telling speech ... full of practical points" and criticize "both local papers" for being "sarcastic" toward him. "Labor men must expect that sort of thing," the paper quipped. This turn in the attitude of the *Week* likely reflected a shift in management during the preceding decade as the newspaper migrated during the war to become the official VTLC organ. Indeed, in July 1918, it would be suppressed under the federal orders respecting censorship for publishing excerpts of the Allies' secret treaties. See "Sotto Voce," *Week*, 17 November 1917, 4; "Federal Elections," *Week*, 10 November 1917, 3; "Factious Opposition," *Week*, 3 August 1907, 16; "The *Week* under Ban," *Victoria Daily Colonist*, 21 July 1918, 6; "Intervention in Russia," *Week*, 20 July 1918, 1; "Here We Are Again!" *Week*, 1 May 1920, 1; minutes, 7 August 1918, box 3, 80–59, Victoria Labour Council Fonds, University of Victoria Archives and Special Collections; and William J. Burrill, "Demise of '*The Week*,'" *British Columbia Historical News* 23, no. 4 (1990): 5–8.

132 "Big Meeting Held during Week in So. Vancouver," *Federationist*, 14 December 1917, 8; "Closing Campaign Rally," *Federationist*, 14 December 1917, 1; "Mass Meeting," *Federationist*, 14 December 1917, 5.

133 "Stewart Miners Are Interested," *Federationist*, 1 March 1919, 8.

134 Jack Dennis, "Letter to the Editor," *Federationist*, 1 November 1918, 6.

135 "Labor Convention Decides to Form United Working Class Political Party," *Federationist*, 1 February 1918, 1, 3, 6; "Labor Political Party Is Planned," *Victoria Daily Times*, 2 February 1918, 12; "Working Class Conference Organizes Political Party," *Federationist*, 8 February 1918, 1; "Federated Labor Party Is Formed," *Federationist*, 8 February 1918, 7.

136 Elections British Columbia, *An Electoral History of British Columbia*, 134; "Hawthornthwaite Meets Williams Tonight," *Federationist*, 11 January 1918, 1; "Hawthornthwaite Elected by Two to One," *Federationist*, 25 January 1918, 1. For Hawthornthwaite's candidacy and controversy surrounding the appointment of Williams to the Workmen's Compensation Board, see "Fighting Irishman Once

More in Battle," *Federationist*, 5 January 1917, 4; also see "Ladysmith Miners, All Hail!" *Federationist*, 26 January 1917, 2; and "J.H. Hawthornthwaite's Record in the Legislature," *Federationist*, 2 February 1917, 5.

137   See "Elect Mrs. Ralph Smith," *Federationist*, 18 January 1918, 7; "Woman Defeats Sergt. Drinnan," *Federationist*, 25 January 1918, 1; Elizabeth Norcross, "Mary Ellen Smith: The Right Woman in the Right Place at the Right Time," in *Not Just Pin Money: Selected Essays on the History of Women's Work in British Columbia*, ed. Barbara Lantham and Roberta Jane Pazdro (Victoria: Camosun College, 1984), 357–64; Betty Griffin and Susan Lockhart, *Their Own History: Women's Contribution to the Labour Movement of British Columbia* (Vancouver: UFAWU/CAW Seniors Club, 2002), 46; and Elections British Columbia, *An Electoral History of British Columbia*, 134. Smith was president of the BC Liberal Party at the time of her death in 1933. Like other political women, she benefited from the celebrity of her husband, whose death created the vacancy culminating in her election under the name Mrs. Ralph Smith.

138   "Has Labor Gone to Sleep?" *Federationist*, 11 January 1918, 6.

139   Influential SPC members, who became prominent during the First World War, voted against the BCFL forming its own political party, including outgoing BCFL president Joseph Naylor, outgoing vice-president Ginger Goodwin, and Ernest Winch, who would soon be elected as president of the Vancouver Trades and Labor Council. Naylor "opposed the formation of a political party ..., calling attention to the Socialist party being in the field, as well as other parties comprising laboring men, and saying that these would oppose the Labor party." In his report as BCFL president, Naylor said that "I believe it is not in the best interests of our movement to fasten a Labor party to our unions." See "Labor Convention Decides to Form United Working Class Political Party," *Federationist*, 1 February 1918, 1, 3, 6; "Working Class Conference Organizes Political Party," *Federationist*, 8 February. 1918, 1; and "Federated Labor Party Is Formed," *Federationist*, 8 February 1918, 7.

140   See "Working Class Conference Organizes Political Party," *Federationist*, 8 February 1918, 1; "Federated Labor Party Is Formed," *Federationist*, 8 February 1918, 7; "Good Wishes for FLP," *Federationist*, 3 May 1918, 5; and "Officers of the Federated Labor Party," *Federationist*, 31 May 1918, 3. According to Dorothy Gretchen Steeves and Martin Robin, Kingsley served as president of the FLP Vancouver local. By February 1919, a notice for the party's upcoming convention in Vancouver would identify Kingsley as president. See "To the Membership of the Federated Labor Party," *Labor Statesman*, 27 February 1919, 6; and "Labor Party to Hold Convention," *Federationist*, 14 February 1919, 1. See also "Federated Labor Party First Annual Convention," *Labor Star*, 13 February 1919, 1; "Vancouver Branch of FLP Gets Started," *Federationist*, 19 April 1918, 1; Steeves, *The Compassionate Rebel*, 37; Robin, *Radical Politics and Canadian Labour*, 150; Irene Howard, *The Struggle for Social Justice in British Columbia: Helena Gutteridge, the Unknown Reformer* (Vancouver: UBC Press, 1992); and Carlos A. Schwantes, *Radical Heritage: Labor, Socialism and Reform in Washington and British Columbia, 1885–1917* (Seattle: University of Washington Press, 1979), 213.

141 "Labor Political Party Is Planned," *Victoria Daily Times,* 2 February 1918, 12.

142 "Officers of the New Labor Party Get Busy," *Federationist,* 8 February 1918, 8.

143 Pritchard interview with McCormack, 16 August 1971, tape 1, t-225, BCA.

144 Allen Seager, "Socialists and Workers: The Western Canadian Coal Miners, 1900–21," *Labour/Le Travail* 16 (1985): 46; "Platform of the Fed. Labor Party," *Federationist,* 11 April 1919, 11.

145 See "Officers of New Labor Party Get Busy," *Federationist,* 8 February 1918, 8; "Federated Labor Party" and "First Meeting of New Labor Party," *Federationist,* 22 February 1918, 1; "Federated Labor Party," *Labor Statesman,* 27 February 1919, 7; "Enthusiasm Shown toward New Party," *Federationist,* 15 March 1918, 1; and various other articles in the *Federationist* from 1918 to 1920; David C. Jones, *Feasting on Misfortune: Journeys of the Human Spirit in Alberta's Past* (Edmonton: University of Alberta Press, 1999), 152–53; and J. Castell Hopkins, *Canadian Annual Review of Public Affairs, 1919* (Toronto: Annual Review Publishing, 1920), 456.

146 "Working Men of British Columbia Need Only to Stand Fast to Have Control of the Government," *Federationist,* 1 March 1918, 2; see also "Saturday, Feb. 23, Opening Meeting of Federated Labor Party," *Federationist,* 15 February 1918, 1.

147 "Live Mass Meeting in Royal City on Saturday," *Federationist,* 15 March 1918, 1, 3.

148 "New Labor Party Meets," *Vancouver Daily Sun,* 16 April 1918, 12; "E.T. Kingsley at National," *Federationist,* 21 November 1919, 1. Prior to its relocation to the new hall on Cordova Street, the Federated Labor Party was headquartered in the Labor Temple on Dunsmuir Street. See "Good Wishes for FLP," *Federationist,* 3 May 1918, 5. For earlier efforts to organize youth, see "Socialist Organization for the Young," *Western Clarion,* 29 December 1906, 4.

149 "Salutatory," *Labor Star,* 16 January 1919, 4.

150 E.T. Kingsley, "Control of the State through Political Action Must Be Secured by Forces of United Labor if Certain Victory Is to Be Achieved," *Labor Star,* 16 January 1919, 1–2.

151 Pritchard interview with McCormack, 16 August 1971, tape 1, t-225, BCA. For a discussion of Kingsley's role as editor, see Chambers to MacLean, 2 April 1919, file 279–1, vol. 602, RG 6, Secretary of State Fonds, LAC; and "Banned Book Is Published Here," *Vancouver World,* 21 January 1919, 3, copied in Office of the Chief Press Censor Files, file 279–1, vol. 602, RG 6, Secretary of State Fonds, LAC.

152 Shortly after the inception of the *Labor Star,* Kingsley expressed optimism about its fortunes, noting that 2,110 copies of the first issue were sold in Vancouver alone. However, in March 1919, in a brief announcing that "the *Labor Star* now possess[es] the full privileges of the mail, such as is accorded by the postmaster-general at Ottawa," Pettipiece advised readers "now bring on the subs. and bundle orders." Although Kingsley anticipated that "patrons and friends can look forward to seeing the present eight pages increased to twelve or sixteen at an early date," the newspaper never expanded beyond eight pages in its two-month existence, and its final issue, on 20 March 1919, was down to four pages, perhaps reflecting a shortage of funds and foreshadowing its demise. See "Confidential Chat," *Labor Star,* 6 February 1919, 8;

"Parm's Paragraphs," *Labor Star,* 13 March 1919, 3; "Confidential Chat," *Labor Star,* 16 January 1919, 3; and *Labor Star,* 20 March 1919.

153 See "Jews – Internationalists!" *Labor Star,* 20 February 1919, 3; "The Educator and His 'Tools of Production,'" *Labor Star,* 6 March 1919, 2; "Sermons Not Heard in Church," *Labor Star,* 13 March 1919, 13; and "Can't Get Ahead of the Game," *Labor Star,* 20 March 1919, 4.

154 N. Lenin, "A Letter to American Workingmen," *Labor Star,* 13 February 1919, 6.

155 "Chickens Come Home," *Labor Star,* 20 February 1919, 3.

156 "Fooling the Animals," *Labor Star,* 20 February 1919, 4.

157 E.T. Kingsley, "The Class War Is Now On!" *Labor Star,* 20 March 1919, 1.

158 See "B.C. Federation of Labor – Proceedings of the Ninth Annual Convention," *Federationist,* 4 April 1919, 2–3, 6–7; "B.C. Federation of Labor – Proceedings of the Ninth Annual Convention," *Federationist,* 11 April 1919, 5–7; "The Origin of the OBU: A Verbatim Report of the Calgary Conference of 1919," *One Big Union Bulletin,* 27 January 1927–12 May 1927.

159 "The Class War Is Now On!" *Labor Star,* 20 March 1919, 1.

160 "Big Majority for the OBU," *Federationist,* 30 May 1919, 1; referendum results, n.d. [c. May 1919], "Appendix A," One Big Union Fonds, UBCSC. The referendum results were influenced by the decision at Calgary to adopt the "BC Method" of ballot counting, which required locals to record abstentions as "yes" votes. See Steeves, *The Compassionate Rebel,* 48. See also Allen Seager and David Roth, "British Columbia and the Mining West: A Ghost of a Chance," in *The Workers' Revolt in Canada, 1917–1925,* ed. Craig Heron (Toronto: University of Toronto Press, 1998), 231–67; Friesen, "Yours in Revolt"; David Bercuson, *Fools and Wise Men: The Rise and Fall of the One Big Union* (Toronto: McGraw-Hill Ryerson, 1978); McCormack, *Reformers, Rebels, and Revolutionaries,* 157–61; Benjamin Isitt, "Searching for Workers' Solidarity: One Big Unionism and the Victoria General Strike of 1919," *Labour/Le Travail* 60 (2007): 11–44; and "The New Unionism," *Red Flag,* 22 March 1919, 4.

161 "The Dominion Hall Instead of Rex Theatre," *Federationist,* 7 February 1919, 8.

162 "Kingsley on the O.B.U.," *Federationist,* 4 April 1919, 1; "The State," *Semi-Weekly Tribune* [Victoria, hereafter not noted], 7 April 1919, 4. For other materials related to his views on the One Big Union, see "Mass Meeting at Victoria," *Federationist,* 18 April 1919, 1; Bercuson, *Fools and Wise Men,* 123; Steeves, *The Compassionate Rebel,* 49; and Robin, *Radical Politics and Canadian Labour,* 177, 190. According to the Victoria *Semi-Weekly Tribune,* Kingsley said that the "OBU has already been tried by the IWW" and that the "only way to succeed is to follow the path of peaceful educational and political activity just so long as free speech, free press and open ballot are permitted. Where these things are denied other methods will become an imperative necessity. Thus the One Big Union is only of value if it aids in the ultimate capture of the machinery of the state by the workers." See "The State," *Semi-Weekly Tribune,* 7 April 1919, 4.

163 George Hardy, "Letters to the *Federationist,*" *Federationist,* 2 May 1919, 6.

164 E. Robb, "Letter to the Editor," *Federationist,* 13 June 1919, 7. For further insight into Kingsley's views on the One Big Union, see "The Class War Is Now On!" *Labor Star,*

20 March 1919, 1; "Kingsley on the O.B.U.," *Federationist*, 4 April 1919, 1; "The State," *Semi-Weekly Tribune*, 7 April 1919, 4; "Mass Meeting at Victoria," *Federationist*, 18 April 1919, 1; and "Kingsley on Capitalism," *Federationist*, 6 June 1919, 8. For secondary sources related to Kingsley's views on the One Big Union, see Bercuson, *Fools and Wise Men*, 123; Steeves, *The Compassionate Rebel*, 49; and Robin, *Radical Politics and Canadian Labour*, 177, 190.

165 "Kingsley on Capitalism," *Federationist*, 6 June 1919, 8. See also "E.T. Kingsley Points Moral of Russia," *Nanaimo Daily News*, 3 June 1919, 4.

166 See E. Robb, "Letter to the Editor," *Federationist*, 13 June 1919, 7.

167 "Dr. W.J. Curry at the Columbia," *Federationist*, 20 June 1919, 1. See also "Kingsley Speaks at the Columbia," *Federationist*, 30 May 1919, 1; Jones, *Feasting on Misfortune*, 152–53; and Hopkins, *Canadian Annual Review of Public Affairs, 1919*, 456.

168 "Kingsley Makes Good Points," *Federationist*, 18 July 1919, 2. For an earlier discussion of Marx's Iron Law (which Marx and Engels attributed to Ferdinand Lassalle), see "Marxian Iron Law of Wages," *Western Clarion*, 5 August 1905, 1.

169 "Kingsley Makes Good Points," *Federationist*, 18 July 1919, 2.

170 "Two Speakers at S.P. Meeting," *Federationist*, 15 August 1919, 1.

171 Gregory S. Kealey, "The Surveillance State: The Origins of Domestic Intelligence and Counter-Subversion in Canada, 1914–1921," *Intelligence and National Security* 7, no. 3 (1992): 179–80.

172 BC Statistics, "Census Population of BC and Canada, 1871 to 2011," http://www.bcstats.gov.bc.ca/StatisticsBySubject/Census/2011Census/PopulationHousing/BCCanada.aspx.

173 Gregory S. Kealey, "State Repression of Labour and the Left in Canada, 1914–20: The Impact of the First World War," *Canadian Historical Review* 73, no. 3 (1992): 285; Arthur R.M. Lower, *Colony to Nation: A History of Canada* (Toronto: Longmans, Green, 1946), 469.

174 Barry Wright, Eric Tucker, and Susan Binnie, "Introduction: War Measures and the Repression of Radicalism," in *Canadian State Trials, Vol. 4: Security, Dissent and the Limits of Toleration in War and Peace, 1914–1939*, ed. Barry Wright, Eric Tucker, and Susan Binnie (Toronto: University of Toronto Press, 2015), 12.

175 Kealey, "State Repression of Labour and the Left in Canada," 286.

176 Peter McDermott, "Enemy Aliens in the First World War: Legal and Constitutional Issues," in *Canadian State Trials, Vol. 4: Security, Dissent and the Limits of Toleration in War and Peace, 1914–1939*, ed. Barry Wright, Eric Tucker, and Susan Binnie (Toronto: University of Toronto Press, 2015), 74.

177 Kealey, "State Repression of Labour and the Left in Canada," 293.

178 Kealey, "The Surveillance State," 180.

179 McDermott, "Enemy Aliens in the First World War," 72.

180 Jeffrey A. Keshen, "All the News that Was Fit to Print: Ernest J. Chambers and Information Control in Canada, 1914–19," *Canadian Historical Review* 73, no. 3 (1992): 318.

181 Ibid.

182 Jeffrey A. Keshen, "Chambers, Ernest John," in *Dictionary of Canadian Biography* (2005), http://www.biographi.ca/en/bio/chambers_ernest_john_15E.html.

183   Ibid.
184   Ibid.; Jeffrey A. Keshen, *Propaganda and Censorship during Canada's Great War* (Edmonton: University of Alberta Press, 1996), 66.
185   Keshen, *Propaganda and Censorship during Canada's Great War*, 66.
186   Daniel Francis, *Seeing Reds: The Red Scare of 1918–1919, Canada's First War on Terror* (Vancouver: Arsenal Pulp Press, 2010), 31; Keshen, "Chambers, Ernest John."
187   Keshen, "All the News that Was Fit to Print," 321–23; Keshen, *Propaganda and Censorship during Canada's Great War*, 72.
188   Keshen, "All the News that Was Fit to Print," 338.
189   Kealey, "State Repression of Labour and the Left in Canada," 291.
190   Wright, Tucker, and Binnie, "Introduction," 17–18.
191   Ibid.
192   *War-Time Elections Act*, SC 1917, c 39.
193   McDermott, "Enemy Aliens in the First World War," 84–85.
194   Robert Bothwell, Ian Drummond, and John English, *Canada, 1900–1945* (Toronto: University of Toronto Press, 1987), 128–29.
195   For an account of the debate among suffragists in Quebec on the limited expansion of the franchise for women, see Tarah Brookfield, "Divided by the Ballot Box: The Montreal Council of Women and the 1917 Election," *Canadian Historical Review* 89, no. 4 (2008): 487–88.
196   Kealey, "State Repression of Labour and the Left in Canada," 288–89.
197   Ben Deacon, memo to Colonel Ernest Chambers, 21 August 1918, file 279–15, vol. 602, RG 6, Secretary of State Fonds, LAC.
198   W.R., "The Liberty Bond-Age," *Western Clarion,* July 1918, 12, copied in file 279–15, vol. 602, RG 6, Secretary of State Fonds, LAC.
199   Malcolm Reid, memo to Colonel Ernest Chambers, 13 August 1917, file 279–15, vol. 602, RG 6, Secretary of State Fonds, LAC. For Mayor Louis Taylor's colourful career, see Daniel Francis, *L.D.: Mayor Louis Taylor and the Rise of Vancouver* (Vancouver: Arsenal Pulp Press, 2004).
200   E.T. Kingsley, "Win the War," *Critic* [Vancouver], n.d., 3, copied in file 279–15, vol. 602, RG 6, Secretary of State Fonds, LAC.
201   For a comprehensive treatment of Lenin's use of the slogan and his disagreements with other socialists, such as Trotsky and Luxemburg, see Hal Draper, "The Myth of Lenin's 'Revolutionary Defeatism,'" *New International* 19–20 (1953–54): n. pag., https://www.marxists.org/archive/draper/1953/defeat/#n1.
202   Kingsley, "Win the War."
203   Whitaker, Kealey, and Parnaby, *Secret Service,* 68; Kealey, "The Surveillance State," 185–87.
204   Whitaker, Kealey, and Parnaby, *Secret Service,* 68–69.
205   Ben Deacon, memo to Colonel Ernest Chambers, 9 February 1919, and Chambers to MacLean, 2 April 1919, file 279–1, vol. 602, RG 6, Secretary of State Fonds, LAC.
206   Wright, Tucker, and Binnie, "Introduction," 9, 13.
207   Kealey, "State Repression of Labour and the Left in Canada," 299.

208 Wright, Tucker, and Binnie, "Introduction," 21.
209 Kealey, "The Surveillance State," 188–91.
210 Kealey, "State Repression of Labour and the Left in Canada," 289.
211 Ibid.
212 "Censorship Notice," 8 October 1918, in Canada, *Canada Gazette* (Ottawa: J. de Labroquerie Taché, 1918), 1461. See also C. Stephenson to Colonel Ernest Chambers, 9 January 1919; "Memorandum for the Office File," 27 January 1919; Colonel Ernest Chambers to August Lemieux, 4 February 1919; C. Stephenson to Colonel Ernest Chambers, 7 April 1919; and Colonel Ernest Chambers to C. Stephenson, 16 April 1919, all in file 279–1, vol. 602, RG 6, Secretary of State Fonds, LAC. In February, Alberta Labor MLA Alex Ross would lambaste the suppression of publications and organizations in a speech in the Alberta legislature, declaring that "we have developed a democracy in Europe but in doing it we have built an autocracy by order-in-council in Canada." See "Press Censorship and Denial of Free Speech," *Labor Statesman*, 27 February 1919, 7.
213 Keshen, "All the News that Was Fit to Print," 331.
214 Keshen, *Propaganda and Censorship during Canada's Great War*, 90.
215 Kealey, "State Repression of Labour and the Left in Canada," 313.
216 Ian McKay, *Reasoning Otherwise: Leftists and the People's Enlightenment in Canada, 1890–1920* (Toronto: Between the Lines, 2008), 429.
217 Petition by Local 74, Alhambra, Alberta, SPC to Minister, 22 December 1918, vol. 229, RG 13, Department of Justice Fonds, LAC.
218 "Bolshevism Is Openly Preached," *Vancouver Daily Sun*, 13 January 1919, 12; Sherwood to Chambers, 6 January 1919; Chambers to Sherwood, 7 January 1919; Sherwood to Chambers, 8 January 1919; "Memorandum for Colonel Chambers," 11 January 1919; Chambers to Secretary of State, 14 January 1919; Chambers to Reid, 14 January 1919; Under-Secretary of State to Chambers, 15 January 1919; Chambers to Secretary of State, 20 January 1919; Chambers to MacLean, 2 April 1919; MacLean to Chambers, 5 April 1919, all in file 279–1, vol. 602, RG 6, Secretary of State Fonds, LAC; Keshen, *Propaganda and Censorship during Canada's Great War*, 90.
219 "The Censorship," *Red Flag*, 11 January 1919, 4, cited in McKay, *Reasoning Otherwise*, 430.
220 "Stop Press News," *Red Flag*, 8 March 1919, 6, cited in ibid.
221 Colonel Ernest Chambers to Deputy Postmaster General, 5 May 1919, file 279–1, vol. 602, RG 6, Secretary of State Fonds, LAC.
222 Colonel Ernest Chambers to Assistant Director of the Naval Service, 26 May 1919, file 279–1, vol. 602, RG 6, Secretary of State Fonds, LAC.
223 Chambers to MacLean, 2 April 1919, file 279–1, vol. 602, RG 6, Secretary of State Fonds, LAC.
224 Keshen, *Propaganda and Censorship during Canada's Great War*, 94–95.
225 Whitaker, Kealey, and Parnaby, *Secret Service*, 74.
226 McKay, *Reasoning Otherwise*, 447.
227 C.H. Cahan, *Socialistic Propaganda in Canada: Its Purposes, Results and Remedies, Address Delivered to St. James Literary Society, Montreal, 12 December 1918* (Montreal:

n.d. [c. 1918]), LAC, RG 24, vol. 2543, file HQC 2051, Part 1 cited in Whitaker, Kealey, and Parnaby, *Secret Service,* 76.

228   Whitaker, Kealey, and Parnaby, *Secret Service,* 72–73; Kealey, "State Repression of Labour and the Left in Canada," 303.

229   Kealey, "The Surveillance State," 186–88. Cahan's final report to the minister of justice went so far as to advocate the prohibition of publishing in any language other than English or French without a federal licence and the prohibition of any poster, leaflet, or pamphlet in a foreign language without prior submission of a translation to the press censor resulting in a certificate. For the orders-in-council, see PC 2381, 25 September 1918, and PC 2384, 25 September 1918, in Canada, *Statutes of Canada, 1918* (Ottawa: King's Printer, 1919), lxxi–lxxii and lxxvii–lxxx.

230   Keshen, *Propaganda and Censorship during Canada's Great War,* 92. Rowell was joined in expressing concern about PC 2384 by fellow Liberal Thomas Crerar, who would go on to be a leader of the Progressive Party in the 1920s.

231   Kealey, "The Surveillance State," 189–91. Cahan's recommendation for an executive position for his son was also rejected.

232   The literature on the Winnipeg General Strike is voluminous and beyond the scope of our book. For an overview, see McKay, *Reasoning Otherwise,* 459–69; and Norman Penner, ed., *Winnipeg 1919: The Strikers' Own History of the Winnipeg General Strike,* 2nd ed. (Toronto: Lorimer, 1975).

233   Gregory S. Kealey, "The Royal Canadian Mounted Police, the Canadian Security Intelligence Service, the Public Archives of Canada, and Access to Information: A Curious Tale," *Labour/Le Travail* 21 (1988): 208–10.

234   Wayne S. Chow, "The Chinese Community in Canada before 1947 and Some Recent Developments," in *Perspectives on Ethnicity,* ed. Regina E. Holloman and Serghei A. Arutiunov (The Hague: Moulon Publishers, 1978), 292.

235   Keshen, *Propaganda and Censorship during Canada's Great War,* 103; Keshen, "All the News that Was Fit to Print," 335–36.

236   Gregory S. Kealey, "The Early Years of State Surveillance of Labour and the Left in Canada: The Institutional Framework of the Royal Canadian Mounted Police Security and Intelligence Apparatus, 1918–26," *Intelligence and National Security* 8, no. 3 (1993): 142.

237   Kealey, "The Royal Canadian Mounted Police," 208–10.

238   Ibid., 210.

239   Ibid., 213. See also A.A. McLean, Comptroller RNWMP, to Commissioner, RNWMP, 17 March 1919, and A.A. McLean, Comptroller RNWMP, to Colonel Chambers, 17 March 1919, reel t-6256, "Labour Organizations and Communism" file, vol. 878, series A-2, RG 18, Royal Canadian Mounted Police Fonds (hereafter RCMP Fonds), LAC.

240   W.A. Pritchard, "After the War Problems," *Western Clarion,* July 1918, 2–4, copied in file 279–15, vol. 602, RG 6, Secretary of State Fonds, LAC.

241   Chambers to MacLean, 2 April 1919, file 279–1, vol. 602, RG 6, Secretary of State Fonds, LAC.

242   Ibid.

243 Ibid. Whether Chambers was implying that the intelligence community ought to regard Pettipiece as a potential informant is unclear from the memo.

244 Chambers to Assistant Director of the Naval Service, 26 May 1919, file 279–1, vol. 602, RG 6, Secretary of State Fonds, LAC.

245 Ibid. See also *"Labor Star* Newspaper," file "9–1694/1919, File Part 1," vol. 2412, RG 13, Department of Justice Fonds, LAC.

246 See Benjamin Isitt, "Mutiny from Victoria to Vladivostok, December 1918," *Canadian Historical Review* 87, no. 2 (2006): 223–64; Benjamin Isitt, "Court Martial at Vladivostok: Mutiny and Military Justice during the First World War," in *Canadian State Trials, Volume 4,* ed. Barry Wright, Eric Tucker, and Susan Binnie (Toronto: University of Toronto Press, 2015), 172–216; and Benjamin Isitt, *From Victoria to Vladivostok: Canada's Siberian Expedition, 1917–19* (Vancouver: UBC Press, 2010).

247 "Speaker Who Finds World Out of Joint," *Victoria Daily Colonist,* 28 January 1919, 5; see also "The Class Struggle and the Bolsheviki," *Semi-Weekly Tribune,* 27 January 1919, 1; "Kingsley in Victoria," *Federationist,* 24 January 1919, 8; and "Hawthornthwaite Replied to in Victoria," *Federationist,* 31 January 1919, 1. Kingsley's remarks were also reported to an official with the Department of Militia and Defence. See Jukes to Davis, 29 January 1919, file 2051–2, vol. 2543, RG 24, Department of National Defence Fonds (hereafter DND Fonds), LAC, as cited in McCormack, *Reformers, Rebels, and Revolutionaries,* 207n82. In February 1919, Kingsley discussed the 60,000-strong Belfast General Strike that had erupted weeks earlier, telling an audience in Vancouver's Dominion Theatre, to applause, that "it was pretty near time the people of this town did the same as the people of Belfast." See "The Dominion Hall Instead of Rex Theatre," *Federationist,* 7 February 1919, 8.

248 "City and District in Brief," *Victoria Daily Colonist,* 31 January 1919, 6; "Aroused by Speeches Defending Red Guard," *Victoria Daily Colonist,* 29 January 1919, 11.

249 "City and District in Brief," *Victoria Daily Colonist,* 31 January 1919, 6; "Meetings Cancelled," *Vancouver Daily Sun,* 2 February 1919, 1.

250 "Aroused by Speeches Defending Red Guard," *Victoria Daily Colonist,* 29 January 1919, 11; "Public Enemies," *Victoria Daily Times,* 29 January 1919, 4; "Campaigners Declare War on Seditionists," *Victoria Daily Times,* 1 February 1919, 18; "City and District in Brief," *Victoria Daily Colonist,* 6 March 1919, 6, regarding a committee established by the Victoria branch of the Great War Veterans' Association to investigate through Comrade Rhodes whether Kingsley's speech was seditious. See also "Put Them Out," *Victoria Daily Times,* 30 January 1919, 10, calling for Kingsley's deportation from Canada; and Charles Provis, "Truth and Free Speech," *Semi-Weekly Tribune,* 20 February 1919, 3, a letter to the editor objecting to Kingsley's statement that machinery had done nothing to improve conditions for workers and suggesting that a government inspector should attend potentially seditious meetings to correct immediately false statements. In contrast to this criticism of Kingsley, strong support could be discerned in some sections of the community in Victoria, including within labour and left-wing ranks, with the *Semi-Weekly Tribune,* the organ of the local labour council, commending Kingsley's critique of capitalist finance in a July 1919 editorial: "Mr. E.T. Kingsley, the veteran economist of Vancouver, is

perfectly right in his contention that so-called 'Capital' consists almost exclusively of figures. That has been the contention of all men who have ever arrived at anything approaching a clear vision of the economic problem." See "Figures," *Semi-Weekly Tribune,* 28 July 1919, 4.

251 "Minutes of the Meeting of the City Council," 3 February 1919, City Council Meeting Minutes, City of Victoria Archives; "Council Favors Ban on Pro-Reds," *Victoria Daily Colonist,* 4 February 1919, 5. See also "Will Urge Ban on Red Meetings Here," *Victoria Daily Colonist,* 31 January 1919, 10; and "Would Repress All Bolshevism," *Vancouver Daily Sun,* 31 January 1919, 1.

252 "Minutes of the Meeting of the City Council," 3 February 1919, City Council Meeting Minutes, City of Victoria Archives. For discussion of the deportation of radicals, see "Deport Alien Enemies," *Victoria Daily Colonist,* 29 January. 1919, 4; and "Deportation," *Victoria Daily Colonist,* 3 February 1919, 4.

253 "Council Favors Ban on Pro-Reds," *Victoria Daily Colonist,* 4 February 1919, 5; "Victoria 'Tired' of Alien Enemies," *Vancouver Daily Sun,* 4 February 1919, 3. Prior to the council meeting of 3 February 1919, the mayor announced a change in procedure, with no delegations from the public being permitted to speak at ordinary Monday-evening council meetings and a special public input session being convened on Fridays instead. This procedural change prevented members of the public from speaking to the resolution prior to council debate and vote.

254 "Will Urge Ban on Red Meetings Here," *Victoria Daily Colonist,* 31 January 1919, 10. See also untitled article, *Federationist,* 8 March 1918, 2, 5, regarding "have you signed the Bible Students petition yet?"

255 "Seditious Talk Must Be Banned," *Victoria Daily Colonist,* 5 February 1919, 1; "'Free Speech' to Labor Champions; but No Sedition," *Vancouver Daily Sun,* 5 February 1919, 1; "Soldiers Are Not Planning Violence," *Vancouver Daily Sun,* 2 February 1919, 1; "Nothing Happened to Disturb the Peace," *Vancouver Daily Sun,* 3 February 1919, 12.

256 "Labor Party at Theatre Royal," *Federationist,* 14 February 1919, 1; "The Dominion Hall Instead of Rex Theatre," *Federationist,* 7 February 1919, 1.

257 "Editorial," *Red Flag,* 8 February 1919, 4.

258 N. Lenin, "A Letter to American Workingmen," *Labor Star,* 13 February 1919, 6.

259 E.T. Kingsley, "Hunting with the Hounds," *Labor Star,* 6 March 1919, 1.

260 E.T. Kingsley, "The Class War Is Now On!" *Labor Star,* 20 March 1919, 1.

261 "Liberty Lost and Lamented," *Labor Star,* 6 March 1919, 3.

262 "*The Liberator: A Journal of Revolutionary Progress*" [advertisement], *Labor Star,* 6 March 1919, 2.

263 McLean to Rowell re "E.T. Kingsley, Vancouver," 15 April 1919, and McLean to Undersecretary of State re "E.T. Kingsley, Vancouver," 15 April 1919, reel t-6256, file "Labour Organizations and Communism," vol. 878, Accession No. A-2, RG 18, RCMP Fonds, LAC.

264 See "Certified Copy of a Report of the Committee of the Privy Council," 12 December 1918, vol. 1930, RG 18, RCMP Fonds, LAC; also see "Monthly Report," F.J. Horrigan to the Commissioner, 13 March 1919, vol. 1930, RG 18, RCMP Fonds, LAC.

265 McLean to Rowell, 1 March 1919, reel t-6256, file "Labour Organizations and Communism," vol. 878, Accession No. A-2, RG 18, RCMP Fonds, LAC.

266 "Parm's Pertinent Paragraphs," *Labor Star,* 6 March 1919, 6; see also "Parm's Paragraphs," *Labor Star,* 13 March 1919, 3.

267 "Re: Federated Labor Party of Vancouver Local," 27 March 1919; "Re: Federated Labor Party," 8 April 1919; "List of Explosives in Vancouver," 24 March 1919; "Re: Theft of Grenades at Vancouver," 3 April 1919; "Theft of High Explosives at Vancouver," 14 April 1919; "Russian Workers Union," 25 March 1919; "Russian Workers Union," 3 April 1919, reel t-6256, file "Labour Organizations and Communism," vol. 878, series A-2, RG 18, RCMP Fonds, LAC; "Irregularities at the Government Wharf, Vancouver," 19 April 1919; "Russian Workers Union," 17 April 1919, reel t-6257, file "Labour Organizations and Communism," vol. 878, series A-2, RG 18, RCMP Fonds, LAC.

268 "Vancouver S.P. of C. Headquarters Raided," *Federationist,* 31 May 1919, 1; "Andrews' List of Undesirable Citizens," *Federationist,* 30 January 1920, 1; "Think Police Acted beyond Their Power," *Victoria Daily Times,* 2 July 1919, 14; "Red-Coats Busy," *Semi-Weekly Tribune,* 30 June 1919, 1; "Red Guards Again," *Semi-Weekly Tribune,* 18 August 1919, 4; Kealey, "State Repression of Labour and the Left in Canada," 281–314; Reinhold Kramer and Tom Mitchell, *When the State Trembled: How A.J. Andrews and the Citizens' Committee Broke the Winnipeg General Strike* (Toronto: University of Toronto Press, 2010); Francis, *Seeing Reds;* S.W. Horrall, "The Royal North-West Mounted Police and Labour Unrest in Western Canada, 1919," *Canadian Historical Review* 61, no. 2 (1980): 169–90.

269 "Mounties Raid Home and Offices of Labor Men," *Federationist,* 4 July 1919, 1; "Vancouver Labor Temple Raided by Police," *Victoria Daily Times,* 30 June 1919, 1.

270 Kealey, "The Early Years of State Surveillance of Labour and the Left in Canada," 131; Whitaker, Kealey, and Parnaby, *Secret Service,* 102.

271 Whitaker, Kealey, and Parnaby, *Secret Service,* 132–33.

272 Ibid., 133.

273 Ibid., 135–36.

274 Ibid., 105.

Chapter 7: The Twilight Years

1 John Sidaway, "Kingsley Led Vanguard in Fight for Workers," *Labor Statesman* [Vancouver], 27 December 1929, 5.

2 We found only a single reference to Kingsley in the *Western Clarion* in the 1920s, at the beginning of a short article on wages that offers offhand "apologies to E.T. Kingsley and others." See William P. Black, "A Dialogue on Wages," *Western Clarion,* 1 December 1924, 6.

3 "Report of Admissions at the Port of White Rock," n.d. [c. October 1913], reel T-5504, Border Entries 1908–1935, RG 26, Department of Immigration Fonds, LAC, viewed in *Border Crossings: From U.S. to Canada, 1908–1935 Online Database,* www.ancestry.com.

4 See United States, "Twelfth Census of the United States: 1900 – Population," Caldwell Village, Noble County, Ohio, 11 June 1900; State of Ohio, "Affidavit for Marriage License," Robert E. Kingsley and Irma K. Becker, 27 November 1905, in *Ohio, County Marriage Records, 1774–1993 Online Database,* www.ancestry.com.

5 United States, "Fourteenth Census of the United States: 1920 – Population," Benson, Nebraska, 19 January 1920, in *1920 US Census Online Database,* www.ancestry.com; United States, "Thirteenth Census of the United States: 1910 – Population," Duluth, Minnesota, 16 April 1910, in *1910 US Census Online Database,* www.ancestry.com. By 1930, Percy would be living again in Minneapolis, where he continued to work as a linotype operator until his death in 1939 at the age of fifty-eight. See United States, "Fifteenth Census of the United States: 1930 – Population," Minneapolis, Minnesota, 3 April 1930, in *1930 US Census Online Database,* www.ancestry.com; Percy Scott Kingsley Death Record, Date of Death 28 November 1939, Certificate No. 005169, Minnesota Department of Health Death Index, in *Minnesota Death Index 1908–2017 Online Ddatabase,* www.ancestry.com.

6 United States, "Fourteenth Census of the United States: 1920 – Population," Minneapolis, Minnesota, Curtis Court Hotel and Apts, 3 January 1920, 4A, enumeration district 95, roll T625_834, in *1920 US Census Online Database,* www.ancestry.com. According to the 1930 US Census, Myra was still working as a public school teacher in Minneapolis at the age of seventy. Intriguingly, her marital status is listed in that census as widowed, indicating that she knew Eugene had passed away, even though she had indicated to the enumerator in 1920 that she was divorced. See United States, "Fifteenth Census of the United States: 1930 – Population," Minneapolis, Minnesota, 3 January 1930, 8A, enumeration district 328, FHL microfilm 2340832, in *1930 US Census Online Database,* www.ancestry.com.

7 "Staggers Reds Says Kingsley," *Federationist,* 6 February 1920, 2. See also "E.T. Kingsley at the Royal," *Federationist,* 30 January 1920, 1.

8 "Kingsley on Paris Commune," *Federationist,* 19 March 1920, 1; "Kingsley on the Commune," *Federationist,* 26 March 1920, 4.

9 "Kingsley on the Commune," *Federationist,* 26 March 1920, 4. See also "Collapse Now Threatened," *Federationist,* 30 April 1920, 7.

10 "Collapse Now Threatened," *Federationist,* 30 April 1920, 7.

11 "Note," *One Big Union Bulletin* [Winnipeg], 15 May 1920, 1.

12 "Collapse Now Threatened," *Federationist,* 30 April 1920, 7.

13 "E.T. Kingsley to Speak on Sunday," *Federationist,* 22 October 1920, 1.

14 Elections British Columbia, *An Electoral History of British Columbia, 1871–1986* (Victoria: Elections British Columbia, 1988), 139–45.

15 See "Sensational Speech at Columbia," *Semi-Weekly Tribune,* 20 January 1919, 1; "Federated Labor Party," *Semi-Weekly Tribune,* 20 January 1919, 4; "Federated Labor Party Repudiate Statement," *Semi-Weekly Tribune,* 27 January 1919, 4; untitled article, *Federationist,* 14 February 1919, 4; "McBride to Speak on Russia," *Federationist,* 28 January 1921, 1; Elections British Columbia, *An Electoral History of British Columbia,* 139–45. For information on Uphill, see Robert McDonald, "'Just a Working Man': Tom Uphill," in *A World Apart: The Crowsnest Communities of Alberta and British*

Columbia, ed. Wayne Norton and Tom Langford (Kamloops: Plateau, 2000), 99–112; Tom Langford and Chris Frazer, "The Cold War and Working-Class Politics in the Coal Mining Communities of the Crowsnest Pass, 1945–1958," *Labour/Le Travail* 49 (2002): 43–81; and "Uphill Has Represented Fernie in Legislature for 36 Years," *Pacific Tribune* (Vancouver, BC), 10 February 1956, 10.

16 "FLP Notes," *Federationist,* 5 November 1920, 1.

17 Elections British Columbia, *An Electoral History of British Columbia,* 139–45.

18 "Kingsley to Speak for FLP," *Federationist,* 27 May 1921, 1; "T.A. Barnard to Speak Sunday," *Federationist,* 3 June 1921, 1; "Tariff Not a Campaign Issue," *British Columbia Labor News* [Vancouver], 2 December 1921, 1, 3; untitled article, *Nanaimo Daily News,* 28 March 1925, 4; "Labor College to Be Formed at Log Cabin," *Summerland Review,* 14 August 1925, 8; "Syllabus of the 1926 Summerland School of Social Science," in Samuel Eldon Charles Wager, "Theosophical Socialists in the 1920s Okanagan: Jack Logie's Social Issues Summer Camps" (MA thesis, Simon Fraser University, 2005), 23, 39. The Summerland School of Social Science was a two-week educational and recreational retreat that the Federated Labor Party sponsored at the "Log Cabin" in the district of Summerland in the Okanagan Valley in the 1920s, bringing together leftists from across the country.

19 "Kingsley Makes Good Points," *Federationist,* 18 July 1919, 2.

20 In contrast, writers such as Dr. W.J. Curry are indicative of the change in radical discourse, claiming that "the ballot alone will never do it; we have got to have the ballot backed up by industrial organization – the O.B.U. if you will." See "Asks Who Made the Grass Dry," *Federationist,* 9 April 1920, 2.

21 "An Appeal to Left-Wing Members of the S.P. of C.," *Federationist,* 6 January 1922, 4.

22 "Conditions for Joining the Communist International," *Western Clarion,* 1 January 1921, 1.

23 "Socialists Hold Mass Meeting," *Vancouver Daily Province,* 22 January 1906, 9.

24 See "Sensational Speech at Columbia," *Semi-Weekly Tribune,* 20 January 1919, 1; "Federated Labor Party," *Semi-Weekly Tribune,* 20 January 1919, 4; "Federated Labor Party Repudiate Statement," *Semi-Weekly Tribune,* 27 January 1919, 4; untitled article, *Federationist,* 14 February 1919, 4; "McBride to Speak on Russia," *Federationist,* 28 January 1921, 1.

25 "Apathy Is Counted Out at Coal City," *Federationist,* 14 February 1919, 3, 6. In a speech in February 1919, in which Hawthornthwaite defended his position against Lenin and Trotsky, he alluded to earlier inner-party conflicts: "This is not the first time I have started something of this kind. This used to happen 20 years ago then you would have old man Kingsley over to straighten it out and all would be well again." Demonstrating his retreat from Marxism, Hawthornthwaite had commented at the founding of the Federated Labor Party in February 1918 that "the Socialist Party of Canada is not suited to this country, and does not fulfill its functions. What is needed is a party which covers a wide sphere and is not confined to one particular class." He said that "one of the greatest troubles [for the Socialist Party of Canada] was that it was founded on German literature." See "Labor Political Party Is Planned," *Victoria Daily Times,* 2 February 1918, 12.

26 See "Federated Labor Party Repudiate Statement," *Semi-Weekly Tribune,* 27 January 1919, 4. For Canadian military activity as part of the Allied intervention in the Russian Civil War, see Benjamin Isitt, *From Victoria to Vladivostok: Canada's Siberian Expedition, 1917–19* (Vancouver: UBC Press, 2010); John Swettenham, *Allied Intervention in Russia, 1918–19: And the Part Played by Canada* (Toronto: Ryerson, 1967); and Roy MacLaren, *Canadians in Russia* (Toronto: Macmillan, 1976).

27 N. Lenin, "A Letter to American Workingmen," *Labor Star,* 13 February 1919, 6.

28 See Allen Seager, "Hawthornthwaite, James Hurst," in *Dictionary of Canadian Biography* (2005), http://www.biographi.ca/en/bio.php?BioId=42322. Seager suggests that Hawthornthwaite's claim could not be independently verified.

29 "Won't Be Steered," *Semi-Weekly Tribune,* 3 February 1903, 3.

30 "Sees Russia Yielding to Communist Form," *New York Times,* 5 January 1921, 13.

31 Although eighteen points appeared in the original *Western Clarion* story in January 1921, they were later expanded to twenty-one after readers inquired about the discrepancy between the Canadian conditions and those published in countries such as France, Germany, Latvia, and Britain. "Conditions for Joining the Communist International," *Western Clarion,* 1 January 1921, 1; "Questions of International Affiliation," *Western Clarion,* 1 March 1921, 4.

32 *Criminal Code Amendment Act, 1919,* SC 1919, c 46. See also Dennis G. Molinaro, *An Exceptional Law: Section 98 and the Emergency State, 1919–1936* (Toronto: University of Toronto Press, 2017); Dennis Molinaro, "State Repression and Political Deportation in Canada, 1919–1936" (PhD diss., University of Toronto, 2015); J.B. Mackenzie, "Section 98, Criminal Code and Freedom of Expression in Canada," *Queen's Law Journal* 1, no. 4 (1972): 469–83; and Peter MacKinnon, "Conspiracy and Sedition as Canadian Political Crimes," *McGill Law Journal* 23 (1977): 622–43.

33 Starnes to Newcombe, 20 January 1921, file 204 "The *Western Clarion,*" box 255, RG 13, Department of Justice Fonds, LAC.

34 Newcombe to Starnes, 21 January 1921, file 204 "The *Western Clarion,*" box 255, RG 13, Department of Justice Fonds, LAC.

35 See "The *Federationist* and Editor to Be Sent for Trial," *Federationist,* 4 November 1921, 1; "Mass Meeting to Be Held on Sunday," *Federationist,* 4 November 1921, 1; "Fed and Editor to Be Sent for Trial," *Federationist,* 11 November 1921, 1; "Freedom of Press Discussed," *Federationist,* 11 November 1921, 1; "*Federationist* and Editor Indicted," *Federationist,* 7 April 1922, 1; V.I. Lenin, *"Left-Wing" Communism: An Infantile Disorder* (1920; repr., Beijing: Foreign Language Press, 1965).

36 "'Left Wing Communism,' Infantile Disorder," *Western Clarion,* 1 March 1921, 1.

37 See Peter Campbell, "'Making Socialists': Bill Pritchard, the Socialist Party of Canada, and the Third International," *Labour/Le Travail* 30 (1992): 42–65; Tadeusz Adam Kawecki, "Canadian Socialism and the Origin of the Communist Party of Canada, 1900–1922" (MA thesis, McMaster University, 1980), 222–26; Benjamin Isitt, "The Search for Solidarity: The Industrial and Political Roots of the Cooperative Commonwealth Federation in British Columbia, 1913–1928" (MA thesis, University of Victoria, 2003), 108–17.

38 "Conditions for Joining the Communist International," *Western Clarion*, 1 January 1921, 1.

39 Ibid.

40 Fred Kaplan, "The S.P. of C. and the Third International," *Western Clarion*, 16 January 1921, 7; Jack Harrington, "The S.P. of C. and the Third International," *Western Clarion*, 1 February 1921, 5; Jack Harrington, "The S.P. of C. and the Third International," *Western Clarion*, 16 March 1921, 3.

41 Chris Stephenson, "The S.P. of C. and the Third International," *Western Clarion*, 16 May 1921, 6.

42 "Soviet Russia Medical Relief Committee," *Western Clarion*, 15 February 1921, 8.

43 Ivan Avakumovic, *The Communist Party in Canada* (Toronto: McClelland and Stewart, 1975), 21; *Canada's Party of Socialism: The History of the Communist Party of Canada, 1921–1976* (Toronto: Progress Books, 1982), 1, 16.

44 "Enter – the Workers' Party," *Western Clarion*, 2 January 1922, 4.

45 "Vote Was in Favour of Third," *Federationist*, 27 January 1922, 1.

46 Ibid.

47 David Akers, "Rebel or Revolutionary? Jack Kavanagh and the Early Years of the Communist Movement in Vancouver, 1920–1925," *Labour/Le Travail* 30 (1992): 9–44; Peter Campbell, *Canadian Marxists and the Search for a Third Way* (Montreal and Kingston: McGill-Queen's University Press, 1999), 99. Campbell credits Akers with directing him to this source: "Report Re: Socialist Party of Canada," 30 December 1921, Kavanagh File, RG 18, RCMP Fonds, LAC. For a discussion of the SPC referendum on affiliation with the Third International, see Ross Alfred Johnson, "No Compromise – No Political Trading: The Marxian Socialist Tradition in British Columbia" (PhD diss., University of British Columbia, 1975), 357.

48 Pritchard interview with McCormack, 17 August 1971, tape 4, t-225, BCA.

49 "The Parting of the Ways," *Federationist*, 6 January 1922, 3. The same issue of the *Federationist* published an appeal to left-wing SPC members, urging them to join the Workers' Party of Canada. The appeal was issued by the Provisional Organization Committee of the party, which included Tim Buck and other national communist leaders. "An Appeal to Left-Wing Members of the S.P. of C.," *Federationist*, 6 January 1922, 4; also see "Winnipeg Has a Workers' Party," *Federationist*, 13 January 1922, 3; "Kavanagh Explains Reason for Formation of Workers' Party," *Federationist*, 20 January 1922, 1; and "Kavanagh and Smith Speak for W.P. of C.," *Federationist*, 3 February 1922, 1.

50 See Jack Harrington, "The Doldrums," *Western Clarion*, July–August 1925, 1; Wallis Lefeaux, "Reflections," *Labor Statesman*, 31 July 1925, 5; J. Sidaway, "The Passing of the *Western Clarion*," *Labor Statesman*, 6 August 1925, 8; and "The Doldrums," *Labor Statesman*, 13 August 1925, 3. For the SPC's demise, see Isitt, "The Search for Solidarity," 157–59; Johnson, "No Compromise," 1; and Ronald Grantham, "Some Aspects of the Socialist Movement in British Columbia, 1898–1933" (MA thesis, University of British Columbia, 1942), 140–46. For the process of political alignment culminating in the formation of the BC section of the Co-operative Commonwealth

Federation, see Walter D. Young, "Ideology, Personality and the Origin of the CCF in British Columbia," *BC Studies* 32 (1976–77): 139–62; and Dorothy G. Steeves, *The Compassionate Rebel: Ernest Winch and the Growth of Socialism in Western Canada* (Vancouver: Boag Foundation, 1977), 70–84.

51 Wallis Lefeaux, "Reflections," *Labor Statesman*, 31 July 1925, 5.

52 J. Sidaway, "The Passing of the *Western Clarion*," *Labor Statesman*, 6 August 1925, 8.

53 Jack Harrington, "The Doldrums," *Western Clarion*, July–August 1925, 1; Jack Harrington, "The Doldrums," *Labor Statesman*, 13 August 1925, 3.

54 "The Passing of the *Western Clarion*," *One Big Union Bulletin*, 13 August 1925, 4. A few months earlier the *Bulletin* declared that the "S.P. of C. is a back number and that the worker [is] no longer interested in what he and his fellow members of the party have to say." See "Of Matter of Fact," *One Big Union Bulletin*, 26 March 1925, 4.

55 "ILP Amalgamation of Several Political Groups," *Labor Statesman*, 12 February 1926, 1.

56 "The ILP," *Labor Statesman*, 19 February 1926, 4.

57 Elections British Columbia, *An Electoral History of British Columbia*, 149–55; Parliament of Canada, "Elections and Ridings," https://lop.parl.ca/sites/ParlInfo/default/en_CA/ElectionsRidings; "Election Results," *Labor Statesman*, 6 November 1925, 1. Rose Henderson, running in New Westminster, had the strongest showing of the five BC CLP candidates, with 3,315 votes to 7,774 for the Conservative victor. For the story of the Canadian Labor Party in British Columbia, see Benjamin Isitt, "Elusive Unity: The Canadian Labor Party in British Columbia, 1924–1928," *BC Studies* 163 (2009): 33–64; and Martin Robin, *Radical Politics and Canadian Labour, 1880–1930* (Kingston: Queen's University Industrial Relations Centre, 1968), 239–53.

58 "Labor Votes for Donaghy Very Largely," *Vancouver Daily Sun*, 14 September 1926, 1; Parliament of Canada, "Elections and Ridings," https://lop.parl.ca/sites/ParlInfo/default/en_CA/ElectionsRidings. See also "Labor Candidate in Vancouver City," *Victoria Daily Times*, 2 September 1926, 1; "Labor Candidate Will Enter Fray in Vancouver, BC," *Calgary Herald*, 2 September 1926, 1; "Triangle Fight in Vancouver Centre," *Saskatoon Daily Star*, 3 September 1926, 12; and "Labor in Field in Vancouver Centre," *Edmonton Journal*, 3 September 1926, 23.

59 See "No Official Labor Candidate in Centre," *Labor Statesman*, 3 September 1926, 1; "Labor Will Contest Several BC Seats" and "CLP Nominating Convention July 30th," *Labor Statesman*, 16 July 1926, 1; "Labor Party Chooses Three Candidates," *Labor Statesman*, 6 August 1926, 1; "Kootenay East Labor Candidate Urges Action," *Labor Statesman*, 13 August 1926, 3; "Vote Labor in the Federal Elections," *Labor Statesman*, 27 August 1926, 1; "Labor Men Have Hopes of Victoria," *Vancouver Daily Sun*, 1 September 1926, 10; "Knight Urges Labor Support," *Vancouver Daily Sun*, 2 September 1926, 22; "Pritchard out to Win in New Westminster," *Labor Statesman*, 3 September 1926, 1; "Labor Candidate for Burrard Speaks at Two Meetings This Evening," *Vancouver Daily Sun*, 10 September 1926, 7; and "An Election Assessment," *Labor Statesman*, 10 September 1926, 1.

60 "No Official Labor Candidate in Centre," *Labor Statesman,* 3 September 1926, 1. Earlier the newspaper had briefly mentioned Kingsley, publishing his vote total from the 1911 federal election in Vancouver City as part of a larger summary of vote totals in various Vancouver-area districts in past elections. See "Federal Election Figures," *Labor Statesman,* 16 July 1926, 4.

61 "Labor Votes for Donaghy Very Largely," *Vancouver Daily Sun,* 14 September 1926, 1; "Twelve Tories in BC," *Vancouver Daily Sun,* 15 September 1926, 1; Parliament of Canada, "Elections and Ridings," https://lop.parl.ca/sites/ParlInfo/default/en_CA/ ElectionsRidings.

62 "Says Vote for Kingsley Will Be Vote against Any Old Age Pensions Bill," *Vancouver Daily Sun,* 9 September 1926, 8.

63 "Työskennelkää ja äänestäkää vain työväen hyväksi" ["Work and Vote Only for the Benefit of Working People"], *Vapaus* [Sudbury], 8 September 1926, 1; trans. Outi Talola. For attempts to suppress *Vapaus,* see Reg Whitaker, Gregory S. Kealey, and Andrew Parnaby, *Secret Service: Political Policing in Canada from the Fenians to Fortress America* (Toronto: University of Toronto Press, 2012), 109.

64 "New Candidate Takes the Field on North Shore," *Vancouver Daily Province,* 7 September 1926, 1.

65 "E.T. Kingsley – Independent Labor Candidate" [advertisement], *Vancouver Daily Province,* 9 September 1926, 11.

66 See Parliament of Canada, "Elections and Ridings," https://lop.parl.ca/sites/ParlInfo/ default/en_CA/ElectionsRidings; "BC Results," *Nanaimo Daily News,* 15 September 1926, 1; and "BC Mainland Results," *Victoria Daily Times,* 15 September 1926, 9.

67 "Neill Endorsed by Alberni Labor Party," *Labor Statesman,* 20 August 1926, 7.

68 "Farmer and Labor Forces Increase Representation," *Labor Statesman,* 17 September 1926, 1.

69 The results in the multiple-member Vancouver City provincial district, which elected five members, show a lower share of the vote, but this was a mathematical reality in which the overall votes were shared among a larger field of candidates, and the share required for victory was substantially lower than that in the single-member districts. When accounting for this variation, the 1907 and 1909 results show relatively higher support for Kingsley among voters than his 1926 candidacy. Elections British Columbia, *An Electoral History of British Columbia,* 99–115; Parliament of Canada, "Elections and Ridings," https://lop.parl.ca/sites/ParlInfo/default/en_CA/ ElectionsRidings; Michael J. Dubin, *United States Congressional Elections, 1789– 1997: The Official Results of the Elections of the 1st through 105th Congresses* (Jefferson, NC: McFarland, 1998), 313,322; "Official Returns of the Election," *San Francisco Call,* 14 December 1898, 5; "Registrar of Voters' Report," in San Francisco Board of Supervisors, *San Francisco Municipal Reports, for the Fiscal Year 1894– 1895, Ending June 30, 1895* (San Francisco: Hinton Printing, 1895), 59; "Results of the Municipal Election Held May 21st, 1900," in Minutes of the Common Council of the City of San Jose, 23 May 1900, City Council Records, San Jose Public Library.

70 "Council Withdraws from Canadian Labor Party," *Labor Statesman*, 8 June 1928, 1. The final break of the non-communists from the Canadian Labor Party in British Columbia occurred in June 1928 when twenty unions in the Vancouver Trades and Labor Council voted to sever its affiliation with the party, with fourteen unions voting to maintain the affiliation (and thirty unions not registering a vote). See also Isitt, "Elusive Unity," 33–64; Robin, *Radical Politics and Canadian Labour*, 239–53; and Gillian Creese, "Exclusion or Solidarity? Vancouver Workers Confront the 'Oriental Problem,'" *BC Studies* 80 (1988–89): 24–51.

71 See Johnson, "No Compromise," 368; Steeves, *The Compassionate Rebel*, 77; Young, "Ideology, Personality and the Origin of the CCF in British Columbia," 139–62.

72 Leo Zakuta, *A Protest Movement Becalmed: A Study of Change in the CCF* (Toronto: University of Toronto Press, 1964). For a similar approach in the international literature, see Roberto Michels, *Political Parties: A Sociological Study of the Oligarchical Tendencies of Modern Democracy*, trans. Eden Paul and Cedar Paul, introd. Seymour Martin Lipset (New York: Free Press, 1962).

73 "Stephen A.M. (1882–1942)," n.d., *ABC Bookworld Author Database*, http://www.abcbookworld.com/view_author.php?id=3277. We thank Mark Leier for drawing our attention to the portrayal of Kingsley in *The Gleaming Archway*.

74 Ibid.

75 Earle Birney, "Report to the Toronto Branch of the International Left Opposition: 24 September 1933," in Bruce Nesbitt, ed. *Conversations with Trotsky: Earle Birney and the Radical 1930s* (Ottawa: University of Ottawa Press, 2017), 68–69.

76 Ibid.

77 Ibid. See also Candida Rifkind, *Comrades and Critics: Women, Literature and the Left in 1930s Canada* (Toronto: University of Toronto Press, 2009), 25; and Raymond Frogner, "'Within Sound of the Drum': Currents of Anti-Militarism in the British Columbia Working Class in the 1930s" (MA thesis, University of Victoria, 1987). Rifkind notes that there was also an election scandal associated with Stephen's campaign for office that contributed to the controversy.

78 A.M. Stephen, *The Gleaming Archway* (London: J.M. Dent and Sons, 1929).

79 For critical commentary on *The Gleaming Archway*, see James Doyle, *Progressive Heritage: The Evolution of a Politically Radical Literary Tradition in Canada* (Waterloo, ON: Wilfrid Laurier University Press, 2002), 84–86; Rifkind, *Comrades and Critics*, 25; and Bart Vautour, "Writing Left: The Emergence of Modernism in English Canadian Literature" (PhD diss., Dalhousie University, 2011), 79–83.

80 Stephen, *The Gleaming Archway*, 33–34. For a more detailed discussion, see Ravi Malhotra, "A Novel of Class Struggle and Romance," *Against the Current* 165 (2013): n. pag., https://www.solidarity-us.org/node/3939. *The Gleaming Archway* also features brief fictionalized portrayals of other Socialist Party figures, including Bertha and Ernest Burns, depicted as Dorothea Barrett and an unnamed husband, "a fuzzy old dreamer who kept a second-hand shop when he wasn't talking Socialism." (Bertha wrote under the pen name Dorothy Drew, and Ernest operated a second-hand store on Vancouver's Powell Street, which served as the headquarters of the SPBC in the

early years. The store, which originally provided meeting space for the SPBC on the upper floor, was located at 132 Powell Street.) See Stephen, *The Gleaming Archway,* 136; Johnson, "No Compromise," 134, 188, 221; "BC Socialist Party," *Independent* [Vancouver], 1 March 1902, 1; "Socialist Party," *Independent,* 12 April 1902, 5; "BC Socialist Party," *Independent,* 15 March 1902, 1; "Socialist Meetings," *Independent,* 31 May 1902, 1; "Important Socialist Meetings," *Western Socialist,* 20 September 1902, 4; and "In the Provincial Field," *Western Socialist,* 17 January 1903, 4.

81 Stephen, *The Gleaming Archway,* 33–34.

82 Ibid., 40.

83 Ibid., 212.

84 "Certification of Registration of Death – Eugene Thomas [*sic*] Kingsley," 13 December 1929, record 23286, vol. 417, GR-2952, BCA. See also Parker Williams, "E.T. Kingsley," *Labor Statesman,* 13 December 1929, 4.

85 "Certification of Registration of Death – Eugene Thomas [*sic*] Kingsley," 13 December 1929, record 23286, vol. 417, GR-2952, BCA.

86 Jerome B. Tritcher and Milton Helpern, "Accidental Carbon Monoxide Poisoning Due to Domestic Gas Appliances and Gas Refrigerators: The Problem in New York City and Its Control," *American Journal of Public Health* 42 (1952): 259–67.

87 Ibid., 259. See also Brooklyn, Department of Health, *Report of the Commissioner of Health on Illuminating Gas* (Brooklyn: Department of Health, 1883).

88 "Labor Writer Dies Suddenly," *Vancouver Daily Sun,* 9 December 1929, 18.

89 "Certification of Registration of Death – Eugene Thomas [*sic*] Kingsley," 13 December 1929, record 23286, vol. 417, GR-2952, BCA.

90 United States, "Fifteenth Census of the United States: 1930 – Population," Minneapolis, Minnesota, 3 January 1930, in *1930 US Census Online Database,* www.ancestry.com. Myra appears to have retired shortly after she was enumerated in the January 1930 census since she is not listed in the 1930 Minneapolis city directory. According to her obituary, she lived with Percy and his wife, Clara, for a time in Minneapolis and then moved to live with her younger son, Robert, and his wife, Irma, in Mentor, Ohio, northeast of Cleveland, where Myra died in 1935. Her funeral was held in her hometown of Caldwell, Ohio (where she had lived with Eugene fifty-five years earlier) on 31 December 1935. See "Mrs. Myra Kingsley," *Minneapolis Tribune,* 30 December 1935, 6; and *Davidson's Minneapolis Directory, 1930* (Minneapolis: Davidson's, 1930), 840.

91 Parker Williams, "E.T. Kingsley," *Labor Statesman,* 13 December 1929, 4.

92 Ibid.

93 John Sidaway, "Kingsley Led Vanguard in Fight for Workers," *Labor Statesman,* 27 December 1929, 5.

94 Ibid. For some of Kingsley's speeches on the Paris Commune, see "Brief Local Times," *Vancouver Daily Province,* 19 March 1904, 16; "Commune Anniversary," *Western Clarion,* 24 March 1906, 4; "News and Views," *Western Clarion,* 9 March 1907, 4; "Last Sunday's Meeting," *Western Clarion,* 16 March 1907, 4; "Local Items," *Vancouver Daily Province,* 16 March 1909, 20; "E.T. Kingsley Lectures," *Federationist,*

27 March 1914, 6; "The Paris Commune and the Bolsheviki," *Federationist,* 15 March 1919, 8; "Rulers Would Do Same Thing Again," *Vancouver Daily Sun,* 18 March 1918, 2; "Kingsley on Paris Commune," *Federationist,* 19 March 1920, 1; and "Kingsley on the Commune," *Federationist,* 26 March 1920, 4. For an example of his writing on the subject, see "The Eighteenth of March," *Western Clarion,* 19 March 1910, 2.

Conclusion

1   "Socialism," *Voice,* 22 May 1908, 3; Ross McCormack, *Reformers, Rebels, and Revolutionaries: The Western Canadian Radical Movement 1899–1919* (Toronto: University of Toronto Press, 1977), 70.

2   For references to Kingsley in the *One Big Union Bulletin,* published in Winnipeg in the 1930s, see "Wages," *One Big Union Bulletin,* 27 November 1930, 4 (a Kingsley article reprinted from the *Western Clarion*); "A Jaunt in BC," *One Big Union Bulletin,* 1 October 1931, 8; and "Lestor's Corner," *One Big Union Bulletin,* 29 September 1932, 3, a letter from "A Kingsleyite." For references to Kingsley's work in the Australian labour press, see Chapter 5, note 6.

3   Bryan Palmer, "Foreword," in *Disabling Barriers: Social Movements, Disability History, and the Law,* ed. Ravi Malhotra and Benjamin Isitt (Vancouver: UBC Press, 2017), vii.

4   See Ravi Malhotra, ed., *Disability Politics in a Global Economy: Essays in Honour of Marta Russell* (London: Routledge, 2017); and Liat Ben-Moshe, Chris Chapman, and Alison C. Carey, eds., *Disability Incarcerated: Imprisonment and Disability in the United States and Canada* (New York: Palgrave Macmillan, 2014).

5   See, for example, Ravi Malhotra and Morgan Rowe, *Exploring Disability Identity and Disability Rights through Narratives: Finding a Voice of Their Own* (London: Routledge, 2013).

6   The mysteriously ambiguous presence of Kingsley's impairments in his narrative is reminiscent of a legendary postcolonial novel by noted Canadian author M.G. Vassanji, *The Book of Secrets* (Toronto: McClelland and Stewart, 1994).

7   Peter Campbell, *Canadian Marxists and the Search for a Third Way* (Montreal and Kingston: McGill-Queen's University Press, 1999).

8   Ian McKay, *Reasoning Otherwise: Leftists and the People's Enlightenment in Canada, 1890–1920* (Toronto: Between the Lines, 2008), 82. See also Ian McKay, *Rebels, Reds, Radicals: Rethinking Canada's Left History* (Toronto: Between the Lines, 2005). Some commentators have bemoaned the *Western Clarion* for being relatively unoriginal in making use of political cartoons only in overtly didactic ways. See David Buchanan, "'Yours for the Revolution': Communication and Identity in the *Western Clarion,*" *English Studies in Canada* 41, nos. 2–3 (2015): 154–56.

9   Buchanan, "'Yours for the Revolution,'" 144.

10   McKay, *Reasoning Otherwise,* 114–20.

11   Kingsley accordingly ought to be seen as challenging stereotypical notions of disabled people who overcome their impairments. On this, see Simi Linton, *Claiming Disability: Knowledge and Identity* (New York: New York University Press, 1998).

12 For important overviews of the rise of the social model, see Joseph P. Shapiro, *No Pity: People with Disabilities Forging a New Civil Rights Movement* (New York: Times Books, 1994).

13 Catherine J. Kudlick, "Disability History: Why We Need Another 'Other,'" *American Historical Review* 108, no. 3 (2003): 763–93; Susan Burch and Ian Sutherland, "Who's Not Yet Here? American Disability History," *Radical History Review* 94 (2006): 127–47. See also Susan Burch and Michael Rembis, eds., *Disability Histories* (Champaign: University of Illinois Press, 2014); and Malhotra and Isitt, eds., *Disabling Barriers*.

14 Although one might see this interpretation as purely speculative, the fictional portrayal of Kingsley as the character Tacey in A.M. Stephen's novel *The Gleaming Archway* corroborates this impression. Buchanan notes how the political newspapers that competed on the left with the *Western Clarion,* such as *Cotton's Weekly,* tended to be more personal, including columns on women's issues. See Buchanan, "'Yours for the Revolution,'" 147.

15 The literature on this point is considerable. See Geoffrey Reaume, *Remembrance of Patients Past: Life at the Toronto Hospital for the Insane, 1870–1940* (Toronto: University of Toronto Press, 2000); Ben-Moshe, Chapman, and Carey, eds., *Disability Incarcerated;* Sarah F. Rose, *No Right to Be Idle: The Invention of Disability, 1840s–1930s* (Chapel Hill: University of North Carolina Press, 2017); and Bob Williams-Findlay, *More than a Left Foot* (London: Resistance Books, 2020).

16 See Richard Allen, *The View from Murney Tower: Salem Bland, the Late Victorian Controversies, and the Search for a New Christianity* (Toronto: University of Toronto Press, 2008), 29, 111; Alexander Richard Allen, "Salem Bland and the Social Gospel in Canada" (MA thesis, University of Saskatchewan, 1961), 26; and Richard Allen, "The Social Gospel and the Reform Tradition in Canada, 1890–1928," *Canadian Historical Review* 49, no. 4 (1968): 381–99.

17 Kim E. Nielsen, *The Radical Lives of Helen Keller* (New York: New York University Press, 2004), xii; Keith Rosenthal, "The Politics of Helen Keller: Socialism and Disability," *International Socialist Review* 96 (2015): n. pag., http://isreview.org/issue/96/politics-helen-keller.

18 For an inquiry by the RNWMP commissioner about whether Kingsley had been naturalized as a British subject, see McLean to Rowell, "E.T. Kingsley, Vancouver," 15 April 1919, and McLean to Undersecretary for State, "E.T. Kingsley, Vancouver," 15 April 1919, reel t-6256, file "Labour Organizations and Communism," vol. 878, Accession No. A-2, RG 18, RCMP Fonds, LAC.

19 Kim E. Nielsen, "Perhaps a Little Bit Crestfallen," in *Helen Keller: Selected Writings,* ed. Kim E. Nielsen (New York: New York University Press, 2005), 88.

20 See also Rosenthal, "The Politics of Helen Keller," suggesting that scholars have overstated her political inactivity in later life.

21 See James Tobin, *The Man He Became: How FDR Defied Polio to Win the Presidency* (Toronto: Simon and Schuster, 2013). For a more recent account of Roosevelt and his impairments, see Anne Finger, "Dancing with a Cane: The Public Perception of

Franklin Delano Roosevelt's Disability," in Malhotra and Isitt, eds., *Disabling Barriers,* 63–77. For a social history of polio, see Anne Finger, *Elegy for a Disease: A Personal and Cultural History of Polio* (New York: St. Martin's Press, 2006).

22 Parker Williams, "E.T. Kingsley," *Labor Statesman,* 13 December 1929, 4.

23 Ross Alfred Johnson, "No Compromise – No Political Trading: The Marxian Socialist Tradition in British Columbia" (PhD diss., University of British Columbia, 1975), 14n16.

Index

Note: "(i)" after a page number indicates a photograph or map. "FLP" stands for Federated Labor Party; "SLP" for Socialist Labor Party; "SPBC" for Socialist Party of British Columbia; and "SPC" for Socialist Party of Canada.

Araceae

Printed and bound in Canada by Friesens

Set in Univers Condensed and Minion by Artegraphica Design Co. Ltd.

Copy editor: Dallas Harrison

Proofreader: Alison Strobel

Cover designer: George Henry Kirkpatrick

Cover images: Eugene Thornton Kingsley,
courtesy *British Columbia Federationist*, 1916